INTERSPIRITUALITY

—— Volume I ——

The Heritage

INTERSPIRITUALITY

—— Volume 1 ——

The Heritage

of
Interspirituality: The Heritage
and
Interspirituality: The Future

Opening Message by His Holiness the 14th Dalai Lama

Foreword by Matthew Fox
Afterword by Ken Wilber

INTERSPIRITUALITY: THE HERITAGE
with voices from over 100 global leaders and their
organizations, initiatives, and events from 1999 to 2015

Interspirituality: The Heritage
Volume 1

Editors
Rev. Shannon Marie Winters MS
Rev. Kurt Johnson PhD
Robert Atkinson PhD
Nomi Naeem MA
Chamatkara (aka Sandra Simon)
Karuna (aka Rev. Caroline Ashley)
Karen J. Gordon
Roger P. Briggs

Print ISBN: 978-1-958921-78-4
Ebook ISBN: 978-1-958921-79-1
Library of Congress Control Number: 2025946851

Published by Light on Light Press
An imprint of Sacred Stories Publishing, Fort Lauderdale, FL
Printed in the United States of America

DEDICATION

These Volumes are dedicated to the over one hundred twenty Featured Authors who have made the Volumes possible. Their articles, excerpts, abridgements, and twenty-five years of correspondence and attachments have enabled creation of a historical and thematic account of the interspiritual paradigm since the 1999 publication of Br. Wayne Teasdale's book, *The Mystic Heart: Discovering a Universal Spirituality in the World's Religions*, that named the paradigm. The Volumes mark the twenty-fifth anniversary of that publication and the tenth anniversary of *The Coming Interspiritual Age*, the book whose generative organization, The Interspiritual Dialogue, founded with Br. Teasdale in 2002, became the charity that is the parent of The Light on Light Press. We honor also the Featured Authors who have co-created the online resource *interspirituality.com*.

TABLE OF CONTENTS
VOLUME I

FEATURES from or about:

Jeffrey Genung 218, 265; Charles P. Gibbs 218, 247; Philip Goldberg 218, 234; Karen J. Gordon 218, 325; Victor H. Kazanjian Jr. 253; William Keepin 218, 348; Frank Levy 218, 259; Kay Lindahl 218, 240; Sally Mahé 253; Netanel Miles-Yépez 218, 362; Rami Shapiro 218, 259; Wayne Teasdale 67, 83, 90, 98, 112, 117, 119, 128, 164, 265, 295; Claudia Welss 218, 228; John A. Wilde 218, 321.

OPENING MESSAGE

HIS HOLINESS THE 14th DALAI LAMA

We humans are social animals; we are part of a community. All social animals have the sense of community. Without a community, one single individual cannot survive. So we must develop a reality where the entire world of human beings are one human community — we are brothers and sisters — one humanity!

As a social animal, human beings need those kinds of human emotions that bring together. Loving kindness brings together; compassion brings together. They minimize destructive emotions. Loving kindness brings together even anger and excess.

In the long run, compassion is much stronger than enmity. And compassion is our true nature. That is a given — human beings being one community, in loving each other. The worst thing is enmity in the name of different faiths — really unthinkable! All religions actually carry the message of *Love* — loving kindness, forgiveness, tolerance.

Biologically, we are all equipped with the seed of compassion. Young children? — no enemy. Young children? — they don't care about differences. They simply appreciate love, affection, a smile, and play together. They don't care about a different faith, different nationality, different color, or different country. In them, the sameness of human beings is very much alive.

Knowledge and education are key ingredients for the future. Step by step, we can make society a happier and more peaceful society. Nonviolence, compassion — with full confidence — these are key factors for the happier individual, happier community, and peaceful world. All religions carry this message of *Love* — kindness, forgiveness, tolerance, compassion.

In taking care of others, you get the fuller benefit. Respect others; love others. With that perspective, the whole atmosphere appears peaceful — for the individual level, family level, community level, and finally, the world level. Essentially, all religions carry this message.[i]

FOREWORD

Interspirituality, Deep Ecumenism and the Future of Humanity

by Matthew Fox

I very much welcome this volume — now ballooned to two volumes because of the energetic response to the project — that gathers many spiritual practitioners to share their thoughts on Interspirituality, Interfaith, and Deep Ecumenism. This is done in the spirit of the late Br. Wayne Teasdale, whom I had the opportunity to meet on several occasions, and in the spirit of his mentor, with whom I was blessed to forge a deep friendship, the late Benedictine monk and pioneer in Interspirituality, Fr. Bede Griffiths.

All of humanity can get excited about the topic treated here from so many diverse perspectives. Why? I see Interspirituality, Interfaith, and Deep Ecumenism as one of the major signs of hope for our species today as we struggle to find our ground — what Howard Thurman called our *common ground.*

As we face all the doomsday scenarios that beset us — including the warming of the planet with its wildfires, droughts, increased hurricanes, floods, and galloping extinctions of other species — we can see that all of these add up to our human species having lost our way, not to mention the fact of our spending $56,000 per second on weapons and war. The odds are not in favor that *Homo sapiens* will survive our own folly and escape the fate of our cousin hominid creatures, about fourteen of which we have counted, who have, alas, all gone extinct.

What resources do we have at our disposal to turn back the looming extinction spasm? How can humans change our ways, be transformed, and grow up fast? The pages of this book offer many answers to those questions. The collective wisdom of the world's rich spiritual heritage calls us at this critical moment in history, beckoning believers and nonbelievers alike to learn from each other what it means to be human at an ever-deeper level.

Deep Ecumenism is a sign of our time and a hopeful sign. How crucial this is! At a time like ours, the voices of doom are very loud and ever present, and despair spreads more swiftly than hope. Despair is so dangerous because, as Thomas Aquinas reminds us, when one is in despair, one does not care about oneself, much less anyone else.

Awakening to Interspirituality and Deep Ecumenism is not an insular event—it follows the habits that all the mystics as well as today's science speak of: the habits of interdependence or interconnectivity. As Hildegard of Bingen put it in the 12th century: "Everything that is in the heavens, on the earth, and under the earth, is penetrated with connectedness, penetrated with relatedness."[1]

Thomas Merton, one of the great pioneers in Deep Ecumenism, in a talk delivered three hours before his untimely death, said that "compassion is a keen awareness of the interdependence of all living things that are all part of one another and all involved in one another."

Today's science is itself promoting compassion when it teaches that interdependence is foundational to how our universe works.

Science and the Webb Telescope are opening our horizons daily to the wonder of this universe we call our home with a new creation story of the 13.8 billion year history that has brought this planet, its galaxy, its sun, and our earthly home into existence.

This perspective — and the beauty and awe that accompanies it — bring hope and even wisdom, just as Rabbi Heschel insists when he assures us that awe is the "beginning of wisdom." It is wisdom we seek if we are to survive as a species — knowledge is not nearly enough.

The spiritual traditions of the world — including science — offer paths and practices that allow us access to awe, gratitude, forgiveness, praise, thanks and, therefore, wisdom. And compassion.

Compassion is the revolution and change of consciousness that our species needs to survive. When the Dalai Lama says that we can do away with all religion, but not with compassion, he is telling us exactly that. There is such a consensus in religions the world over on humanity's capacity for compassion *and* how compassion constitutes the divine in us.

Thus, the rise of compassion is another sign of hope in our times and is born of interdependence. It is profoundly feminine, indeed what Julian of Norwich identifies in motherhood and compassion. The recovery of the divine feminine and a healthy and sacred masculine is essential for humanity's survival.

This third gift of hope in our times, the return of the Divine Feminine, must include the awakening of a renewed (and ancient) masculinity that does not serve gods of war and conquest, dominance, and the reptilian brain ("I win; you lose."), but understands spirituality as strength. It is born of the heart and not of power-over dynamics. Compassion is "passion-with," not "passion over."

The Dalai Lama warns us that the "biggest obstacle to interfaith is a bad relationship with one's own faith tradition." Each believer and practitioner must dig deep into the core depths of their faith. Very often in the West, people out of touch with their own faith tradition are ignorant of its mystical and/or its prophetic tradition. The mystic is the lover; the mystic shouts "Yes!" to life. The prophet is the warrior and shouts "No!" to injustice.

Ignorance about mysticism reigns in Christianity but it can be recovered rapidly. The Four Paths of Creation Spirituality name its structure or skeleton: the Via Positiva of joy, delight and awe; the Via Negativa of darkness, silence, stillness and also grief; the Via Creativa of creativity, where "the divine and the human meet"; and the Via Transformativa of Justice and Compassion. The latter names lead to enacting the common good.

The core message in world religions is invariably about compassion. We heard from the Dalai Lama above, and from Jesus we hear, "Be you compassionate as your Creator in heaven is compassionate." Compassion is how we bring together heaven and Earth, cosmos and psyche, humans and the divine.

How do we turn from scattered minds and hurt and revenge to become practitioners of compassion? Meditation, mindfulness, and contemplation are such a path and so too is our work for justice for, as Meister Eckhart reminds us, "compassion means justice." Compassion is about works of mercy and works of justice, as Isaiah teaches. Caring leads to action — "what happens to another, whether it be a joy or sorrow, happens to me," as Meister Eckhart put it, and "compassion is where peace and justice kiss."[2]

I created the term "deep ecumenism" in my book *The Coming of the Cosmic Christ* written in 1988. It was born of conversations with my Buddhist friend Joanna Macy, who explained to me how the "deep ecology" movement to which she subscribed was an effort to transform the struggle for Earth justice from being simply a secular and political battle to being something deeper, where spirituality played a role. I felt the same way about the "ecumenical movement" — the coming together of religions especially after the failures of religion so manifest in WWII required a deeper dive.

We do not gather with people of other faith traditions to read theological position papers at one another. Rather, common prayer and common action are required, both of which need to come from a deeper place than merely proclaiming our cherished doctrines. Thus, the term *deep* ecumenism. Contemplation and meditation take us to depth places in ourselves, and so too does the common solidarity that is forged when battling powers and forces of injustice.

Interfaith and Deep Ecumenism as a Practice

I have tried in my adult spiritual life to implement deep ecumenism as a practice. My book, *One River, Many Wells: Wisdom Springing From Global Faiths*, tries to do that in an explicit manner by naming eighteen themes that are common to all the world spiritual traditions. In other books, Deep Ecumenism plays a significant role *as a methodology*. My book on *The Reinvention of Work* draws on what the prophets of Israel and Christian mystics say about work and spirituality — but also what the *Tao Te Ching* and *Bhagavad Gita* and Sufism, Hinduism, Celtic, Indigenous, goddess, and other traditions teach about spirituality and work.

I was amazed at how fully all these traditions agree with one another, for example, on the importance of *joy* in work. I invoke this method in many of my other books as well, in books on Education,

Creativity, Sacred Masculinity, and Evil where I bring the seven capital sins of the West together with the seven chakras of the East to create a fresh language for examining evil.

This Volume opens doors to deep ecumenism as a method and a practice. When one is invited to pray with people of other traditions, do it! I am eternally grateful for the hours I have spent in sweat lodges, vision quests, sun dances, and pow wows praying with Indigenous Peoples, for example. So many visions, connections, and archetypes have risen for me from those ancient practices — indeed singers accompanying the sound of the drum, echoing the beating heart of the universe, with songs of ancient ancestors have birthed in me powerful experiences of Spirit.

A powerful practice for me in deep ecumenism has been our Cosmic Masses which we have celebrated about 125 times in North America. Whether at the World Parliament of Religions in Chicago or Toronto, or at Historic Sweets Ballroom in Oakland or Grace Cathedral in San Francisco or the National Cathedral in Washington, DC, or in Unity headquarters near Kansas City or for 1,000 participants at a Sounds True retreat in the Colorado mountains, people from a wide variety of traditions find common prayer in the context of dance, dj, vj, and rap — a form that follows the four paths of creation spirituality which on examination constitute the basic structure of the traditional Mass of the West. Jewish people, Muslims, Christians, indigenous, atheists and humanists, young and old, Hindus, Muslims, Buddhists, and wicca people have availed themselves of this thanksgiving ceremony of the Cosmic Mass. Truly, worship can be interspiritual and deeply ecumenical.

Another practice of deep ecumenism has been the Order of the Sacred Earth that I founded with a twenty-nine-year-old woman and a thirty-one-year-old man six years ago. This movement, which currently hosts about sixty-five different "pods" or communities from several continents, is deeply ecumenical: We take one common vow: "I promise to be the best lover of Mother Earth and the best defender of Mother Earth that I can be." Participants range from people in their twenties to people in their eighties, and the common ground we share is that of passion for saving Mother Earth as we know her. At our first vow ceremony, held on Winter Solstice in a Buddhist temple in Berkeley, about eighty people showed up representing many faith traditions and at least one atheist, a twenty-six-year-old woman who told me she was looking for a community that shared her values and Order of the Sacred Earth was it.

Deep Ecumenism represents a step beyond religious ideologies and doctrines to a movement of common values born of deep emptying and listening and deep responses to common concerns such as the survival of our common home, Mother Earth.

About 600 years ago, Nicolas of Cusa — scientist, mathematician, philosopher, mystic, theologian, and even a cardinal in the Roman Catholic church — spoke the following vision: "Humanity will find that it is not a diversity of creeds, but the very same creed which is everywhere proposed....There cannot but be one wisdom....Humans must therefore all agree that there is but one most simple wisdom whose power is infinite; and everyone in explaining the intensity of this beauty, must discover that it is a supreme and terrible beauty."[3]

Has humanity today found the vision Cusa beheld 600 years ago? Is the Webb Telescope not reminding us daily of this "supreme and terrible beauty" that we call the universe? Is this vision enough to get humanity to move to the next stage of its evolution — a "common creed" of wisdom, gratitude, and compassion?

Let these books further light the way.

INTRODUCTION

One can imagine how challenging it is to write a fittingly brief introduction to two volumes of such significant content. The two volumes themselves are both thematic books and history books, a quite demanding task. We[1] are publishing these on the 25th anniversary of Br. Wayne Teasdale's now classic book, *The Mystic Heart: Discovering a Universal Spirituality in the World's Religions*,[2] and his naming of "Interspirituality." He defined Interspirituality this way:

> The common heritage of humankind's spiritual wisdom; the sharing of mystical resources across traditions [MH p. 268].

and "the Interspiritual Age" as:

> The name for the age we are now entering, where people are no longer isolated within their home tradition but are exploring other traditions, finding what is useful to their own growth [MH p. 268].

Although this has been an incipient context for the creation of these Volumes, Br. Wayne Teasdale was far from alone in his endeavors.

Rather, he was one of a multitude of pioneers and spokespersons for an emerging paradigm regarding where the thousands of religious and spiritual traditions on our planet would go in the inevitable era of globalization and the challenge of an equally inevitable multiculturalism.

These Volumes (which will be consistently referred to herein as "these Volumes") acknowledge hundreds of contributors — and even more in the historical commentaries — themselves standing in a wider context of more than three-score global pioneers, many now passed, who were pivotal in this emergent process. Of these, at least a half dozen also suggested names for this emerging paradigm. Raimon Panikkar had called it the "intraspiritual experience," Matthew Fox "Deep Ecumenism," Thích Nhất Hạnh our "Interbeing," and Thomas Merton the "mystical communion." Eastern writers had added a number of expressions for it as well. The initial website of Br. Teasdale's Interspiritual Dialogue (now over 20 years old and with some sections built on now archaic software no longer available) honored over fifty men and women seen as seminal to the emerging paradigm.[3] All emphasized a "commonality of heart" across all the world's traditions. Of these, he honored two as his own "spiritual fathers" — Fr. Thomas Keating and Fr. Bede Griffiths (Dayananda) about which these Volumes will say much more. Having been mentored significantly by them, he could only see his own work as a continuation of theirs, saying:

> Interspirituality and Intermysticism are terms I have coined to designate the increasingly familiar phenomenon of cross-religious sharing of interior resources, the spiritual treasures of each tradition. In the third millennium, Interspirituality and Intermysticism

will become more and more the norm in humankind's inner evolution [MH p. 10].

Fittingly writing the Foreword for these Volumes is Matthew Fox — the one, now-living pioneer among the half dozen pioneers who offered a name for this paradigm — his being Deep Ecumenism.

Fr. Keating had been conducting the Snowmass Interreligious Dialogues, of which Br. Teasdale was a part, beginning in 1984, from which emerged the "Nine Points of Agreement" in *The Common Heart* (2006) and had been the wellspring of Br. Teasdale's own "Nine Elements of a Universal Spirituality" published earlier, in 1999. The relationship of these interspiritual pioneers — Keating, Griffiths, and Teasdale — is well discussed in these Volumes along with so many others: His Holiness the 14th Dalai Lama (who has offered messages in the Volumes as well), Ken Wilber (who has written the Afterword), and so many more. Ken Wilber had said of the emerging Interspiritual Age: "The Interspiritual Age is ... about just that — the emergence, happening now and gaining momentum — of an interspiritually unified world. It has its basis in a background coming transformation — that of an Integral Age."[4] Thus, the synchronicities discussed by Wilber and Teasdale in their seminal conversations in 2004 (YouTube: "Ken Wilber and Wayne Teasdale") are even further enhanced today.

The "many more" noted above are not only the over one hundred contributors to these Volumes but also the at least three-score "Interspiritual Pioneers" who have been honored in many books and at many websites. These include now Pioneers originally honored at Br. Teasdale's initial 2003 interspiritual website — ISDnA.org (now only partially extant due to the flow of time and antiquated web technologies) although that early photo tribute is still available at TheComingInterspiritualAge.com (2013).

In creating these Volumes over several years, we have reached out not only to the scores of interfaith and interspiritual leaders included in these Volumes but also to many others. Accordingly and inevitably, our results have been able to embrace only those who responded. This causes us also to naturally be prone toward the points of entry and points of view *of* those respondents. Unavoidably then, we have missed others. For such unfortunate omissions, we apologize in advance.

In addition to the over one hundred responses that we have had, we also have had access to twenty-five years of saved correspondence and attachments. And, we have also graciously received the reprinting rights from numerous of our fellow publishers who have, to one degree or another, been part of this emerging landscape — and we are so grateful to them.

In grouping the content of these Volumes, we have had to do so from multiple angles — some thematic, others chronological. Thus, readers will see a combination of content both from multiple thematics and multiple and often simultaneous timelines. The intertwining and close personal relationships of so many major leaders across the world's interfaith and interspiritual communities have also made the intertwining of the stories we need to tell quite challenging, to say the least, also creating complexity [to say the least] in determining what were the best points of entry on this or that at any particular historical time. So, these Volumes are both a thematic and historical compilation. However, because so much has happened in the last twenty-five years of this emergence of Interspirituality, we felt bound by history to create these Volumes no matter what the difficulties, acknowledging as well that the Volumes appear also around the 10th anniversary of the book from one of us, *The Coming Interspiritual Age*.

Below are some main editorial points about structures and usages in these volumes.

Reference to "these Volumes": A two-volume work requires frequent reference back and forth between the Volumes. Thus, when we are referring to the publications *Interspirituality: The Heritage*, and *Interspirituality: The Future*, we consistently use these phrases: "in these Volumes," "in this Volume," "the current Volumes," etc. Readers will note some repetition of key quotations between the volumes, as well as with some elements of the Timelines. This is because we suspect the Volumes might be read separately by some readers.

Interval Notes: To make the vast content of these Volumes further accessible, we join various contents with "Interval Notes" written in a conversational tone, to help readers quickly understand the significance of particular contributions and also meld the Volumes historically chronological with the diverse thematics of the books. As well, before each section of Features by Featured Authors, we share those author's names in a "word cloud" (alphabetically), briefing the reader on the content coming next. This is especially important for informed readers, since they will immediately recognize many of these authors and their significance to the content being discussed.

Features and Sections: As noted just above, Features are the contributions from the named Featured Authors collected in these Volumes. These vary in length and theme and each also represents unique contexts in content and chronology. In addition to solicited Features *for* the current Volumes, Features can be selected quotations from a source outside these Volumes or, if needed, from another part of the present Volumes. Some Features are from as much as twenty-five years ago while others are very recent, all gathered within the Table of Contents structure we have created for these books — section titles and subtitles accompanied by the "word clouds" of author's names that inform the reader of the landscape of contributions that follow. This is also why we frequently join them with the Interval Notes comments to further orient the reader. In our commentaries and referencing, we use the term "section" in its general and generic sense but "Section" when referring to a specific Section that has a specific title or subtitle.

History Sections: The massive amount of material curated for these Volumes, with multiple commentaries by multiple leaders, led us also to create an efficient way of constructing the "History" sections. In these, along with foundational texts written by our above-acknowledged editorial team, we have also woven in collages of content from diverse additional authors, and sources, taking bits from here and there and combining them into a narrative stream that recounts both the content of the history *and* the thematics. The Endnotes related to those sections further elaborate the utilized sources. Nearly all the authors drawn from in these shorter sections are further represented by additional, often longer, "Features" within the Volumes as well (see "Features" below). These are grouped either thematically or chronologically, as appropriate to each of the sections of the books. Notes at the end of each history-related section further guide the reader to the pertinent and applicable, longer contributions from our larger body of Featured Authors.

Excerpts and Abridgments: Because of the need to include extensive and diverse historical content in these Volumes, we sometimes present material (especially previously published) permissioned to us as

Excerpts, Abridgments or Selections. Endnotes clarify contexts on a case by case basis. *Abridgments* are previously published material (originally most often prepared by professional editors) previously published in the form provided us, and thus repeated herein verbatim. *Excerpts* are select quotations or sections from previously published, or soon to be published, material permissioned to us and sequenced herein for the heuristic purposes of these Volumes. *Selections* [often noted under Titles as "Selected from..."] are excerpts like those noted just above, *or* as taken from Features elsewhere *within* these Volumes and reprised again for heuristic purposes. Endnotes further explain each unique case. Since "..." ("ellipsis") is generally used in journalism to indicate "breaks" between excerpted passages, we decided (for purposes of these Volumes) that since "..." do not "look" or read well at the beginning of an indented paragraph, we would place them at the end of the previous paragraph so that paragraphs in excerpted sections of the Volumes could start "cleanly."

Subsequent Fully Illustrated Volume: Unanticipated by us, and especially key to these Volumes, some Featured Authors furnished copious historically valuable photographs and other illustrations with their Features. As well, a number of Featured Authors — writing on very specific interspiritual communities, practices, or modalities — included additional valuable content, including long sections of quotations, practice descriptions, and also poems and prayers. Considering the historical value of these materials but acknowledging that they do not technically reproduce or format well for a non-glossy print book, we plan a third volume to this series to serve these important submissions. These will appear subsequently through Light on Light's electronic [e-] publication capacity at issuu.com/lightonlight. Additionally, for coherence, and to further recognize this content within the current Volumes: (i) various of these submissions appear in Volumes 1 or 2 in shortened versions; (ii) we describe, in Endnotes, additional content that will be further published subsequently; and (iii) there is a concluding section in Volume 2 specifically referring to, and including material from, Features that will be subsequently published. All of these elements have great value for recounting the history of Interspirituality and thus are important to include herein. For brevity and convenience, this subsequent e-volume is often referred to simply as "Volume 3."

Titles: The diversity of religious titles (e.g., Rev., Dr., Fr., Br., Sr., etc. [and that is just re: "Western" titles!] and post-nominal letters [letters appearing after a person's name to indicate a religious order, academic degrees, or titles] are extremely varied, and often inconsistently cited across historical writings. Thus, after detailed examination of all our texts and texts from contributors, we decided: (i) we use them "as is" from sources when these are important to specific historical contexts, about specific events, initiatives, etc. and where their use is important to the content and meaning of the surrounding narrative text; and (ii) we use them "as is" from our Featured Authors' Features. Further, we use them in a particular consistent manner in our own editorial texts, especially when persons appear very often (like "Fr. Thomas Keating," "Br. Wayne Teasdale," etc.) and when, as with Indigenous Peoples, a title like "Chief," in common parlance, is almost always used as a part of their name. However, we also allow some variations when contextually appropriate, like when referring to a person by just their last name (e.g., "Keating," "Teasdale," etc.), or first and last name (e.g., "Thomas Keating," "Wayne Teasdale," etc.). Admittedly, this causes some inconsistencies but it has been impossible for us to vet, and then create consistent usages, from the multitude of already existing historical texts. Thus, "readability" has been one criterion we have always kept in mind.

Endnotes: To mediate space, footnotes and reference lists are joined into Endnotes finalizing each Volume. Sequences of individual Endnotes within Sections and Features are numbered with Arabic numerals; the sequence of groupings of Endnotes and References at the end of each Volume are numbered with Roman numerals as keyed from a concluding sentence in each Section or Feature within the Volumes. To prevent introducing inadvertent errors, we follow the Endnote formats of each Featured Author. Quotations of Br. Wayne Teasdale are from either (i) *The Mystic Heart* (1999) (as permissioned by New World Library [originally for *The Coming Interspiritual Age* (2013)], and/or these new Volumes); and/or from, and often duplicating, or even varying slightly from the above sources (ii) as quoted or sequenced in numerous international website and internet sources that widely quote Br. Teasdale. Accordingly, page notations from, or attributed to, *The Mystic Heart* in texts by our editorial staff are noted within texts as [MH p.#, pp.#'s, f means forward] (and further endnoted as needed); the oft-cited (in books and online) 118 word sequence of quotations of Br. Teasdale from *The Mystic Heart* read at the founding of the Universal Order of Sannyasa [today Community of the Mystic Heart] Washington DC, January 9, 2010 (also communityofthemysticheart. org, History) is noted as [MH, pp. 4-12 sequence]; and because it is widely quoted worldwide, and reoccurs often, in various contexts in these Volumes, we have allowed individual Featured Authors to write page notations from *The Mystic Heart* in their own way; "pers. com." means "personal communication," noting by/to.

A Further Note: We must point out some historical paradoxes of the current moment involved with the timing of these Volumes. We are keenly aware that currently and globally we are in a regressive period seeing a resurgence of *many* elements of older paradigms readily characterizable as an "us versus them" mentality generating dominance behaviors, competition, and conflict. If we see human cultural history as a broad evolutionary process of tendencies toward partnership consciousness and partnership culture on the one hand and domination consciousness and domination cultures on the other (see Endnotes farther below), it appears that after decades of apparent progress, our world seems to be regressing into a backwards direction, of uncertain duration, turning away from the calls and values of inclusion and toward reemergence of substantial conflict and division, further exacerbated by a global communications crisis regarding mis- and disinformation. A group of over one hundred sociologists recently declared this problem "an evolutionary catastrophe."

In *The Mystic Heart*, Br. Wayne Teasdale noted such predicaments emerge from "new set[s] of historical circumstances" [MH p. 4], and this appears to be the case today. We find ourselves on the 25th anniversary of his writing of *The Mystic Heart: Discovering a Universal Spirituality in the World's Religions* in a period of historical regression. Because we do not know the future of the regressive period, or how long it may last, we have judged a need to acknowledge it here and elsewhere in these Volumes, but to not overly belabor it, since none of us know where this current period of regression is leading. Obviously, the predicament itself makes the contents of these Volumes even more historically important. Thus, to maintain acknowledgment and awareness of this current uncertainty, but to not feel compelled to always digress into its details and nuances, we'll take this tack. When needed, we will refer to it simply, using the phraseology of iconic sociologist Riane Eisler (a contributor to these Volumes), as "the current global regression more toward dominance consciousness and dominance culture than toward partnership consciousness and partnership culture."[5] Interestingly, neuroscientists in our own "Interspirituality, Science, and the Future" Section (Volume 2, see "IRAS" at Chatlos, Calvin) note that most current brain studies indicate that a network in the human brain actually "wires" human beings toward altruistic behavior and a high sense of moral imperative. However, this natural "wiring" toward good behavior, and partnership, *can* be overridden by psychological pathologies like narcissism or neurosis. Unfortunately, the latter appear to characterize many of our global leaders today, be they dictators or elected. This research also suggests that "spiritual experiences" are part of our innate wiring, not something humans choose, or just "believe in." This is comforting in an era where, as noted later in this Volume 1 (see "Trends"), sociologists have declared this current direction toward regressive behavior as "an evolutionary catastrophe."

With that said, and in the context of what we have previously said about History Sections in these Volumes and the Features from our Featured Authors, let us begin with some recounting of the general history of what has emerged as Interspirituality.

Endnotes and References for Opening Message,
Foreword, and Introduction[i]

HISTORY

We are at the dawn of a new consciousness, a radically fresh approach to our life as the human family in a fragile world. This journey is what spirituality is really about. We are not meant to remain just where we are. We cannot depend on our culture either to guide and support us in our quest. We must do the hard work of clarification together ourselves. This revolution will be the task of the Interspiritual Age. The necessary shifts in consciousness require a new approach to spirituality that transcends past religious cultures of fragmentation and isolation. We need to understand, to really grasp at an elemental level, that the definitive revolution is the spiritual awakening of humankind [MH pp. 4-12 sequence].

With these words penned some twenty-five years ago, Br. Wayne Teasdale, a contemplative monk also famous for his advocacy of social activism,[1] spurred an already existing global trend toward transtraditional and transcultural spirituality in a world inevitably moving toward globalization and multiculturalism. In the books that he is most known for — *The Mystic Heart: Discovering a Universal*

Spirituality in the World's Religions, A Monk in the World, and *Bede Griffiths: An Introduction to His Interspiritual Thought* — he called the emerging global spirituality Interspirituality and identified it in the message of over fifty major historical spiritual figures from across the multiplicity of our world's spiritual and faith traditions.[2] He also listed fundamental shifts in global awareness necessary for a successful global shift, some of which he noted are already happening. These included:

- Appreciation of the interdependence of all realms of human life and the surrounding cosmos

- Growing ecological awareness, with recognition of the interdependence of humankind and the biosphere, including the rights of all biological species

- Embracing of the shared wisdom in all the world's religious and spiritual traditions, past and present

- Growing friendship, and actual community, among the individual followers of the world's religious and spiritual paths

- Commitment to the depths of the contemplative pursuit and the mutual sharing of the fruits of this ongoing journey

- Creative cultivation of transnational, transcultural, transtraditional, and world-centric understanding

- Dedication to nonviolence, with a commitment to transcend militancy and violence tied to national or religious identities

- Receptivity to a cosmic vision, realizing humanity is only one life form and part of a larger community, the universe.

These shifts, he suggested, mark the threshold required for healthy globalization and the birth, through the world's Wisdom Traditions, of an unfolding Interspiritual Age. Further, he said that such shifts were possible, if not inescapable, because of the world's "new set of historical circumstances" [MH p. 4]. He was not the first to suggest a term for what was emerging in this new universalizing of the global spiritual experience in the interfaith paradigm; at least five other interfaith leaders had suggested a new term for this emerging new generality amid the global interfaith phenomenon, as we will detail farther below.

A New Millennium

Today, it is widely acknowledged that a universal spirituality is, in fact, arising on a global scale, uncannily reflecting Teasdale's suggestion that "the only viable religion for the Third Millennium is spirituality *itself*" [MH p. 26]. This vision that has been resonating across the world's interfaith community — and particularly in an emerging "interspiritual paradigm" — is identified by many as a "spirituality of the Heart," and one reflecting the emergence of a new global "unity consciousness." This trend, identified by developmental philosophers as "a great conveyor belt" toward a successful global civilization,[3] is attributed to multiple and convergent causes. In the evolutionary consciousness discussion, and the consciousness sciences, it is generally recognized as being the natural next step in our cognitive evolution. Social scientists see it as a global adaptation driven by inevitable trends toward globalization and multiculturalism. Some spiritual and religious leaders see a "divine purpose" at work, some even considering the "spiritual perfection" of our species. If such a "world awakening" is possible, moreover real, there are diverse and complicated implications for our complex world — including the arenas of religion, science, social structure, governance, economics, culture, and more.

Since 1999, numerous books and media articles[4] have presented responsible surveys of global factors, trends, and statistics that might be influencing and contributing to this emergence, guided significantly by the reservoir of collective human wisdom available from the world's perennial Great Wisdom Traditions. Absent such a moral and values-related contribution by the world's religions, it is suggested the world appears destined to march toward globalization led only by self-serving special interest groups, and political and financial institutions. This would leave the public at the mercy of uncoordinated planetary resource exploitation and consumerism, coupled with a cacophony of competitions and conflicts over politics, financial wealth, natural resources, and the various other currencies of international power.

Trends

The historical oeuvre of interspiritual writing to date, and in a global context, suggests a number of generalities that now appear self-evident. These include these apparently undeniable trends:

- Globalization of planet earth is inevitable; the question is what kind of a globalization it will be and whether it will be devoid of any significant contribution from the Great Wisdom Traditions.

- Multiculturalism is inevitable. Again, the question is what kind of process will unfold and whether it will be a bumpy ride full of competition and conflict (indeed possibly even outright economic and military warfare) or whether a more reasoned dialogue may emerge, mitigating such negative consequences to some degree.

- The world now faces an array of critical challenges that could affect its long-term stability and peace. These include resource scarcity and competition, drastic global climate and population changes, and political agendas and fundamentalisms tied to narrow and competing national, religious, ethnic, or racial identities. There is also now the relatively recent turn of many nations toward nationalist populism and autocracy, all in the context of the current global regression more toward dominance consciousness and dominance culture than toward partnership consciousness and partnership culture. The duration and eventual result of this trend, further exacerbated by the social media revolution and its mis- and disinformation catastrophe, cannot now be known.

An emphasis common to our world's interfaith and interspiritual communities — that if the world's religions could move away from the atmosphere of competing creeds, dogmas, and end-time scenarios, and take up their role as the world's true Wisdom Traditions — this shift "from head to heart" could help spur a positive world transformation. It is not too late for the religions to take on this role, employing the "unifying" or "Archimedean points" already identified through the world's interfaith dialogue process.[5]

The four principles include:

1. the possibility of a common core to human mystic experience,
2. fundamental teachings held in common by all the world's religions,
3. the shared ethical implications of the teachings of all the great traditions, and

4. the inevitable mutuality across the religions regarding commitment to social and economic justice.

Although *creeds and dogmas,* exclusive by nature at a cultural level, still characterize much of the purely religious side of the world's traditions, there are significant shifts occurring across the world's spiritual communities. These are spiritual- and values-based shifts emphasizing the profound mutual recognition among humans in the realm of the heart and shared understanding of profound and numinous unitive states of higher consciousness common to all the traditions — and today also even in secular experience. These shifts are moving powerfully to potentially alter the global equation. Spiritual emphasis on the experience of the heart and states of unitive higher consciousness are nurturing universally compelling life-altering experiences of interconnectedness, mutuality, and "Oneness." These experiences are reflected in an expanding worldwide popular literature and media regarding the experience of a global collective or gestalt of "We." In turn, these are influencing influential movements for social and cultural change, like the myriads in the now well-known lists in the 2006 bestseller *Blessed Unrest: How the Largest Movement in the World Came into Being and Why No One Saw It Coming.*[6]

At the same time, modern science continues to bring forward major discoveries concerning the nature of reality — indeed the unified nature of reality — both at the level of new factual discoveries and also changes in science's methods and philosophies with regard to these. Such discoveries arise from across the physical sciences as well as the biological and cognitive sciences, affecting our understanding of physics, chemistry, cosmology, our anthropological origins, and changes in the structures and assumptions of the philosophy of science itself.

New Self-Evident Truths

In this globalization phenomenon, "new self-evident truths" have appeared to be emerging for some decades, albeit recognizing as well the current regressive period noted previously. Historically, the merging rational and analytical mind of the Renaissance and early European "Enlightenment" created a gestalt in which individuals began thinking strongly in terms of their worldviews and life options, not just those of the privileged or governing elite, and saw the emergence of self-evident truths with regard to the value and rights of individuals. So also today, new self-evident truths seem to be arising. But this time they appear to involve the meaning of collectives and the roles of individuals and institutions within collectives and in responsibility to a collective. The dynamic historical flux of this may itself account for the more currently emerged regressive period noted above.

Recent books, like so many cited within these Volumes, have presented arrays of statistics, surveys, and opinion polls showing these trends. They show that, overall, our human brain-mind is moving toward a gestalt that sees profound interconnectedness, indeed even Oneness — a unity consciousness. These show that, worldwide, these holistic trends have been powerfully moving toward the falling away of old sectarian and parochial lenses, definitions, and worldviews and that this has been happening across every arena in global life — religion, culture, social structures, governance, economics, and many more. In light of these trends, documented for multiple decades now, history will likely have to record how much sway the current regressive trend actually held. If we look at similar regressive trends like those championed culturally by "the Axis" powers before World War II, that trend of facism, authoritarianism, and militarism lasted about three decades and resulted in some ninety million deaths. And we must also recognize that the decades of progressive trends noted generally above also included significant subcultures of political or religious fundamentalism throughout, that were exercising their militarism under the 1st World label of "terrorism." Paradoxes abound, as contained in the popular aphorisms "one person's religion is another person's cult" or "one person's terrorist is another person's freedom fighter."

In the arena of religion, there have been not only the positive trends reflecting emerging views that are transtraditional, transcultural, transnational, and world-centric but also keener understandings of the nature and problems of fundamentalism, especially as it can lead to social and cultural conflict, terrorism, and war. For example, in polls from the years before the recent apparent regressive trend, 78% of those polled internationally believed there are "unifying principles" concerning reality; 71-80% believed that multicultural understanding is fundamental to a positive world future and that the world should be pursuing a unified vision; some 80% also believed that the religions should be talking to each other with regard to visions of the common good. Up to 78% described positive experiences when either personally investigating or interacting with a religion different from their own. And some 40% identified regular practices in their lives that have a background in a religion other than that of their direct heritage. Meantime, some 50% or more identified religious fundamentalism as a danger including not only religious fundamentalism but also scientific fundamentalism.[7]

Religions and Peace

Theologian Hans Küng is famous for his phrase, "There can be no peace among the nations without peace among the religions and there can be no peace among the religions without dialogue between the religions."[8] His Holiness the 14th Dalai Lama, in his messages prefacing this book, echoed this clearly as well. In the past especially, though still in many cases today, religion was the source of division centered on different claims about absolute truth. The paradox is that when any religion takes this approach, it may fail to practice the more basic message of its teachings, which is centered on love, kindness, compassion, mutuality, nurturing, and the value of human beings — indeed, the value of all life and of the planet itself.

It's precisely this U-turn back to their roots that some of the religions have been taking in more recent times, and is the one, it would seem, that all the religions must take in the New Millennium for the good of our world. In fact, as Br. Teasdale proclaimed in his book, *The Mystic Heart,* it is the calamitous and challenging "new set of historical circumstances" that require this change in emphasis and direction. In a larger world, allowing separation of our globe's many cultures and religions, and in an illusion of infinite natural resources, it was perhaps possible for entire cultures to act in selfish and self-serving ways. But in a world of finite, potentially exhaustible resources — and one necessarily united across cultures by communication, commerce, travel, and shared global challenges like climate change, environmental pollution, over-population, resource scarcity, and more — these competitive and conflictive behaviors are no longer reasonable or sustainable.

In this context, if religions continue the old way of stressing their different claims to truth, they will continue to be part of the world's critical problems. If religions emphasize love, kindness, mutuality, nurturing, the value of everyone, and interdependence, they can still be part of the solution for the planet. At the core of Interspirituality is the simple and yet profound experience of the Oneness of everyone and everything that exists. This sense of Oneness dates back to the earliest spiritualities on the planet, and yet is as modern as the 20th and 21st centuries. In our time, it has now been confirmed by science, which sees everything in the universe as part of a single fabric.

As Br. Teasdale said in his seminal writings on Interspirituality, "This journey is what spirituality is really about" [MH p. 4], and "This revolution will be the task of the Interspiritual Age" [MH p. 12]. The emerging interspiritual experience meets this challenge head-on. Through cooperation and co-creation, the diverse inner experiences and wisdom of our species can become a transformational asset for our future. An outspoken and challenging voice, Teasdale also warned that it would take great courage for members of any world religion or spiritual tradition to follow a more universal path. Nevertheless, he was convinced that this path is the destiny of all the world's religions. The role of global interfaith movements, and their synergy with the diverse efforts of the world's widespread Peace and Sustainability movements, are critical to this positive manifestation planetwide. Without these cooperative efforts, we may face not only critical global challenges, but also, in our inability to meet them with the creativity that has aided our species' survival in the past, we may face the ultimate possibility of eventual extinction.

Endnotes and References for "History" Section[ii]

INTERSPIRITUALITY ITSELF

Interspirituality could be seen, historically, as emergence of a deeper sense of, and emphasis on, an international perspective and experience of the world's spiritual and religious traditions in their emerging global context. Growing rapidly, especially in the last few decades, out of the world's post World War II interfaith movement, Interspirituality emphasizes the experiential, heart, and consciousness-related qualities of the world's many spiritual traditions and deemphasizes the specific creedal and dogmatic claims of the religions. Thus, in its present form at a global level, Interspirituality is not really a "way" so much as a *trend*, as religion and spirituality make a natural and inherent adjustment to our world's rapid movement toward inevitable globalization and multiculturalism.

The emergence of this trend is timely. It's widely acknowledged that a universal spirituality is, in fact, arising rapidly worldwide — a global shift to the heart of true spirituality at the core of all the world's religions. This new spirituality of the heart also reflects an emerging new global unity consciousness. As stated by interfaith pioneer Br. Wayne Teasdale, who coined the term Interspirituality in a 1999 book

The Mystic Heart: Discovering a Universal Spirituality in the World's Religions:

> The real religion of humankind can be said to be spirituality itself, because mystical spirituality is the origin of all the world religions. If this is so, and I believe it is, we might also say that interspirituality — the sharing of ultimate experiences across traditions — is the religion of the third millennium. Interspirituality is the foundation that can prepare the way for a planet-wide enlightened culture, and a continuing community among the religions that is substantial, vital, and creative [MH p. 26].

Overall, the vision of Interspirituality is well summed up in this paragraph by Teasdale as well:

> We are at the dawn of a new consciousness, a radically fresh approach to our life as the human family in a fragile world. This journey is what spirituality is really about. We are not meant to remain just where we are. We cannot depend on our culture either to guide and support us in our quest. We must do the hard work of clarification together ourselves. This revolution will be the task of the Interspiritual Age. The necessary shifts in consciousness require a new approach to spirituality that transcends past religious cultures of fragmentation and isolation. We need to understand, to really grasp at an elemental level that the definitive revolution is the spiritual awakening of humankind [MH, pp. 4-12 sequence].

Many Champions

The vision of an emerging Interspiritual Age has arisen from leaders across the world's religious, spiritual, and philosophical traditions, anchored in the foresight of a globalizing world and a deep sense of the underlying commonalities held by all the traditions.

Br. Teasdale's naming of Interspirituality was preceded by a host of earlier visionaries and leaders in all the world's religious and spiritual traditions. Interestingly, the names emerge from across all the world's religions since their initial arising in what has become known as the Axial Age — the period from 800-200 BCE. Across these many traditions, the forerunners of Interspirituality were visionaries who realized that a common experiential thread underpins all spiritual experience and is the harbinger of an eventual "great coming together." In fact, a list (and photos) of some fifty of these pioneers can be seen on the internet at several interfaith and interspiritual websites.[1] The fifty-some most commonly listed, in no particular order and using their names as cited, include Alison Davis, Vivekananda, Neil Douglas-Klotz, Chiara Lubich, Matthew Fox, Roberto de Nobili, Pascaline Coff, Madame Blavatsky, Ajatananda, Amma, Aurobindo, The Mother, Babaji Nagaraj, Baha'u'llah, Felix Adler, Yogananda, Ken Wilber, Harold Vogelaar, Huston Smith, Rudolf Steiner, Wayne Teasdale, Atmananda Udisin, Brahmabandhab Upadhyay, Ram Dass, Satchidananda, Frithjof Schuon, Pandurang Shastri Athavale, Baba Virsa Singh, Pythagoras, Ramakrishna, Russill Paul, Raimon Panikkar, Ma Jaya Sati Bhagavati, David S. C. Kim, Willigis Jäger, Alejandro Jodorowski, Leon Klenecki, Thomas Merton, Donald W. Mitchell, Carl Jung, Thomas Keating, Jules Monchanin, Henri Le Saux (Abhishiktananda), Francis Acharya OCSO, Hazrat Inayat Khan, Juliet Hollister, Mahatma Gandhi, Andrew Harvey, Thích Nhất

Hạnh, Bede Griffiths (Dayananda), Joseph Gelberman, and H. H. the 14th Dalai Lama.

What is fascinating about such a long list is that if you went to the internet and found out about each of these pioneers, they would each comprise a book (or more) in themselves. And you would also find their names cited in various ways, taking into account the common parlance of other traditions, formal religious titles, and so on. Further, this gives some perspective on the amount of content that is involved in assembling a history of Interfaith and Interspirituality, since obviously such lists inadvertently also omit other persons of significant importance, or from other general time periods.

Many of these pioneers were associated with the global manifestations extending from the 1962-1965 historic Vatican II Council. The latter had profound effect on religions around the world, further nurtured by ecumenical leaders of global stature like His Holiness the 14th Dalai Lama and so many others. Scholars note that this vision framed the international discussion of the so-called "foundationalist theologians" after Vatican II, who envisaged the possibility of a global religious pluralism ultimately joined in heart and consciousness. Further, these unifying principles characterize the best vision of philosophy and futurism as well — from the perennial humanist goal of "a global ethical manifold" to Ken Wilber and the integralists' positing of a conveyor belt to an Integral Age.

This rapid expansion reflects two major actualities, both of which hold long-term historical implications. First, what Br. Teasdale termed "Interspirituality" was not new. Earlier, Raimon Panikkar had called it the "intrareligious" or "intraspiritual" experience, Matthew Fox "Deep Ecumenism," and Thomas Merton the "mystical communion." Eastern writers had added a number of expressions for it as well. The emerging paradigm actually reflected the aforementioned vision of well over fifty major historical figures who emphasized the "Common Heart" across all the world's traditions. Thus, it is no surprise that today we see Interspirituality nearly everywhere, under a variety of names and with the brandings of diverse groups and leaders worldwide; not just as Interspirituality but as "global-, ecumenical-, universal-, transtraditional-, or world-centric spirituality," along with the "spiritual but not religious," the "nones," and "multiple belonging."

The roots of Interspirituality also run deep in secular society. The same ethos that marks Interspirituality was at the heart of the 19th century American Enlightenment flowing from the pens of Ralph Waldo Emerson, Henry David Thoreau, and Walt Whitman, who identified the insights of interconnectedness and the praxis of love. With the culmination of the 19th century and the beginning of the 20th, the same ethos became the message of humanism (be it secular or religious humanism). The motto "deed over creed" was coined by Ethical Culture founder Dr. Felix Adler. The epiphany of the "overview effect," of the Earth from the moon, through Apollo astronaut Dr. Edgar Mitchell, led to the founding of IONS (the Institute of Noetic Sciences) [1973] exploring the intersection of science and human experience, particularly focusing on the implications of consciousness, intuition, and interconnectedness. Its sponsored book *Global Mind Change* [1988] by Willis Harman became an influential precursor of the emerging integral paradigm detailed further in these Volumes.

Indeed, a host of historical visionaries across the millennial Wisdom Traditions forecast the arising of a global universal spirituality — specifically in the last centuries, pioneers such as Teilhard de Chardin in the West and the Indian independence leader and sage Sri

Aurobindo (with his companion, The Mother) in the East. From these and other wellsprings have also evolved what has become known as the burgeoning and multifaceted "evolutionary consciousness movement."[2] The trend, identified by developmental philosophers as a great conveyor belt toward a successful global civilization,[3] is attributed to multiple and convergent causes. In the evolutionary consciousness movement, and the consciousness sciences, it's recognized as the natural next step in our cognitive evolution. Social scientists see it as a global adaptation driven by unavoidable trends toward globalization and multiculturalism. Of course, many proponents of religions see a divine hand at work.

Not an Abandonment of Religion but a Shift of Emphases and Priorities

What is envisioned in Interspirituality is not an abandonment of the phenomenon of religion (the phenomenon of spirituality appears wired into what humans are), but a "return to Source," an emphasis on the *best* that all the world's religions have always offered in the arenas of values, ethics, and ideals. This historical shift can be attributed to many causes. Indeed, if a world awakening — what some are also calling a "Second Axial Age" — is arising, there are vast and complicated implications for our complex world, including the arenas of religion, science, social structure, governance, economics, culture, and more. Certainly, all compassionately spiritual traditions affirm that there is an ultimate goodness that we are to help make fully present in the world, and that we can develop an identity more consciously informed by a deeper source, a higher power, a greater self — whatever it may be called. The task of a global spiritual revolution appears to be the awakening of this deeper reality common to the world's many religious traditions and an emphasis on living in accordance with it. For those involved with Interspirituality, this requires a major effort to bring our awareness out of preoccupation with petty and self-centered concerns into a compassionate connection with all life, living in ways that all can live.

According to documents of the United Nations Department of Public Information, major influential elements in this progress toward an emerging universal spirituality, global sense of shared universal values and ethics, and potent action toward world change have included The Charter for Compassion, The Earth Charter, and more recently the Interspiritual Declaration (the latter of the emerging global interspiritual experience).[4] These three efforts and their global constituencies express, inspiringly, the emerging spirituality, ethics, and values needed for a sustainable future.

Trends in a Global Interspirituality

The Coming Interspiritual Age surveyed global factors influencing and contributing to the emergence of world change centered on significant input from the reservoir of that collective human wisdom generally known as the world's perennial Great Wisdom Traditions. It asked if there is an inherent role for spirituality and religion from this innate reservoir of human wisdom that forms the underpinning of our species' millennial history — albeit obscured by a plethora of social and cultural factors.

Absent such a contribution from the wellsprings and ideals of the world's values and ethics traditions, it suggests the world appears destined to march toward globalization led by self-serving special interest groups, and political and financial institutions, leaving the public at the mercy of uncoordinated planetary resource exploitation and consumerism, coupled with a cacophony of competitions and conflicts over politics, financial wealth, natural resources, and the various other currencies of malevolent international power. Overall then, what is envisioned is the global emergence of a stronger and stronger "contemplative voice" to help guide our human destiny — and perhaps just in time.

Interspirituality has arisen internationally, especially in the last three decades, from within the contemplative core of the world's many religious traditions. Its modern well-known proponents across the Western religions, of course, include in large part the close association of Wayne Teasdale with Bede Griffiths and Thomas Keating, and their immediate historical association with Raimon Panikkar, Thomas Merton, and others. These were the pioneers of East-West contemplative and mystical dialogue, and Thomas Keating pioneered not only the East-West Centering Prayer Movement but also the more than two decades-long Snowmass Interreligious Initiative. The latter — particularly from its "Nine Points of Agreement"[5] (which we will enumerate in subsequent sections) — can be seen as spawning the current increasingly dynamic interspiritual experience, especially after the works of Teasdale and others further popularized the concept. Searches at Google, when it was still providing those results, normally turned up some one million entries tagged Interspiritual and Interspirituality and myriad far-flung organizations and networks associated with these trends.

These same trends have also brought women, and profound understanding of the feminine, indeed "Divine Feminine," into more proper balance across the traditions and among leaders and visionaries — a historical and cultural omission that had resulted from the centuries of the male-oriented cultural narratives in global landscape of dominance hierarchies. We herald this in these Volumes and strive to be a part championing that urgently needed balance.

The momentum of the interspiritual experience also results because the world's spiritual heritages — driven by the contemplative and mystical voices of the world's religions — do not stand alone. Rather, they are a part of a larger surrounding context of myriad other progressive visions. These have gathered in recent decades across innumerable other fields of human endeavor and culture — as featured in Paul Hawken's bestseller *Blessed Unrest: How the Largest Movement in the World Came into Being and Why No One Saw It Coming* [2006]. Consistent with Namaste publishing's mandate to its book *The Coming Interspiritual Age* — to see if data supported the visions in its previously published bestseller *A New Earth* by Eckhart Tolle — statistical and other surveys recorded in *The Coming Interspiritual Age* clearly showed global confluences, trends, and recognizable progress across science, sociology, history, and consciousness and brain-mind studies, all of which portrayed developmental threads inevitably part of an international unfolding of a growing planetary multicultural and globalization process.

A number of conclusions about these global trends appear self-evident. What is characteristic of them as a whole are rather obvious conclusions testifying to the precariousness of our time. These include:

1. *Globalization* of planet earth is inevitable. The question is what kind of a globalization it will be and whether it will be devoid of any significant contribution from the Great Wisdom Traditions.

2. *Multiculturalism* is inevitable. Again, the question is what kind of process will unfold and whether it will be a bumpy ride full of competition and conflict (indeed possibly even

outright economic and military warfare), or whether a more reasoned dialogue may emerge, mitigating such negative consequences to some degree. Myriads of statistical studies support the reality of these trends, and although we don't have space here to cite many of these fascinating overviews, we refer the reader specifically to statistics and tables in several of our recent publications.[6]

3. Well-vetted *Points of Agreement* already exist across the world's religions, most basically the "big four" derived from all the post Vatican II global discussions already cited above. These are: (1) the possibility of a common core to human mystic experience, (2) fundamental teachings held in common by all the world's religions, (3) the shared ethical implications of the teachings of all the great traditions, and (4) the inevitable mutuality across the religions regarding commitment to social and economic justice.

While it's true that creeds and dogmas, exclusive by nature at a cultural level, still characterize much of the purely religious side of the world's traditions, significant movements across the world's spiritual communities — emphasizing the profound mutual recognition among human beings in the realm of the heart and the primary understanding of profound similarities across the traditions' understandings of unifying states of higher consciousness — are also moving profoundly to potentially alter this equation. Spiritual emphasis on the experience of the heart and states of unitive higher consciousness appear to universally nurture profound life-altering experiences of interconnectedness, mutuality, and Oneness. These experiences are reflected in an increasingly expanding worldwide popular literature and media regarding the experience of a global collective or gestalt of We.

Thus, in sum, we can list the fundamental shifts in global awareness necessary for the successful arising of a global universal spirituality — or Interspirituality. They include the following, many of which are already unfolding before our eyes in these current times:

- Appreciation of the interdependence of all realms of human life and the surrounding cosmos
- Growing ecological awareness, with recognition of the interdependence of humankind and the biosphere, including the rights of all biological species
- Embracing of the shared wisdom in all the world's religious and spiritual traditions, past and present
- Growing friendship, and actual community, among the individual followers of the world's religious and spiritual paths
- Commitment to the depths of the contemplative pursuit and the mutual sharing of the fruits of this ongoing journey
- Creative cultivation of transnational, transcultural, transtra-ditional, and world-centric understanding
- Dedication to nonviolence, with a commitment to transcend militancy and violence tied to national or religious identities
- Receptivity to a cosmic vision, realizing humanity is only one life form and part of a larger community, the universe.

For many, these shifts mark the threshold required for healthy globalization, and the birth, through the world's Wisdom Traditions, of an unfolding Interspiritual Age.

Endnotes and References for "Interspirituality Itself" Section[iii]

Universal Principles

A common thread seen throughout the texts of these Volumes will be that they involve an assembling of visions and related action from multiple global spiritual and thought leaders and their attendant organizations and impact networks. Their statements and attendant actions involve stated universal principles. The conclusions about universal principles or self-evident truths parallel those derived from science, where that discipline uses the terms "a generality," a "general pattern," or a "law of science." Such terminology from science reflects that our human *objective* ways of knowing derive from observation, and testing, of countless "particular or component patterns" that point toward the generality, the general pattern, or thus, a law of science. This activity is so common in modern science and economics that today a further term for such syntheses, "design principles," has also emerged and some of these have won Nobel prizes.[1]

A fine, free e-publication compiling *Universal Principles and Action Steps* proposed by myriad international leaders, organizations, networks, NGOs, etc. was published by the interspiritual and United Nations community for the 2018 Toronto Parliament of the World's Religions — about which publication we will say much more farther below — and it served a daylong pre-event at the Toronto Parliament as well as wide following usage at the various international "COP" conferences [United Nations Conference(s) of the Parties]. Another manifestation of this view of universal principles is the "Unitive Narrative" of the international Evolutionary Leaders Circle, another document drawn from both the Great Wisdom Traditions and the cutting edges of most current science. It grounded a 2024 conference at Cathedral St. John the Divine in New York City the day before the

United Nations 2024 Summit for the Future and included prominent members of the global interspiritual community.

In sum, such principles assemble and emphasize the great ethical and wisdom teachings of the religions, but also the profound contributions of the arts, including literature, poetry, music, art, dance, and all the other manifestations that mark the best attributes of our species — *Homo sapiens* — as an unparalleled species at least on this planet.

Thus, it is not by accident that such unifying ethical principles represent one of the aspects of inherent religious unity that was realized by fruitful discussion across the world religions after the pivotal 2nd Vatican Council (Vatican II, 1962-65). Global discussions following Vatican II (often called "the Foundationalist Discussions")[2] defined three potential unifying or "Archimedean" principles possible among all the world's religions. These include:

1. Their common mystical core, experiential unity consciousness;
2. Universal ethical teachings and behavior aspirations; and
3. Mutual commitment to the self-evident truths of economic and social justice.

In the West, participants in these post Vatican II conversations included such historical luminaries as Thomas Merton, Wilfred Cantwell Smith, Harvey Cox, John Cobb, Langdon Gilkey, Juan Luis Segundo, Karl Rahner, Jeremy Bernstein, Raimon Panikkar, and Hans Küng.

Ultimately, of course, the potential of each of such principles in manifesting actual unity or a successful healthy global cosmopolitan culture remains a question. This very question vexed the early explorers of this Foundationalist conversation. Generally, at the time of the world's post Vatican II discussions, the more conventional theologians among the Foundationalists, those more bound by conventional creed or belief, concluded that unity points might actually not be possible. Generally, however, the mystics and liberation theologians — among them Thomas Merton and Raimon Pannikar, together with the liberation thinker Harvey Cox — took the experiential position that the shared existential / mystical core of all the world's traditions was synonymous with actual commitment to building a world based on the shared values of all the traditions. Shared values and ethics of love, kindness, selfless service, and equanimity are central to the teachings of all the great traditions. Further, they have been principal to the historical reform and revival movements that have characterized all the traditions as well.

When forgotten by the traditions themselves, or made subservient by political or financial pathology, these same values sprang up in independent movements. Humanism is perhaps the best example — the legacy of Ethical Culture and other humanist movements, which declared that this shared ethos was in fact the core of religious experience itself: deed over creed. These values are widely held in common, simply for sociological reasons. From Einstein to Schweitzer, King to Mandela, the number of social heroes who have embraced such universal values is huge. Indeed, this sense of shared ethos spawned many social movements across the globe in turbulent times of social and political change that typified the latter half of the 20th century. The unifying principle generally acknowledged as an Archimedean point of the world's religions — the shared commitment to social and economic justice — was thus universally shared with these wider more secular movements. Our world widely being in a current, apparently regressive, period opens many questions. We will have to see how persistent and widespread this current regressive period continues to be. It does reflect that our world is choosing between two meta-directions — dominance consciousness and dominance culture or partnership consciousness and partnership culture.

Br. Teasdale, who named the Interspiritual experience as the direction that religion must go to accommodate the needs of authentic globalization and multiculturalism, said in *The Mystic Heart: Discovering a Universal Spirituality in the World's Religions:*

> This revolution will be the task of the Interspiritual Age. The necessary shifts in consciousness require a new approach to spirituality that transcends past religious cultures of fragmentation and isolation. We need to understand, to really grasp at an elemental level that the definitive revolution is the spiritual awakening of humankind [MH, pp. 4-12 sequence].

He emphasized throughout *The Mystic Heart* the critical balance of advancing individual spiritual maturity simultaneous with collective social evolution if we were to enter a successful global age. Not every individual might be able to personally access experiential unity consciousness, so the challenge to the religions must be to educate about their shared values and lofty ethical goals, not simply to emphasize their differences in terms of theologies, creeds, or apocalyptic scenarios.

Br. Teasdale listed, or included discussion of, fundamental shifts in global awareness that would be necessary for successful globalization and multiculturalism. These became what is known in common parlance as the "Nine Elements of a Universal Spirituality" (following on the "Nine Points of Agreement" [Among the World's Religions], the "Eight Shifts Needed in World Consciousness," the "Five Evolutionary Developmental Elements," and subsequently the

"Seven Elements of Interspiritual Education" about which we will say more immediately below. As a member of the Snowmass Dialogues, the Monastic Interreligious Dialogue, a Trustee of the Global Parliament of the World's Religions, along with numerous colleagues with diverse other interfaith backgrounds, Br. Teasdale's statements of basic principle unfolded during the initial period after the publication of *The Mystic Heart*, 1999-2006, to be further amplified in the global interfaith and interspiritual communities thereafter.

We turn to these now. This is important and of moment because international bodies, like the United Nations and other NGO communities working worldwide, now recognize many of these interspiritual conclusions as internationally vetted "consensus statements" concerning values, ethics, and ideals and cite them along with others so acknowledged, like the Universal Declaration of Human Rights, The Earth Charter, the Charter for Compassion, foundational documents for the UN Conferences of the Parties, and so on.

Endnotes and References for "Universal Principles" Section[iv]

Points of Agreement

Br. Wayne Teasdale's seminal work on Interspirituality heralded: "We are at the dawn of a new consciousness, a radically fresh approach to our life as the human family in a fragile world. This journey is what spirituality is really about. We are not meant to remain just where we are. We cannot depend on our culture either to guide and support us in our quest. We must do the hard work of clarification together ourselves. This revolution will be the task of the Interspiritual Age. The necessary shifts in consciousness require a new approach to spirituality that transcends past religious cultures of fragmentation and isolation. We need to understand, to really grasp at an elemental level that the definitive revolution is the spiritual awakening of humankind" [MH, pp.4-12 sequence]. This would manifest, he said, because of a "new set of historical circumstances" [MH p. 4], something that particularly rings true today.

They are fundamental shifts in global awareness necessary for a successful global shift, some of which Br. Teasdale noted as already happening. The most well known, associated with *The Mystic Heart* and published in 1999, are the "Nine Elements of a Universal Spirituality." They include nine generalized behavioral traits that would be expected to naturally arise from full realization of the highest values generally held in common across the world's Great Wisdom Traditions.

The "Nine Elements," often treated in subsequent literature as a "list" were actually numbered subtitles across three chapters of *The Mystic Heart*, from pp. 109-157. Teasdale distilled them by reference into another now well-known list: the "Nine Points of Agreement" (aka the "Nine Points of Agreement Among the World's Religions," or "The Snowmass Agreements"). These were widely known from the work of the Snowmass Interreligious Dialogue (later called the Snowmass Interspiritual Dialogues), first from eight points and finally by nine, that were not officially published until 2006. Br. Teasdale reported to colleagues that he derived the "Nine Elements of a Universal Spirituality" by generally asking, "If the world's religions actually agreed on the 'Nine Points of Agreement,' what would that imply regarding how people would behave — what their lifestyles would reflect?"

Along with the "Nine Elements of a Universal Spirituality" and the "Nine Points of Agreement" there are three other lists of points or principals, culled later from the texts of *The Mystic Heart* by Kurt

Johnson, David Robert Ord, and faculty at the One Spirit Interfaith Seminary in New York City, noting that just as the "Nine Elements of a Universal Spirituality" were not originally a list but actually subtitled commentaries across three chapters of *The Mystic Heart*, there were other embedded lists within Teasdale's *Mystic Heart* text as well. These include "The Eight Shifts Needed in World Consciousness," "The Five Evolutionary Developmental Elements," and "The Seven Elements of Interspiritual Education." These are as named in 2013-2021 publications by Johnson and Ord (in *The Coming Interspiritual Age*), the Community of the Mystic Heart (about which we will say much more farther on) and a United Nations NGO-related publication assembled for the 2018 Parliament of the World's Religions in Toronto, Canada and published subsequently in 2021. Therein, all five lists were gathered as "Foundational Documents" under the subtitle "The Interspiritual Declaration" in an e-book on *Universal Principles and Action Steps*.[1] Since their initial or early publications as noted below, many have been published widely in the interspiritual literature. To be succinct, we cite all five lists below, from the 2021 publication:

1. **The Nine Points of Agreement** (source, the 30-yr. Snowmass Interspiritual Dialogue)[2]

    1. The world religions bear witness to the experience of Ultimate Reality to which they give various names: Brahma, Allah, (the) Absolute, God, Great Spirit.
    2. Ultimate Reality cannot be limited by any name or concept.
    3. Ultimate Reality is the ground of infinite potentiality and actualization.
    4. Faith is opening, accepting, and responding to Ultimate Reality. Faith in this sense precedes every belief system.

5. The potential for human wholeness—or in other frames of reference, enlightenment, salvation, transformation, blessedness, nirvana—is present in every human.

6. Ultimate Reality may be experienced not only through religious practices but also through nature, art, human relationships, and service to others.

7. As long as the human condition is experienced as separate from Ultimate Reality, it remains subject to ignorance, illusion, weakness, and suffering.

8. Disciplined practice is essential to the spiritual life; yet spiritual attainment isn't the result of one's own efforts, but the result of the experience of Oneness (unity) with Ultimate Reality.

9. Prayer is communion with Ultimate Reality, whether it's regarded as personal, impersonal (transpersonal), or beyond both.

2. **The Nine Elements of a Universal Spirituality** (source, Br. Wayne Teasdale, *The Mystic Heart: Discovering a Universal Spirituality in the World's Religions*)[3]

1. Actualizing full moral and ethical capacity
2. Living in harmony with the cosmos and all living beings
3. Cultivating a life of deep nonviolence
4. Living in humility and gratitude
5. Embracing a regular spiritual practice
6. Cultivating mature self-knowledge
7. Living a life of simplicity
8. Being of selfless service and compassionate action

9. Empowering the prophetic voice for justice, compassion, and world transformation

3. **The Eight Needed World Shifts in Consciousness** (source, Br. Wayne Teasdale, *The Mystic Heart: Discovering a Universal Spirituality in the World's Religions,* as published in Johnson and Ord)[4]

   1. Appreciation of the interdependence of all realms of human life and the surrounding cosmos
   2. Growing ecological awareness, with recognition of the interdependence of humankind and the biosphere, including the rights of all biological species
   3. Dedication to nonviolence, with a commitment to transcend militancy and violence tied to national or religious identities
   4. Embracing of the shared wisdom in all the world's religious and spiritual traditions, past and present
   5. Growing friendship, and actual community, among the individual followers of the world's religious and spiritual paths
   6. Commitment to the depths of the contemplative pursuit and the mutual sharing of the fruits of this ongoing journey
   7. Creative cultivation of transnational, transcultural, transtraditional, and world-centric understanding
   8. Receptivity to a cosmic vision, realizing humanity is only one life form and part of a larger community, the universe

4. **The Five Evolutionary Developmental Elements** (Teasdale's major 1999 points, as summarized by Johnson and Ord 2013)[4]

1. Human consciousness and heart have been evolving toward a maximum potential regarding the kind of being humans can be and what kind of an earth we can create.

2. This has been going on since the known origin of the cosmos, as material evolution and as evolution of consciousness.

3. This is recognized in a fundamental tenant of the interspiritual vision, that the evolution of world religions has been one unfolding experience reflecting the gradual growth of human maturity.

4. This trend is anchored in the universally unfolding experience of unity consciousness or awakening, the experience of profound interconnectedness, no separation, and the world of the heart.

5. This has implications for the innumerable realms and arenas of endeavor represented by all humanity.

5. **The Seven Elements of Interspiritual Education** (source, Community of The Mystic Heart with One Spirit Interfaith Seminary, as published in Johnson and Ord)[4]

1. Teaching Interspirituality itself (the journey from interfaith to experiential interspirituality)

2. Teaching sacred activism (the inherent connection of being and doing)

3. Cultivating higher consciousness (unity consciousness as an actual experience)

4. Nurturing individual formation (personal maturation in authentic universal spirituality)

5. Teaching Integral (the integral vision and the developmental view of history)

6. Community building (building authentic communities of all kinds)

7. Ministry development (developing interfaith and inter-spiritual ministry from conventional roles—in religious institutions, chaplaincy, hospice—to entrepreneurial initiatives, creating new roles for interfaith and interspiritual ministry).

Endnotes and References for "Points of Agreement" Section[v]

International Conferences and Assemblies

In 1993, Teasdale had been involved with the refounding of the Parliament of the World's Religions in his home city of Chicago. Also in 1993, he had been instrumental in creating, with Julian von Duerbeck O.S.B., a historic interfaith dialogue with His Holiness the Dalai Lama on the "emptying" in truly awakened awareness. This led to the Gethsemani Encounters between Buddhist and other interfaith monastics. By this time, the Snowmass Dialogues had been ongoing since 1984.

After it's early legacy, beginning with the legendary interfaith appearance and message of Swami Vivekananda at the First Parliament in Chicago, in 1893, the tradition, about which we will say much more later, was revived following increased interest in interfaith dialogue promoted especially through organizations associated with the United Nations and interfaith associations such as The Temple of Understanding, which through the 1960s and 1970s promoted various spiritual summits on three continents.

The founder of the Temple of Understanding, Juliet Hollister (of which Fr. Thomas Keating was later a President), is an example of what one person's commitment can bring to the world stage. Seeing the desperate need for the world's religions to step up to global challenges, Hollister worked with Eleanor Roosevelt, Albert Schweitzer, The Very Rev. James Parks Morton, His Holiness the Dalai Lama, and others to revive an activist platform for the interfaith community, founding the Temple in 1960. Interspiritual pioneer Fr. Thomas Keating became its first president. Also, the American interfaith movement gathered steam in the Civil Rights Era with the galvanizing of faith groups around the cause of social justice.

Backgrounding this, much had begun with the Roman Catholic Church's 1965 Vatican II conclave issuance of the *Nostra Aetate*, a new vision of the role of interfaith cooperation in the world. This now iconic event was a testament to Pope John XXIII's historical legacy. This was the beginning of the global "Foundational [or Foundationalist] Discussion," of what the world's religions held in coming about which we will say much more later. In New York City, the leadership of the Episcopal Cathedral of St John the Divine founded a multifaceted Interfaith Center of New York, combining interfaith dialogue with social service visions across denominations. In 2007, a broad world coalition of Muslim scholars issued a statement on interfaith harmony. King Abdullah of Saudi Arabia followed with sponsorship of a world interfaith conference hosted by the King of Spain. His Holiness the Dalai Lama, who had received the Nobel Peace Prize in 1989, hosted world interfaith leaders gathering in India.

Contemplatives, and activists inspired by the contemplative enterprise, were also gathering worldwide, not only through the Snowmass Initiatives but also a variety of emerging Guidelines for

Inter-religious Understanding (or Dialogue), through the Monastic Interreligious Dialogue movement and other far-flung associations. Regular international symposia on contemplative living were sponsored by Mind and Life Institute, along with annual conferences on contemplative outreach by the Center for Contemplative Living. We will share much more about these, and many other interfaith / interspiritual initiatives and activities, which by 2008 — two years after the publication of the "Nine Points of Agreement" were published — were meeting around the world with regularity, convened by some of the world's most well-known contemplatives and mystics for face-to-face dialogue. As Teasdale had predicted, the effect of one-on-one meetings among respected spiritual leaders was becoming a powerful leaven for understanding and recognition around the globe. Among the contemplative leaders and well-known mystics who participated in joint statements from these gatherings were the following: from Islam, Imam Dr. Amir al-Islam, Imam Mohamed Bashar Arafat, Shaikh Kabir Helminski, Shaikah Camille Helminski, and Llewellyn Vaughan-Lee; from Buddhism, Ven. Bhikkhu Bodhi, Ven. Thubten Chodron, Acharya Sam Bercholz, and Lama Surya Das; from Christianity, Fr. Thomas Keating, Rev Cynthia Bourgeault, Rev Joan Brown Campbell, Dr. Thomas P. Coburn, Sister Joan Chittister, Rev Matthew Fox, and Rev James Parks Morton; from Hinduism, Dr. Amit Goswami, Aster Patel, Swami Ramananda, Swami Atmarupananda, and Sraddhalu Ranade; and from Judaism, Rabbi Schachter-Shalomi Zalman, Rabbi Shefa Gold, and Rabbi Naomi Levy.

In 2010, the Temple of Understanding assembled and honored a broad cross section of interfaith visionaries in a well-publicized event in New York City. The centuries-long convergence of the evolutionary conscious, integral, and interspiritual experience was well on its way.

A Needed "Aside": Distinguishing Spirituality from Religion and Further Distinguishing the Interfaith and Interspiritual Experiences

After sharing this stream of history concerning the emergence of the interfaith and interspiritual experience, we need to further illumine two elemental facets — differentiating spirituality from religion and further distinguishing the interfaith and interspiritual experiences. This could be a very long discourse, so to be able to relay it succinctly and briefly, we will turn to how this discussion is introduced to students at interfaith and interspiritual seminaries.

Currently, there are over 4,000 religious traditions. Historically, the number has probably exceeded 60,000.[1] Thus, there are also thousands of extinct religions, a fact we don't often think of. Each of these religions has had a distinct narrative concerning the perennial universal questions of "who we are, where we came from, and where we're going." Commonly, they also have had distinctive origin stories, narratives of the miraculous, even messianic promises, and end-time scenarios. And, they have had variously tighter or looser parameters for how life was lived, how religion was practiced, and how that related to love, fear, or a bit of both. Likely, over the millennia, millions of persons both killed for, and died for, these religions and the ideas or worldviews attached to them. Each undoubtedly had their heroes, both warrior and saint. And likely the saints were incarnations of love and care as much as anything, or anyone, we can point to in our own day. Indeed, Religion and Spirituality are rather strange bedfellows. There are many angles by which we can distinguish religion from spirituality — and each has a different, useful, and informative slant.

As a part of hastening the discussion in this day and age, we can also query AI as to what the difference is — and it is helpful. It says, in a way paralleling what many might say, each in their own way: "While often used interchangeably, 'religion' refers to a structured system of beliefs and practices usually within an organized community, while 'spirituality' is a more personal quest for meaning and connection to something larger than oneself, which can be expressed outside of a formal religious framework; essentially, religion provides a framework for spirituality, but one can be spiritual without being religious in a specific organized religion" [Google AI]. Following on this, we might say the above regarding religion but suggest, regarding spirituality, that *it more involves* the experiential and behavioral essences of love, values, etc., that nearly all religions *point to*. A commentary on the Snowmass Dialogues in the *Contemplative Outreach News* said it well, as we noted previously:

> Within a few days it became clear to attendees that while their religious vocabularies were different, their experiences were not.

From a different, more sociological point of view, religion could also be said to be simply what "spiritual people" do together when they gather, or make community and communities, and thus naturally then develop agreed upon gatherings and observances regarding those activities. In that context, religion could be said to be what emerges when a *story* or *narrative* is attached to the context of these noble and admirable behavioral traits. It could also be said that "the trouble begins" when the allegiance to the story or narrative associated with religions becomes stronger or more compelling than the experiential, behavioral essences of love, values, etc., that all religions point to. This probably explains one of the mantras of humanism: "It's not your God I am afraid of. What I'm afraid of is what you may do in 'his' name." This innate paradox, or bifurcation, between what spirituality is and what religion is has been a tricky one for millennia. As Ken Wilber says, it explains why many of the best, and many of the worst, actions in history have happened in the context of religion. Likely for those nearly 60,000 religions across history that many killed for, or died for, each likely also had saintly, serving individuals. There is also a historical angle. All religions are traceable back to a founder or founders. Generally those groups became religions when, often sometime after the passing of that founder or founders (or even sometimes while they were still alive), things were written down that then became normative with regard to either belief or activity. It's all a very natural phenomenon but it creates some tricky ground for a group of primates known as the species *Homo sapiens*.

To understand better what appears to be a natural progression from religion to spirituality, and from the conventional spiritualities (of this brand or that) to an interfaith and then interspiritual spirituality, this class "handout" from the One Spirit Interfaith Seminary in New York City is helpful:

> Most people come into their interfaith experience from one or the other of the traditional world religions or denominational experiences—Christian, Jewish, Moslem, Buddhist, Hindu, agnostic, atheist etc.
>
> As these people begin to taste other religious experiences (and "experience" is the key word, not just creeds or beliefs), and the rich historical backgrounds behind all these, they find themselves in an interfaith experience.
>
> As a person's spiritual path matures more, they begin to harvest and enjoy the riches of varied religious experiences and points of view. Valuing this richness

more than just that of one tradition is "Trans-traditional Spirituality." Trans-traditional Spirituality begins with generally the same assumptions as Interfaith, but moves toward emphasizing the value in sharing all the varied experiences of the world's traditions. It emphasizes less the interest in deciding, ultimately, who is actually "right" or "wrong," although this consideration still lingers in the background. That concern lingers in the background because this religious experience (actually the heart in this experience) remains shallow enough that there is still a "mental" concern about who is ultimately "right" or "wrong," a concern linked actually to deeply hidden fears about ultimate rewards or punishments.

As people develop in Trans-traditional experience, they begin to understand that there is a common and deep shared "knowing" at the deepest core of all religious experience. This experience — of a deeper holistic spirituality, interconnectedness, unconditional love, and non-separation — becomes the basis of "Truth," not the mental concern about which religious narrative, story, interpretation, speculation, prophecy, practice, method, leader, Messiah, etc. is ultimately "right." This is Interspirituality, a great step into the freedom that grows into Awakening that has even more deep experience of profound interconnection with everything — no separation, no "other." And yes, still also living in the humility of three-dimensional life in a temporary body etc.[2]

As we have said, distinguishing spirituality from religion moves the evolution of religions from the conventional and denominational, to the interfaith and interspiritual. It enlightens the place of the interfaith and interspiritual phenomena in context of the greater understanding of consciousness itself and in step with the greater growth of more holistic- and partnership-based consciousness within the world at large.

When we look at this phenomenon, this gradual evolutionary emergence of the interfaith, and then the interspiritual phenomenon — and the larger context of evolving consciousness — there are at least two centuries of authors and pioneers, and at least 2,000 major books, that articulate this progression. If we look back, we can date the roots of this globalizing realization to the earliest straddling between the world's Great Wisdom Traditions and the implications of the emergence of modern science. In the widest sense, this embraces the broad context of the West's "Enlightenment Period" — generally considered at least the late 1600s to the early 1800s [often called the "long 18th century"] wherein Western politics, philosophy, science, and communications radically reoriented as part of the "Age of Reason" or "The Enlightenment." This puts us squarely in the mid-to-latter 19th century of major interfaith development, and wherein Darwin published his *On the Origin of Species*. This then transitions to the origins of the Evolutionary Consciousness Movement, the Interfaith-Interspiritual Age, Integral Age, or whatever word we may call it by.

Two Centuries and 2,000 Books

Across the landscape of popular books, names like Deepak Chopra, Barbara Marx Hubbard, Lynne McTaggart, Ken Wilber, Don Beck,

Eckhart Tolle, Andrew Cohen, etc. are well known in popular parlance. But there is also a larger significant number of recognizable leaders who have been involved in the high tide of the evolutionary consciousness movement. A group calling themselves the Evolutionary Leaders lists some 300.[3] However, the phenomenon is far more complex. If we look at the origins of the Evolutionary Consciousness Movement, by the mid-19th century, we began to see clear evidence of dialogues and syntheses between the spiritual and the scientific. As the 19th century closed, there had already been one Parliament of the World's Religions (held in Chicago in 1893), inquiry between spiritualism and 19th century science in the founding of Theosophy, and the appearance of pivotal texts on the relationship of objective and subjective knowing by such researchers as William James, Sigmund Freud, and C. J. Jung.

With the onset of the 20th century, there was a vibrant mixing of Eastern and Western understanding, prominent in the literature of the First World, featuring names known to nearly every avid reader: D. T. Suzuki, Evelyn Underhill, P. D. Ouspensky, and Rudolf Steiner, each of whom attempted to bridge the scientific-spiritual gap — as in the internationally influential *Creative Evolution* by Henri Bergson, together with further emergence of the developmental vision in writers like James Mark Baldwin and Jean Piaget.

As the 20th century progressed, Western cultures dominated by Christianity were swept by a similar transcultural dynamism in the religious writings of Joseph Campbell, Martin Buber's *I and Thou*, Alfred North Whitehead in philosophy, Arnold Toynbee's histories of the rise and fall of cultures, and Arthur Lovejoy's classic, *The Great Chain of Being*, known to nearly every student of religion if they have stepped for a moment outside the tradition of their birth. As the Second World War was about to plunge the world into uncertainty, the discovery of LSD and the popularization of other psychedelics, natural and synthesized, introduced a precarious path for the human subjective search. Theosophy's J. Krishnamurti emphasized the enigmatic "pathless land," while Paramahansa Yogananda's book, *Autobiography of a Yogi*, was a runaway bestseller.

As we passed beyond the World Wars and entered an increasingly integrative epoch, integrative texts began to abound. In Europe, Frithjof Schuon wrote on *The Transcendent Unity of all Religions* in 1948. The same year, Thomas Merton entered contemplative monasticism from where he would popularize the subjective journey for millions of readers. In this post-War period, Western psychology reached a clinical high tide, with works emerging on love, sex, learning, and the clinical definitions of psychological illness. We have already referred to Aurobindo's work and that of Teilhard de Chardin, both from this period. The syntheses of Karl Jaspers recounted the rise of the world's religions in the Axial Age and introduced the lexicon of Eastern philosophers to the philosophies of the West.

The phenomena of the 1960s are, of course, legendary in this culmination, including an international countercultural wave that embraced every aspect of culture from music, art, and pop-spirituality to recognition of the perils that might face our species in the future — pollution, overpopulation, resource competition, corporate greed and corruption, and war. In the United States, this was the era of the Civil Rights movement and the work of Dr. Martin Luther King, Jr.

The Evolutionary Consciousness trend did reach high tide in Popular Culture. This cusp between the 1950s and 1960s was also the era of the "Beat" poets or "Beat Generation," remembered by many readers from a clutch of New Yorkers: Allen Ginsberg (*Howl*, 1956), William S. Burroughs (*Naked Lunch*, 1959), and Jack Kerouac

(*On the Road*, 1957). Beat had multiple meanings, initially meaning "beaten down" — a reference to the revolutionary tone of the era. But when the Beat generation merged nearly seamlessly into the hippie and peacenik movements of the '60s, the meaning took a turn. Consistent with the paradoxical language of the Eastern spirituality manifesting throughout the West, beat came to mean "with the beat" of change or evolution. The message of this '50s and '60s radicalism was already consistent with what became the implicit principles of both the evolutionary consciousness movement and Br. Teasdale's view of the emerging Interspiritual Age: peace and tolerance, rejection of materialism and militant nationalism, and an embracing of the heartistic and mystical elements of our humanity.

Many readers will readily recognize their own special experiences of this era. If you read fiction, you'll remember the wildly popular messages of J. D. Salinger (*Franny and Zooey, The Catcher in the Rye*), Hermann Hesse (*Steppenwolf* and *Siddhartha*), and William Golding (*Lord of the Flies*). If you read spirituality, you'll remember Shunryu Suzuki (*Zen Mind, Beginners Mind*), Alan Watts (*This Is It* and *Psychotherapy East and West*), the American tours of Maharishi Mahesh Yogi, and Harvard Divinity School's Harvey Cox's influential cultural overview *Religion in the Secular City*. Aldous Huxley's elaboration of his "Perennial Philosophy" and his *Brave New World* are also famous from this time.

Students of science will recall Rachel Carson's pivotal book on pollution, *Silent Spring*, the Club of Rome's compilation, *The Limits to Growth,* and Paul Ehrlich's *The Population Bomb*. Sociologists often refer to these as the modern era's apocalyptic literature. Followers of psychology will never forget their reading of R. D. Laing's *The Divided Self* and *The Politics of Experience*, along with Thomas

Szasz's *The Myth of Mental Illness.* In the genre of holism, nearly everyone knows Abraham Maslow's *Toward a Psychology of Being* and Thomas Kuhn's *The Structure of Scientific Revolutions,* which helped us comprehend the phenomenon of paradigms.

Few will not know of The Beatles and their flirtation with Eastern spirituality or the wider phenomenon of "psychedelic rock" (witness hundreds of thousands of hits at YouTube even today). In this era of collision between transformative vision and pop culture, rockers The Doors took their name from the prolific pen of a famous visionary contemporary, writer Aldous Huxley, whose *The Doors of Perception* and *Brave New World* had been blockbuster literary successes. Equally remembered are other icons of this flamboyant era: the psychedelic experiments at Harvard University by Timothy Leary and Richard Alpert, and the controversies that swirled around the "hip" pop artists Andy Warhol and Roy Lichtenstein. Each well portrays Marshall McLuhan's memorable mantra of the time: "The medium is the message."

Such popular phenomena sunk the roots of the evolutionary consciousness message further into the substrata of world culture than we often realize. Except for the fundamentalist sectors of the world, which are information proof, these myriad characters and movements left not only an indelible mark of a more holistic vision on the world but also momentum in that direction.

It ought not to surprise us that the cresting of the emerging evolutionary consciousness, of which Interspirituality is a part, began around the year 1970. Much of this demarcation results from the influence of the new physics, and with it a recognition of deep synchronicity between humanity's interior and exterior ways of knowing. It was at this time that the first literature about the Earth as an integrated organism (the eventual "GAIA" of James Lovelock) began to emerge. From 1969, now classic books began to appear, melding these formerly divided cultures of knowing: Charles Tart's compilation, *Altered States of Consciousness*, the work of Elizabeth Kübler-Ross, *On Death and Dying*, and Fritz Perls' gestalt therapy.

In 1976, the implications of the new physics were popularized widely in Fritjof Capra's bestseller, *The Tao of Physics*. The same message was brought to the world's contemplative and monastic communities throughout the 1980s by Interspirituality's own Fr. Bede Griffiths in a series of speaking tours and articles in prominent periodicals. In 1970, Gary Zukav's bestseller, *The Dancing Wu Li Masters*, furthered this conversation on the worldwide stage, winning the American Book Award for Science. This was also the era in which contemplatives around the world, from multiple traditions, began sharing their experiences through the communications of the Monastic Interreligious Dialogue, joining first East and West and then the experiences of the so-called 1st World with those of Indigenous Peoples.

The sheer variety and number of developments in these, and academic fields around the world — more and more finely grained — elaborated the meaning and implications of a world propelling itself toward multiple perspectives and holistic integration. In the endnote attached to this text, we enumerate many of these, divided into numerous categories.[4]

The 1970s also saw the publication of syntheses establishing pivotal paradigms of thinking for the holistic age, from Julian Jaynes' *The Origin of Consciousness in the Breakdown of the Bicameral Mind* to the massively influential Integral Theory beginning in 1977 with Ken Wilber's *Psychologia Perennis: The Spectrum of Consciousness* and continuing on through over 20 books by Wilber now available in nearly 40 languages. From Integral also grew the understanding of Spiral Dynamics developed by Don Beck and Chris Cowan and other views of reality rooted to a great degree in the work of Arthur Koestler, a British polymath renowned for both his works in fiction and nonfiction. Koestler coined the term *holon* in 1967 to refer to the well-known phenomenon of things that constitute a whole and a part at the same time, like organs in the body or the interconnected elements of the ecosystem. As Koestler recognized, the implications of the hierarchies and holarchies comprised of holons was barely beginning to be understood as the integrative and holistic eras unfolded.

With holistic awareness also emerged new understanding of nutrition and alternate modalities in medicine and the healing arts. Who isn't familiar with the works of popular writers like Drs. Andrew Weil, Deepak Chopra, and Kenneth R. Pelletier? Chopra's 1989 publication of *Quantum Healing* is often considered a game changer in understanding the relationship of health, wellbeing, and consciousness. Also emerging from this emphasis was new literature on the healing modalities of feminine spirituality, as in the works of Marija Gimbutas, Anica Mander, Anne Kent Rush, June Singer, Carol Christ, Judith Plaskow, Jean Shinoda Bolen, and Tsultrim Allione. The diversity of these testifies to the global nature of this unfolding.

The integral paradigm emerged during this period and is what then became the wider evolutionary consciousness movement. Exponential growth of this global consciousness movement continued through the next two decades, bringing with the new millennium a diverse landscape of authors, speakers, pundits, and spokespersons. Most of us are familiar with *What is Enlightenment* magazine founded by Andrew Cohen. Many may have attended the period of annual conferences on Science and Nonduality. In a way that wasn't possible even a few decades ago, leaders could now be brought together across great distances to meet personally, discuss diverse issues, and propose mutual and synergistic solutions. In recent years, gatherings such as Integral Institute, The Contemplative Alliance, and Evolutionary Leaders have allowed prominent authors and spokespersons to meet personally and regularly. You will see that we "Timeline" and "Benchmark" many of these historic elements in our accounts within these Volumes.

Most of us need no reminder of the names of these frequently seen celebrities and near-celebrities who spread the message of humanity's developmental transformation. The catchiest names that come to mind in an arbitrary scan across the media landscape include Ken Wilber, Don Beck, Deepak Chopra, Eckhart Tolle, Marianne Williamson, Barbara Marx Hubbard, Lynne McTaggart, Andew Cohen, Dean Radin, Duane Elgin, Briane Swimme, Michael Dowd and Connie Barlow, Matthew Fox, Robert Wright, Yasuhiko Kimura, Llewellyn and Anat Vaughan-Lee, Bruce Lipton, Jean Houston, Michael Beckwith, and Michael Brown, to name just a few.

In addition to individuals we know from our day-to-day media, there are a host of lesser known but immensely important scientists and religious scholars whose contributions have further grounded this holistic message of our world's potential. Among these, Russian-Belgian Nobel Laureate Dr. Ilya Prigogine pioneered study of reality's structures and makeup. Austrian-American Dr. Erich Jantsch elaborated concepts of self-organizing principles. The title of his most famous book, *The Self-Organizing Universe: Scientific and Human Implications of the Emerging Paradigm of Evolution,* illumines the overall vision of evolutionary consciousness. Drs. Francisco Varela and Humberto Maturana pioneered studies of how organisms actually co-create their environments, setting a prescription for how our species might succeed in the future with global problem-solving. Their work seeded the field now known as "autopoiesis," coined by them in 1972.

American-born British physicist Dr. David Bohm in a now famous book, *Wholeness and the Implicate Order*, suggested a synthesis of the new physics, consciousness, and the human brain. Bohm had been hounded out of the United States, his patriotism questioned by the fanatics of the McCarthy era. Hungarian-born scientific philosopher and systems theorist Dr. Ervin Laszlo, who was also instrumental in bringing Eric Jantsch's work to the world, authored over 70 books, extending his pioneering work in systems theory to a comprehensive view of evolution. And from that emergence comes today's Holomovement, about which we will also say much more further on.

As the new millennium dawned, American Passionist Fr. Thomas Berry, a student of both Teilhard de Chardin and native shamanism, articulated a succinct statement of Eco-spirituality, the now famous "Twelve Principles." Motivated by an urgent sense that the planet's commercialism might soon destroy the biosphere, Berry made his entire ministry about the ecological message. His call for a new unity with nature reached millions worldwide, not the least of which was former senator and United States Vice President Al Gore. In 2007, Gore and the Intergovernmental Panel on Climate Change received the Nobel Peace Prize for their work informing the world about the human role in climate change. Just three years before, the Peace Prize had gone to Kenya's Wangari Maathai, founder of Africa's Green Belt Movement, which was initially a women's movement that advocated massive grassroots action as the only sure route to world change.

The public success of Berry, Gore, and Maathai paralleled the predictions of sociologist Paul Ray, published in 2000. Ray identified nearly 150 million Americans and Europeans who share a progressive worldview centered on the issues of spiritual development, ecological advocacy, and the transformative political role of women. Eco-spirituality would eventually find even more fruition in its merging with advancing studies of planetary ecology and the new integral methods. In 2001, the Declaration of Amsterdam joined thousands of scientists in designating the earth an interconnected organism of geosphere, biosphere, and noosphere. By later in the same decade, the founders of the "GAIA hypothesis" (now the "GAIA theory" being tested in numerous scientific forms) even received honors from major scientific societies. Entire new scientific disciplines owed their genesis to this new holistic view — palaeoecology, ecophysics, earth systems sciences, and biogeochemistry. All of these became important in our measures to determine how real and how imminent the danger of global climate disruption. Ecology also joined with Integral. In 2011, the voluminous *Integral Ecology* joined guiding ecological texts on scientists' and university students' bookshelves, doing exactly what its subtitles indicate — uniting multiple perspectives on the natural world. Shamanic practice has also joined with progress in the healing arts as holistic and alternative medical approaches have become more and more welcome in the integrative and holistic epoch. The good news is that both the religious and scientific understanding of what Interspirituality is, as a cultural phenomenon, includes the coexistence and synergy of the varieties (and integrities) of *diverse* religious expressions and narratives *and* the understanding of their underlying unity in our profoundly interconnected world.

In this we can ask, and need to ask, what became of the original intentions and visions of voices in the seminal days of the interspiritual and integral movements? Kurt Johnson addressed this in 2025 in a program by the Edinburgh Centre for Spirituality and Peace, in Edinburgh, U.K. He identified three historical factors that the pioneer writers on Interspirituality did not appear to anticipate. These three were:

1. **Disaffiliation.** The vision of some early pioneers, especially Teasdale and Wilber, was that Interspirituality and Integral Philosophy would usher in "the global intersubjective discussion that the world so desperately needs but to a great extent has never had" [our paraphrase]. It was absolutely accurate that this discussion was and is urgently needed, but what happened was that multimillions worldwide disaffiliated, and thus did not birth millions of the new generations into "the great isms" —while at the same time the ecclesiastical, political, and financial structures of these religions, philosophies, and worldviews remained culturally intact, albeit in far smaller numbers across the wider populations of civil society.

2. **Resurgence of Nationalist Populism.** It appears few anti-cipated the current formidable resurgence of movements of Nationalist Populism reviving formidable civil society support for more fundamentalist worldviews and authoritarianism over democratic institutions and social methodologies. These movements have turned multimillions, knowingly or by social coercion, strongly toward dominance systems and away from the directions toward partnership that were and are inherent in the

interfaith, interspiritual, and integral experiences. Part of this is also the result of a global decrease in general literacy and levels of authentic education. This emergence is strongly connected to the third element below.

3. ***Media Transformation and the Mis- and Disinformation Dilemma***. Also unanticipated was the media transformation away from printed modalities and instead to the world of screens. This transformation has led worldwide to shorter attention spans in our global populace, less access to vetted factual media, and a proliferation — especially through social media — of mis- and disinformation. It has also led the field of psychology to understand the compelling nature of "conspiracy theories" on the human brain. Amazing as it may seem, a 2024 assemblage of global sociologists identified this trend as "an evolutionary catastrophe." The definition of evolutionary catastrophe in science is something that so upsets the norm that there is no guarantee of how, or how long, it will take to restore some kind of new normal.

Like it or not, this spectrum of severe challenges is elementally a part of the interfaith and interspiritual landscape today.

Endnotes and References for "Conferences…" Section[vi]

TIMELINES

We can now turn to sharing more specifically from Timelines relevant to the contents of these Volumes. Because of the complexity of many activities, initiatives, events, etc. — all from diverse and far-flung global "players" (and admitting, as we did in our Introduction, that we would have inevitably missed some, if not numerous, aspects of this global picture) — we can group more than twenty-five years of interspiritual emergence into convenient and informative sequential Timelines. These have been distilled from the contributions in these Volumes, the general global literature, and twenty-five years of correspondence and attachments from a myriad of the pioneers historically involved in these nearly three decades of interfaith and interspiritual activity.

We utilize these Timelines because they cluster all this history into some coherent detail. Consistent with these Volumes marking the 25th anniversary of Br. Wayne Teasdale's book naming Interspirituality, we begin after the 1999 publication of his *The Mystic Heart: Discovering a Universal Spirituality in the World's Religions*. Also noted in the timelines, however, are particular interfaith activities, initiatives, organizations, etc. that preceded *The Mystic Heart* and were either of special mention by Br. Teasdale, or are intimately connected to the later emergence of his work.

At a global level, it is important to notice that these activities (events, initiatives, publications, etc.) in the global interfaith / interspiritual community are paralleled by strikingly synchronic, but institutionally independent, unfoldings in the secular community. Notably, these are all characterized by calls for — in the words of their own publications — a "common core of values, standards and attitudes, a sense of universal moral responsibility and obligations, that would be needed to achieve an enduring global egalitarian civilization." These include: in 1999, the United Nations Declaration and Program of Action on a Culture of Peace, in 2000, the UNESCO (United Nations Educational, Scientific, and Cultural Organization)'s Manifesto on a new global ethic, and, also in 2000, the statements on a viable future from the UN Millennium Summit. Further, in 1993, the Parliament of the World's Religions composed its "Declaration Toward a Global Ethic" also founded on shared ethical principles that religious, spiritual, and cultural traditions considered foundational to a more peaceful and just world.[1]

These timelines are presented in a short "telegraphic" format, especially since the work of most *individuals* connected to them (many of whom are Featured Authors herein) are more fully elaborated throughout the pages of these Volumes.

1999-2003: The period following on the work, since 1984, of the Snowmass Dialogues, Contemplative Outreach, etc., and the 1999 publication of Br. Teasdale's *The Mystic Heart*, saw the founding of major institutions that became foundational to the further development of the interspiritual experience. Their subsequent interactions fostered much of what developed thereafter, including the founding of the following: The Interspiritual Dialogue Network (aka "Interspiritual Dialogue") [incorporated 2002] by Wayne Teasdale and colleagues (and as ISDAC.com [2001] updated to ISDnA.org [2005]); The Spiritual Paths Foundation (aka Spiritual Paths Institute) by Thomas Keating and colleagues, as spiritualpaths.net [2002]); One Spirit Interfaith Seminary (aka One Spirit Learning Alliance or "One Spirit," [2002] and as 1Spirit.org [2002]); Satyana Institute, and as Satyana.org, a primary organizational partner of these others (founded in 1996 by William Keepin and Jed Swift). As well, in 2000, following the publication of *The Mystic Heart*, interfaith pioneers at Scarboro Missions (Toronto, CN) published their first widely disseminated Golden Rule materials, centering on the landscape of thirteen of the world's religions. Following the 9/11 2001 attacks, the iconic "Interfaith Amigos," Imam Jamal Rahman, Pastor Don Mackenzie, and Rabbi Ted Falcon, began their interfaith dialogue and collaboration, promoting understanding and peace among different religions. Earlier, in 1978, His Excellency Mussie Hailu began global Golden Rule work as a co-founder of Pathways To Peace. In 2010, Hailu played a key role in having the United Nations adopt April 5 as International Golden Rule Day. In 1981, Rabbi Joseph H. Gelberman founded The New Seminary for Interfaith Studies in New York City (today the All Faiths Seminary International). Specifically mentioned in *The Mystic Heart*, its graduates founded New York City's One Spirit Interfaith Seminary, the world's largest interspiritual seminary, and one that became intimately involved in the development of Teasdale's interspiritual message, as noted further below and detailed in these Volumes. In 1992, Neale Donald Walsch began publishing *Conversations With God* which spent two and one-half years on the

New York Times bestseller list, a non-denominational, open source, "populist" approach to spirituality; later, in 2003, he and Steve Farrell co-founded Humanity's Team which became a regular collaborator with the interspiritual community; and, in 2003, Br. Teasdale began "Common Ground" activities with The Crossings retreat center in Austin, Texas (founded by local interfaith leaders Kenneth and Joyce Beck). Their programs "embodying Brother Wayne Teasdale's vision of inter-spirituality" [*The Austin Chronicle*] included the annual Austin interfaith "Abraham Walk" and programs co-created with New York's famous Omega Institute for Holistic Studies, another supporter of his early messaging. The Feature in these volumes on interfaith history by Paul Chaffee, founder of *The Interfaith Observer*, recounts the establishment of other important precursors to the interspiritual experience. Also important during this time was the work of Spirituality and Practice a multifaith website and a nonprofit organization founded by Frederic and Mary Ann Brussat who were early friends of Br. Teasdale and the Center for Action and Contemplation founded in 1987 by Fr. Richard Rohr OFM and Brian McLaren (a Featured Author in these Volumes).

2004-2006: Rapid growth of the institutions founded from 2001-2002 spurred by: **(1)** activities at the 2004 Parliament of the World's Religions ("PoWR") (Barcelona); Br. Teasdale and Interspiritual Dialogue, with Theatre Group Dzieci and Russill Paul hosted day event on Interspirituality at Barcelona Parliament; World Commission on Global Consciousness and Spirituality (of which Br. Teasdale was a member) with Dr. Ashok Gangadean, Yasuhiko Kimura, and Andrew Cohen hosted discussion of global interfaith and interspiritual landscape [2004]; this led to Kimura's publication in his *Vision in Action* the paper by Gorakh Hayashi and Kurt Johnson that immediately followed Teasdale's passing; subsequently lost from the internet for decades, it is republished in these Volumes; **(2)** We, the World and We.net founded the "11 Days of Global Unity" celebrations in the United Nations community and hosted its first interspiritual programs with Interspiritual Dialogue [2004]; **(3)** explosive upticks in activities spurred by unfolding cooperation among incipient interspiritual institutions following the passing of Br. Teasdale in 2004, and the organization activities following the various events and activities convened after his passing [2004, 2005] (see more detailed accounts in the Interspiritual Dialogue "Benchmark" section farther below); **(4)** invitation from the Snowmass Dialogues to embrace all of these institutions into the coterie of its subsequent activities and dialogues [2004]; **(5)** *Kosmos* journal founded with the subtitle "An Integral Approach to Global Awakening" (Nancy Roof and members of UN Spiritual and Values Caucuses) [2004]; **(6)** founding of the Claritas Institute for Interspiritual Inquiry, and the Interspiritual Mentor Training Program (Joan Borysenko, Janet Quinn, et al.) [2005]; **(7)** founding of the Institute for Sacred Activism (Andrew Harvey, Diane Berke, et al. [2005]); **(8)** publication of the Snowmass Dialogues (and "Nine Points of Agreement") in *The Common Heart* (Miles-Yépez) [2006] and publication of *Integral Spirituality* (Wilber) [2006]; **(9)** expansion of major activities, and founding of new organizations from these incipient interspiritual communities, both with the United Nations interfaith community and official UN NGO Committees like the UN NGO Committee on Spirituality, Values and Global Concerns [2004-2006]; and **(10)** co-creation of organizations and networks with important elements of the global evolutionary consciousness movement, particularly those of the Integral and Spiral Dynamics community, *EnlightenNext Magazine*, and the founding of the

Evolutionary Leaders Circle by the Source of Synergy Foundation [2006]; and joined in secular context by publication of *Blessed Unrest: How the Largest Movement in the World Came into Being and Why No One Saw It Coming*" (Hawken) [2006]; **(11)** founding of the Coalition for One Voice ("COV") (Sourcewatch.org) [not the same as others of similar name (Wikipedia.org)] by Teasdale colleagues, Deepak Chopra and others, followed by their activities (also with Andrew Cohen, Alex Gray, et al.) as Alliance for a New Humanity and "Passion to Connect" program [2006], COV continues to host a 20K newsletter for the Interspiritual Dialogue to this day; **(12)** Interspiritual Dialogue is a founding member of the World Wisdom Alliance, a worldwide coalition of groups, organizations, and networks working for transformation — WWA was founded at a seminal meeting of such groups in Toronto, Canada [2006]; **(13)** The "Tri-Faith Initiative" was founded (in Omaha, Nebraska, USA) linking the Abrahamic traditions and interfaith centers [2006]; and **(14)** in sequential years, Llewellyn Vaughan Lee, a Featured Author to these Volumes, with his son Emmanuel Vaughan-Lee, created the Global Oneness Project and a Global Oneness Summit, and Neale Donald Walsch and Steve Farrell, regular associates of the interspiritual community, created a Global Oneness Day and Global Oneness Summit in association with the United Nations community [2006, 2010].

2007-2012: Following 2006, further growth of diverse and far-flung interspiritual infrastructure: **(1)** significant interspiritual education and curricular development at Interfaith Seminaries, along with pioneer development of interspiritual ordination [2007 forward]; **(2)** organization and seminary development of interspiritual-integral education and curricular development [One Spirit, 2007]; **(3)** interfaith and interspiritual leaders join the Global Peace Initiative of Women in founding the Contemplative Alliance [2008]; **(4)** Beverly Lazetta and community formally found The Community of a New Monastic Way, pioneer New Monasticism community [2008]; **(5)** collaborations with The Order of Universal Interfaith (OUnI) (2008-2014) on interspiritual-ecospiritual programming and ministries, and "Big I" conferences (2012 forward) until its later separate incorporation in Michigan (2015) [2008], and Satyana Institute hosts "Cultivating Woman's Spiritual Mastery" conference [2009]; **(6)** based on Br. Teasdale's original vision of a "Universal Order of Sannyasa," the founding of the Community of the Mystic Heart, with large initial membership, became a major driver for expansion of the interspiritual experience in these early years [2010]; **(7)** founding of the Global Oneness Summit by Humanity's Team which would involve many interspiritual leaders through the Evolutionary Leaders Circle [2010]; **(8)** *The Interfaith Observer* was established by a group of interfaith leaders (Paul Chaffee et al.) and became a major disseminator of interfaith and interspiritual messaging [2011]; **(9)** Ashok Gangadean of World Commission of Global Consciousness and Spirituality (see Parliament of Worlds Religions [2004] above) joins ISD and FIONS at Wainwright House, NY, for Declaration of Interdependence event (YouTube at "Declaration of Interdependence") [2012]; and **(10)** beginning of "2nd Wave" of popular books on Interspirituality: *Song of the Earth* (Harland and Keepin), *God of Love* (Starr) (2012) [see details further below]; invitation from Namaste publishing (following on their popular book *A New Earth*) to prepare a major book on Interspirituality — published as *The Coming Interspiritual Age* in 2013 (Johnson and Ord) [2012].

2012-2016: **(1)** Continuing new wave of books on Interspirituality — *The Song of the Earth: A Synthesis of the Scientific and Spiritual*

Worldviews (Harland and Keepin) [2012], *God of Love: A Guide to the Heart of Judaism, Christianity and Islam* (Starr) [2012], *The Coming Interspiritual Age* (Johnson and Ord) [2013], *InterSpiritual Meditation* and *Mandala* (Bastian) [2013, 2014], *The New Monasticism* (McEntee and Bucko) [2015], *Let There Be Light* (Stein and Vidich) [2016], *Belonging to God* (Keepin) [2016], *The Art of Community* (Vogl) [2016], *Mature Interspirituality* from the Community of the Mystic Heart (Sw. Shraddhananda, edt.) [2017], from a founder of the Community of the Mystic Heart, interfaith theologian Dr. M. Darrol Bryant, *Ways of the Spirit: Persons, Communities, Spiritualities* [2015], and, ultimately, *The Religion of Tomorrow: A Vision of the Future of the Great Traditions — More Inclusive, More Comprehensive, More Complete* by Ken Wilber [2017]; **(2)** Formation of the United Nations-associated five years of Interspiritual and Eco-spiritual Conferences treated in more detail in these Volumes [2012-2017]; **(3)** Diverse programs and activities initiated after the publication of *The Coming Interspiritual Age*, including numerous online *Namaste Insights* publications including diverse interspiritual pioneers (selectively republished in these Volumes) [2013-2014]; **(4)** Expansion of Interspiritual Meditation and Interspiritual Mandala education programs by Spiritual Paths Institute [2013 forward]; **(5)** Continuing meetings of the "Schoolhouse" near Fr. Thomas Keating's Snowmass Abbey lead to co-creation of the pivotal Dawn of Interspiritual Conference [2013]; **(6)** Spiritual Summit for Social Change, New York City, by Interspiritual Dialogue, Coalition for One Voice, and others [2014]; **(7)** Aspen Chapel "Wisdom School" program on Interspirituality and activism with Interspiritual Dialogue and its United Nations colleagues [2014] and *Anchor* magazine [Still Harbor] special issue following on it; **(8)** Rev. Dr. William Thiele writes *Monks* *in the World* recounting the important spiritual and activist work of his School of Contemplative Living and Satyana Institute hosts Christianity and Islam dialogue: "Two Faiths, One God" conference [2014]; **(9)** Interspiritual Dialogue and United Nations colleagues initiate ongoing collaboration with the Center for Process Studies (Claremont CA) and its related Ecological Civilization program (John Cobb, Philip Clayton, Richard Clugston, Ken Kitatani, et al.) [2015 forward]; **(10)** Interspiritual Dialogue and United Nations colleagues' Self Care to Earth Care Conference in Denver with keynotes by Ken Wilber (YouTube Video "Introduction to Integral Spirituality" with over 300,000 views) and David Sloan Wilson of Prosocial.world [2015]; **(11)** 1God.com founded by Ben Bowler in Australia [2015] (and later, see below, will join with the Interspiritual Dialogue Network, and others, to co-found UNITY EARTH) [2016]; **(12)** Interspiritual participation in the 2015 Parliament of the World's Religions (Salt Lake City) [2015]; **(13)** Founding of ContemplativeLife.org by Jeffrey Genung [2015]; **(14)** Members of Interspiritual Dialogue joined the Gaiafield Project subtle activism initiative [2015]; **(15)** Collaboration with Evolution Institute and emerging Prosocial.world with events at State University of New York, Binghamton; New York City's Felix Adler Ethical Culture Library (April 12, 2016); and Gold Hill Historic Site, Boulder, Colorado (June 12, 2016) [2015-2016]; **(16)** Founding of the Charis Foundation for New Monasticism and Interspirituality by members of the Snowmass Dialogues to vision transition of the Snowmass Dialogues to today's Charis Snowmass Dialogues [2015-2016]; **(17)** Residential retreat of Community of the Mystic Heart with (i) presentation of the Sannyas robes of Br. Wayne Teasdale to Swami Shraddhananda's Sacred Feet Slate Branch Ashram (now Sacred Feet Anugraha House, Kentucky, USA) and (ii) passing of the Acclimation re: the Universal Order of Sannyasa (see item 5 in 2007-2012 Timeline above) of Br. Teasdale Sannyas lineage to the care of Swami Shraddhananda, Sacred Feet, and the full Sannyas program of Sacred Feet [2016]; **(18)** Founding of The Convergence Series on VoiceAmerica by 1God.com and Interspiritual Dialogue and one year of programs on The Interspiritual Age, and emergence of the UNITY EARTH network [2016]; **(19)** Interspiritual Event at United Nations Tillman Chapel in New York City by UNITY EARTH, Interspiritual Dialogue, and the UN NGO Committee for Spirituality, Values and Global Concerns (keynote: Dr. Andrew Vidich, co-author of *Let There Be Light: Experiencing Inner Light Across the World's Sacred Traditions*) [2016]; **(20)** Swami Shraddhananda closes Slate Branch Ashram and opens Anugraha House in 2017 (at jefifoundation. org) — this has since been the headquarters address for Sacred Feet Yoga and The Jones Educational Foundation for the last eight years [2016-2017]; and **(21)** Initial Charis Snowmass Dialogues (I and II [see charisinterspirituality.org (csd-past)]) [2016-2017].

2017-Covid Pandemic [3/ 2020]: (1) UNITY EARTH launches multifaceted "Road to 2020" series of interspiritual and cultural events enumerated further later in these Volumes [2016-2020]; **(2)** Crestone [Colorado] Leadership Conferences joining the interspiritual community further with United Nations NGO and Evolutionary Leaders communities [2017, aka "The Crestone Convergence"] and indigenous leaders [2018]; **(3)** Interspiritual leaders from Interspiritual Dialogue, UNITY EARTH, and United Religions Initiative participate in International Urantia Conference, University of Denver (host Gard Jameson et al.) [2017]; **(4)** Founding of *The Convergence* and *Light on Light* e-magazines by beginning over twenty issues concerning Interspirituality and global issues [2017]; **(5)** *Convergence* magazine special issue on Altruism [2017]; **(6)** *Light on Light* magazine launches with issues on community, spiritual practice, and first special issue with the International Day of Yoga Committee at the United Nations ("UNIDY") [2018]; **(7)** *Convergence* magazine special issues on the "Road to 2020," and the 2018 Parliament of the World's Religions [2018]; **(8)** Dawn of Interspirituality Conference in Latin America convened by Satyana Institute et al. [2018]; **(9)** One-day Pre-Event at the Parliament of the World's Religions (Toronto) [2018]; **(10)** *Convergence* magazine special issues on Conscious Business and New York City and African Union events [2019]; **(11)** *Light on Light* magazine special issues on Sacred Sites, the International Day of Yoga with UNIDY, and Change-makers [2019]; **(12)** Interspirituality and science-related visit and discussion with the Dalai Lama in Dharamsala, India [2019]; **(13)** Tribute Event to Fr. Thomas Keating, Aspen Chapel and Snowmass Abbey [2019]; **(14)** Evolutionary Leaders' Gold Nautilus award-winning book, *Our Moment of Choice*; subsequent *Our Moment of Choice* special issue of *Light on Light* magazine [2020]; **(15)** Humanity's Moment of Choice Radio Program on VoiceAmerica founded [2020]; **(16)** Light on Light Press founded, dedicated to books on Interspirituality and the global paradigm shift [2020]; and **(17)** Charis Snowmass Dialogues (II – VII) [see charisinterspirituality.org (csd-past)]) [2016-2020].

This Timeline will be continued in Volume 2, *Interspirituality: The Future*, through the Covid and post-Covid era, where Timeline dates and Benchmarks are more closely related to the content of that Volume.

Now, let's look at these with much more detail especially with regard to organizations, networks, events, and initiatives. Below, we sequence these in short sections, each noted as "Benchmarks."

BENCHMARKS

Based on the chronologies above, we further detail organizations, initiatives, events, and media which stand out in significance across these timelines. We add to each of these selected short Features and excerpts from our Featured Authors or from historical texts. We then follow with sequences of longer Features from Featured Authors grouped as appropriately as possible by thematic categories and chronologies.

Historic Interspiritual Foundings: 2001-2002

Following on the publication of *The Mystic Heart: Discovering a Universal Spirituality in the World's Religions* in 1999 and its interspiritual message, the years 2001 and 2002 stand out as the founding years of significant interspiritual institutions, the interrelations of which became foundational for much that followed in the global interfaith landscape. There was, as well, clear connection in these developments to global cultural impacts of the now infamous September 11, 2001, terrorist attacks in the United States and their inherent connection to the conflictual elements among the world's religions.

The unfolding interrelations of these organizations and networks opened the way for multiple further organizings, initiatives, events, and activities that would follow in rapid succession, including, in their midst, the eventual publication of the vision of the Snowmass Dialogues in 2006.

Clustering these major foundings also helps us form a baseline for tracing these unfoldings, with descriptions and reviews, from both a chronological and thematic perspective. We see now that these 2001-2002 foundings, quite independent of each other at first, were actually to come together very soon through the ongoing work of the Snowmass Dialogues and the emerging landscape of international conferences like the Parliament of the World's Religions. From these shared interfaith and interspiritual roots, these formative interspiritual organizations were key to creating the panorama of interspiritual institutions that today are ongoing, some twenty-five years later. We note them initially in these brief initial descriptions, then move to more detail farther below, and subsequently share the Feature contributions of their founders and constituencies through the later pages of these Volumes. Notes at the top and bottom of every history-related section will guide the reader to the pertinent and applicable longer contributions from our larger body of Featured Authors.

The One Spirit Interfaith Seminary

The One Spirit Interfaith Seminary ("One Spirit" at 1spirit.org) in New York City became the largest interfaith / interspiritual seminary in the world and generated pioneering interfaith and interspiritual literature and curricula. In addition, with partners below, it generated important initial organizations and networks, like the Community of the Mystic Heart whose hundreds of initial members and programs were important to the early years of interspiritual awareness. There are multiple features from its founders and constituencies in these Volumes.

Spiritual Paths

The Spiritual Paths Foundation (Spiritual Paths Institute) at spiritualpaths.net was founded by colleagues of Fr. Thomas Keating, well-springing from the Snowmass Interreligious Dialogues, and with initial centers of activity in Colorado and California. Its distinguished assemblage of interspiritual leaders and teachers, well represented in these Volumes, is recounted more below in a section on Spiritual Paths. Historically, it has expanded into multiple areas of interspiritual education including Interspiritual Meditation (with Facilitator Training) and the Interspiritual Mandala (with Mentor Certification). It has also sponsored important conferences and events.

The Interspiritual Dialogue

The Interspiritual Dialogue Network was founded by Br. Wayne Teasdale with colleagues from New York City and Chicago. Because of its multiple connections to the United Nations and other international institutions, it spawned a wide variety of ongoing programs that are reviewed farther below, including with One Spirit, The Community of the Mystic Heart, the years of interspiritual and eco-spiritual programs conducted in multiple states in cooperation with United Nations organizations, and, eventually, founding of the Light on Light Press which has won multiple awards for both its magazines and books. Its principal websites are lightonlight.us and from earlier, isdna.org, and its legacy is well represented by multiple Features in these volumes.

Satyana Institute

The three foundational organizations above joined with Satyana Institute (founded in 1996) on initiatives beginning with the 2004 Parliament of the World's Religions (Barcelona) and leading to the Dawn of Interspirituality conferences detailed more throughout these Volumes. The roots of *Satyana* mean "a vehicle for action infused with the grace of spirit," and its primary programs have been Gender Equity and Reconciliation International (GERI) and Dawn of InterSpirituality. Principle leaders of Satyana Institute are well represented in these Volumes.

At the turn of the 20th century and the Third Millenium, these key foundational organizations joined with the Snowmass initiatives, already running since 1984, in generating four decades of paramount interspiritual activity. The emergence of these organizations mirror well the words of Br. Teasdale in *The Mystic Heart*:

> The Interspiritual Age will require institutions and structures to carry, express, and support it [MH p. 248].

The collective work of these groups and associated organizations fills the Timelines presented above, and much of what unfolded over the next years and decades in the interspiritual experience grew from the interactions of these foundational groups, along with others. In 2015, they joined together to create a shared website for Interspirituality, interspirituality.com, noting over one hundred associated organizations and networks. Contributions from these many organizations and their growing work and expanding constituencies make up substantial parts of these Volumes.

Let's take a further look now at all elements of this historical narrative. We'll begin with the Snowmass Dialogues since they are a backdrop for the diverse organizations and personalities who form major parts of Interspirituality's emergence.

THE SNOWMASS DIALOGUES 1984-2015

with Features by Adam Bucko - Kabir Helminski - Rory McEntee - Thomas Keating

and subsequent Features by Edward Bastian - Cynthia Brix
Camille Hamilton Adams Helminski - Kurt Johnson - William Keepin
Netanel Miles-Yépez - Rami Shapiro - Mirabai Starr
Wayne Teasdale - Ken Wilber - Matthew Wright

Those who seek Ultimate Reality perceive themselves as citizens of the Earth. Their first loyalty is to the entire human family. They transcend the particularities of race, nationality and religion without reacting against them or trying to destroy them. They recognize the profound human values that the world religions enshrine. They work to preserve and enhance these values, but not at the cost of dividing the fundamental unity of the human family. They belong to an emerging global community. Of the Snowmass Dialogues: "Within a few days it became clear to attendees that while their religious vocabularies were different, their experiences were not." ~ Fr. Thomas Keating[2]

In this day and age, a succinct historical assessment of the Snowmass Interreligious Dialogues (later called the Snowmass Interspiritual Dialogues and today the Charis Snowmass [or Interspiritual] Dialogues) is immediately available from Google AI:

The Snowmass Interreligious Dialogues were a series of conferences that brought together spiritual leaders from many religious traditions to explore common ground and understanding. The conferences took place annually at St. Benedict's Monastery in Snowmass, Colorado, starting in 1984. Three of its most general purposes were [i] To promote mutual understanding and respect; [ii] To explore spiritual common ground; and [iii] To foster closer bonds of love among people and nations. Original Participants included: Imams, Rabbis, Swamis, Priests, Native American leaders and secular practitioners of transcendental meditation. Outcomes: [i] The Snowmass Conference Eight Points of Agreement [later the Nine Points]; and [ii] *The Common Heart: An Experience of Interreligious Dialogue*, a book that reflects on the conferences.

It further notes additional outcomes and legacies from the Snowmass Dialogues, including the "New Monasticism" discussion (explored further in these Volumes), the subsequent continuation of the dialogues as the Charis Snowmass Dialogues through the Charis Foundation for New Monasticism and Interspirituality, and the founding of the Keating-Schachter Center at Naropa University, also further described in Features herein. Rory McEntee, now Dr. Rory McEntee with his doctorate in open theology, associated with all these initiatives, and who assumed management of the Dialogues after 2013, wrote in Namaste Publishing's *Namaste Insights* magazine, "Archive Edition on Interspirituality" [2015]:

Setting a foundation for what has emerged as the modern [interspiritual experience], for over twenty years, a group of spiritual seekers from many religious traditions met in various places around the United States under the general name "Snowmass Interreligious Initiative." It took this name from the location of St. Benedict's Abbey, the home of Roman Catholic interfaith pioneer Fr. Thomas Keating.

These conferences innovated creative forms for interreligious dialogue, wherein the experience was intimate and trusting, transformative and inspirational. To encourage open, candid and honest sharing, no audio or visual recordings were ever made, until the most recent gathering in 2012, also hosted in Snowmass by Fr. Keating. No articles or books written either, until the document *The Common Heart*, published in 2006. Emerging from these decades of dialogue were the now well-known "Points of Agreement" first published in *The Common Heart* and recently elaborated as to content and implication in *The Coming Interspiritual Age*. The "Points" became a fulcrum for the writings of Br. Wayne Teasdale, also a colleague of the Initiatives, in his further elaboration of a "Nine Elements of a Universal Spirituality" around which his now classic book *The Mystic Heart: Discovering a Universal Spirituality in the World's Religions* was structured. *The Mystic Heart* began using the now universally recognized term "Interspirituality" in 1999, right on the cusp of our current Millennium.

The Common Heart contains an extraordinary exploration of the wealth of the world's spiritual traditions combined with dialogue from the heart about the differences and similarities between the world's spiritual paths and collective reservoir of wisdom. Participants in the volume included Fr. Thomas Keating, Ken Wilber, Roshi Bernie Glassman, Swami Atmarupananda, Dr. Ibrahim Gamard, Iman Bilad Hyde, Pema Chödrön, and Rabbi Henoch Dov Hoffman and Grandfather Gerald Red Elk. The book was edited by Netanel Miles-Yépez, co-founder of the Sufi-Hasidic Fellowship and Murshid of the Chishti-Maimuniyya Order of Dervishes, and Executive Director of the Reb Zalman Legacy Project in Boulder, Colorado. The book is available from Lantern books and is now considered a classic recordation of the pioneering dialogues of the emerging interspiritual movement.

At the dialogue's 2012 meeting, members of the initiative, along with new collaborators, met again in Snowmass and will meet again in 2013 in Washington State. Particular emphasis now is the passing on of this legacy of dialogue and innovation to a younger pantheon of interspiritual leaders who can carry forward the momentum of this initiative which has been so critical to the world interfaith movement.[3]

Prior to his passing in 2018, Fr. Keating had visioned the future of the historically pivotal Snowmass Dialogues for some time, and thus passing of its leadership to the "younger pantheon" noted above. In 2023, due to a declining number of resident monks at the Snowmass abbey in such a large facility, the Trappist order began downsizing the activities of the Abbey and, subsequently, advertised the property for commercial sale. As of the summer of 2025, such a possible sale remains unresolved. With the closing of the Snowmass Trappist abbey in 2023, activities of the dialogues shifted to the Charis Foundation, and it obtained its own retreat and event facility, the Charis Mandala Sanctuary near Des Moines, New Mexico.

We share this commentary also because of two included references. The "Washington State" reference refers to the then-planned Dawn of Interspirituality Conference (2013). It emerged from the groups of interspiritual pioneers meeting regularly with Fr. Keating, spearheaded for this important conference by the Satyana Institute [founded in 1996], about which there are numerous Features in the current Volumes.

From the wellspring of the Snowmass Initiatives emerged a coterie of interspiritual pioneers who, in 2002, founded the Spiritual Paths Foundation, also described in multiple Features herein. Regarding the reference to "a younger pantheon," McEntee and his co-author Adam Bucko (now Fr. Adam Bucko, an Episcopal Priest), wrote (in the same *Namaste* serial) regarding the emerging New Monasticism:

> There can be little doubt that traditional religious frameworks are no longer speaking to new generations as they have in the past, especially in the West. In a recent article in the *LA Times*, Philip Clayton, Dean of Faculty at Claremont School of Theology, writes that the fastest growing religious group in the United States is "spiritual but not religious," containing a shocking 75% of Americans between the ages of 18 and 29. Clayton argues that young people are not necessarily rejecting a sense of God, rather they feel that religious

organizations are too concerned with money and power, too focused on rules, and too involved in the structures of the political status quo...

We believe this understanding of Interspirituality, as a reciprocal sharing of realizations and contemplative gifts, in which each person's insights help to affirm, deepen, and direct the other's journey, is a framework that can be embraced by a new generation of spiritually hungry youth, while also allowing for intergenerational bridges to be built between elders, wisdom traditions, and the youth. We call this process spiritual democracy, putting aside our egos and relating to each other in a way in which we can be surprised by the Divine, through which wisdom can come through everyone participating and God emerges as the "between" between friends. Interspirituality can lead us to the God that is emerging among us, while naturally allowing us to touch the God within and beyond...

There are also different ways of being Interspiritual. One may have a solid grounding in one tradition, and from this foundational point reach out to experience and understand the wisdom of other traditions. This has been the way of many of the founders of the Interspiritual movement, such as Fr. Bede Griffiths and Br. Wayne Teasdale. One may also go the way of "multiple belonging" by fully immersing oneself in multiple traditions, such as Lex Hixon, also known as Shaykh Nur al-Jerrahi, did. This way is eloquently described by Matthew Wright, an Episcopal priest and practicing dervish, in "Reshaping Religion: Interspirituality and Multiple Religious Belonging."...

We explore the deeper contemplative dimension of this interspiritual movement in our manifesto, New Monasticism: An Interspiritual Manifesto for Contemplative Life in the 21st Century (http://hab-community.com/HAB/New_Monasticism.html), as well as the sacred activist dimension and the transformation of traditions in *Occupy Spirituality: A Radical Vision for a New Generation* (forthcoming, North Atlantic Books, Adam Bucko with Matthew Fox)."[4]

Of interest as well, the "Minutes" of the 2013 meeting of the Snowmass Interreligious Dialogue group planning the Dawn of Interspirituality Conference, and other activities, also spell out the delegated responsibilities of that year's attendees. Foreshadowed are a number of then future activities that would unfold over the years reflected in the Timelines we have presented earlier. From those meeting "Minutes" [bracketed comments are ours]:

Facilitating for the Core Group of the Association to "Keep this all in motion": Ed Bastian, Kurt Johnson & Diane Berke (Kurt can work/consult with Diane who we know is very busy). Also, Ed is already in cooperative programs with One Spirit so this makes this group quite "functional."

Coordinating re: Dawn of Interspirituality Conference: Will Keepin and Cynthia Brix.

Coordinating re: Snowmass Interspiritual Initiative

with Fr. Keating: Rory McEntee (who in July also joins Will and Cynthia on staff at Cascadia Center, Washington).

Visioning creative expansion re: additional activities and initiatives: Kate Sheehan Roach [re: Contemplative Journal], Ken Kitatani, Kurt Johnson and Doug King re: United Nations related outreach programs.

These quotations are of particular historical note since, at the time, the Dawn of Interspirituality Conference, and its subsequent conferences, were the next emerging major interspiritual events, the *Contemplative Journal* was founded *at* the Dawn of Interspirituality Conference, and "The Association" referred to in the Minutes was the network whose core team created the eventual Interspiritual Network and its current large website at interspirituality.com.

After this meeting, through 2013-2014, Bastian, Johnson, and Berke hosted a series of meetings subsequent to this gathering in California and New York City (the latter with over seventy attendees from the northeastern United States attending). These concerned forming of an international association around the interspiritual experience and creating a collaborative website to portray the interspiritual experience as it has emerged from the Dawn of Interspirituality Conference.

The meeting Minutes are also apt because they note initiation of the emerging programs and initiatives that emerged then in association with the United Nations interfaith community. The "United Nations outreach programs" refer to what emerged as the six years of programs that interspiritual leaders (affiliated with the UN Spiritual Caucus, which later was associated with the UN NGO Committee on Spirituality, Values and Global Concerns) created with special emphasis on Eco-spirituality and the Sustainable Development Goals.

These began with conferences and events back and forth between New York City (the location of the United Nations) and a half dozen locations in Colorado.

These included the Denver/Boulder Integral Community, Denver's Althea Center for Engaged Spirituality, the Aspen Chapel, Carbondale's Davi Nikent Center for Human Flourishing, and what was then the Aspen Institute in Crestone (now the Crestone Baca County campus of Colorado College in Crestone, Colorado). Crestone had a long association with United Nations entities through early activities of UN Under Secretary Robert Mueller and Crestone interfaith leaders Maurice and Hanna Strong who had collaborated on creation of a network of interfaith retreat centers, and other facilities, in the Crestone community, a Heritage Landmark Site also for Indigenous Peoples.

These programs, as we detail further in the current Volumes, included hosting the pivotal 2017 Crestone Leadership Conference [see a video at YouTube narrated by Ken Wilber, which today has 5,000 views].[5] Similar to the incipient 2013 Snowmass Dialogues meeting noted above, the Crestone Leadership Conference culminated with a list of intended events and activities which have, indeed, further unfolded up to the time of even the current Volumes. The noted event in this series in Denver — the Self Care to Earth Care Conference (2015) — is also memorable because it was where Ken Wilber announced his vision of Integral Spirituality, the video for which (as "Introduction to Integral Spirituality") now has over 300,000 views at YouTube [notably the largest number of views of any Wilber YouTube presentation]. The event is further notable because Wilber's companion speaker was Dr. David Sloan Wilson, famous today for leading mainstream science's understanding of how altruism evolves, and the modern understanding that the process of natural selection in evolution has elements (Group- and Multi-Level Selection) which select "for the good of the whole." These account not only for how altruism evolves but also the importance of cooperation and partnership as "fitness" in nature. This revolutionary work in evolutionary biology was just emergent at that time. Wilson would go on with Kurt Johnson (who also has a PhD in evolutionary science) and Br. Wayne Teasdale's friend and confidant Jeffrey Genung (founder of Contemplative Life) to develop, with others, "ProSocial Spirituality" joining contemplative spirituality and scientific activism as a part of Prosocial World (prosocial.world) for which Genung is currently Executive Director. The current Volumes contain numerous contributions from across this landscape.

Given all this, it is important to list the persons who, from 2013, met yearly — not only as part of the Snowmass Interreligious Dialogues but also in groups assembling annually at the Abbey's "Schoolhouse" facility, just down the road from the Snowmass St. Benedict's Abbey. At these meetings, interspiritual activists gathered annually for several days to a week, meeting with Fr. Keating to, as he often said, "co-conspire" unfolding interspiritual events and initiatives.

With Fr. Thomas Keating, usually ten or so of these "regulars" would gather for the annual planning sessions — alphabetically, Michael Abdo, Cynthia Brix, Adam Bucko, Chad Cascarilla, David Frenette, Michael Fuller, Janet Quinn, Rory McEntee, Netanel Miles-Yépez, Kurt Johnson, Patricia Johnson, Will Keepin, Rita Marsh, Kate Sheehan Roach, and Mirabai Starr. Edward Bastian had also been a part of this group until health matters no longer allowed him to share the high altitudes at Snowmass. This group, in one iteration or another — and joining with the group that was a part of Br. Teasdale's "association" centered in New York (Kurt Johnson, Martha Gallahue,

Gorakh Hayashi, Matt Mitler and Theatre Group Dzieci) — became the groups that also created programming for the Global Parliament of the World's Religions (today abbreviated as "PoWR"). Br. Wayne Teasdale was a Trustee of the PoWR, and his fledgling association incorporated as an interfaith nonprofit in the state of New York in 2002 especially to take advantage of the connections available there with the United Nations community. They took on as their first project what Br. Teasdale intended to be the first major program on Interspirituality since the publication of his book, *The Mystic Heart*, at the 2004 Barcelona Parliament.

That Parliament experience was also pivotal because, in the last weeks before the event, Br. Wayne became too ill to attend. The effectuation of the event fell upon his circle of friends, gathered in Barcelona — many of whom at that point had not previously met each other. Fortunately, the joining of other friends of Br. Wayne (like Dr. Ashok Gangadean, Estaryia Venus, Neill Walker [Edinburgh International Centre for Spirituality and Peace] and Dr. William Keepin [Satyana Institute]) not only made that first Parliament program very well attended but also a great success (featured afterwards in *Kosmos Journal*). The article in *Kosmos* about the interspiritual program at the Parliament is also interesting in its title, given by the editors of *Kosmos*: "Tension in Barcelona." The tension referred to is informative. Commentators on that Parliament tended to note that 30% of the Parliament was a trade show of World Religions, "buy mine, buy mine," etc., 30% was about interfaith cooperation, and 30% wanted to further explore what Interspirituality was pointing to, that is, "Discovering a Universal Spirituality in the World's Religions" (the subtitle to Br. Teasdale's *The Mystic Heart*). We'll reprise more on the 2004 Parliament in the third (fully illustrated) of these Volumes which features our Featured Authors on Interspirituality and the arts. Therein, Matt Mitler recounts the music and drama contribution made by his "sacred theatre" troupe Theatre Group Dzieci. At the Barcelona Parliament, the troupe was also accompanied by Br. Teasdale's close associate from Bede Griffiths' Ashram in India, famed sitar virtuoso and spiritual teacher Russill Paul. Further below, in the Benchmarks piece concerning The Interspiritual Dialogue, which Br. Teasdale co-founded, we quote from these contributions from Matt Mitler concerning Br. Teasdale, Interspirituality and the arts.

That said, the most important historical gravitas from the Parliament was the passing of Br. Wayne Teasdale in October of 2004. This was just as he had been planning to leave Chicago (where he had been residing as the official "Hermit" of the Diocese of Chicago under Francis Cardinal George, the Archbishop of Chicago, who had also heard his vows as a Christian Sannyas [renunciate] in 2003 [see fuller biography in Endnote]).[6] He had planned to enter a more hospice-like environment with friend Jeff Genung who had prepared an in-home facility for him. This also explains why Jeff Genung, to this day, is the holder of most of Br. Wayne's properties and papers, including his Sannyas robes which are now in the care of Sacred Feet Anugraha House of his now also departed friend, Swami Shraddhananda (aka Dr. Sonya Jones), an account we will detail further in the current Volumes.

The story wraps together three months after Br. Wayne's passing with the convening of the memorial event in his memory at what was then Omega at the Crossings, in Austin, Texas. This was a pivotal gathering because it was the first time that the wider association of friends around Br. Wayne met the coterie of colleagues surrounding Fr. Keating. And at this gathering, Fr. Keating committed to simply bringing the Teasdale group into his "family" at the Snowmass Interreligious Dialogues and further expanding the interspiritual work.

Thus, with this gathering, the New York and Snowmass interspiritual families were further joined with the colleagues from the Spiritual Paths Foundation, a beloved group of interspiritual leaders and teachers who had formed through the Snowmass Dialogues. Principally organized by Dr. Edward Bastian, this group included the prominent spiritual teachers Rev. Cynthia Bourgeault, Rabbi Rami Shapiro, Swami Atmarupananda, Shaikha Camille Helminski and Shaikh Kabir Helminski, nearly all of whom are represented by Features in these Volumes.

Let's close this section well-springing from the Snowmass Dialogues with these reflections:

Kabir Helminski's Reflections on the Snowmass Dialogues

We are almost like two species existing side-by-side. One species is focused on the material world of the physical senses, accepting as reality only that which can be measured, motivated by an individual ego self and the emotions it generates: the desire to be free of discomfort and to maximize pleasure, to receive approval and avoid disapproval, to gain attention and to avoid being ignored, and to be in control of people and circumstances.

The other species is motivated by an awareness that there is, perhaps, some nonphysical medium through which we are all connected, resulting in a degree of empathy, sensitivity to "vibes," and glimpsing a sense of purposefulness in the unfolding circumstances of life.

These two kinds of humanity cannot merely be described as secular and religious, atheist or believer. In fact, we don't have an adequate vocabulary to identify these two kinds of identities, these two modes of functioning, but for the moment, let us call the first the "ego identity," and the second, "the awakened identity."

The ego identity tends to act for the benefit of oneself (and one's immediate family), is focused on short-term gain, sees nature and the resources of the planet in terms of their dollar value, sees politics as a zero-sum game, a competition where they are the winners and others are the losers.

The awakened identity is concerned with fairness and justice, sees nature and the planet as a living organism, is capable of looking seven generations forward, is concerned with the reconciliation of conflicts and the healing of trauma accumulated in the course of human history.

Religion itself can fall on both sides of this divide; hence, the wars and so-called "clash of civilizations." Perhaps the essential difference between these two states is the degree to which one is controlled by a sense of self based in egoistic thoughts and emotions, as opposed to a self that awakens to a dimension of interconnectedness, of inter-penetrating identity.

One sense of self is ruled by rigid concepts, engaged primarily in service of self, and governed by animal instincts based in fear and aggression. Another sense of self is guided by the heart rather than the ego, living with an awareness of subtler human faculties and an open nondefensive sense of self.

The clash of these two mentalities, these two states of consciousness, is reaching a climax on our planet. The very survival of humanity may depend on whether enough people can shift consciousness from one state to the other.

The life and example of Fr. Thomas Keating has clearly demonstrated that people who have practiced the contemplative disciplines of various traditions can find the unity of purpose, a sense of brotherhood/sisterhood, and, indeed, a profound respect and love for each other. The question before us is: How can this experience be shared with a wider humanity?[7]

Certainly, this is still the question of our time. Let's turn now to further detailing the organizations noted above as "Seminal Interspiritual Foundings: 2001-2002."

SPIRITUAL PATHS INSTITUTE, FOUNDED 2002

Features in these Volumes by Edward Bastian – Cynthia Bourgeault – Camille Hamilton Adams Helminski – Kabir Helminski – Thomas Keating – Rami Shapiro – John A. Wilde

Spiritual Paths Institute (at spiritualpaths.net) is extraordinarily represented in these Volumes. You've just read the reflections from one of their founders, Shaikh Kabir Helminski, on the historic Snowmass Interreligious Dialogues. The Spiritual Paths Foundation was founded in Aspen, Colorado, in 2002. It was most directly influenced by his participation in Fr. Thomas Keating's Snowmass Conferences for Interreligious Dialogue at St. Benedict's Monastery (aka the Snowmass Dialogues). Its mission and programs were further inspired by Dr. Edward Bastian's career as a Buddhist scholar, filmmaker, and student of world religions.

The Foundation and its Spiritual Paths Institute garnered the talents of such well-known spiritual leaders and teachers as Zalman Schachter, Thomas Keating, Cynthia Bourgeault, Kabir & Camille Helminski, Rami Shapiro, Swami Atmarupananda, Joan Halifax, Laura Cespooch and Edward Bastian, among many others. It is most well known for its seminal books *InterSpiritual Meditation: A Seven-Step Process Drawn from the World's Spiritual Traditions* and *Mandala: Creating an Authentic Spiritual Path: An InterSpiritual Process*, and the education programs created around them, along with a two-year, masters-level certificate training program on InterSpiritual Wisdom co-developed by Rev. Cynthia Bourgeault, Shaikh Kabir, Shaikha Camille Helminski, Rabbi Rami Shapiro, and Swami Atmarupananda. A full accounting of their programs is included at spiritualpaths. net/history. Among the Features in these Volumes, Edward Bastian writes specifically on the origins of its Interspiritual Meditations and Interspiritual Mandala programs, and John A. Wilde contributes in detail on the history and influence of the Institute and its activities.

In our earlier sections of this Volume, we've written about the diverse programs and teacher / leaders of the Institute and its close association with the Snowmass Dialogues. We'll continue that narrative by turning now to the Interspiritual Dialogue association founded also in 2002 by Br. Teasdale with his colleagues in New York City and Chicago. As you will see, its activities also closely related to those of the Snowmass Dialogues, Satyana Institute, Spiritual Paths, and the One Spirit Interfaith Seminary in New York City. In fact, it was these five principal constituencies that joined to found the shared website interspirituality.com in 2015. It is actually a fitting tribute to Spiritual Paths to simply look at the oeuvre of books, videos, and other media from its listed founders and teachers.

THE INTERSPIRITUAL DIALOGUE NETWORK, FOUNDED 2002

Features in these Volumes by Diane Berke – Richard Clugston – Ashok Gangadean
Jeffrey Genung – Gorakh Hayashi – Philip Hellmich – Kurt Johnson
Ken Kitatani – Yanni Maniates – Matt Mitler – Sacred Feet Dharma Heirs
Swami Shraddhananda – Wayne Teasdale – Ken Wilber

The Interspiritual Dialogue Network (ISD, and later ISDnA) was founded in 2002 in New York City by Br. Teasdale and a group of colleagues especially to build from the associations possible there with the United Nations community. By New York law, Teasdale, a resident of Illinois, could not legally be a Trustee but he visited New York City regularly working with the group and its multiple activities further detailed in these Volumes. The group, which Teasdale colloquially called "the association," immediately associated closely with the One Spirit Interfaith Seminary [see the Benchmark Section immediately below] founded at the same time. Interestingly, the original home for ISD was the humanist Ethical Culture societies.

They embraced a multi-faith approach to religions based on Felix Adler's (their founder) vision in *Reconstruction of the Spiritual Ideal*. *The Mystic Heart: Discovering a Universal Spirituality in the World's Religions* had been introduced to Ethical Culture by Martha Gallahue of the United Nations "NGO Spiritual Caucus," and Ethical Culture's Brooklyn, New York, branch invited Br. Teasdale and Kurt Johnson to begin regular interspiritual gatherings there.

What ISD is historically known for, beyond its own founding and activities, are five areas of achievement. First, is the long-term association with One Spirit Interfaith Seminary and the co-development of interfaith and interspiritual education and curricula beginning in 2003. This included collaborations with the Snowmass Dialogues and the education programs of the Spiritual Paths Institute. Second, is the presentation at the 2004 Barcelona Parliament of the World's Religions with the then emerging pantheon of interspiritual pioneers and Teasdale. Third, is the founding of the Community of the Mystic Heart (CMNH) in 2010 (see elements of its history in the entry below). Fourth, is the half-decade series of international conferences and events ISD and elements of the United Nations NGO community and Earth Charter Commission developed, which are detailed in further sections of these Volumes. Fifth is the CMNH, ISD, One Spirit nexus in creating curricula combining the message and content of Teasdale's *The Mystic Heart* and Ken Wilber's *Integral Spirituality*. As is well known, the last major public appearance of Br. Teasdale was the series of discussions with Ken Wilber (available now on YouTube [Integral Life and Integral Guy Playlists]). In his last years, Br. Teasdale was centering on completing his two books, *A Monk in the World* and *Bede Griffiths: An Introduction to his Interspiritual Thought,* and Wilber wrote the Foreword for the former.

These contributed directly to the eventual content in Kurt Johnson and David Robert Ord's influential 2013 book, *The Coming Interspiritual Age,* whose lists of the various "Points" or "Elements" re: Interspirituality have been widely used in subsequent publications and other media.[8]

Following on these inter-connections, ISD and others from the New York City and United Nations community began working directly with Ken Wilber and the Integral Institute in 2007 co-convening several major conferences. Two were particularly noteworthy and synergetic. Following on leading a 2014 program on Interspirituality at the Aspen (Colorado) Chapel which, with members of the Earth Charter Commission, also highlighted Eco-spirituality, ISD convened the 2015 "Self Care to Earth Care" conference in Denver. Here, Ken Wilber presented and recorded his "Introduction to Integral Spirituality." The video of that title now has over 300,000 views at YouTube. Second, in 2017, was the convening of the "Crestone Leadership Conference" (aka the "Crestone Convergence") whose video at YouTube, narrated by Wilber, has some 5,000 views. ISD then created a publishing entity — Light on Light (at Lightonlight. us) — beginning with free e-magazines (at issuu.com/lightonlight) in 2017, and then moving to print books as an imprint of Sacred Stories Publishing in 2020. These books have garnered more than a half dozen Nautilus Awards and, in 2024, received Nautilus's "Best in Small Press" award. Wilber, Deepak Chopra, and other spiritual notables have consistently authored Forewords, Afterwards, Special Commentaries, and "Intervals" for these widely read books. The most recent awards have been for books created with two-time Nobel Peace Prize nominee and systems philosopher Ervin Laszlo.

The wider series of conferences and events were presented in Boulder, Denver, Aspen, Carbondale, and Crestone, Colorado, from 2008 to 2018 (thereafter breaking significantly due to the Covid pandemic). Around 2008, ISD began partnering with an emergent group of leaders called the "Aspen Grove," who were well-connected to both the Snowmass Initiative, the Colorado Integral community, and the California-based SHIFT Network. The Aspen Grove had formed in Aspen, Colorado, through Lori Warmington (a friend of Fr. Keating's) with diverse members from the history of the Snowmass Dialogues and parishioners of Aspen's fabled Aspen Chapel (another entry in these Volumes). The group included Fr. Thomas Keating and previously noted regular attendees at the annual Schoolhouse meetings near the Snowmass Abbey — Michael Abdo, Michael Fuller, Adam Bucko, Rory McEntee, and Kurt Johnson. But it also included New York members, like Kurt Johnson and Martha Gallahue, Chicago members, like Gorakh Hayashi, and California members, like Philip Hellmich (author of *God and Conflict*, who was then Director of Peace for the Shift Network).[9] Thus, several of these members were also part of the 2004 interspiritual event at the Barcelona Parliament of the World's Religions. The latter also included William Keepin and Cynthia Brix who had also been regular attendees at the annual Schoolhouse gatherings, from which sprang the "Dawn of Interspirituality Conferences" of which Satyana Institute was the named primary sponsor. Michael Fuller and Michael Abdo, also closely associated with Fr. Keating and Ken Wilber, among others, brought the integral vision to the Aspen Grove, and Wilber wrote the foreword for the Snowmass Dialogues' *The Common Heart: An Experience of Interreligious Dialogue* edited by Netanel Miles-Yépez which first published the now famous "Nine Points of Agreement."

Subsequently, ISD brought that group east, connecting them to what was then the United Nations NGO "Spiritual Caucus" (then chaired by Steve Nation and Barbara Valocore) for a 2009 major interspiritual gathering at their Lifebridge Sanctuary retreat center near Rosendale, New York. Among so many represented at that event was Lama Surya Das, celebrated author of "The Awakening Trilogy"[10] who is also a contributor to the current Volumes.

These gatherings, highlighting both Interspirituality and Eco-spiritualty, were in collaboration with eco-spiritual constituencies from the heritage and legacy of eco-theologian Fr. Thomas Berry. We will recount much more about these in Volume 2 of these Volumes whose content centers strongly on the connections of Interspirituality and science. Berry and Teasdale were colleagues at Fordham University in New York City, where Berry was a faculty member and from where Teasdale earned his doctorate in theology. The connection of Interspirituality and Eco-spirituality is a fascinating landscape, and the pioneers featured in these Volumes include intertwined elements of the Earth Charter Commission (Dr. Richard Clugston and Ken Kitatani in these Volumes) and the Yale Forum for Religion and Ecology (Drs. Mary Evelyn Tucker and John Grimm et al.). These activities eventually led to the "Rome-Assisi Conferences on Spirituality and Sustainability" associated, among others, with the Vatican Dicastery for *Laudato Si*. These all connect ably through elements of the United Nations, including initially, from 1994 and 2000 respectively, the informal United Nations' "Spirituality" and "Values" NGO Caucuses and their affiliations with UNESCO and UNEP [the UN Environmental Program] and participating members of the Earth Charter Commission. These elements in the UN community, originally the informal "Spirituality" and "Values" Caucuses, later in

UN administrative evolutionary history became associated with the UN Council of NGO's "Committee on Spirituality, Values and Global Concerns." The latter had been founded by Diane Marie Williams, first in the UN Geneva community (2002) and later also at the UN in New York City (2004). Williams, Deepak Chopra, and others also founded what has become "The Evolutionary Leaders Circle (ELs)," a project of Williams' Source of Synergy Foundation. Today the ELs are a network of over three hundred global thought leaders, many of whom are Featured Authors to these Volumes. Nancy Roof, prominent in establishing and sustaining both the UN Spirituality and Values Caucuses, notably founded (in 2001) the renowned *Kosmos Journal*, widely sourced in these Volumes and around the world.

Tribute Event to Br. Wayne Teasdale, 2005

Following Br. Teasdale's untimely passing shortly after the 2004 Parliament of the World's Religions, a tribute event was organized for him at what was then "Omega at the Crossings" (aka "The Crossings") in Austin, Texas, a retreat center associated with the well-known Omega Institute of New York state. The Crossings had been the location of several interspiritual events — the "Common Ground Events," accompanied by "The Abraham Walk" with the Austin Interfaith Community, hosted primarily by Br. Teasdale's Chicago colleagues, and colleagues also from the Snowmass Dialogues, who worked closely with Kenneth and Joyce Beck, the Crossings Founders. While Br. Teasdale and Fr. Keating were both living, the activities from Chicago, New York, and Snowmass were each growing somewhat independently, each doing their own development of events and initiatives.

A significant change came with the September 2005 tribute event for Br. Teasdale. It, just like the Barcelona Parliament event, joined together, in in-person contact, the far-flung personal and organizational friends of Br. Teasdale. All met and worked together personally. The Barcelona Parliament experience had done this for the far-flung associates of Br. Teasdale, and the Tribute Event to Br. Teasdale at The Crossings joined these, for many for the first time, to diverse associates of Fr. Keating and the Snowmass Dialogues. The tribute event concluded with the joining of Interspiritual Dialogue, Br. Teasdale's Chicago colleagues, The Crossings "Common Ground" programs, and others, into one entity — taking a new name "Interspiritual Dialogue in Action" ("ISDnA") and agreeing on creation of a new website (see "The Interspiritual Multiplex" farther below). A governing "Service Council" was created including Kenneth and Joyce Beck, Deanne Quarrie, Charles Ragland and Adam Blatner M.D. (of Unity Church and later founder of the interspiritual website blatner.com) from Common Ground, Gorakh Hayashi (Br. Teasdale's Chicago colleague) and Kurt Johnson and Luca Valentino (who later became a scholar of Dogen) representing Br. Teasdale's "association" in New York. Included in the larger assemblage were Curandero Don Oscar Miro-Quesada (who suggested the acronym ISDnA), Betty Sue Flowers (former Director of the Lyndon Baines Johnson Library and Museum in Austin), pioneer Sound Healer Estaryia Venus (an associate of Br. Teasdale since the Barcelona Parliament), and Dr. Joan Borysenko and Dr. Gordon Dveirin — who soon after would found the Claritas Institute for Interspiritual Inquiry. The Claritas Institute founders are each Featured Authors herein, along with Jeffrey Genung, who would go on to found Contemplative Life (at contemplativelife. org). There is still a one and a half hour video on YouTube from the

Tribute Event (which you can find at YouTube by searching "Tribute to Wayne Teasdale at The Crossing [sic], Sept. 05"). It includes many of the persons noted above.

At and after the Tribute Event, Fr. Keating, recognizing the need to bring these persons together more regularly, offered to fold the varied groups together not only by participation in the ongoing Snowmass Dialogues but also through the special meetings that many attended subsequently at his Abbey's nearby Schoolhouse facility. It was from these yearly planning meetings that the Dawn of Interspirituality Conferences and other significant events emerged. Also, shortly after the Tribute Event, Gorakh Hayashi and Kurt Johnson wrote what may be seen as one of the first accounts of Br. Teasdale's legacy after his passing. It (as "The Heart of Brother Wayne Teasdale's Vision of the Interspiritual Age") was published online by Yasihiko Kimura in his then *Vision in Action* online journal. Since this journal issue has not been available online for many years, and the article has never been in a print publication, we located a copy of the original manuscript and have included it in these Volumes. We have also done the same for another "lost" article by Br. Teasdale himself, "Swami Abhishiktananda: Christian Sannyasi and Advaitin" which was also published online and is no longer available. It had originally been provided by Kurt Johnson to the online *Contemplative Journal* after the 2013 Dawn of Interspirituality Conference. An entry found on the internet confirms that its original online publication has been deleted.[11]

For the members of Teasdale's association, there had been a gap in the last year before the Barcelona Parliament where it was quite impossible for Br. Teasdale to continue the regular meetings he was having between the New York and Chicago groups. The New York group particularly recalls a short note from him, hand-delivered by a

Teasdale colleague from Chicago the first time Br. Teasdale had not felt well enough to travel to New York City. In that note, which was handwritten, Teasdale communicated, "I'm sorry I have not been able to continue to be in regular touch with the association. It is taking all my strength now to complete both the Monk in the World book, and the Bede Griffiths book [Kurt Johnson pers. com. to Light on Light]." This gap continued up to before the Barcelona Parliament, which Br. Teasdale had assumed he would feel well enough to attend. But as it turned out he did not feel well enough to travel and the association found out about a week before that he would not be up to it. This was reflected in the convening of the session in Barcelona where persons who had been planning to be there with Br. Teasdale, like various interspiritual leaders from California, and Dr. Ashok Gangadean, from Pennsylvania, ended up arriving to the surprise that Br. Teasdale was not well enough to attend. As noted in the Benchmark Section on the Snowmass Dialogues, the interspiritual participations at the Barcelona Parliament were historically pivotal — not only the day presentation by Br. Teasdale's "association" and the discussions of the World Commission of Global Consciousness and Spirituality but the performances by Theatre Group Dzieci. Dzieci's founder, Matt Mitler, in his contribution in our third volume well summarizes the significance of that occasion and Br. Teasdale's part in it:

> …The Parliament of the World's Religions would next convene in Barcelona …. Brother Wayne instantly said I should participate.
>
> Later on, having looked over the Parliament's application, I wrote to Brother Wayne that I had far too many ideas for what to present there. He told me to present them all, and that winter, invited me to

Chicago to meet the other planners. Brother Wayne was undergoing medical care at that point but still warm and inviting, and all proposals were approved, all fees waived.

Dzieci ended up going to Barcelona along with the InterSpiritual Dialogue group, where we co-hosted events with them, presented performances of our own *Fools Mass* and *Cirkus Luna*, led para-theatrical workshops, and offered a series of meditative *Morning Observances*. Sadly, by then Brother Wayne had become too ill to attend.

If we are fortunate and questioning, we may be guided on our paths by gifted teachers who transmit with their entire being, who are also students learning alongside us, who tackle great mysteries and embrace fathomless questions — *Who am I? Why am I here? What do I serve?*

And even when those teachers are no longer with us in human form, we may still receive guidance. We may even in some small way, provide guidance ourselves for another generation of seekers — by simply working on ourselves.[12]

There was a pivotal transition time immediately after Br. Teasdale's October 2004 passing and then, again, after the September 2005 Tribute Event. There were numerous meetings of colleagues of Br. Teasdale, one memorable one being at Omega Institute in New York State the spring after his passing. It is especially memorable for four reasons. As Matt Mitler further recounts in his piece in our third volume, Omega (in upstate New York) was where he had first met Br. Teasdale — bringing him by car to the first meeting to plan the Barcelona event at the Ethical Culture Center in Brooklyn, New York City. Br. Teasdale had well-acquainted himself with the work of Theatre Group Dzieci during this ride, and they also had mentors in common, one being Jean Houston. The later Omega meeting was well attended by American Advaita teachers, all who remembered Advaita was part of Br. Teasdale's root spirituality. And, also attending were Sufi leader, teacher, and writer, Llewellyn Vaughan-Lee, a friend and colleague of Br. Teasdale, and persons from Pir Zia Inayat-Khan's "Seven Pillars House of Wisdom" in New Lebanon, New York, whose Interspiritual Institute was dedicated to the legacy of Br. Teasdale.

Kurt Johnson notes [pers. com. to Light on Light] there was, for many years, a photo of persons at that meeting, all sitting about a picnic table. But it has not been seen in years and is likely also lost. But, one thing learned by such gatherings was that Br. Teasdale, perhaps a bit like Johnny Appleseed, had scattered his influences and inspirations widely among colleagues, friends, and constituencies. But he often did not mention such persons to each other, and had quite different conversations with each. At the time of that above-mentioned gathering at Omega Institute, Kurt Johnson noted he did not know of Pir Zia Inayat-Khan's friendship with Teasdale. But soon thereafter both he and Pir Zia, and Adam Bucko, Michael Holleran, Charles Gibbs, Aster Patel, Dena Merriam, and others in these Volumes, became part of the Contemplative Alliance assemblage, which its founder Dena Merriam writes about in these Volumes. Interspiritual Dialogue also continued ongoing relationships with Imam Jamal Rahman and the Interfaith Amigos (see the Timeline [2001-2002]) and Ashok Gangadean of the World Commission of Global Consciousness and Spirituality (see the Timeline [2004]). Theatre Group Dzieci, whose founder, Matt Mitler, also writes for these Volumes continued regular international performances. Dr. Gangadean was part of the Spiritual Summit for Social Change in New York City cosponsored by the Interspiritual Dialogue (see the Timeline [2014]), and Kurt Johnson joined him for an interspiritual event at Haverford College in Haverford, Pennsylvania, as well. Both Iman Rahman and Dr. Gangadean are among these Volumes' Featured Authors. Br. Teasdale indeed was a central "glue" in the early emergences of the interspiritual paradigm following publication of *The Mystic Heart*. Very memorable from the Omega Institute gathering was a moment at the end, likely pointing to the urgency of the interfaith and interspiritual messages of our times, when after a long discussion about "where to go, what to do" following on Br. Teasdale's passing, Sufi leader Llewellyn Vaughan-Lee rose and said, very loudly, with some dismay, "It is not enough." Twenty years later, we think this observation rings quite true. The times are critical, and there is so much work yet to do.

THE ONE SPIRIT INTERFAITH SEMINARY, FOUNDED 2002

Features in these Volumes by DeShannon Barnes-Bowens – Diane Berke
Andrew Harvey – Kurt Johnson – Leslie Reambeault – Melissa Stewart

We've intentionally weaved the accounting of the Interspiritual Dialogue network of Br. Wayne Teasdale with that of One Spirit, since *The Mystic Heart: Discovering a Universal Spirituality in the World's Religions* was also part of its spiritual inspiration. You will see that articles by key persons in the history of the One Spirit Interfaith Seminary are very well represented in these Volumes, and we have already pointed to One Spirit's historic contributions to the development of interspiritual education, interspiritual curricula, and joint interspiritual/integral studies. Among these contributions is, from its interfaith and interspiritual curricula, "The Seven Elements of Interspiritual Education." It was historically added to the pantheon of "Universal Principles and Action Steps" publication prepared before the 2018 Parliament of the World's Religions by intercultural and interfaith groups widely associated with the United Nations NGO community.[13]

The seminary operates under the umbrella of the One Spirit Learning Alliance in New York City. Prior to the Covid era, it occupied a large in-person facility. After Covid, it transitioned to an online curriculum. Its ordination program in Interfaith and Interspiritual Ministry at The One Spirit Interfaith Seminary is a two-year program. It has also emphasized "Sacred Activism," its founder, Rev. Dr. Diane Berke, being a long-term associate of Andrew Harvey's Institute for Sacred Activism (at andrewharvey.net/sacredactivism). Berke and Harvey, both Featured Authors to these Volumes, have each, and together, taught and written extensively on these themes. The seminary's activities and outreaches have especially emphasized antiracism, diversity, equity, and inclusion and ministry to marginalized communities.

Rev. Berke founded the One Spirit Interfaith Seminary in New York City. She was also the Spiritual Director of the seminary and the One Spirit Learning Alliance. She had previously been part of the core staff at New York City's pioneer "New Seminary." The role of the New Seminary, founded in New York in 1981 by Rabbi Joseph Gelberman as an interspiritual pioneer, was noted by Br. Teasdale in *The Mystic*

Heart. After the September 11 attacks, Berke felt a renewed urgency to support the emergence of Interspirituality in a broader creative framework and founded One Spirit. Its success is not only attested to by its thousands of graduates and ordinees, but also the remembrance of its inspiring commencement ceremonies which annually filled the huge Riverside Church in New York City. One Spirit rapidly became the largest and likely most well-known seminary operating with a specifically interfaith and interspiritual curriculum and ordination program. It was closely related to the founding and activities of the Interspiritual Dialogue network [ISD] also founded in New York at the same time — since it directly connected to the work of Br. Wayne Teasdale — and Diane Berke and Kurt Johnson were among the co-founders with Teasdale of ISD. Kurt Johnson joined the faculty at One Spirit soon thereafter. The One Spirit community was similarly instrumental in the founding of the Community of the Mystic Heart (CMNH), an important early association and ongoing experiment in New Monasticism that at one point gathered upward of 400 interfaith and interspiritual clergy as members. Both New Monasticism and Community of the Mystic Heart have more detailed entries below.

One Spirit is only one of many interfaith and interspiritual seminaries and, aside from that fact, in more recent years — as the interfaith and interspiritual messages have embedded more and more deeply across all the world's traditions — so many historically prominent seminaries and religious educational institutions have broadened their curricula to this more world-centric context. That is one of the pieces of good news when we talk about the emergence of an Interspiritual Age, another term coined by Br. Teasdale. Diane Berke and Kurt Johnson wrote a significant update on the expansion of interfaith and interspiritual seminaries and curricula for *The*

Interfaith Observer in September 2012. *The Interfaith Observer* (TIO) is an important resource for tracking the history and growth of Interspirituality. Accordingly, we:

- share this extensive Endnote that indexes all of the major articles published in TIO by the important interspiritual voices represented as Featured Authors to these Volumes.[14] This includes a feature by Diane Berke and Kurt Johnson on the global interfaith seminary landscape with internet links to each; and

- in another Endnote, we provide a succinct digest of today's existing interspiritual seminaries and interfaith educational curricula drawing from a compilation of the Rev. Phillip Waldrop of the World Alliance of Interspiritual Clergy as fully published earlier in one of our Light on Light associated e-publications.[15]

These are important historical elements in the discussions of interfaith and interspiritual seminaries and their formative roles regarding the interspiritual experience. In fact, the subtitle of the banner head at interspirituality.com underscores this as "Serving the Emerging Global Interspiritual Paradigm."

We are also happy to share a tribute to Diane Berke and the One Spirit community in the "Interspiritual Pioneers" subsection of our "Reflections and Pointers" Section in Volume 2 of these Volumes. It is taken from the article in our forthcoming Volume 3 on *Interspiritual Community*, from the Feature there: "Interspirituality — In and Out of the Classroom" by Leslie Reambeault and Melissa Stewart, also previous Directors at One Spirit Interfaith Seminary. And, selections from a Feature by DeShannon Barnes-Bowens, another One Spirit Director, appear in our Volume 2, in (i) our Roundtable on First

Peoples, and (ii) our Section on Interspiritual Community; the Feature will be published subsequently in full in Volume 3.

Returning to The New Monasticism

Let's return now to the New Monasticism. Such initiatives began to crest especially in 2012-2013, first in serial publications and ultimately in book form with *The New Monasticism: A Manifesto for Contemplative Living* by Rory McEntee and Adam Bucko, published on April 10, 2015, by Orbis Books.

Before this, citations of new monastic experiments in the Catholic traditions date at least to the 1970s and 1980s in the United Kingdom and the mid-1990s in the United States. In the interfaith and interspiritual contexts, Bede Griffith's community in India is often cited as exemplary. His Shantivanam community in Tamil Nadu, South India, also known as the Saccidananda Ashram, was established around 1950 by French Benedictine monks Father Jules Monchanin and Father Henri Le Saux (Abhishiktananda). Along with Father Bede, they are historically renowned for impelling convergence of Christian-Hindu contemplative experience and universally honored among Interspirituality's pioneers. Br. Teasdale's penultimate book publication, during his life, was *Bede Griffiths: An Introduction to His Spiritual Thought* (2003). And his important piece on Abhishiktananda (Fr. Henri Le Saux), lost for nearly ten years, is republished in these Volumes. Well-springing from personal experience in Fr. Bede's community during his lifetime are such well-known names in Interspirituality (and science) as Wayne Teasdale, Andrew Harvey, Russill Paul, and Rupert Sheldrake. Fr. Matthew M. Cobb of the Bede Griffiths Trust writes extensively on this history in these Volumes, particularly in light of the decades-long international phenomenon, the "Monastic Interreligious Dialogue" (today DIMMID), about which we will share much more in a separate section farther below.

As well, Raimon Panikkar spoke of the "new monk" in 1980, and a well-recognized initiative since the early 1980s has been Beverly Lanzetta's "Community of a New Monastic Way," further formalized in 2008, which continues to this day. It has been further invigorated by her 2018 book, *The Monk Within: Embracing a Sacred Way of Life*.[16] A widely quoted booksellers' notation summarizes well the landscape of the New Monasticism.

> *The Monk Within* is written for the person seeking a deeper, contemplative orientation to daily life. Yearning for inner realization of divine wisdom, this "new monk" draws on four interlocking themes: embodied spirituality grounded in the sacred web of life; the mystical path of the feminine, inspired by women's monastic communities; the archetype of the monk that is the deep truth of every person; and the interdependence of the world's wisdom traditions, expressed through interfaith, interspiritual dialogue.

And, of which, the *American Benedictine Review* [12/2021] said, "Beverly strikes me as the twenty-first-century heir to the twentieth century's great spiritual teacher, Thomas Merton, who also believed that a profound experience of the divine is attainable by all who draw on a daily regimen of silence, solitude, prayer, and reflection." Netanel Miles-Yépez writes of her, and other New Monasticism pioneers, in his Feature "The Interspiritual Milieu" later in this Volume.

In the 2000s — the time frame of much of these Volumes' timelines — the American Academy of Religion provided programming on the New Monasticism with accompanying documentations of its history and many examples.[17] There are exemplary initiatives within the Protestant denominations in the 1990s.

Of course, global and regional cultures, and their attendant religious cultures, have changed dramatically in the last century, certainly changing the landscapes of the meaning of a "new" Monasticism. Certainly, the general direction of both the interfaith and interspiritual experience clearly invited the "discovering a universal spirituality in the world's religions" — the very subtitle of Br. Teasdale's *The Mystic Heart*. In *The Mystic Heart*, Br. Teasdale said, "Every one of us is a mystic" [MH p. 3]. He defined mysticism as "The desire for, awareness of, and insight into the ultimate reality, however, this may be understood" and the mystic as "Any individual with a direct experience and awareness of the absolute, the divine, or boundless consciousness" [MH p. 270]. As well, his book, *A Monk in the World*, pointed clearly in this direction for the average person.

Given this, there is no doubt a certain result would be a myriad of contemporary humans asking — in the context of the deepest inner subjective experience of our species — how cultivation of these potentials relates to the cultural containers of past and future. Traditional monasticism has been one of those containers but today myriads of humans are asking how one might venture into these frontiers of consciousness (as Teasdale said in his definition) outside of those traditional contexts. Certainly, the availability of traditional forms of monastic life — of cloister, celibacy, etc. — is lessening while at the same time "new monastics" face the reality that modern cultures (especially of "lst World" and the West) do not readily support financial or administrative success for persons or groups that want to experiment in shared living and cultivation of quietude. Thus, so many experiments in New Monasticism, outside the contexts of conventional religious denominations, have been relatively short-lived. But no doubt, the future of a New Monasticism is as relevant as ever today, perhaps more so.

In this context, before we turn below to more about *The New Monasticism* from McEntee and Bucko, and their Features as well in these Volumes, we must reprise for a moment Br. Teasdale's dream of a "Universal Order of Sannyasa" — a diverse universal order of explorers of the New Monasticism, about which experiments we'll devote a section much farther below. In short, before we return to it later, what grew from Br. Teasdale's "Universal Order of Sannyasa" went through several iterations attempting to find a way to realistically approach a diversity of paths toward a New Monasticism *and* sustain it also as an ongoing meta-community. As "Community of the Mystic Heart (CMH)," it ultimately created a full Sannyas component under Swami Shraddhananda and her community at Sacred Feet Slate Branch Ashram (now Sacred Feet Anugraha House) in Kentucky, USA, and a looser and more diverse "New Monastics in the World" program. The latter was a dynamic effort that ended after several years simply because not a single member had the time to cover all of the administrative responsibilities required by more than 50 of the then 400 members of CMH adopting their own diverse "personal monastic Rules" all operating independently at the same time.

The full Sannyas community continued under the supervision of Swami Shraddhananda at Sacred Feet's Anugraha House until her passing. At the time of Swami Shraddhananda's transition, and subsequently with her dharma heirs (see their Feature in Volume 2), the future of Br. Teasdale's Sannyas lineage was left as "to be determined" by the Sacred Feet dharma heirs and the Trustees of The Interspiritual Dialogue incorporated by Br. Teasdale and colleagues in 2002. Today,

Sacred Feet's remaining dharma heirs as "needs-be" live separately in various parts of the world. The same is true of the many devotees who were part of the "New Monastics in the World" experiment. This does not mean that these original 400 members and some 50 living under personalized "new monastic covenants" abandoned their deeply spiritual lives. It only means that in today's cultural realities it was impossible to sustain an administrative, or financial, structure for such communities. Many original members of CMH are Featured Authors in these Volumes, and we will be able to devote more detail to their modalities, monastic rules, covenants, vows, etc. in the subsequent third volume noted in the Introduction to these Volumes 1 and 2.

The New Monasticism: A Manifesto for Contemplative Living

The most well-known publication framing the New Monasticism has been *The New Monasticism: A Manifesto for Contemplative Living* by Rory McEntee and Adam Bucko published on April 10, 2015, by Orbis Books. The New Monasticism's New Monastic Manifesto was also published prior to 2015 in serials such as *Kosmos Journal* and also published online by "Working With Oneness" with this Abstract:

> New Monasticism: An Interspiritual Manifesto for Contemplative Life in the 21st Century by Rory McEntee and Adam Bucko. "We assert that new monasticism names an impulse that is trying to incarnate itself in the new generation. It is beyond the borders of any particular religious institution, yet drinks deeply from the wells of our wisdom traditions. It is an urge which speaks to a profoundly contemplative life, to the formation of small communities of friends, to sacred

activism and to discovering together the unique calling of every person and every community."

When published in 2015, the book carried this informative description at bookseller websites:[18]

> Young leaders of the new monastic movement introduce their vision for contemplative life — one that draws from the long traditions of East and West but also seeks an interreligious and "interspiritual" dimension to intentional living in our time. With a preface by Mirabai Starr, a foreword by Sufi teacher Llewellyn Vaughan-Lee, and an afterword by Fr. Thomas Keating.

> The New Monasticism introduces the "new monastic movement," offering the authors' intellectual and spiritual reflections on what contemplative life could look like in the 21st century. With chapters focusing on spiritual practice, vocation, contemplation and activism, dialogical dialogue, the relationship with traditional religious paths, contemplative psychology and the building of intentional communities, the authors seek to "cut across the boundaries of religious traditions, of contemplation and action, and endeavor to create intergenerational alliances between those immersed in the depths of our traditional religious frameworks and those who are being called to contemplative and prophetic life outside of those frameworks."

> While drawing on the work of Raimon Panikkar, St. Teresa of Avila, Pierre Teilhard de Chardin, Ewert

Cousins, Fr. Bede Griffiths, Thomas Merton, Brother Wayne Teasdale, St. John of the Cross and the Russian sophianic tradition, among others, the book also incorporates some popular modern day academic, cultural, and contemplative theorists, such as Ken Wilber and Fr. Thomas Keating, who speak to young people about creating a more sacred and just world while providing them with sophisticated tools for psychological analysis and integrated action. It also offers specific practices for a disciplined contemplative life and inspired social justice activism.

A review at Cambridge University Press[19] reflects the landscape of the interspiritual voices in that book being quite in common with the current volumes:

> The description of interspirituality — and the entire text itself — cites the works of Raimon Panikkar, Teilhard de Chardin, Wayne Teasdale, Ewert Cousins, Thomas Keating, and Ken Wilber frequently (often in long block quotes). Readers familiar with these writers' use of terms such as "global mythos," "Second Axial Age," "evolutionary consciousness," "non-dual realization," "false-self system," and "integral spirituality" may find that this book serves best as a synthesis of the ideas of these writers, packaged within a manifesto for new monastic "spiritual but not religious" seekers. The authors acknowledge three paths for such seekers within a new monasticism: "growing strong roots in one tradition, and from that vantage point branching out to drink deeply of the

wisdom of varying traditions"; "multiple religious belonging" by "fully embedding oneself in multiple religious traditions"; and the authors' own path, an interspiritual path that seeks to "assimilate many of our spiritual lineages without becoming fully embedded in, or beholden to, the religious frameworks that surround them." The authors caution that such a path requires "the guidance of elders on traditional paths and a high level of integrity and responsibility."

In the same context and in the same year, 2015, The Science and Nonduality Conference hosted a panel and plenary discussion on Interspirituality where Kurt Johnson as moderator was joined by two of the authors from the above publications, Matthew Fox and Rory McEntee. In the plenary for the whole SAND conference, Kurt Johnson hosted, and three others from the current Volumes participated: Matthew Fox, Rory McEntee, and Edward Bastian. For the smaller panel presentation and plenary, included below is the description of the gathering distributed at the time of the Conference: [20]

Panel and Plenary on The Implications of a Universal Spirituality

It is widely acknowledged that a universal spirituality is, in fact, arising rapidly worldwide — the only viable religion for the Third Millennium being spirituality itself. This is identified by nearly every conscious person as a "spirituality of the Heart" — and one reflecting an emerging new global "unity consciousness." Such characterizations have been elaborated in the recent book, *The Coming Interspiritual Age* (Kurt Johnson and David Robert Ord) and in many other books (including those of our panelists).

Causes cited are myriad: consciousness sciences suggest it is our ongoing cognitive evolution, social scientists that it is driven also by inevitable processes toward globalization and multiculturalism; spiritual and religious leaders see a "divine" cause at work.

If a world awakening is real, there are vast and complicated implications for our complex world — including the arenas of religion, science, social structure, governance, economics, culture, and more. Confusion can arise because everyone sees simultaneously through three basic lenses — reflected universally in our language structures as "first-," "second-," and "third-person" (which become the "four quadrants," or I/ We/ It/ Its, of Integral Theory and Spiral Dynamics). In result, we see dynamically intertwined global upwellings reflecting these varying lenses: in "I," the urgency toward personal "awakening," in "We," social activisms of all kinds aimed at global change, and in "It / Its," ample evidence that myriad long-entrenched historical institutions no longer serve the needs of a modernizing global civilization.

The panel will discuss the entire spectrum of implications suggested by an arising global "universal spirituality."

Moderator: Kurt Johnson, PhD, co-author of *The Coming Interspiritual Age* and long-term pioneer of the "straddle" between spirituality and science; Rupert Spira, well-known teacher of Awakened Awareness and renowned ceramicist; author of *The Transparency of Things*; Matthew Fox, PhD, renowned radical theologian and author of the current book *Occupy Spirituality: A Radical Vision for a New Generation (Sacred Activism)* (co-author Adam Bucko) and other spiritual classics like *One River, Many Wells* and *The Coming of the Cosmic Christ*; Edward Bastian, PhD, co-founder and CEO of Spiritual Paths Institute; author of *InterSpiritual Meditation* and the interspiritual education modules "The Interspiritual Mandala"; Rory McEntee, current moderator of the Snowmass Interspiritual Dialogues [formerly the Snowmass Interreligious Dialogues founded by Fr. Thomas Keating and colleagues]; Cassandra Vieten, PhD, CEO of the Institute of Noetic Sciences, clinical psychologist, and co-author with Marilyn Schlitz and Tina Amorok of *Living Deeply, The Art and Science of Transformation in Everyday Life*.

In this context, let's return now to the Community of the Mystic Heart's experiments with the New Monasticism, especially in four contexts. They are the following:

1. Br. Teasdale's vision of a "Universal Order of Sannyasa" and the experiments of the Community of the Mystic Heart;

2. The historical centrality of the Monastic Interreligious Dialogue [from @1957 to present under various names] and its central relationship to both Br. Teasdale and Fr. Thomas Keating;

3. The "lost article" by Br. Teasdale on a historical central figure to the Monastic Interreligious Dialogue — Swami Abhishiktananda (aka Fr. Henri Le Saux) which we are publishing for the first time in print media in these Volumes; and

4. Another "lost article" published for the first time in print in these Volumes — a piece by Gorakh Hayashi (Br. Teasdale's close colleague in Chicago) with Kurt Johnson published online soon after *The Mystic Heart* by Yasuhiko Kimura (in his journal *Vision in Action*) but lost since then for nearly twenty years.

THE MONASTIC INTERRELIGIOUS DIALOGUE

Features in these Volumes by Matthew M. Cobb - Wayne Teasdale

For those in the monastic life at the formative years post Vatican II, the emerging Foundationalist Discussion, and other emergent global dialogues like the Monastic Interreligious Dialogue (today "DIMMID"), became prominent in the lives and interrelations of monks and nuns around the world. It is mentioned prominently as a major formative force, by both Br. Wayne Teasdale and Fr. Thomas Keating.

If you go to the internet today, you will see the activities of The Monastic Interreligious Dialogue (dimmid.org) and its publication *Dilatato Corde* recorded in detail since 2011. When you look at its Pioneers, they reflect many of the same names as the pantheon of interspiritual pioneers — Fr. Thomas Merton, Fr. Bede Griffiths, and

Swami Abhishiktananda (aka Fr. Henri Le Saux). The direction of its foundation began with Vatican II and the 1957 Papal Encyclical *Fidei Donum*. This led to the formation of the "Aid for the Implementation of Monasticism" (AIM). Originally, the Dialogue was a subcommission of AIM. Then, in 1994, it was set up as an independent Secretariat in liaison with AIM. During the AIM period, there were many sponsored conferences aimed at helping monks and nuns from across the globe's spiritual traditions engage in interfaith and intermystical dialogue. A particularly noted conference in these series — in Bangkok, Thailand, in 1968 — was the scene of the tragic accidental death of Thomas Merton. The official organization DIMMID, as the *Dialogue Interreligieux Monastique* - Monastic Interreligious Dialogue, unfolded from 1974-1979. It was through DIMMID that Br. Teasdale organized the previously noted Dialogue with His Holiness the 14th Dalai Lama on mystical awakening. Then, in 1994, DIMMID became an independent Secretariat.

Before the internet era, many monks and nuns remember early activities of the Dialogue through then often mimeographed communications passed around within monastic communities. This was in the 1970s. Kurt Johnson [pers. com. to Light on Light], then an Anglican Holy Cross monk, remembers these being passed around by hand among the monks and nuns along "Monastery Row" (Highway 9W) in New York State, USA. More than a half dozen monasteries and convents were in a row there, along the Hudson River where originally they had been accessible only by boat.

Communications from the Monastic Interreligious Dialogue were often received in the mail, mimeographed, and passed hand to hand among friends in those monastic houses. This was in the early time of East-West discussion among monastics. Many, if not most, monks and nuns were regularly reading esoteric literature, and what was "hot" in the East-West dialogue at that time was always of great interest. When Kurt Johnson later met Br. Wayne Teasdale, the remembrances of the early days of the Monastic Interreligious Dialogue immediately came up.

COMMUNITY OF THE MYSTIC HEART
Founded originally as the
Universal Order of Sannyasa 2010

Features in these Volumes by JoAnn Barrett – Diane Berke
Interspiritual Monastics in the World – Kurt Johnson
Sacred Feet Dharma Heirs – Swami Shraddhananda

The Community of the Mystic Heart was an important association in the formative years of the interspiritual experience following the publication of Teasdale's *The Mystic Heart*, with an active membership of over 400 by 2013. Because its core membership was mainly ordained interfaith and interspiritual clergy, from the variety of international interfaith seminaries, it served the groundswell of interspiritual activity in the early 2000s. It had active roles in the Dawn of Interspirituality conference, participations in the Parliament of the World's Religions up through 2015, held its own residential retreats, and published the book *Mature Interspirituality* (edited by Swami Shraddhananda) in 2017.

As documented in more detail in the previous section "The New Monasticism," CMH created a full sannyas component under the leadership of Swami Shraddhananda and her Sacred Feet Slate Branch Ashram (now Sacred Feet Anugraha House, in Somerset, Kentucky,

USA) which continued as a residential and retreat facility until her transition in 2021. As noted previously, Br. Teasdale's Sannyas robes are kept to this day at Sacred Feet, and, in a special ceremony in 2016, the Acclimation of Br. Teasdale's Universal Order of Sannyasa, from its 2010 founding by some seventy founders gathered in Washington DC, was passed to the care of Swami Shraddhananda, her dharma heirs, and the Trustees of those who had founded The Interspiritual Dialogue with Br. Teasdale in 2002. Swami Shraddhananda was survived by three ordained Dharma Heirs to Sacred Feet Yoga: Jenny Amrita Williams, Somerset; Sandra Chamatkara Simon, Pittsburgh, PA; and The Right Rev. Bishop Christine Deefholts, aka Sw. Prakashananda, the United Kingdom. They are the publishers of *Sacred Feet Yoga Teachings with Meditations by Swami Prakashananda*.[21]

Community of the Mystic Heart also created several experiments in "New Monasticism" as visioned in Br. Teasdale's conception of the Universal Order of Sannyasa. These are detailed more below, previously in our section on The New Monasticism, and in the third volume on "Communities" announced in our Introduction to these Volumes. Its many activities only became outpaced by the growth of the larger appreciation of Interspirituality in those years, eventually making its active presence less pivotal to the growing interspiritual experience and the "aging out" of its founding members, many of whom were already elders in the growing interspiritual experience.

What became the Community of The Mystic Heart was grounded in Br. Teasdale's vision of a "Universal Order of Sannyasa" (UOS) (from his books *The Mystic Heart* and *A Monk in the World*). In 2010, it was established by members of the Interspiritual Dialogue association (isdna.org) (ISD) which Br. Teasdale co-founded with associates in 2002. In Br. Teasdale's writings, The Universal Order of Sannyasa envisioned Interspiritual Monastics in the World living a life of sacred unconditional service to world transformation, much in the mold of traditional Sannyasa, the robes of which Br. Teasdale wore himself in accordance with Christian Sannyas vows he took in 2003 under Francis Cardinal George of the Roman Catholic Diocese of Chicago, which diocese Br. Teasdale served ecclesiastically as "official hermit." The vision of Christian Sannyas, as articulated by Br. Teasdale, was much in the mold of the Shantivanam (India) community of his own mentor Fr. Bede Griffiths (aka Swami Dayananda). This tradition survives to this day, although in modified form since Bede's transition, and is summarized in detail also in Br. Teasdale's book *Bede Griffiths, An Introduction to his Interspiritual Thought* and is also treated in detail by features in the current Volumes by Andrew Harvey and Matthew M. Cobb, along with many reflections and references from the "New Monasticism" in the Features by Adam Bucko, Cynthia Brix, Jeffrey Genung, Kurt Johnson, William Keepin, Beverly Lanzetta, Netanel Miles-Yépez, Sacred Feet Dharma Heirs, and New Monastics in the World.

By its nature, Teasdale's vision of his Universal Order of Sannyasa was generic and far-flung in its vision:

> The Interspiritual Age will require institutions and structures to carry, express and support it. I suggest that a fundamental institution should be an interspiritual order of monastics or contemplatives open to all people — men and women, married and single, young, middle-aged, and old, confused and clear, adherents or not, with faith or agnostic — united in their desire for a deeper, more meaningful life [MH p. 248].

You will see more about that in the further Features in these Volumes noted just above, some of whose authors were involved directly with the experiments around the Universal Order of Sannyasa vision, and others who took their own directions with the vison of a "New Monasticism" evolving alongside that of the revered traditions from the past. However, the expansive and far-flung vision of Teasdale's Order, catering to the many kinds of lives that might be lived by a "Monk in the World," inevitably also created some cultural difficulties, leading to a renaming of the originally founded 2010 "Universal" order visioned by Br. Teasdale. Obviously, the prospect of any such initiative in the future still remains to be seen but many appear to be hungering for it. We discuss this further in our Section on "Interspiritual Community" in Volume 2 *and* in our anticipated Volume 3 (which will center particularly on the theme of community).

Original Founding and Subsequent Renaming

On January 9, 2010, over seventy ordained interfaith and interspiritual clergy inspired by Br. Teasdale's vision of a Universal Order of Sannyasa gathered at All Souls Unitarian Church in Washington, DC, for its founding. Following a deep review of the vision as articulated in Br. Teasdale's *The Mystic Heart* and *A Monk on the World*, the Order was consecrated by unanimous acclamation. Two months after its founding, UOS responded to esteemed requests by some traditional Sannyasa of India to not use that term "Sannyas" in the broadly universal context and form suggested by Br. Teasdale. The name was then changed to Community of the Mystic Heart (CMH). A group of about a dozen continued with the original name and are represented on Facebook by the name Universal Order of Sannyasa (UOOS), also acknowledging the original founding date of January 9, 2010.

By its fifth induction ceremony in November 2011, there were nearly 300 members of Community of the Mystic Heart, and after the Dawn of Interspirituality Conference, almost 400. Originally, the kinds of membership in CMH were various, to satisfy very differing needs of members responding to their own callings of spiritual practice and sacred activism in the ever-developing interspiritual context worldwide. In time, CMH developed two complementary tracks: a more traditional "Full" and "Lay" Sannyas group under the leadership of Swami Shraddhananda of Sacred Feet Slate Branch Ashram (now Sacred Feet Anugraha House) (jefifoundation.org/) in Kentucky, and a larger group pursuing diverse visions of the kinds of life and work implied by Br. Wayne's writings in *The Mystic Heart* and *A Monk in the World*.

It was these core groups that hosted retreats and also published *Mature Interspirituality* through Sacred Feet which, to this day, holds the original Sannyas robes worn by Br. Teasdale. As noted in TIMELINES, at a residential retreat of Community of the Mystic Heart in April 2016, Jeffrey Genung [later founder of contemplativelife.org] presented the Sannyas robes of Br. Teasdale to Swami Shraddhananda and her Sacred Feet Slate Branch Ashram (now Sacred Feet Anugraha House) as part of a special ceremony that passed the Acclimation of the Universal Order of Sannyasa from its 2010 founding (see item 5 in 2007-2012 Timeline above), and thus Br. Teasdale's Universal Order of Sannyas lineage, to the care of Swami Shraddhananda, Sacred Feet's full Sannyas program, and the Trustees of The Interspiritual Dialogue as founded by Br. Teasdale and his associates in 2002.[22] Swami Shraddhananda, her Dharma Heirs, and Jeffrey Genung are all Featured Authors to the current Volumes.

Today, as well, several of this core group are now part of the editorial teams at Light on Light Publications and Media, the publisher of these Volumes. This followed the eventual aging and transitioning of several key members, including Swami Shraddhananda in 2021. In 2023, Sacred Feet Publishing released *Sacred Feet Yoga Teachings with Meditations by Swami Prakashananda*.[23] In 2025, Chamatkara, another dharma heir of Sacred Feet, edited for Light on Light the popular *Light on Kundalini: Your Lifestyle Guide to Yoga and Awakening* by Karuna, of the Sikh tradition. All three of these writers are Featured Authors to these Volumes, and Karuna has served as Host Editor for Light on Light's annual series of e-publications with the International Day of Yoga Committee at the United Nations.

Community of the Mystic Heart's more general "Interspiritual Monks in the World" programs are detailed substantially, especially in the light of New Monasticism, in the "Subsequent Fully Illustrated Volume" announced in our Introduction. This Volume 3 centers on Interspiritual Community and allows the deserved space for details of vision, purpose, practices, modalities, training, and vows (and with reflections, prayers, art and photography) from communities like Community of a New Monastic Way, the relatively new Charis Foundation for New Monasticism and Interspirituality, Community of the Mystic Heart's near ten-year experiment with Interspiritual Monks in the World, and others. Such details, all quite inspiring, well represent communities who have experimented with an interspiritual vision of New Monasticism, while sharing in common their not having direct (although often indirect) association with the many opportunities for the monastic experience across our globe's well-established denominational traditions.[24] As we have discussed already, in the current economic structures of most of the West, ultimately the difficulty of financially sustaining a community, especially with property and infrastructure, becomes prohibitive. In the case of the diverse and geographically far-flung Community of the Mystic Heart, it ended up proving impossible to have an effective administrative team for over 50 persons who had dedicated themselves to separate, personalized, monastic Rules. The work of all these communities is an inspiration in the direction of all who vision a New Monasticism. One can track various other New Monastic experiments that also sprung from Br. Teasdale's initial vision, like Monks Without Borders-USA, and the Peoples Monastery of New York City (whose founding was also consecrated by Community of the Mystic Heart in 2011).

These are by no means the only known and important experiments in New Monasticism, another reason for our subsequent Volume 3 on Interspiritual Community. For instance, reprising Br. Teasdale's title *A Monk in the World*, in 2014, Rev. William Thiele, PhD, founding spiritual director of the School for Contemplative Living, pastor of Parker United Methodist Church and Adjunct Professor at Loyola University in New Orleans published *Monks in the World: Seeking God in a Frantic Culture* to great interest among the interfaith and sacred activism communities. Quoted at Amazon, Franciscan interspiritual pioneer Fr. Richard Rohr said of the work: "This is the kind of practical and practiced wisdom that the world and the churches need today. William Thiele is making an art form of it — for all of us!" We're pleased to share Features from Dr. Thiele in our subsequent Volume 3, and they are also highlighted, as selections, in our "Interspiritual Community" Section of our current Volume 2.

Ultimately, the channels of Br. Teasdale's Universal Order of Sannyasa and the Community of the Mystic Heart, with its Sannyas component with Swami Shraddhananda's community, shaped further in 2025. Jeffrey Genung, founder of contemplativelife.org and with whom Br. Teasdale planned his hospice, has now joined the Trustees of Br. Teasdale's original Interspiritual Dialogue association, and its Board for Light on Light Publications and Media, along with Sw. Shraddhananda's dharma heirs. Continuing as the keepers of Br. Teasdale's Sannyas robes, certainly continuing his inspiration, and with new retreat facilities now in hand, another experiment from that corner of the interspiritual community may also be at hand. Fr. Adam Bucko, co-author of *The New Monasticism*, now with the Episcopal diocese of Long Island, has obtained facilities for a new experiment as well. These, along with the recent announcements of vision from Dr. Rory McEntee, Netanel Miles-Yépez, Alejandra Warden and others associated with the Charis Foundation for New Monasticism and Interspirituality, are exciting, and we hope to track their progress further in our Volume 3.

After the 2005 Tribute Event to Br. Teasdale
Further Initiatives

Features in these Volumes by JoAnn Barrett - Joan Borysenko - Cynthia Brix
Adam Bucko - Gordon Dveirin - Philip Goldberg - Andrew Harvey - Gorakh Hayashi
Roger Housden - Kurt Johnson - William Keepin - Lama Surya Das - Beverly J. Lanzetta
Rory McEntee - Dena Merriam - Roger Ross - Deborah Steen Ross - Ruth Broyde Sharone
Swami Shraddhananda - Mirabai Starr - Robert Toth - Matthew Wright

The inspiration of the well-attended Tribute Event to Br. Teasdale led not only to the joining of many leaders to the then ongoing Snowmass Interreligious Dialogues (which then took the name Snowmass Interspiritual Dialogues) but also led to the emergence of further important initiatives.

The Interspiritual Multiplex Website of ISDnA

Co-hosting the Tribute Event, attending members of the Interspiritual Dialogue (ISD) increased their membership and updated their name (by acclimation at the Tribute Event) to Interspiritual Dialogue in Action (ISDnA). This was prompted by the donation at the event of a new, higher end website created then in 2005 by a colleague of Br. Teasdale's, Aaron Froehlich, a web designer at Cornell University. It replaced an earlier site by Teasdale and his Chicago and New York colleagues at isdac.com. The new site allowed the building of an expansive interspiritual website which culminated in 2008 by ISDnA working with the staff at the One Spirit Interfaith Seminary. This was the voluminous "Interspiritual Multiplex" which provided extensive materials across all the world's spiritual traditions. The Multiplex was very popular also with its regular newsletters, which reached an audience of 20,000. However, it was an early open-source software and thus, although widely used and cited, could not be perpetuated beyond 2020 when this software was no longer utilized by the internet service community. Thus, it served well for a dozen years, but what remains today at isdna.org is only the foundation of the 2005 site, and the open-source Multiplex is no longer available. Fortunately, however, the 2015 website co-sponsored by the wider international interspiritual community emerged soon at interspirituality.com.

The Claritas Institute for Interspiritual Inquiry

Attending the Tribute Event were *New York Times* bestselling author Dr. Joan Borysenko and her partner, transformative educator Dr. Gordon Dveirin. They presented there on their founding of the Claritas Institute for Interspiritual Inquiry and its Claritas Interspiritual Mentor

Training Program. Subsequently, they wrote about this on the occasion of *Namaste Insights* special e-publication on Interspirituality which we have drawn from extensively in these Volumes with *Namaste Insights'* permission. They have also contributed a new Feature to the current Volumes.

Drs. Borysenko and Dveirin were close friends of Br. Teasdale and recounted their co-hosting of an interspiritual event in Vancouver, Canada, in 2004, which, again, was one of the last events Br. Teasdale participated in as his health began to fail. The event included Br. Teasdale, Cynthia Bourgeault, and H. H. the Dalai Lama's brother Tenzin Choegyal and followed on another event they had all attended with H. H. the Dalai Lama and two fellow Nobel Laureates, Desmond Tutu and Shirin Ebadi, who had been awarded honorary Doctor of Laws degrees from the University of British Columbia (UBC). They recounted how these two 2004 events with Br. Teasdale inspired them to found the Claritas Institute for Interspiritual Inquiry, to further promote dialogue and understanding between different spiritual traditions and explore the essential unity that lies at the heart of all spirituality — the core of Br. Teasdale's universal message. Below, we share some sections of that original *Namaste Insights* article [short comments in brackets are our own]. The original article was still available online until very recently, another reason we are so pleased to share parts of it here.[25]

> The name Claritas was inspired by one of three aspects
> of beauty described by Thomas Aquinas: Integritas
> (wholeness), Consonantia (harmony), and Claritas (the
> inner light or luminosity that shines through when the
> prior two conditions are present).

The first program we offered was the yearlong Claritas Interspiritual Mentor Training program. We invited Janet Quinn, PhD, RN, a nurse educator and experienced spiritual director [you will note her also in the list of regular attendees after the Tribute event to the Schoolhouse planning gatherings at Fr. Thomas Keating's Abbey], to join us in designing and leading the program.

…Our yearlong training program was comprised of 3 weeklong, in-person retreats, and a series of online sessions featuring presentations and conversations with spiritual luminaries including Fr. Thomas Keating, Rabbi Rami Shapiro, Episcopal priest Cynthia Bourgeault, Rabbi Zalman Schachter-Shalomi, Chief Jake Swamp of the Wolf Clan-Mohawk nation, Sister Rose Mary Dougherty, and a splendid group of Sufi, Buddhist, and Hindu teachers.

…We learned and grew along with the two cohorts of the Claritas program, continuing to practice the open mind, open heart curiosity learned from Father Thomas Keating, nurturing the divine potential in ourselves and others, bringing goodness and beauty where we can.

Drs. Borysenko and Dveirin's remembrances of Br. Teasdale and their current comments on the global interspiritual landscape continue in their contribution to the present Volumes, in Interspiritual Pioneers in Volume 2 and in much more detail on Claritas Institute in Volume 3, the volume centering on specific interspiritual communities.

Participations in the 2015 Parliament of the World's Religions (Salt Lake City)

The 2009 Parliament of the World's Religions was in Melbourne, Australia, too far afield for most in the interspiritual community at that time. But, you will see that soon after, the American interspiritual community was to join with the Australian interfaith and interspiritual constituencies in a major way.

The Salt Lake City Parliament is well remembered by many as the Parliament whose content demands and massive attendance led to administrative fiasco. There were long delays in processing proposals and, sometime before the actual gathering, many who had submitted proposals received an apology that their submission had not had a chance to even be reviewed. Thus it was, for the stellar cast of interspiritual leaders, so many of whom we have introduced above and whose contributions fill these Volumes. But we want to share what might have been. We feature it here, somewhat out of chronology, because it involved nearly all of the interspiritual leaders introduced in these Volumes so far, and is an essential "might have been" footnote.

The title of the submission from the combined constituencies of the Interspiritual Dialogue, Spiritual Paths, One Spirit Interfaith Seminary, and Satyana Institute was "Interspirituality: a Paradigm of Hope for the 21st Century," and we share below elements from the proposal itself. It is notable that the submission forms for the 2015 Parliament, which had been created by an outside tech firm, did not contain the category Interspirituality, only the traditional denominations. Thus, the Proposal was submitted under "Other," which may also explain why it was among those reported later as never reviewed.

> This is a Workshop being proposed by 11 leaders, authors, and teachers who have been major founders

of the emerging "Interspiritual" paradigm, including some who presented on Interspirituality at the 2004 Parliament in Barcelona.

...It is a 90-Minute Workshop being proposed by 11 leaders, authors, and teachers, who have been major founders of the emerging "Interspiritual" paradigm, and who are hosts of the major interspiritual websites: interspirituality.com, isdna.org, spiritualpaths.net, mirabaistarr.com, adambucko.com, etc. and recent hosts of the Dawn of Interspirituality Conference (Oct. 2013) (satyana.org).

...The Presenters are Mirabai Starr, Dr. Diane Berke, Dr. Ed Bastian, Dr. Kurt Johnson, Adam Bucko, Rory McEntee, Matthew Wright, Cynthia Brix, Dr. Will Keepin, Karuna, and Swami Shraddhananda. Dr. Johnson is co-author of the award-wining book *The Coming Interspiritual Age* (featured in the Parliament's newsletter, 2014).

There were, however, individual and small group presentations at the Salt Lake City Parliament. These included one on the legacy of Br. Teasdale's vision, which featured Swami Shraddhananda, Kurt Johnson, and Rev. JoAnn Barrett (of the Interfaith Institute of Long Island, New York, and founder of Long Island's dynamic Gathering of Light Interspiritual Fellowship) and Dr. Joni Dittrich (aka Rajashree Maa), psychologist and author of Light on Light Press's recent book, *May the Loveforce Be With You*, on a new Divine Feminine Reiki Lineage.[26]

Another major feature of the participation in the Salt Lake City Parliament was important activity in advance of the United Nations

Climate Change Conference, also known as COP21 or CMP11, held in Paris, France, almost immediately after the Parliament. It resulted in the adoption of the famous Paris Agreement, the international treaty on climate change. The Interspiritual Dialogue with its long history of co-working with the United Nations community since the time of Br. Teasdale, and well described in these Volumes, held nightly meetings at the Salt Lake Parliament for coordinating activism at the Paris Conference advocating for an international agreement. A large registration area in the central foyer of the Parliament coordinated meaningful "lobbying" participations at the Paris Conference from the global religious and sacred activism community.

Pivotal New Emergences

Features in these Volumes by Robert Atkinson – Cynthia Brix – Adam Bucko
Paul Chaffee – Andrew Harvey – Gorakh Hayashi – Roger Housden – Kurt Johnson
William Keepin – Lama Surya Das – Beverly J. Lanzetta – Dena Merriam
Rory McEntee – Roger Ross – Deborah Steen Ross – Ruth Broyde Sharone
Mirabai Starr – Robert Toth – Wayne Teasdale – Matthew Wright

Following on the Tribute Event to Br. Teasdale, the melding of cooperation around ongoing Snowmass Dialogues and the frequent meetings of pioneer interspiritual leaders at Fr. Keating's Schoolhouse, and elsewhere, there was an emergent new era arising in the interspiritual paradigm. The multiple new structures and institutions that Br. Teasdale had said would be needed to carry Interspirituality's partnership message were arising in new organization, new seminaries, new events and conferences, and newly emerging spiritual leaders. Much of that has been detailed above.

In 2011, Kurt Johnson received a call from Constance Kellough, the founder of Namaste Publishing. Constance is well known as the person who "discovered" Eckhart Tolle when *The Power of Now* was in the manuscript stage and had created Namaste Publishing to publish the book, as *The Power of Now: A Guide to Spiritual Enlightenment* in 1997. It was such a success, it was published again in collaboration with New World Library in 1999. The book was for several years a *New York Times* bestseller and was followed soon after by *A New Earth: Awakening to Your Life's Purpose* (2005). The success of these books and the well-known programs with Oprah Winfrey on worldwide television are legendary, and Eckhart Tolle went on to well-deserved global celebrity as a voice of transformative messaging from the core of our planet's millennial Wisdom Traditions. For those who know his books well, he would also aptly fit Br. Teasdale's profile regarding Abhishiktananda (Father Henri Le Saux) — as being an "Advaitin." That is most simply a term from Sanskrit for an enlightened one.

Constance Kellough and Kurt Johnson had met previously at a gathering with Fr. Thomas Keating at the Snowmass Abbey, and she knew that Johnson was also a scientist, with a PhD in evolution and ecology and a position at the American Museum of Natural History in New York City, along with teaching at One Spirit Interfaith Seminary. He had also written a large number of formal scientific papers and some successful popular science books as well, perhaps most well known being his books on the scientific career of renowned Russian-American novelist Vladimir Nabokov (famous for his book *Lolita*, among many others). The latter gained international attention in 2011 when a DNA study at Harvard University unexpectedly determined that an elaborate, but long dismissed, view by Nabokov concerning the evolution of fauna and flora of South America was in fact true. The matter was followed up in a later book by Yale University Press.[27]

Kellough's main interest, especially in the science, was that Tolle's very popular books had been enormously inspirational but, simply by style and genre, not the kind of books that presented "hard data," especially scientific data, about the trends (toward a New Earth, etc.) that they suggested. Was there good hard data to show that, indeed, the world was moving in these transformative directions? If so, this was a book that Namaste Publishing wanted to create. Wishing a relatively quick turn-around and knowing such a book would require copious research, she introduced Johnson to David Robert Ord, an editor at Namaste, an ordained Christian Minister, and a polymath in his own right, who had worked editorially on the Tolle books. Johnson and Ord met for several weeks in person and then, working together over the next year, created the book *The Coming Interspiritual Age* — the term that Br. Teasdale himself had coined for "a new earth." Since it appeared right at the beginning of 2013, it makes the publication of the current Volumes also near the 10th anniversary of *The Coming Interspiritual Age* and the 25th anniversary of Br. Teasdale's *The Mystic Heart*. Having met Johnson *at* a Snowmass Dialogue, Kellough was also aware of Johnson's close connection to Br. Teasdale. The two, and others, had formed the Interspiritual Dialogue in 2002.

Thus, as many know, much of the material in *The Coming Interspiritual Age* was material from Br. Teasdale, which he had shared with his colleagues but had not been well enough to write down in those last two years of his life. This is when he had told his association he had to concentrate fully on finishing *A Monk in the World* and *Bede Griffiths: An Introduction to his Interspiritual Thought*. Gorakh Hayashi and Kurt Johnson, in their earlier, subsequently lost, online publication after Br. Teasdale's transition, had begun sharing some of these undisclosed elements from Teasdale's life and thought during his last two years.

Let's turn now to those items — Br. Teasdale's "lost" article on Abhishiktananda and the Hayashi and Johnson "lost" early paper, and then to a series of important pieces from across the spectrum of the global interfaith community *just* as *The Coming Interspiritual Age* was published. That is when *Namaste Insights* e-magazine created two online issues on Interspirituality from interfaith authors around the world. Those were still available online until June 2025 when it was discovered they had been taken down from the third-party platform on which they were originally available (and are presumably now lost). Fortunately, from 2023-2025, with Namaste Publishing's permission, we had captured selected articles from those volumes and also recorded their original Tables of Contents. But, with no warning of when they would be taken down, we were unable to save the rest. Certainly, the availability of articles originally published online abrogates with time. Fortunately, we have various articles to share from those volumes, especially from authors who otherwise would not be represented in these current historically significant Volumes on Interspirituality's history.

For historicity, since these articles are no longer on line (although we are taking steps to see if they can be retrieved), we want to share the list of authors from around the world who contributed to the interspiritual discussion in that time period immediately around the publication of *The Coming Interspiritual Age*: Eckhart Tolle, David Korten, Nancy Roof, Matthew Fox, Iman Abdul Malik Mujahid, Deborah Moldow, Jonathan Granoff, Lama Surya Das, Ashok Gangadean, Dena Merriam, Oscar Miro-Quesada, Paul Chaffee,

Philip Goldberg, Marcel Kuijsten, Matthew Cobb, M. Darroll Bryant, Rami Shapiro, Thomas Hübl, Ken Wilber, Llewellyn Vaughan-Lee, Valerie Kaur, Thomas Keating, Andrew Harvey, Charles Gibbs, Alison van Dyk, Constance Kellough, Mirabai Starr, Kurt Johnson, Nina Meyerhof, Robert Toth, Russill Paul, Cindy Wigglesworth, David Robert Ord, Diane Berke, Edward Bastian, Cassandra Vieten, Neill Walker, Leo Semasko, Adam Bucko, Phillip Hellmich, Rupert Spira, Catherine Ingram, Will Keepin, Cynthia Brix, Bruce Schuman, Elizabeth Banner, Stephen Olsson, Timothy Miner, Shyla Nelson, Ron Friedman, Victoria Friedman, Zach Perlman, Ina Anahata, Esu Anahata, Harry Gensler S. J., Matt Mitler, Marjorie Lipari, Rory McEntee, Kate Sheehan Roach, Diane Dunn, Ralph Singh, Marc Ian Barasch, Loch Kelly, Kristin Hoffman, Weston Pew, Jeff Schmitt, Dorothy Cunha, Janet Quinn, Maurizio Benazzo, Zaya Benazzo, Jody Lotito-Levine, Andrea Matthews, Thomas Lynch, Cynthia Lynch, Gorakh Hayashi, Sharon Hamilton-Getz and Rick Archer, many of whom join us again in these Volumes over ten years later.[28]

Endnotes and References for
"Timelines" and "Benchmarks" Sections[vii]

Below, after our republishing the above-detailed "lost" articles — on Swami Abhishiktananda by Br. Wayne Teasdale, and Gorakh Hayashi and Kurt Johnson's original article following Br. Teasdale's transition in 2004[1] — are twelve Features from the immediate time period following the 2013 publication of *The Coming Interspiritual Age*. Adapted from their original appearances in two issues of *Namaste Insights* online magazine,[2] these track the emergence of the interspiritual experience, especially in the many new books and serials that appeared during the years of our previously denoted TIMELINES, from generally 2004-2016. The "Additional Resources" noted at the end of many of these Features are from the original publications (with any links updated). They are, as cited therein, gathered within the *Endnotes and References* noted at the end of this Section.

The "Lost" Articles by Br. Wayne Teasdale and Gorakh Hayashi and Kurt Johnson

Swami Abhishiktananda: Christian Sannyasi and Advaitin

by Wayne Teasdale

Many years ago, during the pontificate of Pope Paul VI, one of the most misunderstood of popes, Murray Rogers, an Anglican priest who lived with his wife in a small community in India — and had come to be a close friend of Henri Le Saux — had an audience with Pope Paul. Murray Rogers shared with me this amazing encounter, amazing because the entire time of the meeting — nearly an hour — was taken up with the subject of this Frenchman who had gone out to India. The pope, who read widely in French, had read nearly everything Henri Le Saux had written, and was deeply interested in his experiment on the subcontinent. He discerned its possible significance for the future of Christianity and Hinduism. I am also told that the enigmatic Pope John Paul I studied the story of Henri Le Saux in detail, reading from the original French.

Henri Le Saux, or Abhishiktananda as he came to be known in India as his sannyasic name, was an extraordinary Christian-Hindu mystic, a rare being who lived a totally acosmic and interior life, a mystical inner experience that was not of this world, but the source and basis for it. He was a bridge figure who was able to appropriate both traditions in their deepest wellsprings in the eternal mystery of contemplation. Abhishiktananda was undoubtedly the greatest pioneer on the frontiers of consciousness in the latter half of the 20th century. His singular achievement was as a cross-cultural mystic-sage spanning the gap, experientially and interiorly, between *Advaita* and Christian personalism represented in the trinitarian vision.

He was born on August 30, 1910, in St. Briac on the northern coast of Brittany. His parents, Alfred Le Saux and Louise Sonnefraud, named their firstborn Henri Briac Marie Le Saux. Eventually the family expanded to seven children, five girls and two boys. He grew up in a devoutly Catholic home and was exposed to folk music and Gregorian chant from a tender age. Henri felt called to the priesthood from the time of his early childhood. In 1921, his parents sent him to the minor seminary (high school) in Chateaugiron, from which he graduated in 1926, and then proceeded to the Major Seminary in Rennes. He was a very distinguished student. Henri discerned a more ultimate context to the monastic life, and he wanted to explore this possibility. So, he declined to continue his studies for the diocesan priesthood, and confided in his parents his desire to be a Benedictine monk. His parents opposed his decision, but in 1929 he entered the Abbey of Sainte Anne de Kergonan not far from Plouharnel on the western coast of Brittany. There he was to remain until his departure for India in 1948.

He took to monastic life with a zeal, earnestness, and generosity. On May 30, 1935, the Feast of the Ascension, Henri took his final or solemn vows as a Benedictine monk. He was then ordained to the priesthood on December 21st of the same year. He was made librarian, and this afforded him considerable leisure time for reading and study. He became quite a patristic theologian; that is, an expert in the mystical theologians of the early Church who figured largely in the development of monastic life and spirituality. Then in 1939, the Second World War intervened, and he was briefly in the military. He returned to the monastery in 1940, but it was taken over in 1942, and the monks had to move to Netumieres, not far from Vitry. There they stayed until the end of the war. After the war the monks returned to the abbey, and from 1946 until 1948, Henri was again librarian and professor for the novices and junior monks, teaching them Church history and Canon Law. His mother died in 1944, and his father passed on in 1955, after Henri had been in India some seven years.

Call to India

Henri Le Saux had an irresistible call to go to India. He had been corresponding with Father Jules Monchanin, a saintly and brilliant French priest who had gone to India as a missionary only to encounter a culture and spiritual life so profound and authentic as to change his approach entirely. He went from an attempt to convert Hindus to one of attempting to understand them, and relate India's spiritual wisdom to Christian theology and spirituality. Jules Monchanin left France for India in 1939, and before his departure for India, his great friend, the Jesuit theologian and writer Henri de Lubac, put the task to him: "to rethink everything in the light of theology, and to rethink theology through mysticism." Father Monchanin discovered the mystical depth of both the Hindu and Christian traditions. He was able, with Henri Le Saux who joined him in 1948, to express their focus in India as contemplatives: "Our *Advaita* and the praise of the Trinity are our only aim." Here he was able to convey where the essential encounter of these two traditions must take place. Jules Monchanin invited Henri Le Saux to join him in founding a Christian monastic outpost in Tamil Nadu near Trichinopoly.

Before actually establishing their monastic ashram, they decided to visit a number of Hindu ashrams. Henri Le Saux had heard much about Sri Ramana Maharshi, the silent sage of Tiruvannamalai, and while still in France had read everything he could by and about him. It was the bishop of Trichinopoly, Bishop Mendonca, who had suggested to the two prospective founders that they go to Tiruvannamalai, spend time there, and especially to have the *darshan* of Ramana. They went there together for a week in January 1949, and in his book *The Secret of Arunachala*, Father Le Saux wrote:

> Even before my mind was able to recognize the fact, and still less to express it, the invisible halo of this Sage had been perceived by something in me deeper than any words.
>
> In the contemporary Sage of Arunachala it was the unique Sage of eternal India that appeared to me.
>
> It was a call which pierced through everything, rent it in pieces and opened a mighty abyss. (*The Secret of Arunachala*. Delhi: ISPCK, 1979, pp. 8-9.)

Henri Le Saux went back alone to Tiruvannamalai, to the holy mountain of Arunachala and Ramana in August 1949, the year before the Indian saint's death. Arunachala had finally got hold of him. He would spend long periods in meditation in the caves of the mountain, and there he was plunged into an incredible vortex of interior depth out of which he never emerged. India had taken him after his inner awakening through Ramana. He records in his diary: "My heart is now divided between the sacred river (the Kavery) and the sacred mountain (Arunachala)."

In 1950, the two of them founded their community near Kulittalai, not far from Trichinopoly, and called it Saccidananda Ashram, or Shantivanam, its more popular name. Shantivanam is situated on the banks of the Kavery, one of India's seven sacred rivers, and the site of many saints and sages through the millennia of India's spiritual history. They decided to enculturate their monastic life to the customs and forms of Indian monastic observance, and so each of them took *sannyasa*, or renunciation, becoming thereby Christian *sannyasis*. This meant a life of utter simplicity, poverty, asceticism, and contemplation. They wore the *kavi*, the orange saffron of a Hindu monk, and both adopted new names as is the tradition when embracing sannyasa. Jules Monchanin became Swami Parama Arubiananda, or "the Bliss of the Supreme Formless One," while Henri Le Saux assumed the name of Abhishiktananda; that is, "the Bliss of the Anointed One," a reference to Christ.

They incorporated Sanskrit and Tamil into their public worship. At the same time, they celebrated the Indian rite of the mass which was also expressive of India's genius for the Spirit. This rite of the mass has elements from the temple *puja*, or the offerings to deities that go on all over the country in the millions of temples and shrines that populate the land. It should be noted that the economic life of the ashram has always approximated that of the poorest village in India. The diet is strictly vegetarian, and the focus of life in the ashram is on prayer, or rather contemplative meditation.

Abhishiktananda had always experienced a deep anxiety and ambiguity about Shantivanam. Ever since his awakening in the presence of Ramana, he knew an intense attraction to the Indian approach of mystical contemplation, or meditation, and was drawn more and more to the acosmic, solitary life of the sannyasi, although he was a very gregarious renunciate, much like Thomas Merton. In 1957, Jules Monchanin died. Abhishiktananda was constantly taking trips away to enter more deeply into meditation, asceticism, or the practice of *tapas*, or austerities, meeting other sannyasis, gurus, and giving retreats and lectures. He was also a very productive writer. Starting in 1958, and for the next ten years, he divided his time between Shantivanam in the south, and a hermitage in Uttarkashi in the north, a place in the Himalayas in Uttar Predesh. He preferred so much the solitude of the north, hidden away from the world and from the steady stream of visitors that came to Shantivanam.

In 1968, Abhishiktananda resigned from the leadership of the ashram at Shantivanam, and gave the ashram to Father Francis Mahieu, or Francis Acharya, a Belgian Cistercian monk who, with Father Bede Griffiths, had founded Kurisumala Ashram in the southern state of Kerela near Vagamon some ten years previously. Francis Acharya sent Father Bede to take charge of Shantivanam that same year, and Bede remained the guru of this place until his death in May 1993. Under Bede's leadership the ashram knew an extraordinary growth, and it became an international center of spirituality.

Abhishiktananda was now free to pursue his real vocation: to enter ever more deeply into advaita within the cave of the heart, the *guha*, in that utter solitude of the Godhead. He wanted to "disappear into the Himalayas," and he did succeed in spending nearly eight months of the year in solitude from 1969–1971. At Gyansu, a kilometer from Uttarkashi, he was given a tiny hermitage, and he loved passing the time there in contemplation. Foreign visitors were not allowed into this area of India, so he was left in relative peace. Abhishiktananda had a heart attack on July 14, 1973, in Rishikesh while running after a bus. He died five months later on December 7th.

Abhishiktananda's Struggles

Abhishiktananda paid a huge price for his cross-cultural mystical journey. It was at times for him a terrible agony, particularly after he experienced advaita. He thought he was losing his faith, and he worried about his salvation. He wasn't sure if he were deceived or not. His inner struggle began when he encountered Ramana Maharshi in January 1949. He knew India's mystical life was true, and it conflicted with his simple, but profound Christian faith. He came to realize that both advaita and the Trinity were true, and he was trying to reconcile them within his own being. That was a large part of his inner agony. He had a tremendous loyalty to Christ and the Gospel. He celebrated the mass and said the rosary every day, but he was also a pure advaitin. His inner awakening at Arunachala made it clear to him that the venture at Shantivanam was for him a half measure; he had to go all the way, and that meant association with other sannyasis in the north who were exploring the depths of advaita in their own solitary habitats.

In one of the last things he wrote, a paper for an east-west monastic conference at Bangalore in October 1993 — a conference he was unable to attend because of health considerations — Abhishiktananda waxes eloquently about the nature of his advaitic experience, and clearly articulates the challenge it poses for Christianity in its implications. He says of advaita:

> In this annihilating experience, the person is no longer
> able to project in front of himself anything whatsoever,
> to recognize any other "pole" to which he will refer
> himself and give the name of God.

Once he has reached that innermost centre, he is so forcibly seized by the mystery that he can no longer utter either a "Thou" or an "I."

Engulfed in the abyss, he has disappeared to his own eyes, to his own consciousness.

The proximity of that mystery which the prophetic traditions name God has burnt him so completely that there is no longer any question of discovering it in the depths of himself or himself in the depths of it.

In the very engulfing, the gulf itself has vanished. If a cry were still possible — at the moment perhaps of disappearing into the abyss — it would be paradoxically: "But there is no abyss, no gulf, no distance." There is no face-to-face, for there is only That-which-Is and no other to name It. "Advaita!" ("Experience of God in Eastern Religions," *Cistercian Studies*, vol. IX, 2 & 3, 1974, pp. 151-2.)

This description is in some ways rather shocking for a Christian, Muslim, or Jew who is rooted in a simple monotheistic faith. It seems the complete opposite of the theistic experience. Does God have a place in advaita? And what of the Incarnation; that is, of Christ? Does he disappear in the intensity and unity of non-dual awareness? It is well to remember that there are six classical schools of advaita, and many modern interpretations. Abhishiktananda's is one of them. Is God lost in the ultimate reaches of one's own being? Can this being be said to be ours? Or is it in fact the Godhead's? Abhishiktananda says in his description that we disappear even to ourselves, to our own consciousness. He asks very important questions about God, and then identifies God with the Godhead in the utter intimacy of pure mystical unitive awareness where transcendence is swallowed up into pure immanence. Abhishiktananda puts it:

> Yet where is "God," who is "God," when there is nobody to call him so?
> Here is the pure silence of the Godhead, without any name to define it, without any personalization which could allow one to invoke it, discovered in the disappearance of one's self into the depths of the abyss of one's being. (*Ibid.*)

This names a high state of consciousness in which the person's identity is merged with the Divine Identity, but when there is only this supreme Identity, then the human achieves its place within It, or the human comes home to its proper Identity. It is a wholly transpersonal aspect of the Godhead. It is fascinating because Meister Eckhart himself describes such states of consciousness. He speaks about returning to the abyss and desert of the Godhead, and that when he returns to the Ground, the Godhead, God passes away! If there is ultimately only God, or the Godhead, how can we speak of God as an Identity to which we are related? The God beyond God is the Godhead, the Source that is personal and transpersonal. It is with these kinds of insights and experiences that Abhishiktananda was struggling so intensely.

It is important to remember that Abhishiktananda saw some sort of correlation and possible ontological equivalence between *Saccidananda* and the Trinity. Saccidananda, India's profound understanding of the inner self-awareness of the Godhead, the very content, if we may speak thus, of advaita itself. Saccidananda is composed of three Sanskrit words: *sat*, which means pure existence, or pure being itself, the very intrinsic reality of existence as its own property of self-possession, something which can only be said of the Divine, and not of the human. The human *has* existence as a gift, whereas God *is* existence itself. That is sat. But then there is *chit*, the pure self-awareness of existence in itself, the infinite consciousness and knowledge of being the very fullness itself. Still more, there is *ananda*, or pure, unlimited bliss. Together in one infinite, eternal reality they are this Saccidananda: the total bliss of being infinitely aware of having the identity of the fullness of pure existence itself, Saccidananda!!!

Abhishiktananda suggests that Saccidananda is a primordial experience of the Trinity. Sat is similar to the Father, the Source of being and existence. Chit is like the Son, the Incarnate Logos through whom the universe comes into being and form, while ananda is like the Holy Spirit, the infinite joy and love of the triune community at the heart of the Godhead, the very Godhead itself in its personal and relational mode of expression, its inner identity, how God is God. Somehow Abhishiktananda saw and experienced the inner, ultimate truth of these two formulations. It was utterly clear, a lucid realization of interior experience, that these two were in some essential way if not the same, at least similar, pointing to the reality of the Divine Identity, the supreme Source of everything.

He saw the truth of both, but he didn't know how to express it. Saccidananda itself is an attempt to convey the inner awareness of the Godhead, but it is also the advaitic mystic's inner awareness when he/she has gone beyond the limited identity of a merely human way of thought and experience. I believe that Abhishiktananda did manage to integrate these two experiences and the simplicity of his Christian faith, and he was able to do this in the depths of his own being, beyond all words, concepts, or any form whatsoever. He came to a place of consciousness that brings together Hindu and Christian mysticism to a new species of contemplative understanding that is both and beyond both. He saw, especially after his heart attack in 1973, that life is simply about awakening, or waking up where we are to the reality of being itself, a reality which is beyond the categories of life and death. Life and death are not ultimate, only the awakened state is, and that is our true nature. The Buddha and Christ also addressed this true nature, a nature I would hesitate to call a self.

Before attempting to apply his advaitic intuition in a practical way, I'd like to say something about the place of the guru, the nature of this extraordinary kind of being, for Abhishiktananda was very emphatic about the importance of the teacher, or spiritual master to one's own inner growth to ultimate awareness. Abhishiktananda maintains:

> The guru is one who has himself first attained the Real and who knows from personal experience the way that leads there; he is capable of initiating the disciple and of making well up from within the heart of his disciple, the immediate ineffable experience which is his own — the utterly transparent knowledge, so limpid and pure, that quite simply "he is."
> The meeting with the guru is the essential meeting, the decisive turning point in the life of a person.
> But it is a meeting that can only take place when one has gone beyond the level of sense and intellect.
> It happens in the beyond, in the fine point of the soul, as the mystics say.... (In) the meeting of the guru and disciple there is no longer even fusion, for we are on the plane of the original non-duality.

Advaita remains forever incomprehensible to him who has not first lived it existentially in his meeting with the guru. (*Guru and Disciple*, trans. Heather Sandeman. London: SPCK, 1974, p. 29.)

The guru has attained the Real of *brahmavidya*, or mystical knowledge from direct experience of the Absolute, or the Brahman. He or she has attained to advaitic consciousness. Only such a one can trigger this same awareness in a disciple, when such a one is ready. Because the guru and disciple are existing together on a unitive level of life and experience, the guru can impart this *jnana*, this advaitic awareness to his student. They have been living it, living and breathing in its intensely immediate atmosphere. Their encounter and life together in that timeless, eternal relationship is decisive for the disciple because it demonstrates ultimate truth existentially in a mystical space within the ordinariness of life. But their meeting, their life together in the Spirit does not occur on a rational or sensate level. It is beyond sensation, the reason, intellect, beyond imagination, and in some way, even beyond will, because it transcends personal identity. It is the living experience of ultimate reality in the consciousness of advaitic unity, or non-duality. Advaita is the ground of their fruitful relationship, and the emergence of the disciple into spiritual maturity.

Practical Application of Advaita

It is clear from reading the Christian mystics, and those of other traditions, notably the Hindu, Buddhist, Taoist, and Sufi schools, that some sort of advaitic awareness is at work. The unitive level of experience is essential to the mystical process in every tradition. Abhishiktananda's incredibly rich appropriation of non-duality is a great challenge to Christian theology and spirituality. It calls the

Christian experience to the task of a contemplative deepening in such a way that it takes into account and uncovers the non-dual experience at the heart of the Christian mystical life, and indeed at the heart of the Gospel itself. We can see this same non-dual awareness, the original state, or ultimate, eternal consciousness at work in Tibetan Buddhist mysticism, for instance, especially in its understanding of what it calls *Dzogchen*, the perfection of the nature of the mind, which is consciousness itself.

Advaitic awareness is certainly consonant with the new discoveries in physics, cosmology, biology and psychology, where it has been found that a deeper unity holds all reality together, and this unity is in some sense *in* consciousness itself. Culturally, it encourages a greater and more focused appreciation of interdependence as more than a creation of economics and the omnipresence of the media, entertainment industry, and the internet. These latter phenomena are the results of that primal non-duality, that vast system of cosmic community to which we all belong, the totality of all being that can be. Abhishiktananda uncovered for the West this eternal wellspring, and now it remains to "translate" it into a language the West can hear, and Christianity, Judaism, and Islam can accept.

The Heart of Brother Wayne Teasdale's Vision of the Interspiritual Age
By Gorakh Hayashi and Kurt Johnson

Many of us are familiar with the new age joke-riddle: "What did the Zen Buddhist say to the hot dog vender?" Answer: "Make me one with everything." We laugh because of the witty convergence of meanings. The Zen Buddhist wants to become "One" with all that is as well as have his "one" delicious hot dog. In other words, he wants to eat his own cake and at the same time, share it with the totality. And, as a pacifist, he really doesn't want to fight about it. In a world of global stress with its race for resources, even for survival, we too long for a peaceful, compassionate, practical answer, an answer not just for me or us but for all. And as Al Gore reminds us around global warming, it's no longer a question of noble dreams but of brute survival. We are in a place where a "win/win" situation is utterly imperative, where "what's good for me" and "what's good for all" *must* come together. How do we honor our individual and national needs and, at the same time, respect the needs of all others, including those most different from us? In his core text, *The Mystic Heart*,[1] the late Brother Wayne Teasdale offers a seminal and visionary answer.

Above all, Wayne Teasdale was a mystic, a seeker of the One. He was also, like Gore, a pragmatist. He often quoted Martin Luther King: "The choice is between non-violence and non-existence" (MH p. 7). For Wayne, we awaken and survive through the mystic Heart. For him, the Heart is a "metaphor for the mystical organ of integration with the divine, or for ultimate realization" (MH p. 268). The Heart then connects us with the "ground of Being" and through that ground with "all that is," both imminent and transcendent, material and spiritual, practical and visionary. For Wayne, this synthesis is not so much a mental construct as a "felt" or "whole body-mind" response. A mystic is anyone whose life purpose is to enter the Heart, the space of Oneness, and live and act from this place of integration, serving the needs of self and other, individual and collective, the many and the One.

Wayne saw this non-dual movement converging in many areas at this time on the planet:

- the emergence of ecological awareness and sensitivity to the natural organic world;

- a growing sense of the rights of other species;

- a recognition of the interdependence of all domains of life and reality (and we would include here the arts, sciences, social sciences, education, politics, etc.);

- the ideal of abandoning a militant nationalism and recognizing our essential interdependence;

- an evolving sense of community among the religions through relationships between individual members as well as a growing receptivity to the inner treasures of the world's religions; and

- an openness to the cosmos, with the realization that the relationship between humans and the earth is part of the larger community of the universe (in this regard, Wayne did not discount the possibility of connection with and support from angelic beings, ascendant masters and even extra-terrestrials!).

Wayne saw all these converging movements leading to a major historical paradigm shift: "We are at the dawn of a new consciousness, a radically fresh approach to our life as the human family in a fragile world" (MH p. 4). He named this fresh, never-before-seen era the "Age of Interspirituality." This new epoch could have been named for any of the previously mentioned changes, but for Wayne, Interspiritual is the most encompassing and fundamental term. As a "monk in the world," he was quite sensitive to the dominance of materialism, consumerism, and sensate pleasure in current values. He wanted to highlight Spirit, not matter, Essence, not appearances. Using physicist David Bohm's terms, he wanted to touch the implicate and not merely the explicate order to affect true, lasting transformation at the root level.

Wayne felt that through dialogue between religions, through sharing the treasures of the various mystical and religious traditions, the essential and spiritual ground of all values could be touched. He loved to quote Rabbi Gelberman from New York City, who said: "In exploring other traditions and in embracing them, remember, it isn't a question of *instead of* — Buddhism instead of Christianity, or Christianity instead of Islam — but rather of *in addition to*, that is in addition to Buddhism, Christianity, in addition to Christianity, Islam. We don't reject our tradition, but build on it" (MH p. 49). Having more faith in individuals than in institutions, however, Wayne felt this dialogue could best occur through personal and individual sharing, particularly through the exchange of practices between followers of different faith traditions. The more Jews and Muslims, Protestants and Catholics, Hindus and Buddhists could pray, meditate, and sing together in mutual worship and celebration, the more friendships would grow, alliances could solidify, and the Mystic Heart would expand. This for him was the primary interspiritual dialogue, in the moment here and now, as if were there no history of this path or that. Consistently, Wayne made a distinction between the "church" as a religious, historical institution, and "Spirit," the alive, authentic heart connections between individual seekers. He often equated the latter with mysticism and the non-dual path and the former with religiosity and the dual.

As a mystic, Wayne had to find the essential building block of all Reality, the all-pervasive source of the One in the many. Like many mystics before him of multiple traditions, he came to identify this as Consciousness. Choosing Consciousness as the basic "stuff" of all Life foregrounds the subjective rather than the objective, the knower rather than the known. This radical emphasis on mind over body, subject over object, challenges the view of traditional science, although it totally resonates with the findings of quantum physics. This is how Wayne explains it in his chapter unit, "Everything Depends on Consciousness": "All that we experience — or know, think, imagine, remember, feel, and dream — we experience because we are first *aware*. For us, everything requires and depends on consciousness to be. The perception of an external world, the existence of others, even the fact of our own bodies, are presented to us through the agency of our consciousness" (MH p. 65). Further on, he writes: "That which makes perception possible is the basis of reality. Reality, cosmos, life, and being all rest on mind. Consciousness makes perception and everything else happen. Every system of thought that exists — every theory, science, art, literature, culture, religion, spirituality, family life, our personal experience, all experience — requires consciousness. It is the most fundamental insight in human life, and nothing is beyond its truth" (MH p. 66).

For Wayne, it is this underlying dimension of Consciousness grounded in subjective perception and awareness that will provide the non-dual basis for interspiritual dialogue between all the domains of life. He demonstrates how the new science, quantum mechanics, with its "unified field" theory and "role of the perceiver," confirms this radical perspective: "Subjectivity is intimately part of the theoretical and experimental phases of quantum research. The researcher is part of the quantum phenomena observed or predicted by probability. The observer affects the results of what is observed, and intentionality appears to be at work in particles, waves, and atomic structures. They are perhaps as conscious as we are, and make decisions as we do, but in and through their mode and degree of thought. It is more and more evident that consciousness is at work even on every level of phenomenon" (MH p. 74).

As with particles, waves, and atomic structures, so too with spiritual seekers, paths, and religious traditions — it all begins and ends with Consciousness. In Chapter 3 of his *The Mystic Heart*, "The Mirror of the Heart: Consciousness as the Root Identity," Wayne specifically focuses on Hinduism, Buddhism, and Christianity as representatives of all faith traditions, identifying Consciousness as the common ground not only of these three religions of the Book, but by implication, all spiritual paths, indeed, all domains of life. How does he do so?

Beginning with Hinduism, he focuses on the four *mahavakyas,* the four great statements or utterances of the Vedas, perhaps the earliest of all extant recorded scriptures. The first mahavakya declares: "Brahman is Consciousness." The Absolute, the all-pervasive and encompassing Self or Totality, is Awareness, the great Light of Consciousness. The second mahavakya says, "Atman is Brahman." The essence of the individual self, the Atman, the individual Witness, is identical with the aware Essence of Brahman — one and One merge. Wayne further points out that for Hindus the *guha* or cave of the Heart is where this meeting takes place. The third mahavakya occurs as a conversation between the sage, Uddalaka, and his son, Svetaketu, the archetypal Guru-disciple relationship. In teaching his son about the subtle essence of Atman, Uddalaka says: "The finest essence here, *this*, constitutes the self (Atman) of the whole world (Brahman), and that same essence are you, Svetaketu." The Guru tells his ready disciple, "Thou art That," and the boy awakens to his true nature. Thus we, the individual self, despite our apparent limitations and imperfections, are One with the Totality, One with Atman and Brahman. The purpose of the Sadguru is to foster this recognition. The fourth mahavakya pushes this pure identification even further by having each seeker subjectively claim It: "I am Brahman." As Wayne so elegantly puts it: "This daring assertion falls in the context of the Brahman reflecting on itself, but the implication is that each one of us can arrive at this same self-knowledge around our ultimate identity in God and as God — as Brahman" (MH p. 54). In all likelihood, this is Wayne's own experience and Self-assertion. He lived continuously in the awareness that he was One with the supreme Knower, with all-pervasive Light.

How does Wayne see this same Great Light as the root of Buddhism? Like many others, he returns to the inner experience of Siddhartha Gautama Sakyamuni, the Buddha, who shared with many his experience of "nirvana," of awakening. The essence of Gautama's Enlightenment was his recognizing his core and ground to be this Light, "the revelation of our ultimate nature as this vast awareness" (MH p. 58). Becoming fully "awake," fully "sentient" in the Buddhist sense is to recognize our essence in and as Consciousness. And what do the Buddhists do with matter, substance, apparently solid and individual forms? Wayne underscores Buddhist "shunyata," the impermanence of all passing phenomena, as proof of their insubstantiality, of their "emptiness." Just as thoughts and feelings are ephemeral, passing, and hence unreal, so too are apparently solid objects, the fleeting names and forms of things, since they too transmute, dissolve, and eventually disappear. Buddhist "shunya" or emptiness, however, is not total nothingness nor complete absence; beneath this emptiness of individual and impermanent forms lies a deeper inter-connectedness of Being, of "co-dependent arising" as the Buddhists call it. The transient world of passing forms and this deeper inter-connectedness of Being together form what the Buddhists call "imminent emptiness." What is it which experiences and recognizes this imminent emptiness? It is again Consciousness, the Light of Awareness, which the Buddhists call "transcendent emptiness," "cognizing emptiness," the emptiness which is fullness, which does not pass away. As Wayne expresses it: "Ultimate, or transcendent emptiness is equivalent to *parinirvana,* or the goal of existence as boundless consciousness beyond desire and personal identity" (MH p. 57). In this way, Wayne identifies the mutual ground of both Buddhism and Hinduism as pure and universal Consciousness.

How does he do the same for Christianity? He begins with Plato and Aristotle who he says share the same core dualism of mind/soul as separate from body. For Plato, this dualism is antagonistic; the soul is a prisoner of the body. For Aristotle, the relationship is more cooperative. The soul is both the animating and the intelligent substance or force. First it provides movement and mobility to "primary" matter; it "enlivens" it. It also provides a cognizing or intelligent aspect, once again, awareness or Consciousness. For Aristotle, this is the higher function of the soul, "active reason." It is active reason or mind which separates from the body and has an independent and perpetual existence: "When mind (soul as active reason) is set free from its present conditions, it appears as just what it is and nothing more; this alone is immortal and eternal...."(MH p. 63). Once again, this time within the context of Western philosophy, mind or consciousness has been recognized as the essential or enduring aspect of Reality.

Wayne, however, identifies Thomas Aquinas, the synthesizer of neo-Platonic and Aristotelian insights with Christianity, as the first to bring mind or Consciousness into Western theology. For Aquinas, the highest function of the soul or mind is to know God. We do this through our "intellectual substance." "And this will be most clearly fulfilled in that vision, when the intellect, by gazing on the First Truth, will know all that it naturally desires to know...." (MH p. 63). In this way, Wayne identifies intellect — mind — as the enduring essence in both Western philosophy and in Christianity, as the faculty which allows man to know and be in relationship with the eternal Godhead. Thus, Consciousness becomes the common ground uniting the three religions of the Book.

With Consciousness identified as the mystical or non-dual glue, there still exist certain historical, doctrinal, and institutional differences between the three. How might these sources of potential disagreement and conflict be resolved through interspiritual receptivity and dialogue? Wayne wrote in *The Mystic Heart* that through thoughtful and sensitive discussion along with shared practices, the strengths of each tradition could first be recognized and then synthesized into a greater whole. Again, it is Hinduism in addition to Buddhism in addition to Christianity. At the most general or meta level, what can each of these three paths learn from and offer to one another, both historically and in the now?

Wayne begins by pointing out the dependency of Buddhism on its Hindu roots in India for both context and practices. Buddhism, however, with its absence of a Godhood and of an individual, permanent self could and did offer a critique of institutional Hinduism's hierarchical and separatist caste system. If there was no difference between God and man — simply realized or non-realized Buddha nature — and all individual selves were temporary and thus unreal, how could one person or class of people be deemed superior to another and therefore closer to God, who did not even exist? And, of course, it was the Brahman priests, the highest caste, who appropriated the name of the deity for themselves, that supported and maintained this system.

Thus, for Wayne, Buddhism had political and social roots as well as metaphysical ones. In this way, Buddhism could add to and expand Hinduism's traditional perspective and values.

What could Christianity add to historical Hinduism and Buddhism? Wayne believed that Christianity contributed its gospel of love, of social equality and compassionate service. He directly states that it was Christianity that introduced love into *Hinayana* Buddhism's more ascetic and other worldly thrust. Though Buddhism challenged Hinduism's class system, at the same time, with its *samsara* and *nirvana* emphasis, it also focused on escaping the world. Wayne quotes the anonymous writer of the *Meditations on the Tarot: a Journey into Christian Hermeticism:* "When the Gospel was preached by the light of day in the countries around the Mediterranean, the nocturnal rays of the Gospel effected a profound transformation of Buddhism. There, the ideal of individual liberation by entering the state of nirvana gave way to the ideal of renouncing nirvana for the work of mercy towards suffering humanity. The ideal of Mahayana, the great chariot, then had its resplendent ascent to the heaven of Asia's moral values" (MH p. 6-7). For Wayne, the bodhisattva ideal of a selfless return to the earth plane until all sentient beings are freed was stimulated by the Christian message of love and compassionate service. This was Christianity's gift to Buddhism, and by implication, to Hinduism as well. This is but one example of how, for Wayne, receptive and authentic dialogue between the different faith traditions could not only avoid partisan conflict and struggle but also contribute to a more expanded and fulfilling vision of interspiritual Oneness and solidarity.

Although we see Hinduism, Buddhism, and Christianity in their more mystical and non-dual expressions — for example, the *shaivite* traditions in Hinduism, the *mahayana* approach to Buddhism, and the way of the *mystic* in Christianity — as having a common ground, a core Oneness in Consciousness, we would here like to look more historically at the doctrinal and institutional differences Wayne noted. We hope to identify more abstract or meta sources of differentiation and perhaps, of ultimate synthesis. We see these more meta-categories as Hinduism's "transcendent" emphasis, Buddhism's essentially "imminent" focus, and Christianity's journey from "imminence" to "transcendence" through the "purification of the Heart."

The teleologies or final ends of these approaches are relevant here. Hinduism seeks merger with Brahman, the transcendent Light of Consciousness, beyond the play of individual and worldly forms. Above all, the Hindu seeker wishes to get off the "wheel of becoming" and merge with the infinite Absolute. This transcendent emphasis also appears in Hinduism's four asramas or stages of life: student, householder, forest dweller, and renunciant. The final and highest stage is asceticism, when one has completed all worldly responsibilities and turns exclusively to Spirit for meaning and release. Only then is supreme and eternal samadhi or Liberation possible. In contrast, *Mahayana* Buddhism, based as it is on Siddhartha Gautama's experience of awakening in this world without God or deities, emphasizes imminence. Gautama's teachings end with recognizing one's own Buddha nature or mind in this world by turning inward, not in the pursuit of other-worldly *nirvana*. Again, in Hinayana Buddhism, closer to its roots in classical Hinduism, the focus was more transcendent, to leave samsara behind through extreme asceticism. With mahayana's *bodhisattva's* ideal of compassionate return, the emphasis is again on imminence, on life on this plane. In Christianity's embrace of both imminence and transcendence through the purification of the Heart, we find the two combined.

Wayne was fascinated by historian Arnold Toynbee's suggestion that the "meeting of Christianity and Buddhism would be the most significant event of our period of history" (MH p. 46). Why was this meeting so significant to both of them? Again, Wayne saw Consciousness as key. He writes, "Christian mysticism only ends where Buddhist mysticism begins, and ends—its goal" (MH p. 48). Wayne has earlier established Consciousness as the goal and essence of both traditions. Why does he here say that though Christianity ends in Consciousness, as in Aquinas' active reason beholding the Divine Light, it begins in a different place? We believe Wayne was making a distinction here between institutional or dualistic Christianity and its mystical or non-dual branches. Buddhism begins with one's inherent "Buddha nature or mind" and ends with a more expanded version of it: we are *all* Buddhas, all One with Being-Awareness. Although Christianity also started out with a unitive creation myth with its pristine Paradise and harmony between God and man, institutional Christianity came to embrace the ontology of the Fall. Here it became dualistic, God versus man, man versus woman and the other creatures of the earth, ultimately Good versus Evil. Such dualism always implies a win/lose situation: man must surrender to God or God must surrender to man. Eventually one or the other must be negated. Thus, Christianity in its ontology of the Fall begins in oppositional dualism, and then through the intervention of Christ, the God-man, ends in Re-union, in Paradise regained. Buddhism never postulates an ontological dualism even at the beginning: our essence has always been our Buddha nature, and we merely come to recognize it along with its universal presence. Institutional Christianity, however, even with its final embrace of the beatific vision, can never completely leave its dualistic roots. Even at the end, Man can at best behold the

Godhead, never become fully One with It. Even the most evolved of the Christian mystics would hesitate before the boldness of Hinduism's fourth mahavakya: "I am Brahman; I am, indeed, God." They can look upon the Great Light of Godhead but never absolutely and eternally enter It. This same dualism appears in the Church's perpetual struggle between Good and Evil, ultimately in the eternal separation of Heaven and Hell. It is, perhaps, Buddhism's essential non-dualism, without God and empty of individual forms, which is its potential gift to an interspiritual Christianity. What reciprocally might Christianity offer Buddhism?

We believe Wayne points to it when he discusses Aquinas' synthesis of neo-Platonic philosophy and Christian theology. He acknowledges the role of mind or consciousness in the final approach to God: "And this will be most clearly fulfilled in that vision, when the intellect, by gazing on the First Truth, will know all that it naturally desires to know…"(MH p. 63). For Aquinas, however, the Heart as well as the mind enters this experience: "Contemplation of God in total enjoyment in love, the maturity of a selfless intimacy with the divine in which the person transcends selfishness. It is love. The intellect and heart are united in knowing the absolute directly" (MH p. 63). Wayne underscores this combination by mentioning it again in his description of the mystic and philosopher Spinoza: "The philosopher Spinoza was suggesting this experience when he spoke of the intellectual love of God. The highest kind of knowing unites love and knowledge: It is more than love, because vivified by the intellect, and more than reason, because expanded by love" (MH p. 63). How has the "mind" of God become the "intellectual *love*" of God? How has Consciousness come to have a Heart? Perhaps, this is Christianity's contribution to both hierarchical Buddhism and world-renouncing Hinduism?

How does love come to be the central message of the Gospels? We believe it is the very dualism of the Fall that engenders it. For God to be reconciled to fallen man, unconditional love and forgiveness are required. This is already apparent in the parable of the prodigal son, who comes to realize there is no real separation from the Father, who has always been present and available. Still the son must first believe, ask for and accept this boundless, conditionless Love. It is the temporary separation which brings into full consciousness the need and centrality of Love. We also see this in Christ's cry of abandonment on the cross: "My God, my God, why has thou forsaken me?" Since in Hinduism, Brahman is already the Essence of all individual selves and, in Buddhism, "Buddha nature" is man's intrinsic state, no such core separation and consequent need for love are emphasized. Sinful, fallen man's distance from perfect, unchanging God, however, demands such pure and self-transcending love. Christianity's dyadic symbolism of the parent/child bond also supports this. The parent/child tie is the most fundamental of all love bonds, and where that seems absent, great longing and urgency is generated. Metaphorically, to reconnect with Hinduism's universal Self or reawaken to Buddhism's universal Light is less personal and pressing than Christianity's intimate familial re-union. And again, since in Christianity the separation is a matter of relationship and heart longing, not simply of right understanding, Love becomes the bridge and the way. Christianity's personification of a dualistic God-man relationship along with the myth of the fall then may account for its special gift to Buddhism and to Hinduism, the articulation of the need for and centrality of Love as the catalyst to redemption and re-union. For Toynbee, this may be what Christianity has to offer Buddhism.

Once we have identified transcendence, imminence, and Love's journey between as the core elements of interspiritual wholeness, might there not be a deeper way to combine and even synthesize the three? Again, Wayne points the way in his discussion of the Christian-Hindu crossover, Abhishiktananda, who recognized the resonances between Christianity's Holy Trinity: Father, Son, and Holy Spirit and Hinduism's Great Self, "Saccidananda," Being, Awareness, and Bliss absolute. Wayne writes: "The experience of Saccidananda carries the soul beyond all merely intellectual knowledge to her very center (the guha, cave of the Heart), to the source of her being. Only there is she able to hear the Word which reveals within the undivided unity and advaita of Saccidananda, the mystery of the three divine persons. In Sat, the Father, the absolute Beginning and Source of Being; in Cit, the Son, the divine Word, the Father's Self-knowledge; in Ananda, the Spirit of Love, fullness and Bliss without end" (MH p. 34). The three common elements are: 1) Being as ground and source, 2) Awareness through differentiation and self-consciousness, and 3) Bliss through the fullness of Love. These same three appear again in Mahayana Buddhism as 1) Being, collective and individual in imminent emptiness, 2) Awareness as transcendent emptiness, and 3) Bliss as the bodhisattva compassionate ideal of universal awakening and merger. Further, in all three instances, it is through the experience of Love — the Heart — that Being and Awareness become connected and as One.

In Christianity, Being and Awareness are united through the longing of the Son for the Father, the Father for the Son, God for man, man for God. The Holy Spirit expresses and finally actualizes this longing. Spirit is the "daemon," the go-between first desiring and finally uniting transcendence and imminence, immortal and mortal, man and God. Similarly, in non-dual Hinduism, Brahman, the Universal and Absolute Self, and Atman, the individual self, seek to recognize and celebrate their Oneness. Again, Love or desire serve as the catalyst and vehicle, *mumukshutva,* the longing for Liberation, in the *jnani* or Hindu contemplative paths and *bhakti* or devotion in the paths of the Heart. Finally, in Mahayana Buddhism, the longing of transcendent emptiness to release and liberate all individual forms of imminent emptiness is realized through the compassionate service of the *bodhisattva* ideal. The triune synthesis then of Christianity's Father, Son, and Holy Spirit, Hinduism's Satchitananda, and Mahayana Buddhism's transcendent and imminent emptiness through compassionate service happens in the integration of Being and Awareness within the Heart. In all three, individual Awareness longs for all-pervasive Being, and when realized through Love in the space of the Heart, universal, eternal, and supreme Bliss arises.

Why is this experience so rare and unsustainable? All three traditions agree: when the focus is on individual desire and gratification alone, there can be no real re-union nor perpetual fulfillment. In Christianity, selfish desire and action lead to sin and irrevocable separation. In Hinduism, the *ahamkara* or individual ego seeking self-gratification can never know the great Self and must, therefore, constantly return to taste yet more *maya* or illusion. In Buddhism, self-grasping attachment to the material plane ignoring co-dependent arising, transcendent emptiness, and collective awakening leads inevitably to separation, impermanence, and suffering. On the other hand, when individuality in all three traditions moves beyond itself and embraces the well-Being of the whole, when the many and the One again reunite, then Christian beatitude, Hindu *ananda,* and Buddhist Awakening become the norm and we have "world without end." Once again, we have returned to our new age joke, "make me one with everything," and the critical dilemma of our times: how can we enjoy our individual hot dog and also share it with all others?

For Wayne, we do this by entering the mystic Heart and knowing and experiencing our fundamental Oneness in Consciousness as the ground for co-creative action and manifestation. How might we make this synthesis more understandable and tangible, more operational? We return to the body / mind problem in yet another form. How can matter and consciousness, substance and thought, the physical and spiritual needs of both the individual and the collective be joined and synthesized? How do we move beyond living and thinking in polarities and instead embrace an ontology of Oneness? How do we find a unified ground of meaning and purpose that lets us eat our cake and still have enough to share with others? How can we truly understand how matter and mind, body and Spirit, individual and collective co-exist as One and further, how do we find tools and practices to assimilate and implement this benevolent and at the same time survival-generated perspective?

Kashmir Shaivism, a highly sophisticated non-dual Hindu philosophy originating in 12th century India, provides possible insights and methodologies. When we combine these with hypotheses of contemporary quantum mechanics, a viable explanation begins to emerge. *Pratyabhijnahrdayam*, one of Shaivism's core scriptures, says, *"Citi* herself, descending from the plane of pure Consciousness, becomes *citta,* the mind, by contracting in accordance with the object perceived" (Siva, 53). Here we have an explanation of how pure, all-pervasive Consciousness, Wayne's core essence, becomes the mind — limited, individual awareness — by contracting through the perception of and participation in discrete objects. Pure Consciousness, all-pervasive Light, becomes individualized minds, Aristotle's active reason, by coming into relationship with differentiated matter. In other words, when universal or Big Mind focuses on concrete objects rather than on the Great Light of Consciousness, it contracts and becomes small mind, our own limited awareness in a world of concrete names and forms. In Buddhist terms, transcendent emptiness or awareness, when it begins to focus on the impermanent realm of separate objects, becomes itself differentiated and individuated, losing its transcendent dimension, its formless freedom.

Quantum mechanics with its metaphors of Light and space, energy and matter, waves and particles suggests a parallel process. The key is Consciousness or Light condensing into greater densities, manifesting in different expressions or forms, yet remaining ever One. We have a spectrum model, a single essence differentiating into varieties of itself, like the different colors of a color wheel, rather than a system of duality and opposition. Both quantum physics and Kashmir Shaivism connect this with vibrational frequencies. When Light moves so fast as to appear motionless and still, it approximates unchanging substance, unmoving potentiality. It becomes all-pervasive ground and potential source, God the sustaining Father, Sat or all-pervasive Being, transcendent emptiness in the three faith traditions. In quantum mechanics, this unmoving ground may be the limitless space into and from which the rapidly moving photons enter and disappear.

In the three religions, when Light begins to move a bit more slowly, it differentiates itself from non-dual Essence, and now distinct and apart in Oneness can know itself for the first time. Hindu Sat has condensed into Chit, pure Awareness, Christian Father separated into Son as pure Spirit/Word, and Buddhist transcendent emptiness coalesced into formless Inter-being now capable of knowing Itself.

In quantum theory, this may be the point at which photons start to emerge and vanish within the space field. When Light further slows and condenses, it coalesces into universal energy, Shakti, Chi, or the Tao in the Eastern religions, living Spirit in Western Christianity and quantum energy in Western science. As it continues to condense and differentiate, it becomes first separate and individual thoughts, feelings, and sensations and finally concrete objects, separate bodies, the imminent world of passing names and forms. This all parallels quantum mechanics condensing of moving particles into matter. We have a new paradigm of seeing mind and body, awareness and being, energy and matter, even waves and particles, as no longer different and mutually opposed but rather as one continuous spectrum of Light vibrating at different frequencies and densities. By combining the insights of Kashmir Shaivism and quantum mechanics, we can see how Wayne's intuition of Consciousness as unified, ineffable ground simultaneously manifesting as matter, energy, individual thoughts/ feelings, electrons, and even sub-atomic particles becomes viable. We have a way of explaining how the One can also be the many.

We still have the concern of how to make all of this operational and practical. After the success of *The Mystic Heart*, a central focus for Wayne was answering the many questions he received about how this cogent vision could be actualized as part of the world transformation he also envisioned. Addressing this in discussions after *The Mystic Heart,* Wayne stressed a view anchored in his mature appreciation of the simultaneity of immanent and transcendent, relative and absolute. Recognizing the breadth of social crises and challenges worldwide, he called for a potent new initiative by all the traditions aimed at maturing the individual *and* the collective simultaneously. This call was a vigorous extension of the challenge that *The Mystic Heart* aimed at the world's religions, and specifically at their contemplative core. "We need to understand, to really grasp at an elemental level," he wrote "that the definitive revolution is the spiritual awakening of humankind" (MH p. 12). If, as Wayne had stressed throughout *The Mystic Heart*, the pivotal transformative asset of the world's religions was the commonality of their mystical experience of Oneness ("unitive awareness," MH p. 80f) and its inherent manifestation as transformative unconditional service to the world (MH Chapter 7, "The Spirituality of Action"), a new synergy of these dimensions must be the urgent imperative for all the world's traditions. Attention to the contemplative core could no longer be merely anecdotal or acknowledged by the traditions as being limited to the possible experience of just a few. "This journey is what spirituality is really about," Wayne had written (MH p. 18). "We are not meant to remain here…. We cannot depend on our culture either to guide and support us in our quest. We must do the hard work of clarification ourselves" (MH p. 120). This renewed attention to the Heart was the first of what Wayne called his "two-pronged" challenge. Regarding the contemplative core, his central term "the mystic Heart" pointed the Way. To enter, live, and act fully from the space of the One Great Heart is to reconcile the apparent opposites of Awareness and Being, knowing and feeling, self and other and to embrace and live the common ground of universal peace, love, and joy. As individuals, we can experience this quite directly and immediately — "becoming," merging into Being of imminence meeting transcendence, of man becoming God in "felt Awareness," "conscious Presence," "differentiated Totality" — the individual Heart expanded and merged into the Heart of Kosmos. This was one indispensable asset the world's religions could bring to the process of world transformation.

But, as second prong, Wayne recognized another emphasis required by the centuries of inertia caused by sectarian separation and discord. Such attention to individual spiritual work must be enacted, Wayne said, with simultaneous and equal emphasis on the traditions creating and proffering a new revolutionary narrative with paramount emphasis on shared core values and, most challenging, a common realization from the experience of the Heart that, in a world of shrinking space and resources, the exclusive claims natural to the evolution of the religions must now be recognized as a possible pathology, one of several possible sources of mass conflict which could lead to our planetary extinction. "This revolution will be the task of the Interspiritual Age," he wrote. "The necessary shifts in consciousness require a new approach to spirituality that transcends past religious cultures of fragmentation and isolation" (MH p. 12).

Of this balanced attention, Wayne had written in *The Mystic Heart*: "If transformation is only a matter of consciousness, then there is always the risk that the change many never touch the deeply hidden intentions of the heart. If the will is not involved in the radical change the spiritual process initiates, then the resultant "enlightenment" is only partial. Clearly, if the mystical process is to be complete, it must include a profound transformation in the will. Achieving the ultimate awareness of the way things are is simply not enough" (MH p. 89). Br. Wayne knew that tremendous courage would be needed for the religions of the world to become part of the revolution to initiate an Interspiritual Age. Writing to his own constituency, the Roman Catholic Church: "It will take enormous vision and courage to walk this path in history. It brings to mind Christ's words: 'Unless a grain of wheat falls into the earth and dies, it remains only a single grain, but if it dies it yields a rich harvest'" (MH p. 248). Wayne was challenging the world's religions to take this revolutionary path, a path he felt would make their confounding diversity an asset, not a liability, to the world's future. This was the center of Wayne's attention after the success of *The Mystic Heart* and as he began preparation for his contribution to the 2004 Parliament of the World's Religions (a process which involved both of the present authors).

In preparing for the Parliament with his fledgling "interspiritual association" (which after his transition became InterSpiritual Dialogue in Action, www.isdna.org), Wayne brought to his last planning session (New York City, October 2003) the report of his "Omega Vision" or "Omega Formula." He said he had received this simple formula in a recent spiritual experience and he wondered out loud, in his usual humility, "if it might serve for Interspirituality the same purpose E=mc² had served for science." We share it here for the first time:

$$\Omega > \sum E^n$$

It means: "Always, Omega is greater than the sum of all experiences" (Ω / Omega; > / greater than; $\sum$ / sum of; E to the nth / all experience).

For Wayne, this was the view of the mature soul, whether referring to an "Omega point" in individual spiritual knowledge or the cumulative knowledge of any or all traditions. It was also a fulcrum for mature humility, an acknowledgement of fundamental "unknowing" from which it would not be possible to posit an exclusive claim.

Wayne was not only serious about the two-pronged requirement for maturing world spirituality to help usher in a transformative Interspiritual Age, but also he was concerned that if the world religions could not assume this universal redeeming role, it might well pass to another historical vector, one he saw already growing from individual personal transformations to grassroots circles of transformation and broader associations, networks, and coalitions. These, he wrote, "could then join together in collaborative efforts to reverse the negative habits that produced the ecological crisis, countless wars, and the many forms of injustice, oppression, and inequity" (MH p. 249). "The Interspiritual Age," he said, "will require institutions and structures to carry, express and support it" (MH p. 248). From sharing spiritual practices of the Heart, to true interspiritual dialogue from the core essentials of religious experience, Wayne believed the "treasures of the world religions" could forge a common ground and actual impetus toward realization of his dream of a new civilization grounded in the mystic Heart (MH pp. 4-5).

Thus, we stress in conclusion of this paper, that the world-embracing, cosmocentric vision of Br. Wayne, elucidated in *The Mystic Heart* and thereafter in discussion with his many friends and colleagues, deserves substantial further elucidation and study. Such enterprise has been overlooked somewhat since his 2004 transition, both because of the suddenness of his passing and also because much of the depth and detail of his vision is scattered across the many pages of his books, written in inspiring style, but not necessarily rigorously enumerated in structure. It is not enough to simply remember Br. Wayne as an inspiring figure. His succinct comprehension of the world's spiritual traditions in the context of unitive awareness, coupled with his balanced call for the socially transforming energy that inherently emanates from this realization, is a distinct contribution to current holistic and integral approaches to world transformation. Fully aware of what was required of these approaches, Wayne said, "This new paradigm must be able to accommodate all human experience, knowledge and capacities" (MH p. 65) "built both on intellectual integration and direct experience" (MH p. 35) and "make available to everyone all the forms the spiritual journey assumes" (MH p 26). We will comment more on this in the future.

Shortly before his transition, Gorakh Hayashi asked Wayne whether he had any final teachings he wanted to share with the world. Wayne paused, reflected, and then wrote: "The Divine is infinite sensitivity." Again, Wayne grounded even absolute Consciousness in the tender knowing of the Heart. For Wayne, the key to all of this is uniting body and mind, matter and Spirit, feeling and intellect through entering and living the way of the mystic Heart. In the penultimate words of his seminal text, Wayne alludes again to this core teaching: "Spirituality, finally, is awareness and sensitivity, and sensitivity is itself awareness-in-action. It is this quality that we most require in our time and in the ages to come, but it is a quality refined only in the mystic heart, in the steady cultivation of compassion and love that risks all for the sake of others. It is these resources that we desperately need as we build the civilization with a heart, a universal society capable of embracing all that is, putting it to service in the transformation of the world. May the mystics lead the way to this rebirth of the human community that will harmonize itself with the cosmos and finally make peace with all beings" (MH p. 249-250). And lest we are daunted by this title of mystic, Wayne has earlier reassured us: "Every one is a mystic. We may or may not know it; we may not even like it. But whether we know it or not, whether we accept it or not, mystical experience is always there, inviting us on a journey of ultimate discovery" (MH p. 3). May each of us become what we all already are.

Remarks, Endnotes and References[viii:1]

Select Serial Features that Appeared in 2014 after the Publication of *The Coming Interspiritual Age*

Features[3] by Mirabai Starr - Dena Merriam - Ruth Broyde Sharone - Roger Housden
Matthew Wright - Lama Surya Das - Beverly J. Lanzetta - Andrew Harvey - Roger Ross
Deborah Steen Ross - Robert Toth - Adam Bucko - Rory McEntee - Kurt Johnson

Love Language:
The Inter-Spiritual Heart of the Mystics

by Mirabai Starr

Mira has offered herself to her Lord.
The single lotus will swallow you whole.

From "Mira the Bee"

For decades I was conditioned to believe that to engage a mature spiritual life I needed to "pick one tradition and go deep," which implied that my attraction to the teachings and practices at the heart of all religions was superficial and indolent. Also, that the path of non-dualism — with its affirmation of undifferentiated consciousness — was superior to my devotional disposition. Also, that my experience of longing for God was an illusion — some kind of unconscious blend of unresolved childhood abandonment and magical thinking. In other words, the energy that fueled my journey was predicated on a perfect storm of delusional inclinations.

It was only when the fire of loss swept into my life and burned the scaffolding to the ground that all conceptual constructs came tumbling down and these insidious messages revealed themselves as 1) unkind, and 2) untrue. From the ashes of grief a transfigured, more authentic self began to rise, and she felt no obligation to choose sides. She was a Jew and a Sufi, a believer and an agnostic. She practiced Vipassana and Centering Prayer, observed Shabbat and received communion. She rested in blessed moments of unitive consciousness and sang the praises of Lord Krishna.

I am not alone. A tribe of people is coalescing around the world to celebrate a reorientation from religious separation to interspiritual connection. While many of us have been pilgrims on this path for decades — sometimes feeling alone in the wilderness, sometimes gathering with other seekers who are similarly drawn to worshipping the sacred in every single holy house we encounter — now, at last, our numbers seem to be reaching a tipping point and what was a fringe phenomenon is becoming a global movement.

The interspiritual path is characterized as much by what it is not as what it is. It is not a new religion; in fact many of its most enthusiastic adherents consider themselves "spiritual but not religious." It has no creed or dogma, no tenets or prohibitions. No special attire sets it apart and no single symbol represents its core philosophy. Its membership is as diverse as the full spectrum of humanity. It is not about belief, but action. And the only action required is love.

The mystics of every tradition — and those whose hearts thrum with yearning for God but do not have any religious affiliation — embody this Way of Love. The language the mystics speak is the Language of Love. Drenched in love-longing, the mystic dissolves into the ocean of the One. Mystical poetry transcends theological distinctions and neutralizes ideological ultimatums. These love poems to God do not describe Ultimate Reality: they evoke it. The poems of the mystics slip past the thought-guardians and batter down the gates of the heart. In crying out to the Holy One, the ecstatic poets offer us a direct connection with the object of their souls' deepest desire, and ours. Mystical poetry generates a sacred field, and invites us to step in.

See if these snippets knock on your heart-door:

This longing is dear to me.
This longing makes every place sacred.
This longing,
Too large for heaven and earth,
Fits inside my heart,
Smaller than the eye of a needle.
(Rumi)[1]

When he spoke my soul vanished.
I look for him and can't find him.
I call, he doesn't answer…
I beg you, daughters of Jerusalem,
If you find my love
You will say that I am sick with love.
(Song of Songs)[2]

All night I could not sleep
Because of the moonlight on my bed.
I kept on hearing a voice calling:
Out of Nowhere, Nothing answered "yes."
(Zi Ye)[3]

Oh, living flame of love,
how tenderly you penetrate
the deepest core of my being!
Finish what you began.
Tear the veil from this sweet encounter.
(John of the Cross)[4]

Listen, my friend,
This road is the heart opening,
Kissing his feet,
Resistance broken, tears all night.
(Mirabai)[5]

... and finally, insane for the light,
you are the butterfly and you are gone.
And so long as you have not experienced this:
To die and so to grow,
You are only a troubled guest on the dark earth.
(Goethe)[6]

The highest calling of the mystic is not to become enlightened, but rather to become nothing, to utterly disappear into the One. What madness! And yet the mystical path is all about paradox. When lover merges with Beloved, all separation melts and only love remains; there is no one left to long nor any object of longing, and this, to the mystic, is good news. Mystics claim their experience of union is ineffable, and yet they cannot resist expressing their encounter in lush poetic language. Mysticism is characterized by annihilation: the soul is the moth inexorably drawn to the flame. In burning to death, lover is transformed in Beloved, individual self yields to its oneness with the Divine, the dream of exile ends and the spirit comes home to its source.

It is here, in the center of the perennial paradox, that it becomes obvious all spiritual paths emanate from and return to the same universal heart. This is where the only possible response to the quiet blessing of union with the One is the passionate outpouring of love-language. Here, longing for God is not a malady to be cured or a broken thing that needs repairing, but a shattering of the cup of the heart so that, within the vast spaciousness that opens, the Mystery may come pouring in and lift us into the arms of Love itself.

Endnotes and Additional Resources[viii:4]

The Contemplative Alliance: The Role of Contemplative Practice in Transforming Society
by Dena Merriam

The idea to form a Contemplative Alliance, bringing together deeply committed meditation practitioners from across the religious traditions, emerged from the recognition that a new spiritual voice is needed, one that reflects the changing spiritual landscape of America. It was also felt that as a collective we need to tap the wisdom and understanding that comes from deep contemplative practice to guide us through the challenges we now face.

It is clear to many of us that we are at a crossroad and are being called to make significant shifts in thinking and behavior. There has been no strong voice to articulate what these shifts entail, and thus there is no model, no clear vision of where we need to go or how we are to get there. Contemplative practice can contribute to this process of creating and clarifying a collective vision in numerous ways.

American society and much of the developed world have been operating with a certain set of thought patterns that have been reinforced again and again through most of the institutions and structures of our society. These thought patterns make up the prevailing narrative of our culture: they define the values and goals of our society and what a good life should be. They define prosperity in a very narrow way focusing exclusively on economic growth and expansion, unlimited consumption, the commodification of nature, and the sense that the right to pursue such growth and consumption is almost a "sacred" right, not to be challenged or questioned. We now see these thought patterns beginning to break down. This is manifesting as deepening cracks in our economic and political institutions. The onset of climate instability, the oil spill catastrophe in the Gulf of Mexico, financial fluctuations, far reaching degradation of the environment, the potential scarcity of vital resources like water — all of these are signs of shifts in the external landscape, which are but reflections of shifts in the internal landscape. To understand what is taking place, we need to look more closely at the internal world and see what is coming apart and what is coming together in our collective thought patterns. There is a struggle between the old and the new, and that which is seeking to be born needs support and guidance.

Those who work in the spiritual field know that changes take place first at the level of thought and then manifest as behavior change. Thoughts have force and the power to manifest and so it is said, "As we think, so we are." Collective fear, pain, or anger manifests in a particular manner and shapes an external reality. Similarly, changing the way we regard and interact with nature would manifest certain outcomes. Changes in the way we regard prosperity would also manifest as a shift in habits and behavior patterns. A redefining of prosperity and our national well-being would help reshape the values and direction of our country. A redefining of prosperity does not mean denying the importance of material development, but it may mean bringing into balance our material welfare with other equally vital determinants of well-being.

Clearly, changes in the way we view prosperity would have economic implications for our country that must be considered. In Germany, for example, the government is trying to convince the population to start again a national shopping spree. The recession led to reduced consumption, and now the government wants consumption to return to its pre-recession levels. But the Germans are being more cautious and have entered a mindset of conserving rather than consuming. Business will suffer unless consumption picks up. Can the society shift from one based on the production and consumption of goods to a new basis, one that is more sustainable? While this shift would produce short-term pains, it would produce long-term gains for the society. But who has called for a serious reflection of what this entails and for steps to make such a transition?

The current recession presents an enormous opportunity to redefine prosperity and reshape our values to be more in keeping with the central tenets shared by all the spiritual traditions. We have the opportunity now to balance economic growth with spiritual growth as a society and culture. We have the responsibility to work more consciously with our communities in shaping the thought patterns that can guide this effort.

As a contemplative community seeking to be of service at this time, what role can we play in bringing forth the ideas and concepts that will help transform the way we live and function as a society? This will be the theme of our inquiry when we gather. In preparation, we ask that you reflect on the following questions:

1. What is the single most important change in thinking that can help move our society toward greater well-being?

2. To create this change in thinking, a few key messages must penetrate the collective — what would these messages be?

3. How can we best work to foster new thought patterns that can then manifest as changes in our society?

4. What would prosperity look like in a more balanced society where material and spiritual development go hand-in-hand?

5. As we seek to envision a more sustainable society, what would it look like?

There is no greater need now than cultivating a global understanding of human unity. Faith communities should lead this effort as our spiritual values — such as compassion, love, and peace — are universal and can bring us together as a human community. Why then is this so problematic for many religious leaders today? Why is religious identity more important than human identity at a time when the problems we face, such as climate change and growing economic inequity, are global and can only be solved through collective efforts? Although many religious leaders give lip service to the concept of human unity, resistance to actual integration remains. In reality, many still fix their religious identity, or even concept of "salvation," in the root tradition from which they come. If we connect equally with those of another religion, does our commitment to our own religious community weaken? This fear inhibits the deepening of interreligious ties — and it's a challenge the interfaith community must work to overcome by demonstrating that religions are in fact complementary, not competitive.

When I recently mentioned at an international interfaith meeting that we must move beyond merely respecting other faiths to a deeper appreciation of their truth and beauty, I was told this was going too far. I was told the goal of interfaith is to stem hatred, not erase boundaries. I strongly disagree. The goal of interfaith is to come to love the "other," and for this we must come to appreciate the worldviews that other religions offer. This is a huge but much needed step for humankind.

I have been involved in the interfaith movement for more than fifteen years, and I have seen progress, though slow, as religious devotees struggle to engage with one another under the rubric of "tolerance" first, then "respect." But they still shy away from full acceptance of the other.

Since the beginning, my work has been to engage the voices that have been left out of interreligious dialogue — those of women and practitioners of the Eastern traditions, in particular Hindus and Buddhists, who together make up nearly one and a half billion people. It is for this reason that I founded the Global Peace Initiative of Women (GPIW) to help identify and bring to the fore women religious and spiritual leaders. We did this by organizing dialogues in conflict areas — such as Israel and Palestine, Iraq, Sudan, and Afghanistan — that were shaped and led by women spiritual leaders.

Fifteen years later, I find that there is now much greater effort to engage women at the international level. We are often approached to recommend women for interfaith meetings, as there is greater awareness now of their necessary involvement. But there is still resistance to placing the Eastern faiths on equal footing. This has long baffled me as these traditions are so rich in wisdom and insight and so greatly add to any dialogue. To help achieve this East-West balance, GPIW founded the Contemplative Alliance, which highlights the unifying contemplative practices shared by the major religions. We first launched in 2008 at the Aspen Institute in Colorado, and since then we have organized ten such conferences and dialogues around the United States.

When I attend international meetings, I often point to the progress that has been made in the U.S. where Buddhist and Hindu practices of meditation have become mainstream and are gaining respect equal to other religions. A growing community of people is now at ease with the crossing of religious boundaries and the integration of Eastern practices with their Abrahamic beliefs. Now more than ever, we are able to take what we need for our own spiritual unfolding. We should not take this freedom for granted — it is still rare in most of the world.

I see this integration as a very positive step as it can aid in deepening our understanding of human unity, the common vision, and shared values underlying all religious traditions. In the past, religious institutions focused on their differences. This served to separate and polarize people. If we are to solve global problems as a global family, we must shift from a paradigm of separateness to one of unity — by evolving from an emphasis on doctrines that separate to values that unite.

"The truth is one but the wise know it by many names," say the Vedas. Decades of interfaith work have produced fruit. It is now time to openly acknowledge that there is no loss, only gain, when the religions come to truly know and love one another.

Imagining the Future of the Interfaith and Interspiritual Movements
by Ruth Broyde Sharone

The ink is not yet dry on the page of interfaith evolution. As the Pew Research Foundation has documented, religious affiliation has declined substantially among adults, and notably among youth. Some 40 percent of those surveyed on college campuses did not identify with their parents' religion or any other religion, causing them to check the "none of the above" box, and earning them at first the ironic title of "nones" when in fact they might have been dubbed the "alls." When interviewed, they said they considered themselves spiritual seekers or spiritual independents. They made it clear their relationship to structured religious practice and one-and-only-one religious affiliation was no longer relevant. It just didn't turn them on. Their search for spiritual meaning, however, had increased, but they were no longer looking to their parents for answers to the most profound questions of their lives: Why am I here? What is my connection to the rest of the people on the planet and to the planet itself? How should I live my life?

This development of less religiosity and more spirituality has also been reflected in the interfaith movement itself but in a distinctive incarnation. What began more than a century ago as an exploration between Christians and Jews, or Christians and Muslims, next morphed into the Abrahamic encounters with all three monotheistic religions becoming full partners in dialogue. The first Parliament of the World's Religions, held at the World's Fair in Chicago in 1893, was also a significant watershed event, bringing together for the first time religious leaders from the East and the West. Since then, more and more communities have been included in our gatherings and deliberations . . . Unitarians, Buddhists, Hindus, Sikhs, Bahai's, Zoroastrians, and Indigenous representatives. Then came the next wave: Pagans, Wiccans, Scientologists, members of Global New Thought, and most recently the Atheists, Secular Humanists, etc. It seems everyone has been invited to the table at last.

Eboo Patel, founder and executive director of Interfaith Youth Core (IFYC) underscores this idea. "Religious diversity today . . . also has to include the various ways people affiliate vis-a-vis religion, meaning including secular humanist, agnostic, and spiritual seekers. It has to include . . . Sunni and Shia, Catholic and Evangelical, Theravada and Mahayana. And finally, it has to take into account intersecting identities, how religion intersects with other identities like race, class, sex, and gender. This is all to say that an interfaith leader's radar screen for religious diversity has to register far more than just Muslim, Christian, and Jewish."

Paul Chaffee, editor of *The Interfaith Observer*, which did an extensive overview of *The Coming Interspiritual Age*, wrote in the October 2014 issue:

"Today, an unparalleled racial, ethnic, religious, and cultural diversity, ignited by immigration policy reform in the 1960s and empowered by the globe-shrinking influence of high tech, is making 'dual identity' something new and vital. Myriad possibilities emerge. Rather than repeating the predictable patterns of new immigrants, young second and third-gens can draw from a variety of 'identities,' values, shared traditions, and interfaith relationships. . . They have come through a cultural furnace, learning how to live well in the midst of conflicting cultural norms, expectations, and habits, a skill-set the whole human family needs to learn if we're to last."

At the most recent AAR (American Academy of Religion) Conference in San Diego, one of the workshops was devoted to exploring and analyzing the new phenomenon of one person having dual loyalties such as Hinduism and Christianity, or Judaism and Buddhism. Those studying the issue appeared to be experiencing more difficulty than the practitioners themselves. How does an individual with dual religious identities simultaneously carry out the practices and rituals from both faiths, the religious scholars wanted to know.

As we interfaith activists have watched the interfaith community expand to contain all of the faiths and reflect our enormous diversity, we have simultaneously witnessed an internal, unstoppable movement toward greater spirituality as adherents move away from dogma and religious teachings to embrace a wider spirituality — a development which brings its own set of challenges. Many religiously identified interfaith activists view this current movement toward spirituality with great suspicion and trepidation, often referring to interspiritual seekers as "dabblers in woo-woo."

Similarly, people in the spiritual movement are often a bit too eager to bury religion, as did a friend of mine recently who was keynoting at an interspiritual conference in New York. "Religion is dead," was his opening statement. Perhaps the only interfaith representative in the audience, I objected publicly. "Your opening pronouncement is not an ideal ice-breaker to initiate a dialogue between the interfaith community and the interspiritual community," I remonstrated. "There are bridges that still need to be built between the two communities, and effective communication skills and language will be required to achieve that."

As I observe the trending currents in both the interfaith and interspiritual communities, and the intertwining relationship developing between the two especially in the ecological sphere, I am convinced that what will eventually emerge is something new we have not yet imagined. This could be something unique, something that will demonstrate our creativity and flexibility, something that will affirm our humanity and connection to the Earth and secure our commitment to be conscientious custodians of our planet. What that is may be reflected in these recent comments by H. H. the 14th Dalai Lama:

I believe there is an important distinction to be made between religion and spirituality. Religion I take to be concerned with belief in the claims to salvation of one faith tradition or another — an aspect of which is acceptance of some form of meta-physical or philosophical reality, including perhaps an idea of heaven or hell. Connected with this are religious teachings or dogma, ritual, prayers and so on. Spirituality I take to be concerned with those [qualities] of the human spirit — such as love and compassion, patience, tolerance, forgiveness, contentment, a sense of responsibility, a sense of harmony, which bring happiness to both self and others.

Additional Resources[viii:5]

Interspiritual: The Silence Behind the Word
by Roger Housden

What would Rumi or Hafiz say? What would John of the Cross, Meister Eckhart, Eckhart Tolle, Adya Shanti — what would they say? I will hazard a guess: that the *Interspiritual* points to the deep heart of silence; not any kind of silence, but the knowing silence which breathes its vivid awareness through all traditions, whatever name they go by. And I think they would also say that in any attempt to name it, the prosaic will need to give way to the poetic — poetic not as in a poem so much as in a lilt on the term of speech that lifts the sayer as she says the word into some felt apprehension of the reality behind it. The term Interspiritual is a clumsy duckling of a word, a placeholder for the term that is waiting to emerge. For now, it will have to do.

Over the last few decades, the reality it points to has been steadily divesting itself of its various guises and stepping fully embodied out into the light of day in the form of an increasing number of teachers and guides who represent not any particular religion necessarily, but the fragrance of a ripened human heart. Rather than an intellectual appreciation of other religions than one's own, or even a willing participation in their rituals and practices (though it may include that), Interspiritual to my mind points beyond belief, beyond any religion in particular, to the awakening of gnosis in the individual human being.

A ripened heart may or may not emerge through a dedication to religious practices. For Wordsworth, it grew in the presence of nature; for Eckhart Tolle, on a park bench. Currently, it seems to be evident in the form of more and more people who feel the inner life of spirit — undefined by any specific belief, dogma, or ritual — to be the pole star of their life, an internal magnetic pull that exerts an influence on what they say, what they do, and what they think. The effect of that pull is to draw us down into interior silence and stillness, equanimity, generosity of spirit, loving compassion for self, others, and the world. John of the Cross speaks of it as *"the fire that burned inside my chest."* Rumi speaks of it this way:

> *This longing you express*
> *Is the return message.*

There are rituals in every religion that have always served in part to ignite the fire in the chest and to draw us into communion with the ineffable core of our own being. Any form, however, becomes more rigid and literal with time, and it is not difficult after a few centuries or millennia for the forms to obscure the very ineffability they are pointing toward. It has always been difficult, too, for religious hierarchies to be able to consider the notion that what their rituals and practices really point to is not some Divine Being or heroic Jesus or Buddha out there so much as the divine being that each and every one of us already is. Of course, this is entirely understandable, since the hierarchical power structure would crumble if there weren't a division between those who knew and those who didn't; between those who could dispense wisdom and knowledge from some higher source to those who are not privy either to secret (esoteric) teachings or, more prosaically, are not hooked up to the power lines running from the head of religious state on down.

This is precisely what has begun to change so dramatically in the last few decades. People everywhere are becoming more and more inclined to take up Walt Whitman's affirmation that everyone should be their own priest. If all religions were banished, the religious sensibility would still exist. Life's beauty and mystery naturally inspire in us reverence and wonder, and we can intuit that nothing, but nothing, including ourselves and our own little life, is outside of or exempt from an inherently intelligent, perpetual unfolding in the present moment. We can recognize that despite our loneliness and feelings of separateness, all of us are intimately joined in one great unity of life, seen and unseen.

A sensibility like this makes us prone to wonder, to pondering questions rather than wanting comforting answers. It makes us prone to beauty, to experiences of being lifted beyond our sense of who we are into a larger, more inclusive life, which leads to love. It makes us prone to stillness and clarity, to joy, and to feeling deep compassion for the tribulations of others and the suffering inherent in living. All of these responses to life are inherent in any religious tradition, for they are all expressions of transcendence; and yet, they themselves are not dependent on religion. The experience of transcendence is intrinsic to being human.

In recognition of the spirit of the times we live in, Interspirituality must surely also include and affirm a secular spirituality, one that brings heaven down to earth in our everyday lives, that is practiced by individuals according to the promptings of their own ripening heart, drawing on the resources of any religion or none. There are as many pitfalls in this development — narcissism, self-absorption, the illusion without any authoritative oversight that one is in a more knowing condition than is actually so — as there are in religion itself. But an emergent spirituality requires us to be willing to take the risks along with its blessings. Ultimately, I believe that Interspirituality calls us to recognize the extraordinary mystery that we are living in this very moment, without wrapping it up in a neat bow of explanation. In a gesture of wonder and awe, it invites us to bow, not necessarily to any god or deity, but as W. S. Merwin writes in his poem *For The Anniversary of My Death*, "bowing not knowing to what."

Additional Resources[viii:6]

Second Axial Awakening
by Matthew Wright

Running through the history of our planet is a current of spiritual awakening. Beginning as a trickle, it flows through the cracks of history, touching at first individuals, now washing out, over and through interconnected circles, building in force, moving to gather up all things in its embrace.

The current flowed in the first great Axial Age, awakening us to a new depth. Abraham and Sarah left tribe and tribal gods to seek after the One. The Indian rishis retired to their caves in search of the Self. The Buddha left wife and child in the palace and set off on his quest for enlightenment. Ties with family, tribe, and Earth were broken and a new possibility emerged.

We climbed ladders of ascent and journeyed into subtle realms of Spirit. We touched the Transcendent. And often we imagined that we had discovered the purpose of our existence: escape from this world, a flight to the Beyond. We struggled to break the cycle of suffering and rebirth and to attain to the heavenly prize.

All the while the water continued to quietly flow, its force increased through the door that was opened. Not at all what we had imagined — an escape route — this channel instead allowed the qualities of Spirit to flow more fully into this world, guiding the evolution of our planet toward its fullness as an ever-deepening revelation of the Divine Heart.

This is the story I imagine as I ponder the subtle shift being felt around our planet today. For the longest swath of our history, we've imagined the spiritual journey as an individual quest for salvation or enlightenment, with the ultimate goal of escape, or liberation, from the world of matter. Whether we've seen the problem as samsara and suffering or fallenness and sin, something is wrong with this place — and we want out! Images of separation and exile have long dominated our spiritual consciousness.

But slowly over the past century, and now with increasing speed, a sense of oneness is emerging in the consciousness of our planetary body. We are realizing instead that we *belong.* Multiple strands of knowledge point us to this truth: from environmentalists, recognizing that we are part of a global ecosystem; to quantum physicists, uncovering the deep interconnection at the most subtle levels of matter; to evolutionary biologists, revealing life's unfolding as a vast, single process. Slowly we are beginning to discover that there is ultimately no separation within the field of existence — only one seamless dance. We belong deeply to this world, interwoven fully into its fabric.

This realization is forming the headwaters of a Second Axial Age, another great shift in consciousness equal in weight to that which gave rise (roughly between 800 and 200 BCE)[1] to the impulse that eventually manifested as our existing great religious structures. With that first great turn of the wheel, we opened to the beauty of the individual and the possibility of the Transcendent, and a new human journey began. But in the process we lost much of an earlier, collective sense of belonging rooted in tribe, and a deep, felt sense of connection to Earth.

In this next great turn in the spiral dance, we are picking up what was lost — no longer at the tribal, but at the global level. We are entering a period of deep integration, weaving together the primal, collective, and cosmic with the rational, individual, and transcendent — binding together Heaven and Earth. The Divine Heart is moving toward the fullness of its expression in form. With this new turn of the wheel, we release our sense of exile and settle in for the work at hand. Our Second Axial awareness begins from a new starting place: union. We have never been separate: not from one another, not from the Earth that holds us, not from the Infinite we long for.

Instead, we discover that our longing is itself the longing of the Divine Heart, struggling to come to birth in the world of form; it is the very current of awakening that drives the planet toward its fullness. We have misunderstood this longing as a defect — a symptom of our exile. It is instead the deepest sign of our belonging to the work of this world. It is the driveshaft of the entire evolutionary process as we move toward our awakening as a single planetary body.

We have not been left unprepared for this work. While the Second Axial impulse is only now gaining global traction, it has been subtly shaping the spiritual currents of our planet for the last two thousand years. We see it forcefully in the rise of the Bodhisattva vow within Mahayana Buddhism: a shift away from individual enlightenment and escape into Nirvana, toward a pledge to remain in the phenomenal world for the service of collective awakening.

We see it in the birth of Christianity, directly in the life of Jesus, who rejected a First Axial ascetic path in favor of one that fully embraced the world — he feasted, danced, and wept, all the while associating with those designated outcasts and sinners. He refused to recognize the expected divisions between sacred and profane. This full-on embrace of phenomenal existence was enshrined in Christianity's core doctrine of the Incarnation — that "the Word became flesh" in the world "God so loved" — but the Second Axial impulse of its founder was repeatedly roped back into the existing First Axial road maps.

Most clearly, perhaps, we see the Second Axial emergence in Islam and its mystical tradition, Sufism. The Islamic world took the rhythm of monastic prayer and offered it in the marketplace. Like Christianity, it broke out of the ethnic and tribal identity of its parent religion, Judaism (which itself never completely lost touch with its pre-Axial earthiness and embrace of the world). Islam's mystical path, based on the life of a prophet who was husband, lover, parent, warrior, and statesman, found it practically impossible to give way to the First Axial impulse toward asceticism and monasticism. Sufism pledged to keep the contemplative life fully integrated into the life of the world. It was in many ways the first wave of what many today are calling "the new monasticism."

Today we can claim these streams for what they are: the early in-breaking of Second Axial consciousness, a dramatic shift away from the dualistic separation of "Spirit" from "world." Channels for these waters are the ones we must dig and deepen. As this Second Axial Awakening takes hold on the global scale, we must begin the work of reimagining and realigning our First Axial religions. What will change when we see these great traditions as so many currents within a vast planetary movement of awakening and integration? How will we carry their wisdom forward in an age characterized by a primary consciousness of union, belonging, and interconnection?

I believe that our hope still lies in our religions, and that we abandon them at a great loss. They hold much of the wisdom we will need in this next great transformation. But the invitation now is to a dance, not a lecture. The traditions will no longer be only the teachers, but the students as well. As they teach us, we will teach them. The evolution, like all such dances, will be mutual. The wheel will turn once more, and the waters will flow powerful and strong, the Divine Heartbeat loud and full.

Endnotes and Additional Resources[viii:7]

A Thumbnail Sketch of the History and Future of Interspiritual Dialogue in a Fragmented Era

by Lama Surya Das

Venerable Thích Nhất Hạnh says that 80 percent of everything we think is wrong. I think he's being generous. My late great mom, Joyce Miller of Long Island, used to say: "Jeffrey, what other people think is none of your business." Sage advice! Once, when my parents grudgingly visited me in Japan in 1975, she said: "Jeffrey, I don't know about God and Buddha, but I certainly believe in all that is good and true."

Does humanity and the planetary environment as we know it have to die to be reborn? Is this our KarmAgeddon?

In our increasingly shrinking, interconnected world, we need to evolve from dependence to independence, and even further toward realizing genuine freedom and autonomy within interdependence. I believe that it's incumbent upon each of us to strive to do so and together become wise Bodhisattvas, collective leaders and altruistic awakeners rich in both smarts and heart. Indra's cosmic net and universal hologram presaged the Internet in many ways, leveling the playing field and empowering each and all of us as the center of the universal mandala, far beyond ordinary solipsism.

Today, we could well strive together to transform social media into spiritual media by skillful use of the bandwaves, galvanizing into action our committed grassroots networks to genuinely occupy this media-spirit, over which the one percent will not easily relinquish control.

Mahatma Gandhi said that there are seven blunders causing the violence that plagues the world: wealth without work; pleasure without conscience; knowledge without character; commerce without morality; science without humanity; worship without sacrifice; and politics without principles.

The future starts now. History is composed of an infinite series of last moments. What is the future of anything? That is partly what we ourselves manage to cocreate. Blessed are the flexible, for they shall not be bent out of shape. The word religion stems etymologically from the Latin "religio," to unite or bring together. Unfortunately, religion today too often seems part of the problem rather than contributing to helpful solutions. Extreme views and anachronistic forms of intolerant and dogmatic religiosity seem bent toward bringing humanity to the very brink of self-destruction. As I have just said, blessed are the flexible, for they shall not get bent out of shape.

Interfaith dialogue has given way to "interspiritual" dialogue (ISD), at least on these shores, ever since Brother Wayne Teasdale raised its standard and rallied hearts and minds, bodies and souls to that prophetic vision that was to become our happy cause. Following in the large footsteps of Father Bede Griffiths, an Indian *sadhu* and Christian saint, decades back he sparked a quiet renaissance in the evolution of religion and spirituality in our troubled time. This ISD movement and coalition challenges us all to develop a profound sense of universal responsibility; joyfully further common efforts to solve common problems; and link heads and hands, hearts and minds, and "walk our talk" through collective soul-power. It's an excellent antidote to the stress and malaise, cynicism, and overwhelming feelings of powerlessness, hopelessness even, that enervate so many today in the face of global socioeconomic problems, environmental degradation, the gelding of institutional religion, and our political oligarchy.

I believe this essentialized global spirituality is the new frontier — inner space, deep and subtle, beyond the polarities of outer / inner, above / below, masculine / feminine, or the fractious "-isms" and schisms of world religions. If and when we plumb this evergreen mystery of our miraculous existence and true nature, we are always amazed at the marvels of spiritual rebirth and transformation.

ISD is really nothing new. Ancient and timeless spiritual traditions have coexisted and communed together for millennia, even before the Axial Age, 2,500 years ago, when most of the major world religions were founded.

Good spiritual friends are the whole of the holy life.
Find refuge in the Sangha, in kindred spirits, and in
community.
—The Buddha

And whoever saves a life, it is considered as if he saved
an entire world.
——The Talmud

In this remote neck of the woods, on the Western frontier of the
nascent American colonies — Concord, Massachusetts — Ralph
Waldo Emerson epiphanically perceived his spiritual mind as "God's
transparent eyeball." Along with Henry David Thoreau, Margaret
Fuller, and utopian Bronson Alcott, he helped introduce "Hindoos"
and Buddhism (the Lotus Sutra) into the American melting-pot. Pierre
Teilhard de Chardin, Alan Watts, Huston Smith, Joseph Campbell,
Baba Ram Dass, Brother David Steindl-Rast, Allen Ginsberg, Rabbi
Zalman Schacter, Father Thomas Keating, the Dalai Lama, and even
more recently some notable Jewish-Buddhist-Hindu hybrids took the
high road and traveled this same interspiritual peace-path.

Native American shamans and indigenous wisdom traditions
abounded on these shores, before John Muir took trees and waters
from the Catskills to California for his boon companions. Jane
Goodall says: "Out in nature you can become a whole human being
with heart and brain and spirit all connected and whole." She would
know. Like the harmonious, unimpeded intercourse among the earth,
water, fire, air, and space elements, ISD and the creative synergy of
spiritual cross-fertilization long predate the advent of humanity on
this warm planet. It's anyone's guess as to whether the current man-

made agitation displayed by the forces of nature will settle down and rebalance, or whether they're already past the tipping point as we stagger along enjoying the dreams of our somnolence.

Timeless wisdom traditions are another natural resource that we overlook or ignore at our peril. This timely treasure has hardly been recognized as endangered, though we'd do well to research, develop, mine, and explore and even exploit our own innate, natural resources, for a change — hopefully to help tip back the imbalance in favor of sanity, sustainability, and a more equitable and peaceable future.

Our world is increasingly interconnected, interdependent. Though people generally think of Buddhism as an introspective and meditating religion, His Holiness the Dalai Lama himself often says — humbly yet with genuine authority — that we need each other to become enlightened.

> *For where two or three come together in my name,*
> *there am I with them.*
> —Jesus

The Greek root word for communion, *koinonia,* may just as easily be rendered as "transformation," "communication," "joint participation" or "companionship" — suggesting joined spirituality and collective awakening. My old friend Baba Ram Dass recently reminded me of our beloved late guru, Neem Karoli Baba (Maharajji), quoting the monkey-god Hanuman who personifies our own animal nature in selfless service and devotion to the divine: "When I forget who I am, Lord, I serve you. When I remember who I am, I *am* you." We may feel from It, but it is never far from us.

I pray:

> *Lord of peace and bliss,*

Show me your face, hold my hand —
Let me be-Hold thee.

Meanwhile, some of us are fiddling while Rome heats up and burns. The bad news is that 80 percent of Kansans believe in Creationism rather than Darwinian evolution. The rich continue to get richer and the poor poorer in this world, and quantity not qualities continues to rule. Although the good news includes that Mindfulness stock has been rising in the West of late, and the field is well-trodden — especially by Insight meditation practitioners — one wouldn't want to reduce it to mere "mental floss" for daily hygiene, like yoga practiced merely for health and looks, or simply the Religion of Sitting. Personally, I'm far more interested in being a Buddha than a mere Buddhist, or becoming solid and still as a stone Buddha statue in the garden.

We must become twenty-first-century Buddhists:
compassionate and actively engaged, nonsectarian;
studying modern science and democracy; appreciative
of the diversity of peoples and faiths.

I believe deeply that we must find, all of us together,
a new spirituality. This new concept ought to be
elaborated alongside the religions like secular ethics
in a way that all people of good will would adhere to it.
—Tenzin Gyatso, The Dalai Lama of Tibet

Prayer is like talking to God, meditation is like
listening.
—Father Thomas Merton

Let me make a couple of grand and even seemingly outrageous assertions. First, we're all Buddhas, by nature; we only have to recognize and awaken to that fact — realizing who and what we are and how we fit into the bigger picture, and how it abides in each and all of us, transcendent yet immanent. Second, nowness-awareness is the ultimate therapy. In the total and ultimate now, present and future — karma (conditioning and reactivity), memory, self-story — are not binding, and the inherent freedom and fullness of being is available. "Being there while getting there, every single step of the way" is one of my favorite personal expressions of what I'll call nondual wisdom or transcendental awareness — beyond subject, object, and interaction. You can't obtain it but can *be* it, at home and one with yourself in your own life.

Additional Resources[viii:8]

The Birth of InterSpiritual Meditation
by Ed Bastian

Back in 1997, I was invited to be a part of Father Thomas Keating's groundbreaking Snowmass Conference. In the early 1980s, Father Thomas, one of the founders of the Centering Prayer movement and a former Cistercian abbot, began inviting spiritual leaders from many different religious traditions to a private retreat at St. Benedict's Monastery in Snowmass, Colorado (described in the book *The Common Heart: An Experience of Interreligious Dialogue,* 2006). Over the course of four days, representatives of different religious traditions would sit together in meditation and then dialogue about their respective spiritual practices and experiences, often finding common ground, and more often, forming intimate and lasting friendships. That year, Father Thomas invited me to join them, to "be the Buddhist," as one of the founding members couldn't make it. I didn't feel particularly qualified, but after a few deep discussions with him about my growing interest in interfaith work, he convinced me that it would be useful for me to attend and see how it worked in the Snowmass Conference.

I felt incredibly honored. I had heard so much about the Snowmass Conference over the years. It had a reputation for doing the kind of deep contemplative work that was not to be found in other interfaith groups, and I was not to be disappointed. Both the meditation and the dialogue were profound experiences for me. Although I had been interested in interfaith work for a while, I really had no idea that there existed such extraordinary commonalities between the great contemplative traditions, especially among their mature practitioners. It also became clear — much to my surprise — that all of the religions represented had deep and profound practices of meditation, all aimed at developing inner peace, wisdom, and compassion.

On the morning of the second day of the retreat, we convened for a meditation before breakfast, then another meditation before beginning our morning conversation. It was during that second meditation session and the ensuing dialogue that something quite spectacular happened within me, a profound awakening that changed the course of my life. Through these meditation sessions — even though it was only the second day — I was gradually becoming aware of a kind of "InterSpiritual Consciousness" emerging in shared time, space, and silence. And by experiencing and dialoguing about one another's distinctive practices, I found that each of us was helped to discover new depths in our own individual spiritual practices. Moreover, I began to see that the religions of the world were not isolated institutions, but interdependent phenomena within a vast spiritual eco-system. This revelation led me to envision the Spiritual Paths Foundation and the

Spiritual Paths Institute as vehicles of InterSpiritual education and understanding.

It was not that I suddenly realized that all religions are the same; they're not, but there is something in the human spiritual consciousness that is shared by people of all traditions. This realization hit me so powerfully that I began to think: If I could just bring together great teachers — following the example of the Snowmass Conference — to dialogue and meditate together before a public program, the shared feeling would be palpable, and would surely have a profound impact on the program and all those in attendance. This would then become the true basis of an InterSpiritual understanding and peace — not just the words, the tolerance, and the commonalities, but a common experience of sharing at depth. Once people share at this level, they can no longer treat each other inhumanely on the basis of differences in religion. This was really a breakthrough for me and catalyzed me to move forward in creating the Spiritual Paths Foundation and its first InterSpiritual seminars.

Not long after, I sold my business and began devoting all my time, energy, and resources to the founding of this new organization. This gave me the space to reexamine a process of spiritual education and practice I had begun developing ten years earlier (while I was still working at the Smithsonian). In this, I proposed that all of us have predominate spiritual learning styles and fundamental spiritual questions, and that our unique spiritual paths are conditioned by these styles and questions. I hoped that the Spiritual Paths Foundation might develop programs and learning materials to help each person discern and piece together their own unique path.

In 2000, I began to seek the advice and wisdom of spiritual elders like Father Thomas, Geshe Sopa, Rabbi Zalman Schachter-Shalomi, and numerous other colleagues and friends. I also set about building a unique internet-based resource to facilitate the seeker's inquiry, and created the first offerings of the Spiritual Paths Institute, a series of InterSpiritual seminars for the public. These were to be modeled on the kind of dialogue I had witnessed as a member of Father Thomas' Snowmass Conference.

To each seminar, I invited "exemplars" from the world's great spiritual traditions to spend several days together. In the course of these days, we meditated together, shared meals, formed friendships, and began a private dialogue that culminated in a public seminar. At the seminar, each teacher gave their own perspective on the particular spiritual theme (i.e., spiritual style or question) and later participated in a focused InterSpiritual dialogue before an audience. After the audience had heard all the speakers, they were given the opportunity to ask their specific questions of the speaker who had touched them most in a smaller group setting. In this way, we could explore themes and questions from many different spiritual perspectives and in a very personal way.

To date, over fifty profound spiritual teachers representing the world's major contemplative traditions have meditated and taught together before thousands of students in Spiritual Paths programs and seminars. But even as the topics of our discussions changed from seminar to seminar, my primary interest in meditation remained. At every opportunity, I queried these teachers about the unique meditative practices of their traditions, taking notes and comparing their processes and experiences with those of the Buddhist tradition. Immediately, I was struck by remarkable similarities and began to discern a common structure or process, one that I already knew from Buddhism. Only now, I could see that it was not Buddhist at all, but a kind of universal structure of spiritual development, one that might be used to allow people of different religious commitments to share the same meditative process in a group setting.

This, I felt, was a real breakthrough. For during the Snowmass Conference, when I first became aware of the possibility of an InterSpiritual Consciousness, it was not immediately clear how this profound experience could be transmitted to others. After all, that was a small retreat for spiritual professionals, deeply grounded in their individual religious and contemplative traditions, often longtime meditators who could easily sit down in silence together and attune to the shared consciousness created by the group. The half hour or hour that we spent in meditation together was not formal; we simply sat in silence and meditated or prayed according to the ways in which we had been taught in our traditions. With such an experienced group, it was easy to enter into the silence with the expectation of reaching similar depths, or to share a practice, knowing that the structure would be noted by each person according to its function within their own tradition.

But how was this to be done with a group that might be as diverse in experience and ability as they were in cultural backgrounds and religious commitments? The seven-part process that evolved from my dialogue with the Spiritual Paths teachers and my own meditative experiments provided the answer. Because it is a process with discernable steps and functions common to all contemplative traditions, it can be taught to a diverse group of people without interfering with individual beliefs. As everyone follows the same steps, practitioners with varying levels of experience can at least be assured that they are sharing the same ride.

Moreover, even the individual without a clearly defined spiritual path can participate with little disadvantage. For the process only asks one to appeal within for the accoutrements most suitable to their own journey. Thus, I had stumbled upon a direct and practical means of creating true InterSpiritual understanding, a means of sharing spiritual experience that was not dependent upon (or in conflict with) religious dogmas or specific techniques evolved within different religious traditions. It was something new, and yet, something that had been there all along — an InterSpiritual Meditation process.

Additional Resources[viii:9]

The New Monasticism
by Rory McEntee and Adam Bucko

"The monk is a lay person...An order of monastics is essentially a lay order. Some monks may live in monasteries, but increasingly the majority will live in their own homes or form small communities — a monastic order in the world."[1] These words were spoken by the Catholic monk Bede Griffiths toward the end of his life. He went on to express a new vision for monastics, one in which communities and individuals live spiritual lives independent of religious organizations or institutions, independent of celibacy and overarching rules and dogmas — free to follow their own conscience and guidance of the Holy Spirit in living a sacred life, yet united in the common cause of building a sacred world. We envision these "new monastic" lives as being fully engaged in contemporary life, involved in relationships, exploring new ways of walking the spiritual path, and committed to sacred activism. Father Bede goes on to describe these "monastic orders in the world":

Some communities may remain very loose, some may become very close. Each one has to evolve as the Spirit moves it. ... [W]e must keep that freedom of the Spirit by learning from one another, coming together day by day and discerning ... all in a growth process. ... It is so easy to get into rules and organization and so to narrow the freedom of the Spirit. ... It is by learning really to trust the Spirit, in our prayers and meditation, and to share this trust with one another that a new language will gradually form. ... Social action should flow from our contemplation. It should not be a sideline or something inherently different, but should be integrated in our prayer and meditation ... unless meditation is fed by concern with people's problems and the world's problems it loses its depth. There is no rivalry between contemplation and action.[2]

Father Bede compares these communities to those of the Sufis, practitioners of the mystical branch of Islam, who are often married, have families, and are deeply engaged in the world, organized in communities which help them to live from the depth of their commitment to contemplative life.

Our book *The New Monasticism: An Interspiritual Manifesto for Contemplative Living* (Orbis Books, April 2015) is a rallying call for these new types of spiritual life and community, lives that are dedicated to building a sacred world through commitment to one's spiritual maturity, the growth of community life, and to living out these values while fully engaged in the world. "In the world" can be many different things, but for us at its heart lies a passionate embrace for the transformation of our societal, political, and religious structures.

Our book helps to build a foundation for this movement, offering the beginnings of a theological, philosophical and contemplative understanding to its underpinnings, while at the same time providing concrete methodologies and injunctions for its praxis.

It also stands as an authentic expression of our own experience of the Path, articulating a vision which cuts across humanity's wisdom and religious traditions, bringing us into the midst of something new, a revelatory impulse of the Spirit that as of yet has no home. While embedded within our wisdom and religious traditions, it is beholden to none, encompassing modern scientific and psychological truths, sociological and cultural insights, political and economic realities.

By monastic, we denote a level of commitment to one's spiritual life. What does it mean to be a monastic after all? It is not necessarily one's particular beliefs that make one a monastic, nor is it one's lifestyle. It is a total life commitment to the development and maturation of one's spiritual life. This is a journey which takes us into the fullness of our humanity, allowing divinity to flower within us in increasing degrees of love, compassion, joy, sorrow, and wisdom. The monastic is the one who devotes his or her life to this ideal, and allows all life decisions to flow out of this commitment. The root of the word "monk" is monachos, which means "to set oneself apart." For us, this is not so much a physical separation as a setting oneself apart from our cultural conditioning — from an unquestioning, and un-questing, view of life, one that drives us to adulate material success, seduces us into participating in the devastation of our planet, hardens our hearts to the plight of the poor and oppressed, and divorces us from our innate capacity for spiritual growth and maturity.

By New, we refer to the phenomenon of this spiritual vocation being lived out "in the world." This means that one's spiritual journey

is inextricably linked to the day-to-day reality of most people's lives —
and in an evolutionary sense, to moving our human family into greater
depth and maturity. We have found that many people today are feeling
the same calling of the monks of old, yet do not find themselves drawn
to a monastery, or to celibacy, or to disengagement and liberation from
the world. They instead feel a radical urge to be embedded in the world,
with the hardship of financial realities, the ups and downs of political
unrest, the blessings and difficulties of relationships — all in the midst
of a contemporary society that does not support such a calling. It adds
a level of complexity to the "monastic vocation," perhaps many levels.
Yet those of us who feel this calling could never do otherwise, for deep
in our souls we know that our journey to wholeness lies in bringing
forth the radical profundity and divine, transformative energy of our
paths firmly into the world.

Raimon Panikkar, one of the greatest inter-mystical theologians
of the 20th century, has called this a movement from simplicity
through renunciation to simplicity through integration.[3] Rather than
renouncing the world, the new monastic wishes to transform it. The
world is no longer something that can be used merely as a stepping
stone to one's own enlightenment, but rather the transformation of the
world itself is given an equal ontological status to one's own. In other
words, this new way sees one's spiritual path inextricably linked with
the transformation of our global community into a connected, mature,
and harmonious whole.

Perhaps even more radically, the new monastic may or may not be
drawn permanently into a particular religious tradition. While certainly
open to embracing a single religious tradition, this new way also
allows for the emergence of untrodden paths, where the boundaries
among the traditions become porous, yet not without meaning. Our

traditions are seen as a common inheritance for humanity, each with its own integrity, yet also belonging to a universal heritage of human wisdom. They offer us guidance and skill sets with which we may look into our own interiors, and revelations as to what those interiors hold. At their best, they are a storehouse of wisdom for the human family, cartographers of the individual and collective souls of humanity. Within the fulcrum of tensions and synergies born through their mutual interaction, new movements and "complexified forms of religious consciousness" are emerging.[4]

Finally, a note on the word Interspiritual; Interspirituality plants us firmly outside of a fundamentalist adherence to our own particular religious tradition or spiritual path, demanding that we take seriously the revelations, realizations, and contemplative gifts of all authentic wisdom and religious traditions, as well as revelations from science, ecology, art, culture, and sociology. It recognizes the potential for human spiritual growth and maturity, and allows for the diverse ways that human beings, at their best, have cultivated tools to accelerate that growth process. It acknowledges unique transmissions of wisdom and divine attributes among the traditions, and opens up the possibility for us to make use of these collective streams in new and unforeseen ways. It puts a premium on a reciprocal sharing of these gifts in ways that change those who *participate in the* process. As such, it can lead to renewals and transformations of the religious traditions themselves.

Interspirituality, for us, primarily denotes an emergent attitude of presence-based exploration among and between wisdom traditions and individual spiritual paths, engaged with social theory and cultural critiques, scientific insights and developmental psychology, political and economic discourse — calling us to "dialogical dialogue" with one another and potentially leading to new insights, new types of communities, and "communicative action." This understanding of Interspirituality, as a reciprocal sharing in which each person's insights help to affirm, deepen, and direct the other's journey — is *a* framework which can speak to a new generation of spiritually hungry youth, while allowing for intergenerational bridges to be built between elders, wisdom traditions, secular traditions, and the younger generation. It allows for a diversity of spiritual paths and religious understandings and for intimate communities to be built within, and embodied by, that diversity. Rather than separating ourselves according to our religious beliefs, traditions or particular spiritual practices, we can build communities that center around this reciprocal sharing of gifts and support for one another's vocations in the world — and thereby begin to build the Kingdom of Heaven "one friendship at a time."

Endnotes and Additional Resources[viii:10]

Interspirituality—A Vision of Wholeness
by Beverly J. Lanzetta

Interspirituality is a vision of wholeness on the other side of all that is partial and fragmented, and a promise of a unified creation exalted as the highest form of communion in the world's sacred texts. It rests on a contemplative foundation, on the wayless way where name and attachment are given away in order to seek the holy and to be holy. As it exhausts all theories and views, Interspirituality does not bring together diverse traditions and spiritual practices to forge a common religion. Rather, it is a quality of heart that honors the multiple ways in which mystery presents itself, without demanding a final truth or an ultimate name.

A global, interspiritual contemplative path is not defined as over, against, or a revision of any other religious or spiritual heritage. It is not initiated to justify new insight against current theology, test its mettle against virtues and commandments, or measure its truth with reference to scriptures of ancient and modern civilizations. While verification and comparison have a vital role, they do not come first. The cry of passion never tilts in the direction of the past; the awe that overwhelms us suffers no comparison with neighboring religions or truths; and the impossible moment, when we are flooded with a reality beyond our understanding, does not succumb to testing or repetition. Now, more than ever, we need to trust those times.

As a practice of spiritual nonviolence, this journey of openness to other religions or to a spiritual life without religion arises from a wounding felt deep within the self that calls into question and suffers over the exclusion, indifference, superiority, injustice, and oppression that inhabits religions and turns the heart against itself. It is God's dark night in us, an impasse between spiritual paradigms that is leading us to a new and deeper understanding of the sacred and of our part in the transformation of the world.

Together we are birthing an interspiritual path that requires a commitment perhaps unprecedented in history. While religions speak of a transcendent god beyond us, a savior who rescues us, or an absolute toward which we must strive, the mystical path of the heart begins from the process of birth, recognizing that within our beings, spirit is aflame, and new revelation is gestating. We may not yet be able to speak, we may be lost or afraid, but this new revelation is the sacred sound of our souls.

For this, we are forging an interspiritual language that respects and honors the universal, sacred message found in the wisdom of the cosmos, the life forms of the earth, and humanity's shared religious inheritance. It is a pure gift, this discovery of a new spiritual path within the depth of consciousness. Learning to be silent before awe, we practice a faith that is not over, against, or privileged toward any named faith. Rather, we are champions of faith itself, of the mysterious challenge we humans face to trust in the unseen in order to make visible the Spirit on earth and to follow the unnamed, who calls us by many names. We come together as pilgrims, as apostles, to share our journey toward a global spiritual perspective, and to open our hearts in solidarity with each other and with the steady force of life itself that draws us toward a common destiny.

We are not here for ourselves alone. It is incumbent upon us to realize how our actions or inactions profoundly affect our soul health, relationship with all beings, and the diverse and complex biosphere of the earth. We need a voice and a vision from which to awaken the heart of the world and to rescue ourselves from endangering the spirit of life. Injustice and war strike more deeply into the sacred web of creation, generating a hopelessness and despair that wound all our souls. The integrity of our planet and the fate of ecosystems are dependent on an excavation of our hearts and minds — and our souls and spirits — to discover a more generous benevolence and a sturdier vow of humility.

At the core of our collective journey is a vow. If we place Divine Mystery at the center of our hearts, then we truly are living a religious consciousness, whether or not we belong to a named religion. If we place the earthly realm and its entire human and more-than-human inhabitants on an altar of devotion and consecrate our lives each day to their benefit, we are living a spiritual path — a personal, organic spiritual path. When our daily life becomes a prayer, then we are a prayer of love and healing for the world.

Additional Resources[viii:11]

Fr. Bede's Great Gift to Me
The Vision of Sacred Activism
by Andrew Harvey

The seeds of the vision of sacred activism were planted and deeply took root in my soul when I met my great teacher, Fr. Bede Griffiths. One of the greatest mysteries of the path is that the Divine will guide you to meet, at the time when you are ready and receptive, the beings who can lead you forward. I came to meet Fr. Bede through an invitation from a friend who wanted to make a documentary about the life of this interspiritual visionary and mystic, and asked me to be the interviewer for the film.

For ten days, I had the amazing, illuminating, and transformative experience of being with this extraordinary, radiant, funny, wise, humble man at his ashram in Southern India, only fifty miles from where I was born. At the time, Fr. Bede was eighty-five years old, and I was forty-one. In his presence, I felt I had met a true spiritual father, who set me on the path of what I consider my true life's work: the vision of sacred activism, doing everything I possibly can, through passion and grace, to help to birth a new, Divine Humanity.

On the last day of filming, I went in to see him before the film crew arrived, and he looked up at me and said, "You know, Andrew, we are in the hour of God." I asked him what he meant by "the hour of God," and he responded, "We're in the hour of God because we are coming quite soon to the moment in which we will have to decide between adoration and suicide."

He went on, "There are three possibilities before the human race. The first one is that we'll wake up, fall on our knees, beg for grace, and God will transfigure us and make us instruments of a great revolution of peace in action. That is highly unlikely at the moment. Human beings change slowly, and even in desperate circumstances cling to their pride and ignorance. I certainly know that I have."

"The second possibility," he continued, "is that we'll continue in our mad addiction to greed, power, and domination, and engineer a crisis that will destroy us and take a great deal of nature with us. That's what seems likely many days as I sit in this hut meditating on what I've known and experienced during my life." He paused to let that sink in.

Then he smiled — he gave this tremendous, radiant smile — and said, "But that's not what is going to happen, I think. You see, Andrew, the God that I have come to know is a God of infinite love, infinite mercy, and infinite resourcefulness. I have been saved again and again from the worst in myself. Even my worst mistakes and most destructive and stupid thoughts and actions have turned out to create, through some mysterious paradox, doors into deeper compassion for all beings and into action born from this compassion."

He continued, "What I believe is going to happen is what happened to me. Three years ago, I was sitting on my balcony meditating, and suddenly, I was struck by a tremendous force that seemed to be coming from my left and pulled me out of my chair. It was terrifying. I had had a stroke. I thought I was going to die, and I prepared myself for death saying all the traditional prayers. I felt bewildered and disturbed, as if my whole being had been plunged into chaos. Suddenly, the inspiration came to me to surrender to the Mother; I heard an inner voice say quite clearly, 'Surrender to the Mother.' And somehow, without really knowing how, I did."

"Instead of dying, I had an experience of being invaded and overwhelmed by waves and waves of love, a power and passion of love that I had never experienced before. I found myself crying out, 'I am being overwhelmed by love! I am being overwhelmed by love!' And I knew that the love that I was being overwhelmed and possessed by was the love of the Mother — the Mother of All, the Mother of the Universe, the great embodied Godhead glowing in and through everything. Through it, my being was being opened to the radiance of the Mother alive in every tree, plant, rock, and sentient being, and in this very body."

"The consciousness I am being brought into since this experience is unlike anything I experienced up until the time of my stroke. It is a non-dual embodied consciousness in which I experience a profound and mysterious unity with everything and everyone. Distinctions are not lost in this awareness; in fact, everyone and everything becomes more individual, sacred, precious, and holy because I am seeing that every sentient being and every pebble and fern is a unique creation of the Divine Light, infinitely loved and cherished, and entirely inhabited by the Light. I have come to believe that what is beginning to happen in me is destined to happen on a growing scale in humanity."

"And this, Andrew, is the third possibility before us, the one I believe will happen. I believe that the world will be taken into the depths of a global dark night crisis, which at many times as it gets more and more intense will feel like the end — the end of every possibility. But it will not be the end ... because, just as in the inner path of the mystic, the dark night is actually — if you can stand it and live through it with grace and joy and faith and the capacity to surrender both to the suffering it brings and the resurrecting power of the Divine — the dark night is the birth canal of an unimaginable transformation into embodied divine consciousness."

"So I believe that the world is in a vast evolutionary crisis which will go through a terrifying dark night. But that will not be the end, it will be the beginning of something absolutely extraordinary, and amazing, and unimaginable, through the extravagant grace of the One. God is everywhere working a massive Resurrection, and it is the destiny of our time to be the birthing-ground of this Resurrection."

I took that in, and then he said words which he wrote with a diamond pencil on my soul forever. He said, "You know, Andrew," — and he was gleaming, because he was very mischievous; he was a very holy, grand being but at eighty-five he was also a divine child — "I think that I'm at last understanding the Second Coming. You know what's going to happen, I think. It's certainly not going to be the return of Christ as a person. Jesus in time and history opened this path for us, irradiating the entire universe by the resurrection light, and I think we can say that that job was well done. But what's going to happen, I believe, because of the agony and difficulty and wildness and horror of the dark night, many of us are going to be sent on a journey in which we discover in ourselves an unimaginable passion and energy of hope and joy and hunger to recreate the world in justice, and kinship, and celebration, and peace."

"The birthing of a Divine Humanity on a large scale, this rising of the golden yeast of love consciousness at its most impassioned and beautiful and focused and holy and clear in millions of people — that will be the Second Coming, the Great Healing that leads to the Birth. This is a miracle greater than any 'outer' rescuing by God could ever be. We are going to be rescued from 'within' though a massive alchemical process in which the whole of history will take part as a midwife of the new."

"What is going to be very difficult for human beings to accept and manage is that this Great Healing will have to manifest first as an immense crisis or series of crises that will plunge all previous human agendas into chaos. For the Birth to take place, there is a necessary death of all previous visions and ways of acting, a deconstruction of the false self and a dying to the tyranny of the ego. This is not punishment but the fiercest and ultimately most merciful grace, which is known in all mystical traditions."

"Knowing this mystery and that it ends not in annihilation but in the birth of the Divine in matter, in the body, is, I believe, the greatest imaginable source of hope."

We ended our conversation as we heard the film crew shuffling and coughing outside the door. They had been waiting patiently for us to finish, to begin the final day of filming for the documentary.

A week later, back in Paris where I was living at the time, I learned that Fr. Bede had suffered two more strokes and was dying. I felt a great need to see him one last time, and within a few days was by his bedside. He was in a terrible state. One side of his body was paralyzed, and the intellectually brilliant part of his mind had been largely shattered. Yet despite great pain, he was also, for long moments, in a state of grace, overflowing with love for all those around him. He would hold the hands of his disciples and friends and weep with joy, gazing into their eyes with pure and luminous wonder and childlike trust.

On the last night I was with him, I sat alone by his bedside in the early hours of the morning, watching him toss and turn in half-sleep. At around two o'clock, he awoke, reached for my hand, and caressed it. Then quite suddenly, as if commanded by someone I could not see or hear, he sat straight up in his bed and said loudly, over and over again: "Serve the growing Christ! Serve the growing Christ! Serve the growing Christ!"

I experienced these four simple words, which crystallized for me everything he had said in our conversation in his hut, as a direct transmission by Divine Love itself. I knew, through the grace I felt pouring down on us both in that moment, that "serve the growing Christ" meant that our terrible and wonderful time was the destined birthing ground of the Divine Human (the "growing Christ"). And I realized that anyone who was brought by grace to the realization of this truth was called upon to do three related things: to serve the growing Christ in themselves through meditation, prayer, and surrender to the Divine; to serve all other beings as growing Christs; and to serve the growing Christ in history through sacred action.

This profound understanding of our time — the vision of the birth of a Divine Humanity emerging from the Dark Night we are experiencing individually and collectively — and his own humble yet powerful embodiment of this amazing possibility for all of us were Fr. Bede's great gifts to me. My profound gratitude and love for him inspired me to dedicate the remainder of my life to serve this vision through teaching and inviting others to the path of sacred activism.

We are now among those millions of beings who are being crucified and resurrected by the tremendous ordeal the whole of creation is going through. So the worst of times is potentially the best of times, the dark night is a savage grace and a birth canal, and our job, it seems, is to go through whatever we need to go through to be able to find in ourselves the courage, the hope, the joy, the power we never imagined ourselves capable of, together, inspiring and encouraging each other.

Interfaith to Interspirituality
A Natural Progression

by Deborah Steen Ross and Roger Ross

The word Interfaith has been around for many years. It became popular in the 1970s, thanks to Rabbi Joseph H. Gelberman (of blessed memory), who with clergy of many faiths, created first Interfaith salons and then the first Interfaith Seminary to help people understand and respect each other's faiths.

And for years that was enough.

In the past few years, however, the energies of our planet have changed and sped up. A larger more expanded understanding of the Heart of all religions, and an understanding that we are not separate from one another — no matter what faith we are — is needed. Now we move forward into a new paradigm.

Kurt Johnson, in his book *The Coming Interspiritual Age,* writes about Interspirituality as:

> *Spirituality so based on the heart and unconditional love that it would be impossible to feel separate from anything.*

We believe that Interspirituality means more than that. It is the confluence of hands, hearts, and minds coming together to create something new — something that is connected with all of Life on an energetic and mystical level that transcends the everyday, which recognizes and accesses the Divine in every religion, every person and with the Earth itself.

The world's mythologies all ask the same questions: "Who are we? Where do we come from? Where are we going? What are the rules we need to follow to get us there?" To help ourselves change this paradigm, we must also ask, "What is the higher energy that is the SAME, that is the freeing factor at the heart of all these questions and religions?" Br. Wayne Teasdale called it "the Universal Law of Mysticism." We call it "Divine Awareness," for each other and the Earth.

If we look to the Earth and the Earth-based First Beliefs, they come from a place of observation of the everyday, every moment, changes around the person and his/her environment. It does not come from rules and regulations of what to see, how to see, what one must do to be in favor with a supreme being of a particular religion. It is the mindfulness of Love in our observations every moment — around us, with us, into us, with every breath, in every aspect of our walk in the world. This is true worship, true spirituality.

It is what Barbara Marx Hubbard, well known Futurist and Lecturer, touches on in her book, *Emergence: The Shift from Ego to Essence,* when she talks about holding that spark of Oneness within us, within our Divine Essence and learning and becoming a Universal Human. How do we stay mindful at every moment of our higher energy place in the situations we find ourselves every day? How can we keep our energies wrapped in Divine Love and coming from a place of Higher Consciousness, and still operate in a 3D reality, or even in a crisis situation?

At New Vision Interspiritual Seminary in Elmsford, New York, we are teaching these concepts to our ministerial students. We teach the deeper understanding of world religions, Nature-based and traditional, and how to be an interspiritual Minister and function in this day and age, where every day is an exercise in mindfulness and knowing how to stay in our Divine Essence.

We have added a Healing Module to our Program as well, that enables students to learn how to send Divine / Universal Energy to situations, people, and the Earth at every moment and for all situations — for the highest good of all concerned.

We have created what we call the Seven Root Planetary Challenges that are being named and worked with through prayer and energy sendings daily. These seven points represent Fragmented Energy Challenges that support duality and divisiveness. Divine, Universal Energy is being sent to these, at noon in each time zone. We are sending to Transformation, from Fragmentation to Wholeness, for the highest good of all.

1. PATRIARCHY vs. MATRIARCHY – BALANCE
2. MY VERSION OF GOD IS BETTER THAN YOUR VERSION OF GOD / THE ONLY VERSION ALLOWED
3. THE ONE WITH THE MOST MONEY / RESOURSES DIRECTS ALL THE POWER (Illuminati, gold, diamonds, oil, water, 1 percent of elite controls)
4. SOCIAL ORDER – SUPERIORITY OVER OTHERS (color, caste, race, women, animals, planet)
5. DEMISE OF ECO-SYSTEMS – dolphins / whales, seals, rainforests and creatures in them, Nature in general from oil spills and pollution, clear cutting, "Global Warming"
6. FEAR MONGERING – fear controls everything, blaming one race or religion, scapegoating
7. NATURAL DISASTERS – changes in the Earth's topography, floods, earthquakes, droughts, tornados, hurricanes/cyclones, fires

On page 286 of *The Coming Interspiritual Age*, Kurt Johnson asks the following questions:

How can humanity break the historical pattern of religion high jacking spirituality into exclusivity and aggressive, even violent behavior?

What is the formula for linking humankind's interior and exterior senses and skills?

Globally, what new awareness must arise, and what are the attendant skill sets that must accompany it, if humankind is to survive and thrive?

Some of the things we are teaching in our Seminary address these questions:

1. The ability to really "listen" to another person and to our still small voice within
2. To stay in a calm, elevated place in the midst of what appears as chaos, and understanding that chaos births change
3. To always be looking for and seeing the highest and best in every person, in every situation
4. To keep others calm and tuned in
5. The ability to send prayers and energies for the highest good for all concerned
6. Knowing how to be a group leader – creating Wisdom Circles or Cooperation Circles to enhance and hold higher energies and where people can come together physically to initiate acts of interspiritual cooperation and peace building (for further information on this see United Religions Initiative – uri.org)

Interspirituality is the next step in Human Evolution, and the emerging consciousness of all human beings and the planet.

Additional Resources[viii:12]

Pioneers in Hindu-Christian Interspirituality
by Kurt Johnson, Robert Toth, and Adam Bucko

Merton, Griffiths, and Teasdale

Father Thomas Merton, Father Bede Griffiths, also known as Swami Dayananda, and Brother Wayne Teasdale — in the lives and legacies of these three interspiritual pioneers, peacemaking is the congruence between the moral implications of deep contemplative experience (particularly the realization that "there is no separation") and its reflection in our actions in the world:

> With Trappist monk Thomas Merton, we behold this in his lifelong friendship with a Hindu monk named Bramachari, a friendship which shaped Merton's views of both the contemplative journey and the legacy of Mahatma Gandhi.
>
> With Bede Griffiths in his community Shantivanam (which means "forest of peace"), we witness such peacemaking in his teaching about theosis, meaning "transfiguration," an evolutionary vision of humanity at peace in a cosmos of peace.
>
> And Griffith's student Wayne Teasdale marks "deep non-violence" among his "Nine Elements of a Universal Spirituality," as well as peacemaking in the life of "full commitment," described in his classic titled *A Monk in the World* (2003).

There are many more than these three who have nurtured the dialogue between Christianity in the West and the Vedic traditions in South Asia. On the Christian side of the relationship, though, these three may be the most important spiritual midwives to a 21st century understanding of spirituality, social justice, and East-West religion and spiritual practice.

As a seventeen-year-old student at Oakham in England, reading reports of Gandhi's visits to England, Thomas Merton began a lifelong study of the Mahatma and his work. Merton recognized the Hindu principles that inform the practice of nonviolence: a commitment to the force of truth (satyagraha), to non-injury (ahimsa), and to action without attachment to results (nishkama karma). In "A Tribute to Gandhi," Merton wrote, "Gandhi's whole concept of man's relation to his own inner being and to the world of objects around him was informed by the contemplative heritage of Hinduism, together with the principles of Karma Yoga which blended, in his thought, with the ethic of the Synoptic Gospels and the Sermon on the Mount."

He concluded: "Gandhi was right, that India was, with perfect justice, demanding that the British withdraw peacefully and go home; that the millions of people who lived in India had a perfect right to run their own country." Merton would find, as his own life and ministry unfolded, that encounters with persons of deep mystical experience, whatever their religion, would serve to deepen his own experience and faith.

In Merton's classic *The Seven Storey Mountain* (1948), he tells that his friend Brahmachari counseled, "There are many beautiful mystical books written by the Christians. You should read St. Augustine's *Confessions* and *The Imitation of Christ*."

The writings of the Indian scholar and philosopher Ananda Coomaraswamy were also influential. In 1961, Merton wrote, "Ananda Coomaraswamy is in many ways to me a model: the model of one who has thoroughly and completely united in himself the spiritual tradition and attitudes of the Orient and of the Christian West, not excluding also something of Islam… Such men can become as it were 'sacraments' or signs of peace, at least. They can do much to open up the minds of their contemporaries to receive, in the future, new seeds of thought."

Bede Griffiths, Also Known as Swami Dayananda

Father Griffiths' journey to India as a Benedictine monk, he said, meant finding "the other half of my soul." Born Alan Richard Griffiths in Britain in 1906, he studied literature and philosophy at Oxford, tutored by C.S. Lewis, who became a lifelong friend and spiritual fellow-traveler. After sampling Christian spiritual communities across England, Griffiths, like Merton, embraced the monastic life of the Roman Catholic Church. As a Benedictine, he took the religious name of "Bede" and was ordained a priest in 1940. Griffiths found himself compelled to explore the Eastern mystical traditions, yoga, Indian scripture, and Jungian analysis.

In 1955, a year after writing his first well-known work *The Golden String* (1954), Griffiths moved to Bombay. After visiting a number of Indian spiritual centers, he joined other monks in Kurisumala and remained for ten years. During this time, he developed activities and liturgies that acknowledged both Hindu and Christian mystical roots. He took up the ascetic life of the Indian "sannyasa," dressed in the Kavi (the orange robes of the Sannyas), and adopted the Sanskrit name Dayananda, meaning "the bliss of compassion."

Father Bede travelled often between India and Europe, initiating East-West dialogue based on another influential book, *Christ in India* (1967). To further cement this cross-traditional legacy, he located his final ministry at Shantivanam, an ashram in Tamil Nadu founded by pioneer Christian monks working within the Hindu culture and mystical traditions. These included Hindu-Christian icons Father Jules Monchanin and Father Henry le Saux, also known by the Hindu guru name Abhishiktananda.

From Shantivanam, Swami Dayananda joined with other pioneers in the Christian-Hindu dialogue, including Raimon Panikkar, and published the books *Return to the Center* (1982) and *Vedanta and the Christian Faith* (1991). This work became the seed of the "Christian-Ashram Movement" from which came the diverse and influential ministries and activities of his students, including such luminaries as Wayne Teasdale, Andrew Harvey, Russill Paul, and Rupert Sheldrake.

Wayne Teasdale Points to Interspirituality

Brother Wayne Teasdale is best known in the West for launching what has become known as the "interspiritual movement." This began with his 1999 book *The Mystic Heart: Discovering a Universal Spirituality in the World's Religions* (1999), where he explored what he identified as Interspirituality and predicted an emerging Interspiritual Age. Teasdale, naming Bede Griffiths and Thomas Keating, founder of the Centering Prayer Movement, as his spiritual fathers, wrote the influential spiritual activist treatise *A Monk in the World*, as well as the best overview of Griffith's vision, *Bede Griffiths: An Introduction to His Interspiritual Thought* (2003). A decade later, an early colleague of Teasdale, Kurt Johnson, co-authored with David Ord *The Coming Interspiritual Age*, a detailed elaboration of Teasdale's thought and activist vision.

Combining the heritage of his two mentors, Griffiths and Keating, Teasdale adapted the "Nine Points of Agreement" from Keating's two decades-long Snowmass Inter-Religious Initiative into his "Nine

Elements of a Universal Spirituality." While Keating's Nine Points were matters of conceptual agreement across the different traditions, Teasdale's Nine Elements were matters of character that distinguish both the aspirations and fruits of the contemplative enterprise. In doing this, Teasdale helped solidify Merton's legacy, bringing into clear focus Merton's contribution to the post-Vatican II "Foundationalist Discussion," where he suggested the likelihood of a universal mystical experience common to all traditions — what he called the "communion of mystical-contemplative experience."

Unhappily, Brother Wayne's life was cut short by cancer in 2004, just as his work was becoming influential.

There were others, but these three pioneers provide an arena, a template, on which the historically diverse Christian and Hindu traditions can work out their apparent cosmological and theological differences. These divisive disparities were, to the likes of Merton, Griffiths and Teasdale, secondary artifacts of trying to place words and concepts upon the ultimately singular mystical comprehension shared by all. It was to this end that Teasdale dedicated his 2003 explication of Griffith's interspiritual vision.

Following on the above twelve Features adapted from online serials following the 2013 publication of *The Coming Interspiritual Age*, and under a new section title "Moving into a New Era," we return to invited commentary for the current Volumes concerning the emerging interspiritual experience after the transition of Br. Teasdale and through the continuing work of the Snowmass Interreligious Dialogues and so many other elements of the emerging interspiritual paradigm in the TIMELINE period subsequent to approximately 2015.

Endnotes and References for "Lost" and "Serial" Articles Section[viii]

MOVING INTO A NEW ERA

Features by Robert Atkinson - Ben Bowler - Paul Chaffee - Matthew M. Cobb
James Finley (Karen J. Gordon) - Jeffrey Genung - Charles P. Gibbs - Philip Goldberg
William Keepin - Frank Levy - Kay Lindahl - Netanel Miles-Yépez - Rami Shapiro
Wayne Teasdale - Claudia Welss - John A. Wilde

After publication of *The Coming Interspiritual Age*, there was considerable media activity spurred by its publisher, Namaste Publishing, who had published the well known best-selling books by Eckhart Tolle — *The Power of Now* and *A New* Earth (see previous "Pivotal New Emergences" subsection and its citations) — along with *The Presence Process* by Michael Brown and *The Conscious Parent* by Shefali Tsabary. These authors all appeared on the then hugely popular Oprah Winfrey television show. Winfrey's now iconic television series, which included the influential "Oprah's Book Club," was widely syndicated and won multiple Emmy and other awards. This publicity also resulted in multiple international events and additional publications in Namaste's e-magazine *Namaste Insights*, edited by the co-author of *The Coming Interspiritual Age*, Rev. David Robert Ord. The twelve Features just above were drawn from that oeuvre (2013-2015). Those years thus form a good natural boundary for us to turn now to Features solicited directly for these new Volumes' further historical retrospective on the interspiritual experience. These next Features generally take up the emergence of the interspiritual experience after its initial entry into the general public parlance, especially after Br. Teasdale's widely read book and all the happenings that followed it, as chronicled in the Timelines and Benchmarks of our Volumes 1 and 2.

Appropriately, we begin with a Feature from the founding publisher and editor of *The Interfaith Observer*, Paul Chaffee. *The Interfaith Observer* pioneered important early coverage of the interspiritual phenomenon. Following thereafter are Features by additional Featured Authors also well-known across the world's interfaith, interspiritual and transformational communities. These include persons closely associated with many of the historical "Interspiritual Pioneers" honored in our Section by that name in Volume 2.

Interspirituality – Hiding in Plain Sight
by Paul Chaffee

The September 1893 World's Parliament of Religions in Chicago is commonly noted as the birth of a global interfaith movement. India's Swami Vivekananda's electrifying speech opened the Parliament on 9/11/1893, beginning with "Sisters and brothers of America..." His compelling words, the *New York Times* reported, inspired a two-minute standing ovation. Vivekananda was invited to speak near the end of each day's activities, a strategy devised to keep registrants from skipping late afternoon sessions.

The huge enthusiasm of the thousands gathered in Chicago was a measure of the hunger in some for a religious world dominated by mutual respect and collaborative service, not competition and violence. Hunger, too, for a heart-driven faith rather than a doctrine-defined tradition.

Less impressed were religious leaders responsible for the health, vitality, and authority of their individual traditions. Indeed, Vivekananda called for a universal faith. Way too much power is vested in most Abrahamic institutions for their leaders to tolerate the idea of a global faith for humankind. Yet religion's failure to respond to the interfaith spirit theologically or organizationally did nothing to slow down the existential yearning in millions of us for a world where religion exemplifies peace and mutual respect and a tradition that doesn't make its own spirituality the *sine quo non* for everyone.

My own encounter with religious traditions first came as a teenager in a confirmation class at the International Church in Bangkok. The class was terrific. But at our last session the pastor showed up and enthusiastically talked about our becoming church members in a couple of weeks. Incensed, I went to my Dad, a Presbyterian missionary who spent 25 years in Asia. "I'm just beginning to see what you believe; I don't know what the Buddhists around us believe, much less the rest of the world. And you want me to join?!" "Not at all!" Dad replied. "You join if and when you want to, period." That week he gave me a book about the religions of the world and another on Christian sects.

Up from the Grassroots

Interfaith engagement typically begins at the grassroots. Over the past 50 years, local groups have sprung up spontaneously, mostly self organized. The U.S. and Canada had less than 70 interfaith groups in the late seventies — now it is thousands, clearly responding to a spiritual felt need.

The growth has been global. Chapel of the Snows, one of eight active congregations in Antarctica, is a nondenominational Christian church, but it promotes and organizes itself as an interfaith community.

Hundreds of local church councils changed a bylaw or two and began welcoming rabbis and synagogues. Then, before long, Buddhists, Mormons, Muslims, Sikhs, and many, many others have been welcomed.

Thousands of local service organizations, in small communities and large, have shifted their attention to include non-Christian traditions. City-wide interfaith programs have flourished as well. Councils in Detroit, Houston, New York City, Philadelphia, Phoenix, and San Francisco come to mind, but dozens more are thriving.

Universities have played a critical role in the growth of interfaith culture. Under Diana Eck's leadership, Harvard University established The Pluralism Project, the best, one could say, of thousands of faith and interfaith websites. The Berkley Center for Religion, Peace, and World Affairs at Georgetown University has become an influential voice regarding religious freedom and global development.

The University of Southern California has nearly 90 student-organized religious groups supported by remarkable interreligious courses and programming. The Interfaith Youth Core, recently renamed Interfaith America, has established strong, ongoing interfaith leadership programs at more than 200 colleges and universities in the United States. Interfaith America's ultimate goal: to make interfaith cooperation a social norm.

In a major shift, religious establishments in the West are now mostly opening rather than shutting doors to interfaith dialogue. Rome, for millennia asserting no way to salvation outside the Church, established the *Secretariat for Non-Christians* in 1964, later renamed the *Pontifical Council for Interreligious Dialogue*. A year later *Nostra Aetate* was published by the Second Vatican Council's Declaration on the relationship of the Church with non-Christian religions. It was a green light for Catholic parishes everywhere to engage in interfaith relations. In 1971, the largely Protestant World Council of Churches, founded in 1948, created an office for Interreligious Dialog and Cooperation in 1971.

Getting Established

With all this ferment, it's no surprise that international interfaith organizations emerged during the twentieth century. One of the first was the *International Association of Religious Freedom*, founded in 1900, *"to open communication with those in all lands who are striving to unite pure religion and perfect liberty, and to increase fellowship and cooperation among them."*

The *Fellowship of Reconciliation* started in 1914, the *World Congress of Faiths* in 1936. *The Temple of Understanding*, founded in 1960 by Juliet Hollister, continues promoting international interfaith relations through education and advocacy. A gathering of 200 religious leaders in Wichita, Kansas, in 1988 led to the *North American Interfaith Network* (NAIN), which the *New York Times* called the most important interfaith gathering since the 1893 Parliament. NAIN has sponsored annual conferences almost every year since its founding, usually focusing on the skill sets required for dynamic local interfaith development. These organizations all remain active, and their relationship-cultivation activities have enjoyed residual benefits.

For instance, today when the largely Protestant *Church World Service* commits to helping a neighborhood or community stricken with disaster, it is on the basis of a commitment that the *whole* local religious community will be involved. The *Charter of Compassion* has no religious requirements of its members. But its size, its commitment to universal values such as compassion, and the two million who have signed the Charter, make it one of the largest interfaith efforts in the world.

In the midst of this potpourri of interreligious practice, four organizations have taken leading roles in developing a new global interfaith, interspiritual culture. The 1993 *Parliament of the World's Religions* in Chicago began as a centennial celebration of the initial 1893 World's Parliament of Religions. But 9,000+ attended the birthday fete, the personal networking was intense, and interfaith gained a new credibility. Language for a "Global Ethic" was adopted, a seminal interfaith document, more important today than ever.

The Centennial went so well in 1993 that the organization decided to have more Parliaments, held periodically around the world. Since then, the Parliament has visited Barcelona, Cape Town, Melbourne, Salt Lake City, Toronto, yet again in Chicago, and online during the 2020 pandemic. Fifty years of improving audiovisual technology means that the Parliament's website is chock-a-block with remarkable interfaith video and music resource material gathered at recent Parliaments.

Religions for Peace (RFP) was created in 1970, the creative result of years of interfaith activity, much of it in Asia. RFP has offices and leadership in nearly 100 countries, and they focus on building healthy, creative interfaith activities at the local level. Unlike the majority of interfaith organizations that have an open door for interested participants, RFP is led by religious and cultural leaders.

The *United Religions Initiative* Charter was signed in 2000 after five years of studied examination by interfaith practitioners and newcomers around the world. URI's purpose is to promote enduring, daily interfaith cooperation; to end religiously motivated violence; and to create cultures of peace, justice, and healing for the Earth and all living beings. Today more than 1,100 URI Cooperation Circles enjoy a network of similarly motivated interfaith activists in 110 countries. The secret sauce in the continuing growth of URI, its founders acknowledge, is Appreciative Inquiry, a dynamic growth and development approach to building and healing community.

KAICIID is an intergovernmental agency that opened in 2012 through a joint effort by Saudi Arabia, Austria, and Spain. It was inspired by an initiative from Pope Benedict XVI and King Abdullah of the Kingdom of Saudi Arabia who met in 2007 to discuss the founding of a new interfaith activity.

KAICIID seeks to promote human rights, justice, peace and reconciliation, as well as curb the abuse of religion as a means to justify oppression, violence, and conflict. And because it is a governmental program with strong Middle Eastern support, it has a budget that beggars the rest of the world's interfaith budgets and thereby has been able to build a robust programmatic presence, especially in Asia, Africa, and Europe.

Seeing Each Other

The growing flurry of interreligious activity in the decades since the second Parliament in 1993 can't but please interfaith advocates. However, compared to difficulties the world faces today — including climate, authoritarians, nuclear weapons, and poverty — the task ahead feels overwhelming.

Complicating it all is the rough weather religious traditions are encountering. Issues ranging from abortion to abuse to gender to race to religious nationalism preoccupy religious institutions. Churches in North America and Europe are losing members. The fastest growing religious "group" in the U.S. are the self-described "nones," the non-affiliated, many professing to be spiritual but not religious. Pew Research this past June noted that rates of religious disaffiliation in East Asia are among the highest anywhere; but that the disaffiliated often continue their spiritual practices, such as venerating their ancestors.

Regardless of the difficulties, good news hiding in plain sight abounds. Religious turmoil represents an unparalleled opportunity to take advantage of what we've learned about peacemaking among strangers and even enemies. Creating a world where everyone is respected has always been an interfaith goal, and skills for achieving it abound and are being embraced.

The breadth and depth of interfaith culture developed over the last 35 years has been good soil for those who carry on into a realm called Interspirituality. *Faith* traditions come with their own history, doctrines, and culture. *Spirituality*, by contrast, is primarily personal, whatever the tradition. A Google search for the meaning of spiritual came up with a definition I like: *Spirituality involves the recognition of a feeling or sense or belief that there is something greater than myself, something more to being human than sensory experience, and that the greater whole of which we are part is cosmic or divine in nature.*

A distinctive element of spirituality is that it typically rewards serious practitioners regardless of one's tradition. And, we're discovering, those rewards can be happily pursued in company with followers of other paths. A Buddhist, a Pagan, a Presbyterian, and an indigenous Hawaiian, can each pursue a rich spiritual life *and* be enriched by getting together, perhaps praying together, and becoming friends. This could not happen without Interspirituality.

The details and stories of one tradition will differ from those in another, and yet there are shared values. And love, defined and understood in all sorts of ways, is usually the common denominator at the heart of a tradition. Most traditions have mystics who have delved into life and death, goodness and evil more deeply than the rest of us, and they, too, direct us to the heart. They teach the necessity of contemplation or meditation, critical tools in addressing issues of justice and peace as well as personal fulfillment. These gifts have been accessible for millennia, but for much of that time they've been hiding in plain sight.

Interspirituality

Brother Wayne Teasdale (1945-2004), a Catholic monk who helped plan the 1993 Parliament of the World's Religions, coined the word Interspiritual. In Brother Wayne's masterpiece, *The Mystic Heart: Discovering a Universal Spirituality in the World's Religions* (1999), he writes, "Interspirituality and Intermysticism are the terms I have coined to designate the increasingly familiar phenomenon of cross-religious sharing of interior resources, the spirituality treasures of each tradition." Brother Teasdale makes this distinction about spirituality: "Religion and spirituality are not mutually exclusive, there is a real difference. The terms spirituality refers to an individual's solitary search for and discovery of the absolute or the divine."

This year we celebrate the 25th anniversary of *The Mystic Heart*. In it, Teasdale points to a number of shifts in our understanding, which have led us toward Interspirituality.

- *...the emergence of ecological awareness and sensitivity to the natural, organic world,*

- *a growing sense of the rights of other species,*

- *a recognition of the interdependence of all domains of life and reality,*

- *abandoning a militant nationalism as a result of this tangible sense of our essential interdependence,*

- *deep evolving experience of community between and among the religions,*

- *the growing receptivity to the inner treasures of the world's religions,*

- *and an openness to the cosmos, with the realization that the relationship between humans and the earth is part of the larger community of the universe…*

You can quarrel (a few have) with Brother Teasdale's remarkable survey of the relationship between humankind and ultimate reality, but clearly, he had his hand on some of the critical issues we faced 25 years ago, much more so now. At the same time, he is surveying the human-divine relationship from the ancient past to a hoped-for future.

In an extended discussion of indigenous traditions, he writes, "All indigenous cultures are based on natural mysticism," including "Australian Aborigines, the Maori of New Zealand, the Chewong of Malaysia, the Desana of Northwestern Amazon, the San Bushmen of Africa, and all Native American nations." Western religion's relationship to indigenous traditions has usually been condescending and violent; Teasdale opens the door to a better relationship by recognizing the gifts of wisdom and peace these traditions offer. They've been hiding in plain sight. Some will say that Interspirituality is too out-of-this-world, too woo-woo; the Polynesian healing practice called *ho'oponopono*, a spiritual practice rooted in forgiveness and family harmony, might persuade them otherwise.

I do not see Interspirituality developing into strong established institutions, as has been the case with interfaith development. But an Age of Interspirituality seems very much a reality that is already growing among us all. Leaders like the Dalai Lama, Mahatma Gandhi, Martin Luther King, Rumi and so many more have an inclusive multi-religious spiritual perspective and a passion to heal the world. Millions and more around the world are similarly committed. Brother Wayne Teasdale's tour de force makes the journey more understandable and compelling. So too does Kurt Johnson and David Robert Ord's *The Coming Interspiritual Age*, published ten years ago, a portrait of what Interspirituality is achieving and bright possibilities for where it is heading.

The door my father opened to this teenager led to more than 40 years of cultivating interfaith, interspiritual relationships and communities. The journey has been full of joy and challenges. The best benefit, it's safe to say, is the many deep friendships that developed with individuals from every tradition you can imagine, individuals with gifts often hiding in plain sight.

From Metacrisis to Mind Change: Noetic Science and the Rise of an Interspiritual Age

by Claudia Welss

Pain Pushes Until Vision Pulls

There are moments in history when the noise of collapse is mistaken for the end of the world — systems unravel, certainties dissolve, even language begins to fail us. We are living in such a moment. A collective crisis is compelling our collective transformation. Known as a "metacrisis," it represents systemic failures so deeply interconnected they cannot be addressed separately, so mutually reinforcing they amplify one another. As a higher-order whole with its own emergent dynamics and unforeseen consequences, it encompasses social dynamics, including the effects on our individual and collective psyches, and on our ability to lead meaningful lives or envision a viable future. Yet as a planetary "near-death experience," it is also an initiation, a window into a new wave of human evolution.

Fifty years ago, the visionary founders of the Institute of Noetic sciences (IONS) saw this initiation coming. More than a "crisis of crises," they recognized a crisis of consciousness. As Carl Jung observed, "The upheaval of our world and the upheaval of our consciousness are one and the same." To meet this pivotal evolutionary opportunity, we would need to reclaim our agency — *our innate sovereignty and capacity to transform the ways we collectively perceive and give shape to reality.*

A Gentle Revolution in Science and Spirit

The Institute of Noetic Sciences was founded in 1973 from such a transformation. Two years earlier, while gazing at Earth from Apollo 14, NASA astronaut Edgar Mitchell remembered something ancient — that we belong to the cosmos, that consciousness is not an emergent property of matter but is woven into the very fabric of a living Universe. He later described it as a *Savikalpa samādhi*-type epiphany, from the Hindu tradition: a visceral experience of boundaries dissolving, accompanied by profound bliss, belonging, and the presence of *agape*, or unconditional love, as cosmic organizing principle. Paramahansa Yogananda captures this state in his writings: "The separate wave of the soul meditating in the ocean of Spirit becomes merged with the Spirit."

Now more than a scientific pioneer, Mitchell emerged a mystic and a messenger. His revelation birthed in him a new cosmology that carried an urgent imperative to enlist the tools of science to awaken humanity to its inherent oneness. He came to regard epiphany — and other non-ordinary ways of knowing long described by shaman and mystics — not as anomalies, but as latent evolutionary events in every human life, long enabling us to transcend limitations through direct access to energy and information outside of spacetime. Dismissed by the physicalist laws of science, Mitchell saw them as natural phenomena just awaiting scientific validation — and that when this happened, the impact on science and society would be revolutionary.

Joining Mitchell in establishing the field of noetic sciences was a small band of revolutionaries — key among them Dr. Willis Harman — who foresaw that the next great transformation would be a noetic one: a deep and collective re-patterning of human perception, belief, and identity. Harman, a Stanford systems scientist who challenged conventionally-held assumptions, called for "a gentle revolution" in both science and culture. He argued that many collective beliefs, *including dominant scientific and religious ones*, are false but made difficult to disprove, perpetuated by the subtle interconnectedness of all minds. Late last century, he made a bet that this same metaphysical dynamic could be intentionally harnessed to create a "Global Mind Change":

> *We are living through one of the most fundamental shifts in history - a change in the actual belief structure of Western society. No economic, political, or military power can compare with the power of a change of mind. By deliberately changing their images of reality, people are changing the world.*

This wasn't about a change of opinion, but a reconstituting of reality rooted in a new inner landscape. IONS would not only be about advancing the science; it would also be about its meaningful, practical application in the world. Given the current exponential rate of external change, this century will far exceed the last in its need for rapid and radical change to the global mind — and for consciousness-based strategies to navigate complexity, cultivate resilience, and guide the coherent evolution of our systems and selves in alignment with nature's intelligence.

Synergistic Alliance: Noetic Sciences and Interspirituality

Perhaps in response to the accelerating convergence of global crises, IONS' legacy is now organically converging with a younger noetic movement: interspirituality. As interspirituality transcends dogma to reveal the shared heart of the world's wisdom traditions, noetic sciences move beyond materialism while including it, integrating subjective experience into scientific inquiry to reconcile science with spirit. Together, these movements are stepping in from the margins to help ethically guide the evolution of human consciousness and culture away from the brink.

This convergence aligns with what Integral philosopher Ken Wilber calls the dawn of an "Integral Age" as a foundation for planetary awakening. Wilber urges moving beyond competing ideologies to a shared recognition of what unites us, supported by structures and institutions capable of holding higher consciousness. Integral theory maps reality in four quadrants, comprised of the interior and exterior dimensions of both individuals and collectives. Interspirituality provides a cultural bridge for intersubjective healing, while noetic sciences expand our understanding of human potential and reality itself. Together, they powerfully bridge the third-person domain of objects and systems (science) with first- and second-person domains (self and social), recognizing that these domains must evolve together — our systems can't evolve unless the inner narratives that validate them evolve too. Critically, the evolution of our consciousness must keep pace with the evolution of our technologies.

Quantum physics is a great example of a "new" scientific narrative pointing to a more holistic paradigm, even heralding a *scientific spirituality*. It demonstrates that our everyday sense of material reality is a special, limiting case — that a larger, unseen reality exists, governed by vibrating fields, wholeness in flowing motion, nonlocal connections where time and space are of no consequence and where quantum indeterminacy is a portal for mind-matter interaction. This echoes interspiritual wisdom, inviting more expansive comprehensions of who we are, where we are and why we're here. The metacrisis signals the unraveling of the old mechanistic story, making room for this more noetic narrative.

Conscious Evolution, Coherence and the Science of a Participatory Cosmology

Humility is essential in science, allowing us to hold the paradox of *knowing that we don't know* while still standing for something. As Buckminster Fuller said, "There are no passengers on Spaceship Earth." Because science remains one of the most powerful narrative forces in the Western world, the influence of the dominant paradigm is not neutral. Science shapes not only what we believe to be true, but also what we believe to be possible. Meanwhile, decades of research into scientific phenomena like the "observer effect" and the systemic *wholing* power of energetic coherence — most notably by the

HeartMath Institute (HMI) — suggest that we are always participating, knowingly or not, in the subtle dynamics of reality creation. While we must not wait for scientific proof to act on our own inner compass, IONS has spent over 50 years equipping humanity to make it through this evolutionary window by illuminating the vast potentials within human consciousness and how to embody them. Through rigorous empirical research, theoretical innovation and democratization of noetic insight, we are helping generate a gravitational pull toward a science that includes consciousness in its models of reality. A *noetic narrative* reconciling objective and subjective phenomena expands our understanding of what it means to be fully human — and of how to bring a flourishing Earth from the realm of possibility, to probability, to inevitability.

Modern civilization's organizing principles — based as they are on fundamental separation — are obsolete, unable to accommodate evolutionary pressures like artificial intelligence, UAP disclosure, ecological collapse, and social disintegration. But increasingly we are recognizing the rising chaos and fragmentation not as mere signs of a looming breakdown, but as precursors of an imminent breakthrough: as nature's way of reinvention. It is in nature's tradition to transcend its own limitations. The seed doesn't become a flower despite breaking apart, but *because* of it. As one with nature, we carry this same potential. But unlike the seed, it is now our destiny to consciously choose the direction of our becoming: evolution is a contingency, not a guarantee.

Physical chemist Ilya Prigogine's work on dissipative structures demonstrated that when complex systems are far from equilibrium — as our world is now — small islands of coherence can shift the entire system to a higher order. *I believe we are those islands: agape love is the organizing principle, and coherence its currency, catalyzing the emergence of a higher-order whole.* Consciousness-based research initiatives like *Global Consciousness Project 2.0*, uniting IONS, HMI, and a global network of independent researchers and citizen scientists, offer practical strategies for exploring this possibility scientifically — in this case, a planetary-scale "mirror" suggesting that the energies held in the collective heart of humanity shape our co-created reality.

Because the metacrisis presents as a *higher-order whole*, our most viable path forward is becoming one ourselves. The convergence of noetic sciences and interspirituality offers vital scaffolding, ways to address root cause rather than symptoms. This may be how we transcend all our crises at once — by remembering the fuller story we belong to, and in the words of Elena Mustakova, making ourselves available to "the laws of love driving this evolution."

The Great East-West Transmission
How India Gave Shape to Interspirituality
by Philip Goldberg

In a sense, the Interspiritual movement began more than 200 years ago, when prominent Americans began to acquire a deeper and more accurate understanding of the spiritual traditions born in India. Translations of Hindu and Buddhist texts, along with scholarly commentaries about them, entered the libraries of influential thinkers, and eventually into the hands of Ralph Waldo Emerson, Henry David Thoreau, and other Transcendentalists. That's when the East-to-West transmission of spiritual principles began in earnest.

From that New England source, Eastern wisdom flowed inexorably through a variety of streams and tributaries, penetrating the national soul. It spread to the late-19th century spiritual innovators associated with the New Thought movement — most notably, Madame Blavatsky (Theosophy), Mary Baker Eddy (Christian Science), and Charles and Myrtle Fillmore (Unity Church). It accelerated with the arrival on our shores of gurus, swamis, yoga masters, roshis, rinpoches, and other Asian emissaries, a procession that began in earnest in 1893 when Swami Vivekananda electrified the World's Parliament of Religions in Chicago and went on to establish the Vedanta Society. It took a big leap forward in the 1920s when Paramahansa Yogananda made America his home and headquarters (and later wrote his seminal memoir, *Autobiography of a Yogi,* one of the most influential spiritual books of the 20th century). And it exploded in the sixties with a veritable parade of Buddhist masters and Hindu gurus, highlighted by the Beatles' adoption of Transcendental Meditation and their watershed pilgrimage to Maharishi Mahesh Yogi's ashram. The list of prominent Indian emissaries of the 1970s — Swami Muktananda, Swami Satchidananda, Srila Prabhupada, et al. — is, of course, too long to list here. Ditto all the Buddhist masters, from Shunryu Suzuki to the Dalai Lama.

Each of the prominent teachers brought forward a different aspect of the diverse body of teachings that evolved in the East, and each appealed to a different segment of the population. The transformative impact on Western spirituality was magnified by eminent Americans and Europeans whose lives and work were influenced by their exposure to the East. Many cultural icons applied newly-discovered Eastern ideas to their own areas of expertise and disseminated them — sometimes explicitly, sometimes implicitly — to millions of inquisitive seekers who may not have been attracted to foreign gurus or original texts. As a result, countless individuals were spiritually informed, and frequently transformed, through the work of public intellectuals like

Aldous Huxley, Joseph Campbell, Huston Smith, Alan Watts, and later, Ken Wilber and myriad others; psychologists like Carl Jung, Abraham Maslow, and Richard Alpert whom most of us know as Ram Dass; physician / philosophers like Deepak Chopra and Dean Ornish; poets (Whitman, Eliot, Yeats, Ginsberg); novelists (Hesse, Maugham, Salinger); and, perhaps most explosively, musical giants, including some who crossed paths musically and spiritually with the great Ravi Shankar (e.g., John and Alice Coltrane, Philip Glass, and of course, George Harrison).

Most pertinent in the history of the Interspiritual movement, the East directly impacted key pioneers like Thomas Merton, Thomas Keating, Bede Griffiths, and Wayne Teasdale, along with many of their less-famous Christian, Jewish and Islamic brethren. All in all, the assimilation of Eastern ideas and practices by Americans expanded the awareness of millions of people, and, in the process, the entire spiritual landscape. Needless to say, that dynamic continues today.

The principal teachings that came here from India and other parts of Asia — Vedanta philosophy, yogic principles and practices, and nondual strains of Buddhism — have made Western spirituality both broader and deeper than it would be if those traditions had stayed home.

The broader part is obvious. A few decades ago, interfaith gatherings resembled the setup of a joke: a priest, a minister, and a rabbi walk into a room. Each cleric would politely discuss some aspect of religion from the perspective of his (seldom her) tradition, and everyone would leave feeling good about themselves for advancing the cause of tolerance and understanding. When Muslim clerics started to be invited, interfaith broadened a bit, but it was still an Abrahamic party. Gradually, however, the gatherings came to include Buddhists,

Hindus, Jains, and Sikhs, reflecting America's increased diversity after the overhaul of immigration policy in 1965.

This development was of enormous historical significance because the Indic traditions are not simply variations of familiar religious frameworks; they represent a radically different way of addressing the eternal spiritual questions: Who are we? How do we relate to the rest of the cosmos? What does it mean to engage the innately human spiritual impulse? How do we connect meaningfully to dimensions of reality larger than our individual selves?

Largely because Eastern precepts and practices catalyzed a massive rethinking of religion and spirituality, American spirituality deepened. The importance of this vertical penetration can't be overstated. Because the East has always kept direct spiritual experience front and center, the West was exposed to a vast inventory of practices for nurturing one's connection to the divine. Seekers could now avail themselves of Eastern methods without having to travel halfway around the world (and, if such a pilgrimage was indeed on their agenda, it became a whole lot easier to accomplish). Nor did they have to convert to a new religion or adopt a foreign belief system; they could pick and choose selectively and pragmatically.

One framework in which to place this development is the distinction scholars make between the exoteric and esoteric aspects of religion. The exoteric (as in external) consists of the outer elements such as dogma, doctrine, ritual, legends, myths, and interpretations of history. The esoteric, on the other hand, consists of the internal, experiential components of religion, where practices and methods come into play. At the risk of oversimplifying, it's accurate to say that, historically, the Abrahamic religions emphasized the exoteric while Eastern traditions kept the spotlight on the esoteric, in the process developing a treasure trove of practices that have translated well to other locations, cultures, and time periods.

The ramifications of this development reach far beyond the millions who stretch and bend in yoga postures or who devote time each day to an Eastern form of meditation or mindfulness. It led directly to the rediscovery, development, and ongoing refinement of contemplative Christianity and mystical Judaism (and, to a lesser degree, the Sufi wing of Islam). The burgeoning popularity of contemplative practices within the established religions speaks for itself.

The newfound availability of effective methodologies has democratized spiritual experience the way affordable radios democratized listening to music and the internet democratized information access. I would argue that this was the secret sauce that made Interspirituality not only possible but inevitable.

After all, it's one thing for scholars to comb sacred literature and show that mystics from all traditions have similar-to-identical experiences; it's quite another for ordinary spiritual practitioners to discover it for themselves — and to have their lives transformed in the bargain. For the first time, people who were indifferent to, alienated from, or hostile toward conventional religion had access to authentic spiritual alternatives, some of which were eventually secularized as wellness protocols, thereby making it possible for atheists, secularists, and science-oriented rationalists to be spiritual on their own terms, absent religious dogma.

As a result of these historic developments, we've become in large part a nation of mystics as Brother Wayne predicted in *The Mystic Heart*. The famous Rig Veda dictum, *Ekam sat vipraha bahudha vadanti*, commonly translated as "Truth is One, the sages speak of it by many names," has become not only a commonly accepted premise but also a living reality for a large segment of the population. The result, well-documented in survey after survey, has been a profound shift from exclusivist, outer-directed, belief-oriented religion to pluralistic, inner-oriented, experience-driven spirituality — and from a "nesting" spirituality in which membership and affiliation are paramount, to a "questing" spirituality in which exploration, experimentation, and individual choice are supreme. In other words, Interspirituality.

For all these reasons, history is likely to count the great East-to-West transmission as one of the modern era's prime shape-shifting forces. Some of the hallmark trends in contemporary spirituality — individual choice, inclusivity, disaffiliation, experience-oriented pragmatism, the ever-growing Spiritual But Not Religious cohort — would be unimaginable without it. In fact, the East's perennial insights and methods have so permeated the West that, in both obvious and undetectable forms, they will likely come to represent the normative approach to spirituality.

If the interspiritual age is indeed upon us — and I believe it is — then we should all turn toward India and offer a deep bow of gratitude. Without the diffusion of practical spiritual wisdom from its ancient past to a world the sages of old couldn't have imagined, this new era would be inconceivable, or at least many decades away from becoming a living reality.

The transmission continues to this day, of course, as new adaptations, modifications, and blends keep arising, and advances in communication and transportation technology make the world's spiritual wisdom more and more accessible. Those of us who think this is a very good thing have a duty to ensure that traditional teachings are creatively adapted to our time and place while also preserving their integrity, accuracy, and effectiveness.

Interspirituality:
A Journey Toward Global Harmony, NAIN and URI
by Kay Lindahl

Introduction

The evolution of the interfaith movement is a compelling narrative, especially for those who yearn for global peace and harmony. Along the way, terms like multi-faith, multi-spiritual, interfaith, interreligious, and Interspiritual have often been used interchangeably, though their meanings can differ. Historically, interfaith and interreligious organizations primarily included official representatives of various faith traditions, such as clergy, and staff. Over time, membership diversified, welcoming all who desired to focus on peace through a spiritual lens.

Today, we are witnessing another shift in how we view ourselves spiritually. Studies of religious affiliation in the United States have shown that the fastest growing category is "unaffiliated." According to Rev. Dr. Anna Hall in a May 2024 article in *CPR Connects*, 26% of Americans identified as unaffiliated in 2023, yet 64% consider themselves spiritual. This trend suggests a growing openness toward the term Interspiritual to describe this movement.

My passion for seeking a spiritual approach to activism spans many decades. I have participated in, witnessed, and studied the yearning for global peace and harmony manifesting in our time. It is a blessing to see how the many threads of my interfaith-interspiritual journey are woven into the tapestry of my life.

The Journey

It all began in 1991 with a simple yet profound question: "What would it be like to have a strong spiritual base in our community?" Motivated by curiosity, I extended an invitation to several local religious and community leaders to explore this idea. To my delight, nineteen people attended our first meeting. The conversation was so impactful that we decided we wanted to continue gathering monthly, to get to know each other better, and to wonder how we might collectively be of service in our community.

From these gatherings, The Alliance for Spiritual Community (ASC) was born. We developed and refined guidelines for dialogue, learning to listen and speak with respect. Our efforts led to an invitation to produce the program for our city's annual prayer breakfast, featuring prayers from at least seven or eight different faith traditions. For many attendees, this was their first exposure to religions other than Judaism and Christianity. Additionally, the city invited us to provide speakers for the invocation at city council meetings for several years.

In 1993, ASC co-founded the Religious Diversity Faire, a one-day, county-wide event where religious organizations introduced their beliefs in an interfaith 101 format. Attendees could choose which faith traditions to learn about, fostering mutual understanding and respect among different religious communities. Our outreach expanded and supported the growth of many local city interfaith events throughout the county.

The impact of these experiences opened my mind and heart to the value of celebrating diversity. When I heard about the 1993 Parliament of the World's Religions in Chicago, I knew I had to attend. It was the perfect opportunity to expand my knowledge about interfaith work around the globe. Imagine 10,000 people from all over the world and hundreds of religious faiths and traditions gathered in one place. Having meaningful conversations with people from across the continents and discovering commonalities despite different religious beliefs was a life changing and transformative experience.

Hans Küng's words at the Parliament deeply resonated with me: "There will be no peace in the world until there's peace among religions. There will be no peace among religions until there is dialogue among religions." This statement reinforced my commitment to interfaith dialogue. The Parliament was not just another event; it was a catalyst for a lifelong dedication to promoting peace through understanding.

At the Parliament, I found out about the North American Interfaith Network (NAIN), designed to connect interfaith groups in Canada, the US, and Mexico. I attended their annual conference in 1996, and immediately felt aligned with their mission, which included sharing best practices, expanding visions of interfaith, and making lifelong friends.

One NAIN conference introduced attendees to Open Space, a meeting format where participants create and manage their own agenda around a central theme. It ensures that topics of interest to attendees are addressed and that "water cooler" conversations surface organically and become part of the agenda. This open-ended process of inclusion generates energy, ownership, and creativity not often seen in traditional meeting formats.

Another introduced the World Café method, designed to stimulate ideas through a structured conversational process with small groups in an informal café setting. ASC adapted this approach as an Interfaith Café, supporting the exchange of ideas and perspectives of attendees from diverse faiths and beliefs. Others have found this format particularly engaging for youth groups.

NAIN was also where I heard Bishop Bill Swing share his vision for a United Religions Initiative (URI). Supporting self-organizing grassroots groups worldwide was an intriguing notion. I asked him how ASC could be of service. He invited me to contact the staff which led to a collaboration on circle dialogues, then participation in the creation of the URI Charter.

For the next three years, a diverse group of about 200 people gathered each summer to engage in creative conversation using Appreciative Inquiry. We sat at round tables of eight, conducted appreciative interviews with a partner, and then introduced that person to the rest of the group. This process was repeated at every gathering, affirming the value of relationships and acknowledging the importance of each person's presence.

Sometimes it was challenging as every table consisted of people from all around the world and a variety of religions, ages, and genders. In my first group of 8, we lived on 4 continents (North America, Latin America, Europe, Asia), spoke 5 languages (German, Cambodian, Portuguese, Tribal, and English), and had 4 different religious connections (Buddhist, Muslim, Christianity, and Indigenous.) Yet, by the end of that day, we felt a bond of connection with each other and were able to work together to contribute to the whole, demonstrating the potential for harmony and collaboration through the gift of relationships.

The dynamic and spirit of these conversations was honest, heartfelt, and respectful, even when there were disagreements. Moments of silence guided us when it seemed we were at an impasse. A graphic recorder illustrated what was said in real time on large wall-sized paper, so we could literally see the flow of our conversation. Our collective insights and ideas were crucial to shaping the Preamble, Purpose and Principles of the URI Charter.

We came to trust the integrity of the relationships that developed during our Appreciative Interviews. As we got to know each other, honored each other's dreams, generated new ideas, and designed plans to manifest them, we became partners for this new reality. This approach has influenced all my subsequent work, particularly in group dynamics and my focus on the sacred art of listening. Core values of inclusion, hospitality, and respect for the earth have become central to my personal and professional life.

The next turn of my interfaith / interspiritual journey occurred a few years later at the Melbourne Parliament of World's Religions in 2009. Critical global issues facing women and their children was a topic that sparked an expanded conversation about the Divine Feminine, the full inclusion of women, and feminine principles of leadership. We perceived a hunger among women to engage in conversations at the intersection of spirituality and transformative leadership.

This led to the creation of Women of Spirit and Faith (WSF), an interfaith / interspiritual organization which offers a safe and sacred space where women can explore the edges of their emerging spiritual leadership. This vibrant community of intergenerational women from diverse spiritual traditions is engaged in a bold experiment to discover new ways of doing things that are in alignment with feminine principles, always remaining open to guidance from Spirit. Our work is to offer space for those authentic conversations through small retreats, events, media platforms, and publications.

Reflections

Reflecting on these experiences, the evolution of Interspirituality, both personally within my community and beyond, is like entering into the flow of a river. Each step of the way can be seen as a tributary, adding to greater understanding, connection, and partnership among religions, faith traditions, and people of spirit. My initial question in 1991 sparked a journey that transformed my life and contributed to a broader movement for interfaith dialogue, cooperation, and transformative action.

The formation of the Alliance for Spiritual Community provided a foundation for these efforts. Our guidelines for respectful dialogue created a safe space for religious and community leaders to engage with one another. The annual prayer breakfast and the Religious Diversity Faire were significant milestones, bringing interfaith experiences to the wider community and promoting mutual respect.

Attending the Parliament of the World's Religions in 1993 was a pivotal moment. The event's scale and the depth of conversations expanded my perspective and reinforced my commitment to interfaith work. Hans Küng's message about the necessity of dialogue for achieving peace among religions resonated deeply and has continued to guide my efforts.

The connection with NAIN and subsequent collaboration with the United Religions Initiative further expanded my interfaith journey. Creating the URI charter through Appreciative Inquiry was a profound experience, demonstrating the power of collective visioning and the importance of creating spaces where diverse voices can be heard and respected.

The principles and practices developed during those early years of URI have had a lasting impact. They have influenced not only my approach to interfaith work but also my broader understanding of community building and conflict resolution. The core values of inclusion, hospitality, and respect for the earth have become central to my personal and professional life.

The work of WSF continues to inspire me and gives me hope for the future. Over the years, we have discovered that the impact of our work is multiplied if we gather in small intergenerational groups, using circle principles. The mutual mentoring that occurs anchors each of us in finding our own authentic voice and the gift that we each bring. We have seen that what we practice at a small scale reverberates to the largest scale.

As many of us feel a sense of urgency in the face of global challenges, it is imperative for women to fully take their place alongside men. The way we work as women adds to the wholeness of leadership and makes possible a new paradigm of balanced, responsible, and caring global citizenship. In truth, we women are still learning individually and collectively how to effectively bring forth our leadership. The work of this organization is to support and nurture that learning at every level.

Conclusion

Interspirituality, as I have experienced it, is about more than just dialogue among different faiths. It is about building relationships, fostering mutual respect, and working together for the common good. It involves recognizing our shared humanity and the interconnectedness of all life. This perspective has been transformative for me and the many people and communities I have had the privilege to work with over the years.

The journey of Interspirituality continues to evolve. There are always new challenges and opportunities. The work of promoting peace and understanding among people from different faiths and traditions is ongoing, requiring continual reflection, learning, and adaptation. However, the foundation built through the efforts of countless individuals and organizations provides a strong basis for this continued work as we become interspiritual beings.

The evolution of Interspirituality in my life and community has been a journey of discovery, growth, and transformation. It began with a simple question and has grown into a lifelong commitment to promoting peace through understanding and cooperation among diverse religions and faith traditions. The experiences and lessons learned along the way have shaped my approach to interfaith work and my broader understanding of what it means to build a just and harmonious world.

Further Reflection Questions

My sense is that we are on the cusp of the next turn of the wheel, that a new paradigm is ready to be born.

- What wants to happen now?
- How do we reimagine interfaith / Interspirituality?
- How do we engage the growing number of spiritual seekers who are not part of any religion or faith tradition?
- What do we need to learn about spiritual flexibility and spiritual resilience?

Seeing Into the Life of Things
by Charles P. Gibbs

...that blessed mood,
In which the burthen of the mystery,
In which the heavy and the weary weight
Of all this unintelligible world,
Is lightened:—that serene and blessed mood,

In which the affections gently lead us on,—
Until, the breath of this corporeal frame
And even the motion of our human blood
Almost suspended, we are laid asleep
In body, and become a living soul:
While with an eye made quiet by the power
Of harmony, and the deep power of joy,
We see into the life of things.
— *William Wordsworth*

The words above from William Wordsworth's poem "Tintern Abbey" have guided and sustained me for over half a century. They speak of the deep journey inward that has always led me outward into service to this beautiful, wounded world. The journey of transformation. The journey into Oneness. They helped save me during my late adolescence and early adulthood, years when I wandered lost in the confusion of human society that seemed to offer me no true home, in a world where I felt truly at home mostly in those blessed moments when I was lost in the woods — a nature mystic who could find himself by stepping out of society and losing himself in the natural world. They are words that guided my seventeen years as the founding executive director of the United Religions Initiative. Words that point to what is, for me, the heart of Interspirituality — the essence of love, called by myriad names and by no name at all, that holds all that is in a creative dance — inward and outward — of unity flowing into infinite diversity into ineffable unity.

As I traveled the world for nearly two decades for URI, and in the decade plus since I retired and have served as Senior Partner and Poet in Residence for Catalyst for Peace, I've also carried in my heart a quote I first encountered nearly 50 years ago, attributed only to an anonymous Methodist missionary:

> Whenever I go into a new community, the first thing I do is to take off my shoes to remind myself that I am standing on holy ground. Otherwise, I might make the mistake of believing I brought God with me.

Guided by the open, inclusive spirit of these two quotes, I've had the privilege of being in the presence of many remarkable people of deep spiritual grounding, contemplatives and activists — Anamist, Baha'i, Brahma Kumari, Buddhist, Christian, Hindu, Indigenous, Jain, Jewish, Muslim, Pagan, Sikh, Sufi, Zoroastrian, and countless other traditions. Some famous, some largely unknown. Women and men. Young and old. Every color of human skin and a dizzying diversity of languages. Some with impressive traditional learning, some with impressive academic education, some with deep practical experience — all deeply wise; and many co-founders of URI.

In my time with many of these practical wisdom keepers, there were moments when language and distinctions fell away, and we found ourselves abiding on the ineffable ground of our essential unity — We are one. We have come from and we return to one source, known by myriad names and by no name. We are one humanity, expressed in glorious diversity, held in the essential Oneness of the entire cosmos. And we are called to honor this unity and diversity in the way we live our lives, individually and collectively.

In May 1999, the URI co-sponsored a historic interfaith conference in Itatiaia, a national park in the Brazilian rainforest mid-way between Sao Paulo and Rio di Janeiro. 125 people from 35 different religious, spiritual, or indigenous traditions attended. The gathering provided an opportunity to celebrate existing interfaith work in Brazil, to explore the value of connecting Brazilian interfaith work to the United Religions Initiative's global effort to share the sacred and serve the world, and to begin to forge strategic alliances for future work.

An image of the future URI wished to create materialized on the extraordinary second night of the conference. Participants gathered in a large circle in a clearing on a mountain in the middle of the Brazilian rainforest for a ceremony of healing and peace to be led by representatives of four indigenous nations, which had been pushed to the brink of extinction by the ancestors of many of the people standing in the circle.

A bonfire at the circle's center and full moon alternately concealed and revealed by clouds scudding across the night sky provided the only light. From an inner circle around the fire, members of each indigenous nation offered their sacred dance and chant separately, a relic of ancient animosity. Stamping feet sent vibrations deep into the sacred Earth, touching the woven roots of trees and the even more ancient roots of their Peoples. The vibrations passed through those standing in the larger circle and out into the deep, luminous darkness of the rain forest. Like the smoke of the fire, the chants rose — past the clouds, beyond the moon, to the great spirit of life.

Then came the time to set aside the ancient divisions that had led to the separate dances. Then came the time for healing and peace. Then, for the first time in ancient memory, all four nations danced and chanted together — distinct and one. The dance they shared was both the expression and the fruit of their intention to heal the past and make peace.

Then they invited the whole group to form one circle, to embrace and embody healing of other ancient wounds and commit to peace. To dance together as one humanity — Indigenous Peoples in their native dress, a Zen Buddhist monk in her black robes, a Tibetan Buddhist monk in his deep red robes, two Dominican monks in their black robes, a Hindu swami in his saffron robes, and a Muslim sheikh, like most of the people there, wearing the clothes that pass for normal in cities, towns, and villages all over Brazil.

All sizes, shapes, ages, and colors of women and men, hands joined, dancing together as one community, extraordinarily diverse and yet united with each other and with the deep mystery that emanated from and enlivened earth, rainforest, and sky. In that ecstatic moment, we lived our visions of a better world. One and different at the same time, we were what we sought to become.

For me, in both mystical and practical ways, the path of Interspirituality leads to an exquisite balance of Oneness and diversity. My involvement in URI was based on a belief that providing people with practical opportunities to share the sacred and serve the world, from the gathering in Brazil to countless acts of enduring, daily interfaith cooperation, could grow the field of consciousness of unity in diversity and help make it more manifest. Could help, in the words of URI's charter, "to end religiously motivated violence and to create cultures of peace, justice and healing for the Earth and all living beings."

The dance of diversity and Oneness shaped the heart of my contribution, as one of hundreds in a founding generation, to help cocreate and grow URI. I believe it points to a consciousness that is innate in human beings. At a time when we are balanced on the razor's edge between promise and menace, I believe this consciousness holds the key to a positive future for humanity and the entire Earth community, if only we will cultivate it, each in our own way and collectively, and live into it through our attitudes and actions.

On my first trip to India in 1998, to help sow the seeds of an imagined global interfaith movement, I met with Baba Virsa Singh, a Sikh spiritual leader revered by people of all faiths all over India. In a beautiful, enclosed garden on his ashram, I was shown a statue of Jesus, arms opened wide to embrace all who came to him. As it was explained to me, the statue commemorated Jesus' appearance to Babaji. I was told that Christmas was celebrated as a major festival each year in remembrance of that appearance. And, that Babaji and Jesus still met and talked.

It was startling, humbling, challenging, and inspiring to see Jesus so accepted and honored in a Sikh ashram and to imagine an ongoing relationship between Jesus and Babaji that would be the envy of Christians around the world. A thought formed — *Nobody owns the sacred dimension of life; and, it seems, Christians do not own Jesus.* The beauty of the holy is offered equally to all.

Near the end of my visit to Gobind Sadan, I sat with Babaji. Through a translator, he explained his experience of God, our source, as pure love, and of God's call to us to offer love, light, and service to the world. As he finished, he told me again that God's essence is love — boundless, overflowing love.

All God asks of God's children, he told me, is that they come to God for love. The reservoir of God's love is so vast that if all God's children came to God at the same moment and in an instant received all the love they could ever want or need from God, it would be as if a tiny bird took a sip out of the ocean. Then Babaji admonished me to make sure I laughed enough, and he gave me his blessing.

I often recall my visit to Gobin Sadan with gratitude and wonder. I remember that no one owns God and that Christians don't own Jesus.

I believe that if our hearts and minds are open, we can meet together in God's unfathomable love. In that love, we can work together to make our world a better place for all. The hour is late. Shadows lengthened. While we cannot hurry evolution or the flow of history, we can decide what we believe is at the heart of things. We can cultivate our relationship with that heart. We can seek and serve it in all the Earth community. That is our part. That and trusting that the larger hands that hold all that is are benevolent and that we are their extensions in this world.

This is my experience. It shaped the heart of my effort to help cocreate and grow URI. I believe it points to a consciousness that is innate in human beings and holds the key to a positive future for humanity and the entire Earth community, if only we will cultivate it, each in our own way and collectively, and live into it through our attitudes and actions.

Following on these two Features concerning The United Religions Initiative we hope you will enjoy the specific Feature on URI vision and praxis by Sally Mahé in Volume 3 of this series. Her important and perceptive article on the grassroots authenticity and impact of URI is also excerpted in the Interspiritual Community Section later in Volume 2. Also note the previous Feature therein by Victor H. Kazanjian Jr., another previous Executive Director of URI in the Section of interspiritual articles from the 2018 Parliament of the World's Religions.

The Way of Unity as a Universal Spirituality
by Robert Atkinson

At the turn of the millennium, Brother Wayne Teasdale captured a watershed moment by identifying the inception of the Interspiritual Age. Our common heritage led him to recognize the interdependence of all spiritual traditions, which was not only "an inescapable fact of our contemporary world," but also "a value that promotes stable global peace."

A new set of historical circumstances brought about this shift in consciousness that included the emergence of an ecological awareness of the basic fragility of the earth, a recognition of the interdependence of all domains of life and reality, the desire to abandon a militant nationalism, the emergence of an interspiritual community, and the sharing of mystical resources across traditions.

This shift further defines a new interconnected, universal civilization that draws its inspiration from perennial spiritual and moral insights that have moved from "the heart of all mysticisms" to a collectively emerging unitive consciousness available to all. It confirms that, at the deepest level, all things are one. As Brother Wayne put it, "The unitive level of consciousness is both integration with the divine and nondual awareness or perception."

Unity is the Source *and* Direction of Evolution

In *The Story of Our Time* (2017), I traced the unfolding of globalizing forces that expanded circles of unity and made the interfaith movement possible in the late 1800s with the convening of the first Parliament of the World's Religions in 1893. By the 1990s, the Parliament's Declaration Toward a Global Ethic, the formation of United Religions

Initiative (URI), and many other unitive efforts, clearly signaled the dawn of a new consciousness.

Getting to this point has been a gradual, step-by-step unfolding of stages occurring over a few millennia. Yet it is an awareness grounded in unitive consciousness which formed the entire universe.

Andrew Harvey pointed to this phenomenon in *The Essential Mystics* by characterizing each of the world's spiritual traditions as contributing a unique quality in the process of our collective spiritual evolution, because "each tradition has a different *way* of approaching the unfathomable mystery." This also reveals "a relatedness at the deepest level to all the others."

Chronologically, these contributions Harvey noted are: from the First Peoples traditions, *the way of reverent intimacy with nature*, or being humble before the majesty of the universe; from ancient Greek mysticism, *the way of beauty*, or sensing deeply the splendor of the world; from Hinduism, *the way of presence*, or being in pure awareness of the indivisibility of all things; from Judaism, *the way of holiness*, or seeing the divine as pervading human life; from Taoism, *the way of the Tao*, or living in unimpeded harmony with all things; from Buddhism, *the way of clarity*, or waking up to the pure freedom of unconditional compassion in the world; from Christianity, *the way of love in action*, or becoming transformed to reflect the Creator's unwavering love for the entire creation; and from Islam, *the way of passion*, or knowing the peace that comes in surrendering one's entire being to the Unknowable.

The Way of Unity Emerges Out of Discord

While separation and division persist among the world's peoples, Brother Wayne Teasdale knew that humanity needed another step to get to *the mystic heart* of all traditions that underlies them all.

An ongoing evolutionary flow of ups and downs brings about periodic leaps of consciousness — each moving forward the interconnected unfolding of humanity's spiritual heritage. The evolving thread of different *ways* of approaching the unfathomable mystery had reached a formidable block in the mid-19th century, and a renewal of spiritual verities were needed.

Out of the division, discord, and inequality pervading Persia at that time, Baha'u'llah, founder of the worldwide Baha'i community, refreshed the spiritual teachings that have guided the peoples of the world throughout the ages with precisely what was needed then to focus on unity as the way of healing the ills of an ailing humanity. The *way of unity*, as best characterizes the Baha'i tradition, prepared the world stage for spiritual interdependence.

In this culminating stage of a long evolutionary process, the greatest challenge of our time is more fully reflecting the wholeness-in-motion around us and the unity-in-belonging amongst us in our everyday interactions and relationships.

Baha'u'llah proclaimed, "Regard the world as the human body which, though at its creation whole and perfect, hath been afflicted, through various causes, with grave disorders and maladies... The mightiest instrument for the healing of all the world is the union of all its peoples."

Unity is the all-encompassing, over-arching principle that all progress in the world depends upon — as well as the natural outcome of an organic process of restoring seemingly opposing forces to their inherent wholeness. He further said, "The well-being of mankind, its peace and security, are unattainable unless and until its unity is firmly established."

Following this spiritual regeneration, advances in all realms of human rights occurred, from the end of slavery to women's rights, the first convening of the world's religions, and civil rights.

Yet, all great "ages" take centuries to reach the fullest expression of their potential. A dialectic, nonlinear, spiral-like process governs evolution and human history. As Baha'u'llah also said, "The oneness of humanity will be achieved in evolutionary stages replete with strife, chaos, and confusion."

This holistic — and realistic — view explains why a recurring process of personal and collective transformation is necessary throughout the cycles of evolution, enabling a universal spirituality to emerge and eventually replace a dying, divided order with the Unitive Age.

As evolution is by no means a straight line, the wholeness of Creation is undeniable. Abdu'l-Baha provided a clear and concise expression of this unitive worldview: "The evolution of existence is one. The divine system is one. Whether they be small or great beings, all are subject to one law and system." Here we see all things making up an interdependent whole.

Reality is one and apparent opposites — like yin and yang, feminine and masculine — are complementary, interrelated halves of the same whole, balancing and transcending their assumed duality. History's polar tensions are resolved with a higher level of consciousness than created them; in unitive consciousness there is no separation.

Unitive Principles for a Unitive Age

Humanity's spiritual development has occurred in stages, and we are approaching the age of our collective maturity. As the Baha'i writings say, humanity has passed through the stages of infancy and childhood and "is now in the culminating period of its turbulent adolescence approaching its long-awaited coming of age."

The Baha'i teachings clarify the next step in humanity's evolution: "A world, growing to maturity, must... recognize the oneness and wholeness of human relationships, and establish once and for all the machinery that can best incarnate this fundamental principle of its life." Wholeness, and its inherent unity, is the underlying principle defining reality and what we are evolving toward.

Our emerging Unitive Age will not achieve or maintain harmony and unity until this wholeness is the basis for all our endeavors. Unity on a global scale — in all social, cultural, and economic spheres — means living by common values and principles that bring about the Oneness of humanity.

This final leap of consciousness — to our collective unity and wholeness — requires seeing all things as one, not an easy matter, after millennia of division and separateness. Unity itself is an evolving principle that takes in a vision of ever-expanding circles until there is no "other" left to exclude from the circle of the human family — or from the web of all life.

Unity on this widest scale will be achieved progressively. World unity has many stepping-stones to cross in this arduous journey to wholeness and true interdependence.

The necessary stepping-stones to unity in our time are clear. Unity can only be achieved through wholeness; wholeness requires equality between women and men, balance between the extremes of wealth and poverty, freedom from all forms of prejudice, harmony between science and spirituality, and the protection of nature as a divine trust.

These unitive principles are so interdependently tied together that the realization of one depends upon the realization of all others. The way of unity depends upon unitive narratives, unitive justice, unitive economics, unitive education, and unitive relationships on all levels of society becoming the norm.

These common principles, values, and practices — each essential stepping-stones for world unity — are bringing the peoples of the world together with a unity of purpose: to form the necessary foundation for sustainable peace on Earth.

Every individual will contribute what they are capable of to building a global community in which resources are not concentrated in the hands of a few, but rather in which all have enough of what we all need to sustain personal and collective well-being and harmony. This is the world community toward which humanity is irresistibly moving.

Interspirituality, Perennial Wisdom, and One Foot Judaism
by Rami Shapiro & Frank Levy

"The prefix *inter* in Interspirituality expresses the ontological roots that tie the various traditions together... It conveys a fundamental truth: the essential spiritual interdependence of the religions".[1] Ontology is the study of the nature of reality, and one can make the case, as Brother Wayne does here, that various religions do indeed investigate reality, and that this may lead to shared and overlapping insights. But in and of itself this is not a revolutionary idea. What is revolutionary, and no less true, is what we take to be the deeper revelation of Interspirituality: that the great mystics of the world not only share the same ontological search but discover the same ontological Truth, what we call Perennial Wisdom.

1. All life is a manifesting of nondual Aliveness called by many names: YHVH, Tao, Reality, Brahman, Allah, God, Mother, etc.
2. You have the innate capacity to awaken in, with, and as this Aliveness.
3. Awakening to Aliveness calls you to be a blessing to all the families of the earth[2] by living in accord with the Golden Rule.
4. Awakening to Aliveness and being a blessing comprise your highest calling as a human being.

This articulation of Perennial Wisdom, or what Aldous Huxley calls Perennial Philosophy, is ours, and there are many others, but all of them share the same four basic points. For us, the interspiritual revolution comes to fruition when each religion reimagines itself from this Wisdom and in so doing cleanses itself of the tribalism, violence, and supremacist fantasies that increasingly define them. This essay outlines how this might be done in the context of Judaism.

To seek out a Perennial Wisdom Judaism, we start with something deeper than "who is a Jew" and "what is Judaism." We start with what it is to be human, and to do that we look to *Bereshit*, the first book of Torah whose authors provide us with two mutually exclusive visions of what it is to be human.[3]

The first vision comes from the first chapter of Bereshit where we find humanity alien to the natural world, with no inherent purpose other than to procreate in service of dominating the natural world. This story takes place on the sixth day of creation. The Earth is teeming with life and is judged by its Creator to be *tov*, good — not good in any moral sense, but in the engineering sense of being well-made and well-functioning. Everything is functioning optimally, and then, for no reason whatsoever, God said, "Let us make *adam* / humankind in our image after our likeness."[4] Since everything was operating as intended, what purpose was this *adam* to fulfill?

> They shall rule over the fish of the sea, the birds of the sky, and over the animals, the whole earth, and every creeping thing that creeps upon the earth.[5]

But why? Why do fish, birds, animals, reptiles, bugs, trees, and plants need a ruler? They don't. In this first story, humanity is an alien species coming to Earth from the mind of God with only one aim: "to fill the earth and subdue it."[6] This vision of humanity reflects an existential misunderstanding that fuels all our social, economic, political, religious, and environmental problems, a misunderstanding Albert Einstein called an optical delusion of consciousness separating people from one another and from nature as a whole:

> A human being is part of a whole, called by us the "Universe," a part limited in time and space. We experience ourselves, our thoughts, and feelings, as something separated from the rest — an optical delusion of our consciousness. This delusion is a kind of prison for us, restricting us to our personal desires and to affection for a few persons nearest us. Our task must be to free ourselves from this prison by widening our circles of compassion to embrace all living creatures and the whole of nature in its beauty.

This delusion of dualistic consciousness is most likely the psychological origin of the human as an alien story expressed in Bereshit 1. If we are to free ourselves from this delusion, we must adopt a different story. In the context of a Perennial Wisdom-infused

Judaism, this means shifting from the creation story in Bereshit 1 to the creation story in Bereshit 2.

> On the day God made earth and sky, the earth is barren: there were no trees on the land and no herbs had sprouted in the fields, for God had not sent rain upon the earth and there was no earthling [adam] to work [la-avod] the earth [adamah]. A mist ascended from the Earth and watered the whole surface of the soil. And God formed adam from the adamah, an earthling from the Earth, and blew into adam's nostrils the breath of life, and the earthling became a conscious being. God planted a garden in Eden, to the east, and placed adam there... to work the Earth and to protect the Earth.[7]

In Bereshit 1, humanity has no organic connection to nature and is created for no other reason than to subdue nature. In Bereshit 2, things could not be more different. The earthling, *adam*, is drawn up from the Earth, *adamah*; we are Earth made conscious, and as such we are given the dual mission to work and protect the Earth. The Hebrew word for work here is *la-avod*, the same word we Jews use for divine service. Working the land and protecting nature is holy work.

This story leaves no room for alienation or domination, only service and care. This is the story we need if we are to take up the task Einstein calls us to, the task of freeing ourselves from the prison of dualistic consciousness and its zero-sum mindset of us against them and realizing nondual consciousness and its non-zero mindset of all of us together.

When you make the shift from dual to nondual consciousness, from what Judaism calls *mochin d'katnut* (narrow mind) to *mochin d'gadlut* (spacious mind), you embody the Interspiritual Truth at the mystic heart of the world's religions, what we call Perennial Wisdom.

We call our Jewish expression of Perennial Wisdom "One Foot Judaism": a deeply spiritual, ethically universal, Torah honoring Judaism beyond denomination and tribalism that overcomes the delusion of dualistic consciousness Einstein warned us against.

One Foot Judaism rests on two texts found in the Talmud, an anthology of rabbinic teachings spanning the years 250 BCE to 500 CE and consisting of 63 volumes comprising in the standard printing 2,711 double-sided pages. The first and older of the two stories relates an encounter between a Roman soldier and the two leading rabbis at the end of the last century BCE and the beginning of the first century CE: Hillel and Shammai.

> A Roman soldier approached Shammai as he was working on a construction site and said, "Teach me the entire Torah while I stand on one foot, and I will convert."
>
> Outraged by the audacity of the demand, Shammai grabbed a heavy builder's level and chased the man away.
>
> The Roman then approached Hillel, a woodworker, with the same demand: "Teach me the entire Torah while I stand on one foot, and I will convert."
>
> Unperturbed, Hillel replied, "What is hateful to you do not do to another. That is the entire Torah; all the rest is commentary. Now, go and study it."[8]

The second teaching comes from Rabbi Abaye who lived several centuries after Hillel. His teaching is much shorter although far more cryptic:

There are never fewer than thirty-six righteous people awake to *Shekhinah* [and embodying the Golden Rule] as it is stated: "Happy are they who wait for Him [*lo*]."[9] The numerical value of *lo*, spelled *lamed vav*, is thirty-six [*lamed* / 30 + *vav* / 6].[10]

Abaye's teaching may sound confusing upon first hearing, but the basic idea is this: there are always at least thirty-six people awake to *Shekhinah*, the Divine Presence manifesting as all life the way an ocean manifests as all waves, who live according to the Golden Rule: what is hateful to you do not do to another. In Hebrew, the number thirty-six is *lamed* / 30 + vav / 6, and over time, these thirty-six people come to be called *Lamed-Vavniks* or "thirty-sixers."

Here is how One Foot Judaism is a Jewish expression of Perennial Wisdom:

1. *All life is a manifesting of nondual Aliveness called by many names.* The Name Abaye uses for this nondual Aliveness is Shekhinah.

2. *You have the innate capacity to awaken in, with, and as this Aliveness.* A Lamed-Vavnik is a person awake to Shekhinah / Aliveness in, with, and as all reality. Everyone can be a Lamed-Vavnik.

3. *Awakening to Aliveness calls you to be a blessing to all the families of the earth by living in accord with the Golden Rule.* Being a Lamed-Vavnik means living by the Golden Rule which, as Hillel taught, means living Torah.

4. *Awakening to Aliveness and being a blessing comprise your highest calling as a human being.* Awakening to Shekhinah and being a blessing is what it is to be a Lamed-Vavnik.

If Judaism (and all religion) is to promote human thriving rather than extinction, if it is to reveal the organic unity of *adam* and *adamah*, earthling and Earth, if it is to promote service to life as service to God manifesting in, with, and as life, if it is to help people overcome the delusion of dualistic consciousness that threatens the survival of person and planet, then Judaism (and all religion) must root itself in Perennial Wisdom and become a unique expression of Interspirituality.

Man, Mystic & Movement
Brother Wayne Teasdale & Interspirituality

[adapted from an illustrated text that will be subsequently published in full (in our Volume 3), as detailed in Volume 2][1]

by Jeffrey Genung

There is almost a sensual longing for communion with others who have a large vision. The immense fulfillment of the friendship between those engaged in furthering the evolution of consciousness has a quality impossible to describe. — Pierre Teilhard de Chardin (1881-1955)

In every age, souls arise who serve as a vessel of sacred wisdom and a vision that helps move human consciousness forward toward greater unity and love. Brother Wayne Teasdale is one such soul and Interspirituality one such movement. His journey, and the birth of the interspiritual movement, echoes an ancient African proverb: "It takes a village to raise a child." Although Wayne coined the word Interspirituality in his seminal book *The Mystic Heart* in 1999, the roots of the interspiritual movement run deep, influenced by countless souls across time. If it takes a village to raise a child, it takes a global village to raise human consciousness. A global village of mystics.

Like a radiant star guiding us toward a brighter dawn, Interspirituality has emerged as a beacon of wisdom, hope, and love.

Wayne was like a brother and a close personal friend of my family. He was also a kindred spirit and a wise and humble spiritual mentor. He had successfully battled cancer and fully recovered. Some years later, his cancer of the throat returned with a vengeance. His radiation treatment was harsh and so were Chicago winters. It was heartbreaking to see the suffering he had to endure. My family and I wanted to help. We lived in Austin, Texas, which has mild winters. We thought it would be easier for him to recover in a warmer climate surrounded by his close friends and spiritual community. We were founding members of The Church of Conscious Harmony, a contemplative Christian community that practiced Centering Prayer and the Gurdjieff Work. Wayne was closely connected with the church and considered it as his primary spiritual community. By joining us in Austin, Wayne would be surrounded by warmth and love. A perfect environment for healing.

I invited Wayne to come live with us and he humbly accepted. To prepare for his journey, I traveled to Chicago to pack up his apartment and ship everything to our home in Austin. Unfortunately, Wayne never made it. He experienced a fatal side effect from his radiation treatment. Wayne died in his sleep two weeks before he was scheduled to move to Austin.

In this chapter, I invite you to join me on a journey through some of Wayne's life, his mystic journey and his final sacred passage. We'll explore the paths he walked, the wisdom he shared, and the profound mystical experiences that shaped his soul. We'll delve into the heart of the interspiritual movement he championed, tracing its roots, celebrating its present, and envisioning its future. My aim is to weave together a story of how a global village of mystics is finding each other and working collaboratively to seed an interspiritual movement, one that will blossom into a contemplative renaissance.

The Man

Wayne's story begins in the quiet coastal town of Niantic, Connecticut, where he was born in January of 1945. His childhood was shaped by the loving presence of his Uncle John, a man of deep faith and gentle wisdom, whom Wayne considered a saint. It was Uncle John who first ignited the spark of contemplation within him, nurturing a young boy's natural inclination toward the sacred.

This spark grew into a flame as Wayne pursued his academic journey. From the hallowed halls of St. Anselm College in New Hampshire to the McAuley Institute of Religious Studies in Connecticut, he immersed himself in the world of theology and philosophy, earning a master's degree in 1976. But it was at Fordham University in the Bronx, New York, that his path took a decisive turn. There, under the guidance of renowned scholars, he delved into the mysteries of comparative mysticism and mystical theology, ultimately earning his doctorate in 1986.

At Fordham, Wayne encountered two figures who would profoundly influence his life's work. The first was Father Thomas Keating, a Cistercian monk and a pioneer in the contemporary contemplative movement. Father Keating, with his gentle spirit and profound insights, became a close mentor and friend, guiding Wayne in the practice of Centering Prayer and sharing a deep passion for interfaith dialogue.

The second was Father Bede Griffiths, a Benedictine monk who had established an ashram in India called Shantivanam, a sanctuary where Christian and Hindu spirituality intertwined. Father Bede's vision of a harmonious convergence of faiths resonated deeply with Wayne, drawing him toward the rich tapestry of Eastern traditions.

From 1982 to 1992, Wayne sought a deeper experience of monastic life, joining a lay community called Hundred Acres Monastery in New Hampshire. Founded by Trappist monks, this secluded haven provided fertile ground for his own contemplative practice to flourish. But the call of India, the allure of Shantivanam ashram and Father Bede's wisdom, proved irresistible. In 1986, Wayne began making extended pilgrimages to the ashram, immersing himself in the contemplative practices of the East.

This immersion culminated in a profound transformation. In January of 1989, Father Bede initiated Wayne into the order of Christian Sannyasa, an ancient tradition of renunciation, dedicated to the pursuit of God. With this initiation, Wayne embraced a life of simplicity and service, his heart firmly rooted in the contemplative dimension of spirituality that transcended religious boundaries.

Then in 1991, a new chapter unfolded. The Council for a Parliament of the World's Religions invited Wayne to help plan for the 1993 Parliament in Chicago, a historic gathering of faith leaders from around the globe. This invitation marked a turning point, propelling him onto the world stage as a champion of interfaith understanding. He moved to Chicago in 1992, fully embracing his role of fostering a global community of peace and spiritual awakening.

In August of 1993, the Parliament invited him to serve as a trustee. He wasn't just an organizer; he became a vital voice in the burgeoning interfaith movement. His appointment to the Assembly of Religious and Spiritual Leaders in 1993 solidified his role as a bridge-builder between diverse traditions. His election to the board of trustees also gave him a platform to champion interreligious initiatives. He was also invited to chair the Community of the Next Generation to empower the next generation of spiritual leaders.

But Wayne's influence extended far beyond the Parliament. He also shared his wisdom and passion as an adjunct professor at Catholic Theological Union, DePaul University, and Columbia College in Chicago, igniting a thirst for interspiritual understanding in countless students. His retreats and spiritual direction offered seekers from all walks of life a path to deepen their connection and inner peace. And his leadership in the Bede Griffiths International Trust, alongside Father Thomas Keating, ensured the continuation of Father Bede's legacy of interfaith exploration.

Driven by a profound commitment to nonviolence and peace, Wayne joined the Monastic Interreligious Dialogue (MID), a network of monks and nuns dedicated to fostering understanding between different contemplative traditions. It was here that he collaborated with His Holiness the Dalai Lama to co-draft the Universal Declaration on Nonviolence, a powerful testament of their shared vision, a world free from conflict. This collaboration blossomed into a deep friendship and led to their co-creation of the Synthesis Dialogues, an initiative dedicated to fostering interspiritual cooperation and understanding.

Wayne's dedication to peace extended to the international arena. He worked with UNESCO on The Role of Religions, culminating in the 1994 Declaration on the Declaration of a Culture of Peace. These foundational documents, along with the Universal Declaration on Nonviolence, laid the groundwork for the Parliament's landmark document, *Towards a Global Ethic*. It was signed by hundreds of revered spiritual leaders at the 1993 Parliament in Chicago. This document stands as a universal call for ethical action and interfaith cooperation in building a more just and peaceful world.

All of these threads — Wayne's deep scholarship, his unwavering commitment to contemplative practice, his countless dialogues with spiritual leaders from around the world, and his transformative experience with the Parliament of the World's Religions — converged to create the fertile ground from which he wrote *The Mystic Heart*. In this seminal work, which has become a spiritual classic, he articulated a vision of an evolving spiritual movement, a movement he named Interspirituality. He saw a world where the wisdom of diverse traditions could converge, enriching and deepening our understanding of spirituality itself.

But Wayne was more than a visionary writer and scholar; he also embodied the very essence of Interspirituality in his daily life. He walked the streets of Chicago as a true "monk in the world," a Christian sannyasa living a life of simplicity and service. He was a beloved teacher, a trusted spiritual friend, and a compassionate presence to all he encountered, from the city's homeless to internationally recognized religious figures.

Everyone who met Brother Wayne was touched by his genuine humility, his down-to-earth nature, and his playful sense of humor. He carried his vast wisdom lightly, his heart radiating warmth and kindness. Brother Wayne grounded himself in contemplative practice, which included a daily rhythm of Centering Prayer, the rosary, and living a life of simplicity, which serves as the wellspring of his inner life, evidenced by his deep compassion.

From this solid foundation of contemplative living, deep humility, writing and teaching, he emerged as a highly respected prophetic voice. He fearlessly challenged those in power, particularly religious leaders, urging them to use their influence to create a more just and compassionate world. He called for a transformation of hearts and minds, a collective awakening to the interconnectedness of all beings and the urgent need for global healing.

Sacred Stories

My first encounter with Brother Wayne was like a scene from a movie. Picture this: the year is 1989; the setting is the Harmonia Mundi Contemplative Congress in sunny Newport Beach, California. Imagine a gathering of spiritual luminaries from around the world — monks, nuns, swamis, rabbis, and indigenous elders — all converging to explore the common ground of contemplative practice. The air crackles with anticipation as the conference opens with an electrifying announcement: His Holiness the Dalai Lama has just been awarded the Nobel Peace Prize. And who would be with the Dalai Lama sharing in the joyous news? None other than Brother Wayne Teasdale.

The Contemplative Congress was a truly remarkable event, a melting pot of spiritual traditions and a testament to the growing interspiritual movement. Hundreds of renowned contemplative leaders gathered. It was in this vibrant atmosphere, amidst a symphony of chanting, Sufi dancing, prayer, and deep silence, that I first crossed paths with Brother Wayne. However, it would be some years later before our paths would formally converge.

In 1997, I embarked on a new adventure, becoming an organizing member of a five-year experiment in contemplative community called The Church of Conscious Harmony in Austin, Texas. We were a community of householders, teachers, artists, parents, businesspeople, and seekers. We were drawn together by a shared yearning to make daily practice and God devotion the center of our life. We envisioned a "monastery without walls," a community grounded in the daily practice of Centering Prayer and the teachings of G.I. Gurdjieff. Our community was also closely connected to Father Thomas Keating. He served as our spiritual "Abba" and helped guide and inspire us on our contemplative Christian experiment.

It was through this community that I became friends with Brother Wayne. He was friends with Tim and Barbara Cook, the co-founders of the church. Through this relationship, he quickly became a beloved mentor and guide for our fledgling community. His regular visits to our community were always a source of joy and inspiration. He would lead retreats and share his wisdom in captivating talks. During his visits, he would often stay with my family, allowing our friendship to blossom.

Wayne had become widely known internationally for his insightful writing, inspiring teaching, and his ability to connect people from all walks of life. But beneath his gentle demeanor lay a mischievous spark, a "holy rascal" with a twinkle in his eye and a fearlessness in his heart. He possessed a rare combination of deep humility, genuine authenticity, and a playful sense of humor that disarmed even the most hardened cynic. He combined these gifts with an unwavering commitment to justice, which made him a force to be reckoned with.

He wasn't afraid to speak truth to power, challenging hypocrisy wherever he found it. One memorable example of his boldness occurred during a keynote address to a Jewish audience in Chicago. A gathering celebrating a major Jewish holiday. He seized the opportunity to openly criticize his own Roman Catholic Church for its failure to confront the horrors of the Holocaust. He offered a heartfelt apology to those in attendance. He apologized on behalf of the Church, because the institution itself wouldn't, acknowledging its moral failure to act in the past and its continued silence in the present. It was a powerful moment, a testament to his courage and his unwavering commitment to reconciliation and healing.

Brother Wayne's passion for justice extended beyond interfaith dialogue. He felt a deep responsibility to speak out against oppression and injustice wherever he saw it. He penned letters to spiritual leaders, including the Pope, Cardinals, even the leaders of the Anglican Communion — urging them to take a public stand on the issue of Tibet. He challenged these powerful figures to support the Tibetan people's right to independence and sovereignty from Chinese occupation, reminding them of their moral obligation to address global injustices.

It might be easy to imagine Wayne as a fiery agitator, a thorn in the side of the establishment. But he also possessed a unique ability to challenge authority with humility, love, and respect. Even those he confronted found themselves drawn to his gentle spirit, grounded in an unwavering conviction. He cultivated a close friendship with Cardinal George, the Archbishop of Chicago, who deeply respected Wayne's commitment to justice and his grounding in the contemplative life. Their bond was so strong that Cardinal George presided over Wayne's monastic vows into the Benedictine order, a testament to their mutual admiration and shared faith.

This friendship proved to be a lifeline for Wayne. When he was diagnosed with cancer, he lacked health insurance. Through his profession of vows and the unwavering support of Cardinal George, he was able to receive the care and insurance he needed, a testament to the compassion and generosity at the heart of the Church. This act of kindness underscored the complexity of Wayne's relationship with the institution he often challenged, revealing a nuanced interplay of critique and belonging.

Wayne truly lived as a monk in the world. His tiny one-room apartment in Chicago was a testament to his simple lifestyle. He needed little to sustain himself, content with his books, his writing, and the rich tapestry of human connections. Despite his limited means, he was also incredibly generous, always ready to share what little he had with others.

I had the opportunity to witness his life of simplicity firsthand. He generously invited me to sleep on his couch in his tiny apartment the weekend he was to take his Benedictine vows. At the time, he was cancer-free, having successfully battled his first bout with the disease. However, his dear friend Dr. Martha Howard worried about the health conditions of his apartment. It was cluttered and overflowing with stacks of books, papers, and folders, leaving little room to move. Dust gathered on every surface.

Friends like Martha and Barbara, who had braved the labyrinth of his apartment, were concerned about his living conditions and offered to help clean, but Wayne always politely declined. He knew exactly what was in each pile of papers and books, a filing system that only he understood. During my visit, I had a day to myself while Wayne was out. I offered to tidy up his apartment some. To my surprise, he agreed.

I spent the entire day immersed in his world, carefully dusting, cleaning, and organizing without disturbing his precious stacks of research. By the time he returned, the apartment was transformed. He expressed his deep gratitude for the care I had taken to preserve his unique filing system of folders. He also appreciated how I reorganized his prized possession, his books, which overflowed his small bookshelf, spilling onto the floor, counters, and even chairs. He had a world class collection of contemplative literature that he ultimately bequeathed to the Church of Conscious Harmony.

During my cleaning spree, I stumbled upon a book titled *From Science to God* by Peter Russell. Intrigued, I began reading and was immediately captivated by its exploration of spirituality and quantum physics. Wayne, noticing my interest, generously gifted me the book. Later that evening, we attended a party at a friend's house. As we arrived, we were greeted by three of Wayne's closest friends. When he told them I had cleaned his apartment, they spontaneously dropped to their knees in gratitude, offering a playful pranam. I was touched by their heartfelt appreciation and amused by the dramatic gesture of these three women.

The party was a whirlwind of fascinating conversations and connections. As we moved through the crowded rooms, Wayne introduced me to his "Chicago tribe" — a diverse and vibrant community of artists, activists, and spiritual seekers. And then, with a mischievous twinkle in his eye, he introduced me to Peter Russell, the author of the very book I had just finished reading. It was a delightful synchronicity, and I spent the rest of the evening engrossed in a conversation with Peter about the fascinating intersection of quantum physics and spirituality.

The Mystic

The day of Wayne's profession of vows was a momentous occasion, a convergence of worlds. The Benedictine monastery in Chicago was filled to capacity with his diverse community — friends, colleagues, spiritual leaders, and dignitaries from various traditions. And in true Brother Wayne fashion, he defied expectations. Instead of the traditional black robe of a Benedictine monk, he entered the procession adorned in the saffron robes of a Hindu sannyasa. He was, after all, already a monk, a renunciate who had taken vows under Father Bede Griffiths years earlier in the heart of India.

Now, before Cardinal George himself, he was taking cross vows, bridging two seemingly different traditions. We, the witnesses to this sacred ceremony, felt the sacredness of the moment. This wasn't just a personal milestone for Wayne; it was also a symbolic spiritual gesture, a powerful testament to the emerging interspiritual movement. His life, his very being, embodied the essence of a universal spirituality, a harmonious blending of contemplative traditions in the pursuit of truth and unity.

Wayne was a true renaissance man, a pioneer who navigated the boundaries of faith with grace and wisdom. His journey serves as a shining example of evolutionary spirituality, a testament to the potential for unity within and between the great traditions. He showed us that the path to the Divine is not singular but multifaceted, a tapestry woven from the threads of diverse spiritual experiences. Brother Wayne's cross vows represented several milestones.

> *Presiding Authority*: His Benedictine vows were presided over not by a mere Abbot or Bishop, but by Cardinal George himself, a figure just one step removed from the Pope. This signifies the gravity with which the Church regarded this event, recognizing its potential to reshape the landscape of interfaith relations.

> *Official Sanction:* Wayne's interspiritual ministry, often seen as pushing the boundaries of traditional Catholicism, was not only accepted but actively embraced by the Church hierarchy. This signaled a profound shift, an openness to exploring new avenues of spiritual expression and dialogue.

Integration of Traditions: His earlier sannyasa vows under Father Bede Griffiths had already woven together the contemplative dimensions of Hindu and Christian mysticism. Now, with his Benedictine vows, he further solidified this bridge between East and West, demonstrating the universality of the contemplative path.

Symbolic Attire: His decision to take Benedictine vows while wearing the *kavi*, the saffron robe of a Hindu renunciate, was a powerful visual statement. It symbolized the harmonious coexistence of different spiritual paths, a tangible representation of interspiritual unity.

Fulfillment of Vatican II: These cross vows, in their essence, fulfilled one of the key aims of the Second Vatican Council of 1962: to foster dialogue and mutual respect between different religions. Wayne, in his life and practice, embodied this vision, paving the way for a more inclusive and interconnected spiritual landscape.

The scene was both striking and surreal. Wayne, a radiant figure in his blazing orange saffron *kavi*, processed solemnly down the aisle of the monastery church, a simple candle flickering in his hand. At the altar stood Cardinal George, fully vested in the miter and crozier of a Bishop, his presence radiating authority and tradition. As the ancient liturgy unfolded, its words echoed through the hallowed space, weaving a tapestry of sacred intention.

Wayne, his voice filled with emotion, shared an inspirational reading he had prepared for this momentous occasion. Then, in a gesture of profound humility and surrender, he lay prostrate before the altar as Cardinal George intoned the monastic liturgy, consecrating his solemn vows. There was a palpable energy in the air, a sense of the Holy Spirit's presence permeating the sanctuary. An aura of holiness enveloped us, touching our hearts, minds, and souls.

It was a moment of profound spiritual significance, a mystical passage through a membrane between worlds. It felt as if a new cell was being birthed within the body of Christ, a cell infused with the spirit of Interspirituality, sanctioned from within the heart of the mother church. A seed was planted that day, a seed of unity and understanding that would blossom in the years to come.

I believe history will recognize the significance of Wayne's cross vows, marking them as a turning point for the Roman Catholic Church, the Christian tradition, and the interspiritual movement as a whole. They offer a glimpse of a truly "catholic" — "universal" — Christianity. A faith that embraces the richness and diversity of the world's spiritual traditions while remaining rooted in its own unique identity. Wayne's vows were a harbinger of things to come, a testament to the ever-evolving nature of faith and the boundless potential for unity and love.

The reception following Wayne's profession of vows was a celebration of his life and his unique interspiritual path. During the dinner, a priest friend of Wayne's offered a heartfelt toast, recounting their shared walks through the streets of Chicago. He marveled at how Wayne would not only stop and talk with the homeless individuals they encountered along the way but the friendship he had with them, his heartfelt respect and genuine concern for their well-being. Wayne was able to look into their souls and recognize them in their essence, beyond their circumstances. He recognized their inherent humanity and knew them each by name.

Walking with Wayne

A friend shared a story that perfectly illustrated Wayne's compassionate nature and his tendency to exist in his own time zone. He had been late for a walk with this friend, arriving breathless and excited. The reason for his tardiness? He had been rescuing a falcon! He had witnessed the bird falling from the sky and landing injured in the middle of busy Lake Shore Drive. Without hesitation, Wayne rushed into traffic, comforting the dazed creature and praying for its recovery. Traffic miraculously parted around him as he tended to the falcon, which eventually regained its strength and soared back into the sky. Only then did Wayne continue on his way to meet his friend.

I, too, had the opportunity to experience many long walks with Wayne through the streets of Chicago. We encountered countless homeless individuals along the way, and I never once saw him pass by someone in need without acknowledging them, looking them in the eye, and engaging them in conversation. He didn't just see a homeless person; he saw Christ. He always carried extra bills, ready to offer not just a token gesture but a meaningful gift of support.

Walking with Wayne was a humbling experience, a lesson in compassion and presence. But it also revealed why he was perpetually late for everything. He was often lost in another world, operating on his own unique sense of time and space. And because he was so beloved, people made space for him and his peculiarities.

Once, I was staying with Wayne when he was scheduled to give a keynote address at a dinner conference across town. We embarked on our journey, a combination of walking and train rides, punctuated by numerous stops to connect with people along the way. Needless to say, we arrived late. But Wayne, unfazed, proceeded to captivate the audience, his tardiness forgiven by the wealthy Chicagoans who had paid a hefty sum per plate to hear him speak. He had, after all, been attending to more important matters, encountering Christ in the faces of those he met along the way.

His dear friend Martha shared a similar story about a time she was supposed to drive Wayne to O'Hare airport for a trip to Cape Town, South Africa, to attend a Parliament of World Religions event. She arrived at his apartment, expecting him to be packed and ready to go. Instead, she found him calmly baking Cornish hens! He explained that he was preparing a meal for some homeless friends before leaving. Martha, initially stressed about missing their flight, helped him finish the meal, and they delivered it together to Wayne's friends before rushing to the airport, making their flight just in time.

Miracles and Divine Intervention

Wayne's life was punctuated by a series of miracles and synchronicities. He once shared a story about a near head-on collision with a tractor-trailer. Just as the impact seemed inevitable, an unseen force took control of the steering wheel, miraculously maneuvering the car to safety. He felt a divine presence guiding him, an angel intervening to protect him.

Another memorable story unfolded at a conference in downtown Detroit. Wayne burst into a room where people were waiting for him, exclaiming, "Come quickly! Follow me!" He gathered a group of eight friends and led them on a hurried pursuit through a seemingly dangerous part of the city. He explained that he had found an injured bird earlier and wanted to help it. As they searched for the bird, a group of large African American men gathered, curious about these strangers in their neighborhood. Wayne shared his concern for the bird, and the leader of the group, moved by his compassion, declared, "If you are willing to come into a neighborhood like ours to help a little injured bird, then we are indeed brothers." Together, they searched for the wounded creature, united in a shared act of compassion.

Wayne's unique relationship with time extended to his retreats. During a silent retreat, with everyone meditating in a circle, the loud ticking of a mechanical clock disrupted the stillness. Eventually, Wayne got up and, while everyone was meditating, he quietly picked up the clock and walked toward the kitchen. We heard the refrigerator door open, and then silence: no more ticking clock. It was like Wayne stopped time, silencing the intrusive tick-tock by placing the clock inside the fridge. It was a classic Brother Wayne move.

Wayne was beloved by many. One of his close friends was Tenzin Choegyal (TC), the Ngari Rinpoche, the Dalai Lama's youngest brother. Sometime after Wayne's passing, TC and his wife visited me and my family in Austin. I knew how close he was to Wayne as he introduced us many years before. I wanted to give him something to remember Wayne by. I was inspired to grab a small wooden box containing some of Wayne's sacred keepsakes. When I opened the box, TC's eyes lit up. He reached in and pulled out a string of prayer beads, exclaiming with joy that he had given those very beads to Wayne. It was a beautiful moment of connection and remembrance.

The Parliament of the World's as Sacred Community

Inspired by Wayne's work with the Parliament, I submitted a proposal for a panel discussion at the 2018 Parliament of the World's Religions in Toronto. While writing the proposal, my wife Lisa, who managed the office for the Church of Conscious Harmony, stumbled upon a small unpublished booklet written by Wayne titled "The Parliament as Sacred Community: The Dawn of the Second Axial Age." Rather than throwing it away, she thought I might be interested in reading it, so she brought it home with her that day. It was a remarkable coincidence, as the proposal that I was writing at that very moment was focused on the very topic of Wayne's booklet. He wrote about the Parliament's signature document, The Global Ethic, a document Wayne had helped to create. The proposal was accepted, and at the end of my panel discussion at the Toronto Parliament, we ended up reading the concluding prayer at the end of his booklet.

The Mystic Heart and the Spirit of Friendship

I visited Wayne many times during his writing of *The Mystic Heart* and witnessed his deep immersion in the process of writing this masterwork. He shared with me that it was an inspired work. Prior to his writing sessions, he would enter a meditative state to align himself with what was expressing through him. The foreword to the book by the Dalai Lama and the preface by the mystic Beatrice Bruteau wonderfully set the tone for introducing the topic of Interspirituality. In true Brother Wayne fashion, he included a long list of acknowledgments to his many friends at the beginning of the book, and also included thanks to their pets, reflecting his deep love for all beings.

Wayne had many cherished friendships. He had the capacity to quickly meet people at the soul level. Spiritual friendship was so important to him that he devoted an entire chapter to this topic in his book, *A Monk in the World*. Over the years, he introduced me to many of his friends, some of whom have become some of my best friends. He introduced me to one of my closest friends, Art DelVesco, a dear brother who also became both a meditation partner and business partner. We co-founded ContemplativeLife.org, a nonprofit that serves as a digital hub to connect people and communities with transformative practices. The work of Contemplative Life is in many ways a continuation of Wayne's interspiritual legacy. My friendship and partnership with Art is a testament to Wayne's ability to connect people and inspire meaningful relationships.

Through Wayne's legacy, I also met my good friend Kurt Johnson. It was through Kurt that I was introduced to my colleague David Sloan Wilson. In the years to follow, David and I would go on to co-found Prosocial.world, a non-profit whose mission is to consciously evolve a world that works for all. ProSocial World also forged a partnership with Contemplative Life and created ProSocial Spirituality. This is an initiative that explores the integration of evolutionary science and Elenor Ostrom's Nobel Prize winning 8 core design principles with evolutionary spirituality and Brother Wayne's 9 elements of Interspirituality. A short video produced by the Templeton Religion Trust that provides an overview of ProSocial Spirituality can be located by searching "ProSocial Spirituality" at YouTube. These organizations and their work are contemporary examples of how the interspiritual movement is gaining momentum in the modern era.

A Sacred Passage

Wayne's transition from this world was shrouded in mystery and grace, marked by a series of synchronicities and subtle miracles. When Lisa and I offered him a place to live with us in Austin during his second battle with cancer, we were overjoyed when he accepted. However, we didn't have a spare bedroom at the time. With faith as our guide, we began our search for a new home. We began with a simple prayer: "Lead us to the right and perfect home that will bless our family and meet all our needs."

Our limited budget narrowed our options. It was hard for us to find a home with four bedrooms that we could afford in our neighborhood. After working with an agent and looking at many houses, Lisa was drawn to a house in our neighborhood that had been on the market for two years, an unusually long time for Austin. For some reason, the listing didn't mention a fourth bedroom. Lisa had been in a similarly built home in our neighborhood and believed that it must have a fourth room that wasn't listed. The yard was overgrown with weeds from the many months it was vacant. As we stepped inside, we were greeted by an unexpected sight: crystals hung in every window, as if someone had been trying to infuse the house with positive energy. And indeed, there was an extra bedroom. Above the fireplace was a framed picture of the house with a prayer at the bottom of the photo that was almost word for word of the prayer we started with at the beginning of our search. The inscription read: "May this be the right and perfect house to bless you and your family and meet all of your needs." Tears welled up in our eyes; this was clearly the home that was destined for us. It became our sanctuary that we lovingly referred to as "Wayne's Home."

Final Moments and Surrender

As the time for Wayne's move approached, I traveled to Chicago to pack up his belongings from his tiny apartment, which included his library of contemplative literature. At the time, he was staying in a high-rise apartment with his dear friends Martha and Gene. His body was weakened by radiation and his spirit weary. Seeing him in such a fragile state, unable to eat solid food and relying on a feeding tube, filled me with sadness. At the end of the day after I packed up his apartment, he requested a visit one last time. As we entered, I could sense his heart sinking. He expressed gratitude for my help, but I also felt the weight of his sadness. On our drive back to where he was staying, I asked him what he was learning from his experience at this time in his life. His simple and humble reply: "Surrender." We followed our conversation with a long period of silence.

A Peaceful Passing and a Wilted Flower

I returned to Austin, planning to go back to Chicago in two weeks to accompany Wayne to his new home. A few days passed, and I gave Wayne a call to check in on him. He seemed confused, asking if I was coming to see him that week. I attributed it to fatigue or medication, but after his passing, I realized he had sensed his time was near and wanted to see me one last time. That evening, he died peacefully in his sleep, his palms pressed together in prayer resting on the side of his cheek, reminiscent of the Buddha's posture in his final moments.

Back in Austin, we had prepared Wayne's room with love and anticipation of his arrival. Lisa had placed a beautiful yellow flower in the window of his room, a symbol of hope and welcome. Upon hearing the news of his passing, we noticed the flower had wilted, a poignant reflection of our shared grief. I recalled Wayne telling me about a recent encounter with the Dalai Lama, who had casually mentioned that Wayne wouldn't be around in another year. At the time, Wayne thought that was his friend just being playful, as the Dalai Lama has a wonderful sense of humor. It turned out to be a prophetic message.

Signs of Life and a Blooming Legacy

A few days after returning from Wayne's memorial service in Chicago, Lisa and I were astonished to find the yellow flower in his room had miraculously sprung back to life. It stood tall, turned toward the sun, and bloomed radiantly — a clear sign that Wayne's spirit had fully transitioned. It was as if Wayne was lovingly winking at us from the other side, in the form of a flower.

Wayne's most treasured possession was his large collection of books, which filled four pallets in my garage. In his will, he had bequeathed this library to the Church of Conscious Harmony. In a beautiful twist of fate, our son Jordan ended up cataloging the entire collection that summer as part of his high school senior honors project. It was a remarkable assortment of mystical literature from the great traditions, a testament to Wayne's scholarship and interspiritual vision. Brother Wayne's memorial library lives on in Austin as a resource for other contemplative pilgrims on the path.

The Tahara: A Calling to Serve

When Martha called and shared the news of Wayne's passing, I was filled with sadness. Afterward, I sat in tearful silence grieving the passage of our dear friend. I then reflected on how best to sacramentally prepare his body. Having co-founded First Light Funeral Guides, an organization specializing in end-of-life services, I was familiar with the sacred rites and rituals surrounding death and the holy preparation of the body practiced in various traditions. Later that evening, I felt a wave of inspiration enter my mind, heart, and body. Something washed over me. I felt compelled to travel to Chicago and see what I could do to help ensure that his body was cared for with the utmost reverence and intention. I was all too familiar with what happens behind closed doors in many funeral homes. The mission of First Light was to provide families with affordable and meaningful memorial options and to serve as an alternative to a sometimes predatory funeral industry. I felt called to intervene in Wayne's case and see what I could do to ensure that his body was prepared in a holy and sacred way. That evening, I received a vision for an interspiritual tahara ceremony, a ritual that was both rooted in ancient tradition and also infused with a contemporary understanding of Interspirituality, a ceremony that would honor his sacred passage and prepare his body for a holy burial.

Tahara is a Hebrew word meaning "purity." It is an ancient Jewish funeral rite involving the ritual washing and purification of the deceased. In the Jewish tradition, it's referred to as a mitzvah. A good deed performed to comfort the soul and prepare the body for its final resting place. Years earlier, my brother Don and I performed a tahara for our father, an experience that I shared with Wayne. Afterward, Wayne looked deeply into my eyes and said, "What a priestly thing to do." In that moment, he planted a seed in me that years later inspired me to do the same for him after his passing.

I sat down and began writing the interspiritual tahara liturgy, drawing inspiration from the many traditions that had shaped Wayne's life. At that time, our 13-year-old son, Jordan, came up to me and expressed his desire to accompany me to Chicago for Wayne's memorial. He, too, shared a deep bond with Wayne. I cautioned him about the intensity of the experience, but his resolve was unwavering. Together, we flew to Chicago, ready to offer this final act of love and service.

Martha and Gene welcomed us into their home, offering us the very room where Wayne had passed. Martha shared the details of his death and the arrangements she had made with the funeral home. The next day, we met with the funeral director. I shared with him my experience with First Light and asked if Martha, Jordan, and I could have some time alone with Wayne's body. He graciously provided us with a private room and ample time to perform the tahara. It was during the washing of Wayne's body that Martha, a doctor, discovered the true cause of Wayne's death. He didn't die from cancer as his MRI results from the day before confirmed. It had come back negative; the cancer was gone. Instead, he died peacefully in his sleep from a burst in his carotid artery, a rare but fatal side effect of his radiation treatment.

A Tapestry of Sacred Rituals

The details of the tahara ceremony remain sacred and secret, held in reverence for the ancient traditions that inspired it. What I can share is that the liturgy included a diverse tapestry of prayers, chants, and intentions drawn and woven from a variety of spiritual traditions that touched Wayne's life. We sacramentally cleansed his body, anointing it with chrism oil, the most sacred of oils in the Christian tradition. We chanted mantras and hymns, enveloping him with sacred sounds, invocations, and intentions of love and light. We clothed him in the saffron orange *kavi* he wore during his Benedictine profession of vows and then wrapped him in a white linen cloth, echoing the shroud of Christ.

We moved his clothed body into the casket. At this time, Martha had to leave. Jordan and I finished the ceremony by placing a number of mementos and sacred objects from his closest friends inside the casket. We then sealed the casket, and I offered a final prayer. I humbly asked for forgiveness for anything that I may have missed or done incorrectly. I prayed for his sacred passage into the realm of his next life, expressed gratitude for the love he so generously shared in this life and also prayed for the healing from grief that his many friends are experiencing as a result of his death. A profound sense of the divine presence filled the room as we entered into a period of long and deep silence. Then, Jordan and I embraced, tears flowing freely from the depths of our souls. In that moment, I felt an unparalleled closeness to my son, a sacred kinship forged in shared love and grief. It was a trinitarian experience, a gift from Wayne that we will cherish forever.

Reclaiming Sacred Traditions

In the tahara tradition, it is said that performing this rite of passage is among the greatest gifts one can bestow upon another, second only to giving one's life to save another. They say this because the recipient can never repay or thank you for this act of love. In truth, it was Wayne who bestowed the greatest gift upon us. By honoring him and his body, we were blessed and transformed beyond measure.

This experience offered a glimpse into the beauty and power of ancient death rites and the many sacramental traditions that have been sadly lost in our modern era due to an unhealthy fear of death and dying. Wayne's passage, and the sacred ceremony that followed, has rekindled a hope that we can reclaim these practices, restoring the reverence and intentionality that once guided our approach to death and dying and the sacred rite of passage of preparing the body. It serves as a vision of a future, drawing upon ancient rites and weaving it together with contemporary understanding.

Jordan became my hero that day. His willingness to participate in such a profound and intimate ceremony, to face his own fears and embrace the unknown, revealed a depth of maturity beyond his years. I experienced my young son as an old soul, a compassionate companion who also comforted me in my grief. I am eternally grateful for his presence and the profound bond we forged that day.

Wayne's Memorial: A Gathering of Souls

The following day, a funeral Mass was held at Holy Name Cathedral in Chicago, a grand gesture courtesy of Cardinal George. Holy Name, one of the most renowned cathedrals in the United States, was built after the Great Chicago Fire and served as a spiritual home for generations of American immigrants. It was a fitting place to gather and bid farewell to our dear friend, Brother Wayne, a man who embraced all souls with open arms.

The morning of the funeral dawned with a torrential downpour, rain falling in sheets, obscuring the windshield in a gray haze. As we drove toward the cathedral, a man jumped out in front of our car. It was a close call that left us shaken. We parked and made our way through the deluge, climbing the steps to the cathedral entrance. There, we saw the same man, drenched and wearing tattered clothes, seeking shelter within the cathedral. He was likely one of Wayne's friends from the streets, come to pay his respects. Inside, we noticed a number of other street people gathered toward the back of the church, a testament to the impact Wayne had on those often marginalized by society.

A Final Resting Place and a Heavenly Sign

After the service, a motorcade led us to a cemetery on the outskirts of Chicago, where a friend had donated a plot for Wayne's burial. He was laid to rest near the shores of Lake Michigan, beneath a towering cement cross. A simple committal service was held at the cemetery entrance, after which most of the mourners dispersed. A small group of close friends remained, gathering at his graveside for a final blessing. We stood in a circle, the rain-soaked earth beneath our feet. The rain had stopped but the sky was still heavy with dark clouds. We prayed, chanted, and scattered rose petals around the burial site as his casket was lowered into the ground.

Then, a miracle unfolded. Just as his casket touched the earth, an aperture opened in the clouds above, and a brilliant shaft of sunlight pierced through the darkened sky, bathing Wayne's gravesite in a sunny warm glow. The light illuminated each of us standing in the circle, a tangible manifestation of the divine presence. The wind swirled around us, seemingly coming from all directions. The opening in the clouds remained fixed above, a singular beacon of light in a sea of gray. It was an undeniable sign, a wink from God, affirming the radiant life Wayne had lived and the enduring warmth of his spirit. Our saddened hearts found solace in this celestial embrace, a reminder that his love and light would forever shine upon us.

An Enduring Legacy

As I reflect on Wayne's extraordinary life and enduring legacy, I am reminded of Albert Einstein's words about Gandhi: "Generations to come will scarce believe that such a one as this ever in flesh and blood walked upon this earth." Wayne, too, was such a soul, a beacon of compassion, wisdom, and interspiritual unity. His life was a testament to the transformative power of love, his passing a doorway to a deeper understanding of the sacredness of life and death. May his memory continue to inspire us to embrace the diversity of all spiritual paths, to walk with humility and compassion, and to build a world where peace and understanding prevail.

News of Wayne's passing sent shockwaves through his vast network of friends and colleagues. He was a beloved global spiritual figure, his friendships spanning continents and traditions. While many knew he was battling cancer, few suspected his time was so near. As a close friend and steward of his belongings, I felt a deep responsibility to share the news of his passing with his friends around the world and to offer closure and comfort to those whose lives he had touched.

I sent out a letter with news of his passing to his mailing list. I expressed the profound loss we all felt and also celebrated the radiant light Wayne brought into the world. I included a memorial bookmark I had created, a small token to help remind them of the essence of this extraordinary soul. I received many wonderful letters back from his friends, such as Cardinal George, The Dalai Lama, Beatrice Bruteau, Fr. Thomas Keating, Pir Viliat Khan, and many others.

About a year after Wayne's passing, a memorial gathering was held at The Crossings, a retreat center in Austin founded by his friends Ken and Joyce Beck. It was a large and heartfelt gathering of friends and colleagues, including his dear friends Martha, Father Keating, Dr. Kurt Johnson, and many more. It was at this memorial that I first crossed paths with Kurt Johnson, someone who has become a dear friend and a champion of Wayne's interspiritual vision. Kurt's dedication to carrying forward Wayne's legacy has been instrumental in the evolution of the interspiritual movement. This very anthology, commemorating the 25th anniversary of *The Mystic Heart*, would not be possible without Kurt's selfless service and his tireless efforts. I offer deep bows of gratitude to this holy and wise man.

The timing of Wayne's memorial in Austin coincided with the devastating impact from Hurricane Katrina, which brought a flood of refugees to Austin. The city's convention center and public spaces were overflowing with displaced families seeking shelter and support. After attending the Friday session of the memorial, Martha and I felt that the best way to honor Wayne was to spend the rest of the weekend volunteering to assist with the hurricane refugee crisis that was unfolding in Austin. Tens of thousands of refugees were being bussed into Austin from New Orleans, and the convention center and all other shelters were at capacity.

We made our way to the Austin Convention Center and received a brief orientation for volunteering. We were each assigned our respective stations. At the start of our shift, we were given a red volunteer shirt donated by a local Texas-based company. As we glanced at each other, we burst into laughter. The company's name, emblazoned across our shirts, was none other than "Wayne Industries!" It was a moment of pure synchronicity, a playful wink from Wayne, assuring us that his spirit was present, both with us and with the refugees of the hurricane. We spent the rest of the weekend working the midnight to 8 AM shift, our hearts filled with a sense of purpose and connection to Wayne's legacy of service.

The Toronto Parliament and Wayne's Guiding Hand

Years later, Kurt Johnson invited me to write an article on Interspirituality for a magazine published as part of the 2018 Parliament of the World's Religions in Toronto. He also suggested that I submit a proposal to speak at the Parliament. As I was working on the proposal, my wife Lisa returned home from work. That day she was reorganizing her office at the church and stumbled upon a small booklet by Wayne titled *The Parliament as Sacred Community: The Dawn of the Second Axial Age*. She was going to discard it but thought that I might be interested in reading it, so she brought it home to me. To my astonishment, the booklet mirrored the very themes I was writing about in my proposal, a remarkable coincidence that felt like a guiding hand from Wayne.

I submitted the proposal and received an email from Dr. Myriam Renaud, a Parliament representative, approving it. Excited, grateful, and knowing about Wayne's deep connection to the Parliament, I shared the story of Wayne's booklet with her. She replied that she was very familiar with Wayne's work and that part of her doctoral dissertation had focused on the Global Ethic, a document that Wayne had also worked on. I sent her a copy of Wayne's booklet and a picture of a framed Global Ethic document of Wayne's on the wall in my office. Her response was immediate and filled with laughter. She sent me a photo of the same framed document, also hanging on the wall of her office! It was another extraordinary synchronicity, a testament to Wayne's enduring presence and the interconnectedness of those who share his vision.

A Cosmic Prayer for the Sacred Community

The synchronicities surrounding the Toronto Parliament extended beyond the discovery of Wayne's booklet. At the end of our panel discussion, the moderator, a dear friend and colleague, Kate Sheehan Roach, felt a spontaneous urge to invite the audience into a large circle. Then, in a moment of unplanned inspiration, she asked someone to read aloud the prayer that Wayne had written at the end of his booklet, *The Parliament as Sacred Community: The Dawn of the Second Axial Age*.

This prayer, titled "A Cosmic Prayer for the Sacred Community," was a perfect culmination of our session, its words resonating deeply with the audience. It felt as if Wayne himself had orchestrated this moment, throwing a "forward pass into the future" that we were destined to catch. The prayer, a powerful invocation of unity, peace, and interspiritual understanding, is a testament to Wayne's enduring vision and his ability to inspire even from beyond the veil. Here are the words of this remarkable prayer:

A Cosmic Prayer for the Sacred Community
Brother Wayne Teasdale

0 Blessed One, eternal Source and Lord of creation, sustainer of all worlds. you embrace the whole cosmos within yourself, for everything exists in you.

Let your cosmic winds come and breathe your everlasting Spirit on us. Let us inhale you, divine Spirit and be inspired.

Enlighten us in your truth. Pour your grace into our hearts. Wipe away our sin and all negativity. Transform us into your Love, and let us radiate that Love to all others.

Inflame us with your unending life. Dissolve our limited way of being. Elevate us into your divine Life. Give us the capacity to share that Life with everyone.

Shape us in your wisdom. Grant us your gentle and healing sensitivity towards all creatures.

Give us your joy and laughter. Let us become that divine wisdom, sensitivity, laughter and joy for all beings.

Let us realize fully that we are members of that Sacred Community with all humankind, with other species, with Nature and the entire cosmos.

Grant us a heart that can embrace them all in you. Let us be in communion with you forever in the bliss of That Love: the Love that Dante knew so well "moves the sun and other stars."

Further Evolution of Interspirituality

Evolutionary Spirituality: A Quantum Shift in Consciousness

The interspiritual movement, like a grand tapestry woven through time, neither begins nor ends with Brother Wayne Teasdale. He served as a vital thread, a luminous voice articulating this emerging vision, much like Sri Aurobindo with Integral Yoga and Thích Nhất Hạnh with interbeing. But the seeds of Interspirituality were sown long before Wayne, and their fruits will continue to ripen for generations to come.

Interspirituality, Integral Yoga, and interbeing are all expressions of an evolutionary spirituality blossoming at the cusp of a quantum shift in human consciousness. Just as biological organisms evolve, so too does spirituality. Darwinian evolution, with its principles of variation, selection, and replication, provides a framework for understanding this process. These principles, traditionally applied to genetic and biological evolution, can also be generalized and extended to social, cultural, and indeed, spiritual evolution.

Interspirituality is inclusive, with an emphasis on inter-connectedness. It weaves together universal wisdom, contemplative experience and the practices of diverse traditions, which represents an evolutionary leap in spiritual understanding. It's no coincidence that this understanding is emerging alongside groundbreaking scientific discoveries in quantum physics, evolutionary science, neuroscience, contemplative science, and more, all pointing toward the profound interconnectedness of all beings and phenomena.

Conscious Evolution: A Call to Action

While traditional Darwinian evolution on a biological level unfolds over vast stretches of time, modern evolutionary science reveals that social and cultural evolution can happen quickly, and most importantly it can be conscious and intentional. This offers humanity great hope. Given the existential extinction level threats facing humanity, such as the environmental crisis and the potential for nuclear war, evolving consciously is no longer an option; it's a necessity. However, conscious cultural evolution calls for a transformation of both individuals and societies. It also requires an integration of inner work on oneself and outer action that serves the greater good.

Spiritual Pioneers and the Seeds of Change

When the time is ripe for a new idea to emerge, it often manifests through multiple individuals simultaneously. Spiritual pioneers like Sri Aurobindo, Bahá'u'lláh, Thích Nhất Hạnh, Paramahansa Yogananda, and Wayne Teasdale serve as vessels for these emerging understandings, their voices echoing a collective yearning for deeper meaning and connection. While these individuals play a crucial role in articulating and disseminating new ideas, the seeds of these transformations are often sown long before they take root.

For instance, the seeds of Interspirituality have been germinating for centuries, nurtured by mystics, philosophers, and spiritual seekers across traditions. The movement today is still in its early stages, gaining momentum and finding its unique expression in the 21st century. This very book is an anthology of the interspiritual movement over the course of the last 25 years since the publishing of *The Mystic Heart*. It documents the evolution and maturation of Interspirituality, revealing its diversity and potential to transform human consciousness.

A Timeline of Spiritual Evolution

Spirituality, like all aspects of life, is in a constant state of flux. Major spiritual movements often unfold over centuries, building upon and enriching one another. Interspirituality, for example, has roots in the intra-spiritual movement of ecumenism, which fostered dialogue and unity among diverse Christian denominations. This, in turn, laid the groundwork for the interfaith movement, promoting tolerance and cooperation between different religions. The interfaith movement then gave rise to the interreligious movement, encouraging deeper dialogue and understanding across religious boundaries.

The Parliament of the World's Religions is perhaps the most visible symbol, representing the apex of the interreligious movement. The first Parliament occurred in 1893 in Chicago, IL — the second Parliament, a century later in 1993. It was the 1993 Parliament that served as an incubator for the birth of Interspirituality and a catalyst for Brother Wayne sharing this next wave of spirituality with the world.

Interspirituality builds upon the foundation of interreligious dialogue but goes further, inviting practitioners to delve into the experiential, contemplative, and mystical dimensions of diverse traditions. It encourages us to practice each others' practices, to be nourished by each others' scriptures and wisdom teachings, and to recognize the underlying unity that connects all spiritual paths.

If we look back through the early to mid part of the 20th century, it was relatively uncommon for spiritual seekers to venture beyond their own traditions. However, toward the end of the 20th century and into today, we are witnessing a growing openness and interest in people from all faiths exploring the practices and wisdom teachings of other traditions. This spiritual diversity is a hallmark of Interspirituality and a testament to the evolving nature of spirituality itself.

The Rise of the "Nones," science, and the emergence of a New Spirituality

We are beginning to see a growing interest in the exploration and integration of science and spirituality. This is another example of our evolving consciousness. Over the last two decades, the Pew Research Center has been documenting a rapidly growing trend in the United States: the rise of the "nones," individuals who identify with no particular religion. This group, comprising agnostics, atheists, and those who describe their religious affiliation as "nothing in particular," has grown from 16% in 2007 to 28% in 2024, becoming the largest and fastest-growing segment of the US population. This shift may be attributed in part to a growing interest in evidence-based ways of knowing that comes from science and less reliance on faith and belief-based ways of knowing that comes from traditional religion.

Both science and spirituality seek to understand the mysteries of the universe, but through different lenses of perception and understanding. Science favors empirical data and outward experimentation, while spirituality emphasizes inner experience, wisdom, rites and rituals that are handed down through traditions. These two approaches to knowing, intellectual and experiential, are like the two hemispheres of the brain. They are different but also have the capacity to complement and balance each other. In the modern era through movements such as Interspirituality, we are beginning to see a growing receptivity for both cognitive knowing (science) and contemplative knowing (experiential spirituality) as equally essential ways of understanding and making sense of reality.

The exodus from organized religion may be a growing sign of a yearning for a new type of spirituality, one that values and embraces both scientific inquiry and contemplative experience. The emergence of Interspirituality may be an answer to this call.

Transforming Spiritual Transmission

Throughout history, religious institutions have served as the primary vehicles for spiritual transmission, relying on traditional hierarchies and established lineages. While these tried and true methods have been effective in preserving and transmitting spiritual wisdom throughout the ages, it may not be fully meeting the needs of today's seekers. The rise of the nones suggests a need for new forms of spiritual expression and community to emerge, something that resonates with a more diverse and interconnected world.

Thích Nhất Hạnh proposed that "possibly the next Buddha may take the form of a sangha," a community of practitioners. This vision of collective wisdom and shared leadership aligns with ethos Interspirituality, which emphasizes collaboration and a more collective and contemplative expression of human consciousness.

Converging Streams: Science, Spirituality, the Arts, and Technology

The past century has witnessed profound shifts in both scientific and spiritual understanding. New scientific disciplines like quantum physics, neuroscience, and contemplative science, and many more, are revealing a profound interconnectedness that exists within and between us and the cosmos in which we arise. This echoes ancient spiritual wisdom that comes from many of the contemplative traditions. Similarly, new spiritual paradigms like Integral Yoga, interbeing, and

Interspirituality are emphasizing the unity and diversity that underlies the cosmic mystery.

The convergence of modern science and contemporary spirituality is a new and hopeful development of our time. Also, new expressions of the arts and new innovations in technology are rapidly changing ways of knowing and what can be known and experienced. These four streams of science, spirituality, the arts, and technology each serve as a unique portal into the mystery of existence. If we can begin to approach these four streams in a highly conscious way, we may find that the synergy of these four streams of human experience open a portal into a state of quantum consciousness, a realization of our profound unity where the seemingly impossible is now possible. More than just the mere convergence of these four streams, this transformation will require the conscious integration of the new sciences, evolutionary forms of spirituality, experiential arts, and emerging forms of transformational technology. It will require us to infuse these four streams with a high degree of conscious intention, wisdom, and love to endure that what we design, engineer, and cocreate with these modern marvels are created to serve the aim of conscious and compassionate evolution for all.

A Contemplative Renaissance and the Birth of a New Humanity

The interspiritual movement is poised to catalyze a contemplative renaissance, an era marked by the integration of contemplative science and contemplative spirituality. This renaissance will usher in an age of conscious and compassionate evolution, fostering planetary healing and a deeper understanding of our interconnectedness.

This transformation will include the conscious convergence of science, spirituality, the arts, and technology, each stream contributing its unique possibilities to the whole. The new sciences will illuminate the reality of our interconnectedness. Interspirituality will guide us toward a more contemplative, compassionate, and inclusive experience of a universal spirituality. The new arts will reawaken our sense of wonder and experientially connect us with the beauty, mystery, and sacredness of existence itself. Consciously designed technologies that are developed to foster conscious evolution will provide us with superpowers that increase knowledge, collaboration, communication, and interaction with worlds and realities previously unknown.

The birth of a new humanity and a new civilization will also inevitably involve great pain and disruption on a massive scale. The dismantling of outdated patriarchal structures and the healing of generational trauma will require great courage, compassion, and patience. It will also require a willingness to embrace rapid change as the institutions and structures from a global culture of dominance dissolve and give way to an era of widespread cooperation. The pain will be immense and so will the progress. Through the formation of interconnected networks of compassionate communities, the collective fear that has been manipulating the fate of the human family will begin to give rise to collective spirit cooperation. This will give rise to what Brother Wayne referred to as a "civilization with a heart."

Signs of Hope and the Emergence of a Superorganism

The interspiritual movement is gaining momentum, as evidenced by the diverse voices and initiatives represented in this anthology. This organic emergence of interspiritual groups is a testament to its timeliness and transformative potential. As this movement matures, we will witness the formation of collaborative communities and networks. These networks will resemble an organism, with the potential to evolve into a conscious and compassionate superorganism, working together collectively for the well-being of all beings.

A clear sign that this transformation is underway will be widespread evidence of the embracing and embodiment of feminine principles and energies in all aspects of human society. This transition has more to do with energy than gender although it will involve a cultural shift of both. A great rebalancing of masculine and feminine energies is needed in both men and women and society as a whole. This rebalancing may prove to be the most important shift needed to facilitate the emergence of a new civilization. A clear sign that this movement is underway will also be a rapid increase of women in positions of leadership and authority. This will serve as an outward sign of an inward shift in human culture.

Three Levels of Ecumenism:
A Vision of Universal Unity

In closing, I want to share a profound insight that emerged from a conversation between Brother Wayne and Nudananda, two of my closest mentors. They met only once, sharing a contemplative walk through the streets of Chicago, but their dialogue gave birth to an idea that has deeply shaped my understanding of spiritual evolution: the "three levels of ecumenism."

The term ecumenism, derived from the Greek word *oikoumene* (the inhabited world), originally referred to the movement within Christianity promoting unity and cooperation among different denominations. Nudananda and Wayne expanded this concept to encompass a broader vision of spiritual unity, extending beyond the confines of any single tradition.

First Level: Intra-spiritual Unity: The first level of ecumenism encompasses the movement toward unity within specific spiritual traditions. This includes the efforts to foster harmony and cooperation among diverse Christian denominations, as well as similar movements within other religions. It's a recognition that despite differences in interpretation and practice, there is a shared essence, a common ground that unites those who walk a particular spiritual path.

Second Level: Inter-spiritual Unity: The second level of ecumenism expands this vision to encompass unity among all spiritual traditions. This is the essence of Interspirituality, recognizing the interconnectedness of all paths and the wisdom embedded within each. It's a movement toward mutual respect, understanding, and cooperation. Acknowledging the shared human yearning for connection with the Divine and the diverse ways in which this yearning is expressed. Wayne referred to this as the "religion of the third millennium," a spirituality that transcends the boundaries of individual traditions and embraces the richness and diversity of the human experience.

Third Level: Cosmic Unity: The third level of ecumenism extends beyond the terrestrial realm, encompassing a cosmic unity that includes all spiritual beings throughout the multiverse. Wayne and the monk recognized that our interconnected universe is teeming with life, both physical and spiritual, and that our human family is but one small part of this vast cosmic tapestry. This level represents a quantum leap in consciousness, a recognition of our interconnectedness with all beings, both seen and unseen, earthly and celestial. It's an invitation to embrace our true identity as daughters and sons of the Most High, expressions of universal Love.

Embracing Our Cosmic Inheritance

This vision of three levels of ecumenism offers a profound framework for understanding the evolution of spiritual consciousness. It invites us to move beyond the narrow boundaries of home-team consciousness, to embrace a more expansive and inclusive and cosmic worldview, one that recognizes the interconnectedness of all beings and the underlying unity and diversity that binds us together. It's an invitation to step into our ancient inheritance as cosmic spiritual beings, to embody the common thread of our spiritual essence that flows through all cosmic creation. By awaking to and consciously embodying our common heritage, we participate in the great mystery, the unfolding of universal LOVE.

Some Final Notes

Wayne was a member of Monastic Interreligious Dialogue (MID). He co-drafted the Universal Declaration on Nonviolence with H.H. the Dalai Lama. Wayne became a close personal friend of the Dalai Lama, and, together, they co-founded an interspiritual collaborative called the Synthesis Dialogues.

Wayne introduced the Universal Declaration on Nonviolence to the MID where it was adopted as a formal project. Wayne also served with UNESCO on *The Role of the Religions in the Promotion of a*

Culture of Peace. In December 1994, he helped produce a document called the *Declaration on the Role of the Religions in the Promotion of a Culture of Peace*. These formational documents and corresponding initiatives helped serve as some of the core foundational work that underpinned the Parliament's signature document *Towards a Global Ethic* which had hundreds of revered spiritual signatories and was released at the 1993 Parliament of the World's Religions in Chicago.

Authored or Co-authored by Wayne Teasdale (carried by main booksellers)

Wayne's books, which became so historically influential regarding Interspirituality [see Kurt Johnson's piece in Volume 2 on Raimon Panikkar] and as listed at the main bookseller websites include:

> *Monastic Studies* – by Bernard Orchard; others Jacques Cote, Jean Leclercq, Bede Griffiths, Abhishikananda, Agnes Bokross, Wayne Teasdale; [Number Thirteen, Autumn, 1982]

> *Toward a Christian Vedanta: The Encounter of Hinduism and Christianity According to Bede Griffith*; Asian Trading Corp (January 1, 1987)

> *Cistercian Studies Quarterly* by Wayne Teasdale Jean Leclercq, Marie Anne Mayeski, Robert Musser, Paul E. Lockey, Daniel M. La Corte, James Conner, Jim Grote; Abbey of Our Lady of New Clairvaux, Vina, California (January 1, 1994)

> *Community of Religions* Hardcover – by Wayne Teasdale (Editor), George Cairns (Editor); Continuum (January 8, 1996)

The Mystic Heart: Discovering a Universal Spirituality in the World's Religions; New World Library (January 1, 1999)

A Monk in the World: Cultivating a Spiritual Life; New World Library; First Edition (January 1, 2002)

Bede Griffiths: An Introduction to His Spiritual Thought; SkyLight Paths; (May 1, 2003)

Catholicism in Dialogue: Conversations Across Traditions (Catholic Studies); Sheed & Ward (May 5, 2004)

Awakening the Spirit, Inspiring the Soul: 30 Stories of Interspiritual Discovery in the Community of Faiths; SkyLight Paths; 1st edition (June 1, 2004)

The Mystic Hours: A Daybook of Inspirational Wisdom and Devotion; New World Library (November 16, 2004)

Audio Book: *Bede Griffiths: Interspirituality for the 21st Century*; New Dimensions Foundation

Endnotes and References for "New Era" Section[ix]

Verse on Verse: On Interspiritual Lineage
by Matthew M. Cobb

As the interspirit of Spoken Word, Call and Response, Antiphonal Psalmody, Ancient Oracular and Rabbinical Responses, we respect the honored oral traditions that are still with us, here and now in this present moment, albeit in modern contexts that dispel and disfigure their

meaning and place in our communal life together. As perennialists, the prevailing view is founded on the presupposition that practice is what makes the path appear within a certain culture and language, while on a certain landscape. In the end, all cross cultural experiences have the initial capacity to deepen the root system of the original tradition into which we are born. In the meantime, it is possible to be born again within multiple paths of belonging from a variety of cultural contexts. Furthermore, bearing witness to each other from these various places will only enrich our shared experience of the fruits from the practice, because of the path we follow attuning on one line at a time.

Potential Chorus Lines

Meister Eckhard says, "God only spoke one word and in that word the whole creation, all time and space comes into being, in that one word."

John Cassian says, "In the end there will be one Christ loving himself."

Bede Griffiths says, "The model of the whole universe is distinction in unity: I in you and you in me."

Backdrop for the Continuity of an Ancient Tradition: Remembrance involves a common human nature for an evolution of...

Listen! Just one line is enough for a lifetime of coming and going, isn't it? You see, it's a total intercommunion and interrelationship, waiting to be recovered by an act of remembrance. The one, the ultimate, is present in Creation and in humanity from the beginning. Humanity still has this presence and can awaken because of an act of remembrance to this presence at any time. How far will this awakening spread at a time when there is also a crushing hostile force?

Hold! What is transpiring right now, as we witness not just one line at a time, but multiple lines as they emerge and converge, entangle and mingle to show more of this modern life of relative uncertainty, ambivalence, complexity, and interdependence? Crushing hostile forces and Awakening creative forces appear to be driving us onto the brink of self-annihilation or self-transcendence. Both either / or and black and white thinking are perilous pitfalls, and yet there is the possibility of discernment in the current potential of seeing the outcomes of life choices with more clarity.

Remembrance! Our ancestors walked everywhere, often for several days, and sometimes to meet an oracle or solitary soul for wisdom's sake — to face the demons and befriend them, thereby awakening them because of remembrances of being daemons or creative forces. On each step of remembrance, we also, as modern wanderers, hermits, and preachers, are re-presencing our relationship to wisdom and unveiling our capacity to walk on the edge of modernity to attain again, just one line to walk along the precipice of compassion.

Pause! We carve out space together here, for each other, so let's give thanks for that gift of walking in this ancient manner, as just one line can accompany each of us in accordance to our certain origin place. Walking with discipline and some risk exposure, albeit always on the precipice of the one line that draws us forward in the wilderness of our modern lives, will always cost us something. Let's imagine walking along during these waning days of the wild wild west show of modernity — "I think, therefore I am." Integral whole self, hidden at center of Creator Spirit, as common human nature touching divinity. Walking along together here, being moved by just one line, one spoken word of reality, is sufficient to carry us forward beyond this Cartesian Night Terror (c.f., cogito, ergo sum).

Imagine! These lines that we receive by inheritance from spoken word, oral lineages, are confluential revelatory song lines flowing along quite naturally, as contemplative faculties imbue us with a new vision that offers more allowances than advantages, more acceptance than entitlement? Perhaps, then for the first time, again, we will engage the effectual cooperation of walking back from this modern show on the terrain of someone else's heritage site and sacred place, thereby recovering and restoring us as an integral part of nature, which has the capacity to hold as a reflection, All That Is—Cosmic, Universal, Planetary Field of Mind.

Repent! Isn't that what an act of remembrance (aka, contrition) inhabits for us? An ancient future hidden within the universal movement of a common human nature is essential in order for recovery of insight and restoration of the sacred substance of which we are all made. The form offered herewith is referred to as Walks Back, and the function is contemplation-reflection of the sacred. As form follows function, there is a long line of hidden treasuries of beauty and wisdom found on ancient pilgrimage routes (i.e., land lines), where seekers and sages converge on monasteries and ashrams, heritage sites, and sacred places which continue to reveal both lines of confluence and conduit (i.e., story lines). As we flow together as a common human nature and receive a touch of the divine breath at these intersections of our multiple belongings, we are compelled and impelled from both beyond and within, an internal and external dynamism ever-flowing and ever-turning around center of Creator Spirit.

Seek! From a perennialist's vantage point, all of these ancient pilgrimage routes evoke a second simplicity, whereby we may know again the origin that seeks us. There are hidden within these ancient footprints existential lines of inquiry and discernment that actually make the walker's next hesitant step appear along the terrain of their own soul (aka, anima/animus), which gives pause for a formal cause to rise strong again in an act of remembrance on one's original path.

Ask! There is one line of wisdom that links up the footprints of every pilgrim's peregrination, "Wanderer, your destiny is not found at your destination site, nor is your indulgence merited by your place of fitness, instead look underneath the soles of each hesitant step." In the meantime, trust is the question and love is the solution that opens and turns the spiritual heart toward the impartial fine point of our souljourn, an interdependent Christ — the field of the fulfilment of our common human nature. Consider that disciples of the Christian ashram movement in India are discerning the emergence of a Perennial Christocentric Sadhana (PCS) in the field of interspiritual inquiry, while there already exists a direct offshoot from the life and teachings of Alan "Father Bede" 'Swami Dayananda' Griffiths (December 17, 1906 – May 13, 1993), a Christocentric perennialist oral lineage holder.

Knock! "I'm being overwhelmed by love," cried out Sw. Dayananda to his caregivers only six days after his first cerebral ischemic stroke. "Surrender to the Mother," was how Fr. Bede described his new cosmovision received during his breakthrough experience, which apparently ushered him onto an understanding of both Near Death Awareness and belonging to Christ as the common human nature. Fr. Bede lived his next two years full of energy and traveled extensively to bear witness and spread this revelatory dynamism that changed his heart and worldview.

Enter! Meanwhile, in south India, Fr. Bede often hosted Four O'Clock Talks to greet seekers and sages after chai. Ashramites and wanderers could share what they were learning and discovering along their life-way as the afternoon chai brought everyone together under the shade of the thatched canopy. Many times, synchronicities would appear, and certain guests might offer a contemplative practice with instructions during the Four O'Clock Talks.

Reinhabit! Sipping and tasting your mid-afternoon cup of chai under the thatched-roof shade within Shantivanam at Saccidananda Ashram. In a wellspring of light, a voice announces to everyone, "Come along, darlings, come along." It is Fr. Bede / Sw. Dayananda invoking with the vibratory lilt of an English country school teacher calling the children to return. As Bede walks back to the dharma hall, ashramites and pilgrims coalesce and converge their different life ways, standing up to follow him in order to better understand the mystery of this human journey toward wholeness and Divine Life. It is together here, in the imaginal realm, that we can care to extend our intention to learn from Dayanandaji, as good enough souljourner (ashramite and pilgrim), for another Four O'Clock Talk on what is souljourn (c.f., ashrama and pilgrimage) in the modern context.

Transfigure! Fr. Bede was not a guru, because most of his talks were internal wrestling matches, whereby he was distilling the wisdom from the ancient texts for a place in the modern world. There were also pointing out instructions for those seeking just one line of the truth for the spiritual heart's nourishment. Inevitably, the sharing of some sapiential message ended with Fr. Bede's recapitulation of the paschal mystery. "Go Beyond! Go Home!" Addressing both ashramite and pilgrim, so whether you were coming or going, as seeker or sage, the continuity of the recapitulation of the mystery was essentially found in Letting Go and Letting Come, on the precipice of belonging to a new cosmovision of real humanity.

Experiment! Here are some possible wrestling matches we can imagine encountering today, as we dive deep within the ashram of the wanderer's heart, perhaps taking the form of a beautiful challenge or dark incumbrance, such as:

What is the global capitalist market economy objectifying and speculating over next, while the children and indigenous are keeping vigil on the horizon of extinction? What cosmovisions are emerging in the planetary field to impel us to "Surrender to the Mother" and "Go Beyond"? So, what kind of authority will practical mysticism assert within this interspiritual lineage? Now, what new cosmovision of reality will we inhabit?

Rest! Fr. Bede is still engaging us in the imaginal realm as our natural power of contemplative and comparative faculties awaken to flourish again. Throughout all of Fr. Bede's talks, the formal cause of each human person was a unique expression of the recapitulation of a common human nature, the Christ Event. In this way, redemption is restorative, and salvation is regenerative, because just one line serves as the rapture of the *Return to the Center* of sacred humanity — woman, man, nature, and Creator Spirit. As the pinnacle and crown of the yogic path is samadhi, it is attained by passing through meditation or dayana into the bliss of samadhi, whereby one can make an oblation of fulfilment of life's purpose.

Offer! We are forever indebted in gratitude to Sw. Dayananda for awakening PCS in the form of an interspiritual lineage, whereby embodying meditation prepares us to be recipients of samadhi — an unswerving attention to bear witness to our common human nature, both the Christ Event Horizon[1] born from above and the lotus born Bodhisattva Yana welling-up (jharna) from below. Dayananda in his name, as such, is representing and represencing this possibility of ascending the yogic tree from darana to dayana. Darana exercising the comparative faculty and dayana the contemplative faculty.

Interspiritual Wrestling Matches

On just one line we can embrace the art of possibility, while holding the paradoxical tension between comparative and contemplative faculties.

What if the flow of dayana is represented as an internal harvest time, the cultivation of the fruits of the Wishfulfilling Tree?

Consider! Sw. Dayananda — Fr. Bede transmitting the revelatory context of an interspiritual wrestling match between converging lines on multiple levels, whilst on one field of play. What follows is an interspiritual exercise within an imaginal realm interaction with a devoted servant leader sharing his own intellectual vulnerability in the face of there being "No More Gurus" to magically implant knowledge of the sanata dharma. Just one line is sufficient for us to walk along as we move through the remembrance of an ancient future from secular to sacred, comparative to contemplative. Now, in the 21st century with the Zodiac Age of Aquarius initiating all sentient beings, there are only the inner gurus, inner voice of love and wisdom.

Shift! As the Yoga Sutras (i.e., YS) of Patanjali attest, there are Astanga (8 limbs) on the Wishfulfilling Tree. The 6th and 7th limbs are darana and dayana, while the 8th limb is samadhi (aka, Crown of the Wishfulfilling Tree). Considerate of the context, in the East

- meditation or dayana (7th limb) is what is commonly known as contemplation (c.f., contemplatio in the monastic practice of Lectio Divini) in the West. Whilst, in the West: meditation or darana (6th Limb) is what is commonly known as one-pointed concentration (c.f., ekagraha, YS) in the East. Darana engages volition (i.e., choice), where as dayana engages vinyasa (i.e., flow states of dynamic continuity). At this point, ascending between limbs 6 and 7, a threshold is crossed over. This threshold is also an autogenic shift, whereby there is a correlative transit from alpha to theta brain waves.

Repeat! Meditation in the West (darana) is a process in which we exercise our autonomy and self-determination by passing through the one-pointedness of mind (ekagraha), under the influence of concentration, into a vantage point shift from thinking to feeling — from thinking about the Divine to feeling and experiencing the Divine Presence. It is a journey from the complexity of the mind to the simplicity of the heart. Moreover, there is the high probability of coherence between heart and mind (viz., subtle heart). Beyond the subtle is the spiritual heart, which is on the causal level.

Presence! Darana provides a comparative faculty giving us unswerving bare attention to one-pointedness, whereby the concentration of the mind on one line prepares for the receiving of dayana from the contemplative faculty of the direct intuition of truth. This description of the differences between darana and dayana are intended to extend wide enough to capture a better understanding of dayana, while perhaps hinting at its deeper nuances and viability for comparative studies. The paradoxical tension to be held now is one that is capable of both giving and receiving, arising and passing, externalizing and internalizing from a new vantage point. Moreover, the emphasis on transcendence and immanence in reference to divine attributes can be recapitulated here with an emphasis on omnipresence, as the wanderer Walks Back on just one line.

Contextualize! Locating the *Coming Interspiritual Age* is transpiring to awaken a new cosmovision of reality that recapitulates an ancient future, whereby we dare to start again by stepping from Material Cause to Essential Cause to Formal Cause to Final Cause, standing back to witness the undercurrent riptide of academic-military-industrial complex coercing us toward more species extinctions in order to guarantee progress, sustainable development, and mutually assured growth without end. This is where Fr. Bede's *Return to the Center* provides pointing out instructions via the schools of Indian Buddhism, where an embodied dayana remains the penultimate step on the yogic path to liberation. And yet, this embodiment of dayana is an integral part of the eightfold path and the six perfections, or paramitas. The importance of dayana in the contexts of classical yoga and Sankara — an eternal interaction of spirit and matter (c.f., every prakriti has a purusha and every purusha is a prakriti) — traditions and in Indian bhakti, in both contemporary and premodern contexts, demonstrates its continuity within these other manifestations of the Indian religious heritage.

Iterate! Case in point, Mircea Eliade has extensively documented the development of yoga in relation to the ritual forms and practices of the Brahmanical sacrificial traditions. He traces the methodology of the rigveda ascetic types such as the rishis and munis through the process of ritual interiorization toward more recognizable forms of yoga in Hindu and Buddhist sects and traditions such as Theravada and Mahayana. He characterizes several historical phases of yoga, including Brahmanical, Classical, Sankara, Buddhist, and Tantric, which provide a foundation for understanding the many roles of yoga and meditation in the Indian context.

Expiate! Why is this significant for our wrestling match now? Because, Fr. Bede and the concurrent Indian Ashram movement were and still are criticized for their Brahmanization of a Christian cosmology and ethos, which appears extractive and colonialist. Geopolitically, during the current attempt to Saffronize India as a Hindu Nation, Eliade has resurfaced as an integral part of counteracting fundamentalist extremism, particularly on the issue of possible origins of yoga in the ancient Indus civilization, which for many represent the adjacent possibility of a pre-Vedic substratum of Indian culture. The importance of the so-called Indus yoga seal and the implication that some type of yoga practice is likely to have been present in the Indus context, Eliade largely accepts the pre-Aryan genesis of yoga.[2]

Overlay! *The Marriage of East and West* showcases a new form of complementarity and fulfilment as interdependent pairs. Over the past century, as Eastern forms of meditation (i.e., dayana) have migrated to the West (i.e., contemplatio), we see meditation playing a more expanded role within Hindu and Buddhist communities (i.e., sanata dharma), which demonstrates the tension between adaptation and appropriation in the religious thought and practice of these traditions. The study of meditation is an important point of intersection between cultures, a place of coming together that has both vitality and immediate relevance within the marketplace of spirituality and sacredness of secular society, as well as the development of its cultural and religious horizons.

Speculate! Throughout the secular age in the West, the decline of Christendom has brought many cases forward that no longer accept the one-sidedness of a historical Jesus as an object of cultic worship.

The final and most obvious aspect of late capitalism, however, is the progressive extension of the logic of the marketplace to all aspects of culture, including religion and spirituality. In the "market-like conditions of modern life," as Jürgen Habermas puts it, everything tends to become a commodity that may be bought and sold, from art to politics to religion itself.[3] Now forced to compete in the marketplace alongside other secular businesses and industries, religion itself tends to become yet another consumer product within the supermarket of values. The religious believer, meanwhile, is free to choose from a wide array of possible beliefs and to piece together his or her own personalized/customized spiritual pastiche/playlist.

Future! Max Weber's metaphor of religion striding into the marketplace of worldly affairs and slamming the monastery door behind, becomes further transformed in modern society with religion placed in the consumer marketplace. Individuals are able to select from a plurality of suitably packaged bodies of knowledge in the supermarket of lifestyles. The western religiosity appears caught up in transactional objects of worship (c.f., idolatry) projected as cognitive structures of dogma, which imprison the little "free" wills of believers, rather than awakening hearts to experience the mystery of the Cosmos and human race.

Plant! Considering the Interspirituality of Sachidananda Ashram / Ashram of the Holy Trinity (aka., Shantivanam, Forest of Peace), the mystical consciousness of Christ as a translational subject is awakened. "Christians need to open their hearts to Christ within, experience Christ within as their guru (i.e., teacher or rabbi). This is the function of the ashram."[4,5,6] Christ is experienced not as a teacher outside, but as the inner guru, the Sadguru, who transfigures and transpires us from within the cave of the Heart. Meditation, as a soaking into the depth of reality, thus becomes a mystical experience of the Christ Event Horizon within an embodied cognition of contemplative and comparative functions. In a trustworthy process, this is a revelatory event horizon of one's being, ontological and epistemological salves that anoint our categorical mistake of denying our teleological substance and real presence as theandric *Homo sapiens* (i.e., woman (anima), man (animus), nature and divine).

Root! Through meditation, one realizes that one is a branch on the vine of Christ, a spark of the divine fire that the Spirit of Christ inflames, a stream from the divine fountain that is opened in Christ. At a time when people are giving up on the language of conceptual theology and the symbols of routine liturgy, the church (i.e., human institution) must recapitulate ("Surrender to the Mother" and "Go Beyond") and reveal the mystical dimensions of Christ's real presence in the Christ Event Horizon. It is in this multidimensionality of belonging where interspiritual ashrams and sadhanas (c.f., PCS) make a significant contribution to the evolution of Interspirituality. In the meantime, there is a danger within Christian spirituality to practice Centering on the human Jesus and losing sight of the divine mystery, which is revealed on the Christ Event Horizon. The ashram is leaven, inconspicuous, feeble but essential, and called to bear witness to the mystery of Christ Event Horizon, hidden wholeness of the One Heart, and those in the ashram are called to awaken the church to this mystery.[7]

Place! An ashram is a place of silence, an oasis of stillness, whence all labor (i.e., efficiencies) bow to leisure (i.e., sufficiency). The distinctive feature of an ashram is its culture of meditative pursuits. Seekers come to an ashram in search of guidance on one of four interspiritual lifeways or ashramas. These four ways of living are student, householder, forest dweller, and renunciate. Ashramas find purpose and meaning within ashrams. Albeit quite quiet inside, there is an adjacent possibility that in the phrenetic divergence of modernity, the real ashram is an ashram of one with the inner guru at the center. "Ashram is in the heart of a guru and in his personal contact in the depth with the Indweller."[8] In the process of integral meditation, one deepens one's consciousness to realize the divine depth of reality and expands it to perceive the divine in all things.[9]

Redeem! In an interspiritual ashram, primacy is given to the relentless quest through sadhanas (viz., interspiritual discipline and integral practice). It is a sacred place whereby, above all else, common people can experience divinity, as such, and live in an ever-deepening awareness of real presence — a souljourner's quest from sacramentum to *res*, from rhetoric to reality. This is curated by a simple renunciation and authentic attachment within a setting of silence, stillness, peace, and joy that is committed to lifelong seeking and telling of the truth. When there is final cause for a pause to tend and touch what we are, there is sufficient energy for creative expression to come along, turn around, dismantle, and go beyond.[10] Both ashramite and pilgrim are formal cause for rejoicing, because there exists One Heart Christ Event Horizon for the full participation in the transfiguring and redeeming of the substance of which we are made.[11]

Commune! Now what is requested, is that the word "union" be reconsidered and reconfigured to more accurately represent (i.e., represence, remembrance) not so much a rare and unimaginable operation, but more of something that is both exposed to risk and valued to be worth attainment. In a vague, imperfect fashion, at every moment of this conscious life, within an embodying of both an intensity and a thoroughness in all the more valid moments of that life, we can only know anything by uniting with it; by assimilating it; by an interpenetration of it and ourselves; by suffusion of the woman (anima), man (animus), nature and Creator Spirit. It gives itself to us, just insofar as we give ourselves to it; and it is because our outflow toward things is usually so perfunctory and so languid that our comprehension of things is so perfunctory and languid too.

Converse! "Walking along to the place of the wise, is to escape the flame of separation." Wisdom (i.e., sapientia) is the fruit of communion between Divine Life and common human nature. The signified is samadhi — the fusing of both individual and universal light (i.e., Light on Light) — which sheds light on those who "keep themselves to themselves" and stand apart, judging, analyzing, criticizing, and demonizing the sacred, which they have forgotten or have not experienced. Here commences the work and ministry of Interspirituality, as just one line holds an interspiritual lineage to reveal what is real by dispelling the darkness of ignorance and the fear of the other or the other side. Walks Back to common human nature, Christ Event Horizon — One Verse, One Line at a time.

Endnotes and References for "Lineages" Feature[x]

The Pioneering Interspiritual Teaching of
Dr. Ed Bastian and the Interspiritual Paths Institute

[adapted from a fuller text that will be subsequently published
(in our Volume 3), as detailed in Volume 2[1] — it includes extensive materials on
spiritual practice that we can share in full therein]

by John A. Wilde

A teacher comes, they say, when you are ready.
And if you ignore its presence, it will speak to you more loudly.
But you have to be quiet to hear.
—Robin Wall Kimmerer

Since 2013, I have had the privilege of working closely with Dr. Edward Bastian as he took his innovative InterSpiritual wisdom and practices to the internet. He was that teacher who I was ready for.

Like many of you, I have enjoyed finding wisdom and practices from many sources. Christianity has been my main source for most of my life, but in recent years, and especially since I retired from serving congregations as a Presbyterian pastor, I have been able to expand my exploration of the great variety of wisdom and practices on our planet. Like many of you, I was on the InterSpiritual path long before it was named by Wayne Teasdale in 1999. Like many of you, I have encountered many pioneering teachers of InterSpiritual wisdom and practices from previous centuries as well as the current one. My journey has taken me to amazing places. I have been guided by some great teachers from within and beyond Christianity. Even before I went to seminary and was ordained as a Presbyterian minister, I was influenced by writers including Herman Hesse, Ken Keyes, Jr, and Nikos Kazantzakis who made it abundantly clear that Christianity did not have a monopoly on spiritual wisdom and practices.

During the 1980s when I was serving a church in Dearborn, Michigan, I participated in several courses offered by The Institute for Advanced Pastoral Studies (later re-constituted as the Ecumenical Theological Seminary of Detroit). Dr. John "Jack" Biersdorf taught these courses. He was a United Church of Christ minister who had studied and practiced Buddhist meditation, and I learned a lot from him. He led me to a new appreciation of the great variety of wisdom and practices beyond Christianity. Before he died in 2020, he wrote *The Infinite Reach* where he describes how science and religion are finding common ground.

In the '70s, '80s and '90s, I regularly read *Cultural Information Service*, *Values and Visions* and other educational guides offered by Frederic and Mary Ann Brussat. I found these resources very useful as a pastor. Since 2006, their *Spirituality & Practice* website has been a leading source of wisdom and practices offered by a huge variety of spiritual and cultural teachers from many religions and cultures. Over the years, I have taken many wonderful e-courses offered by *Spirituality & Practice*. Two of these courses led me to Edward Bastian and other Spiritual Paths Institute teachers.

As a young adult, Ed worked with the famous documentary filmmaker Lowell Thomas. In India, he met the Dalai Lama and other Tibetan Buddhist teachers. This led to an immersion in Buddhist wisdom and meditation. Later, Ed furthered his studies in Tibetan Buddhism receiving a Ph.D. at the University of Wisconsin.

Ed became a close friend of Thomas Keating when he was working in Aspen, Colorado, in the '90s. When there was a vacancy for the Buddhist representative in Father Keating's Snowmass gatherings of experienced meditators from many Wisdom Traditions, Ed became the experienced Buddhist meditator. You can read about these meetings in *The Common Heart: An Experience of Interreligious Dialogue* edited by Netanel Miles-Yépez. This experience changed Ed forever and led to the creation of the Spiritual Paths Institute in 2002. After Ed met Wayne Teasdale in 2004, he and the Spiritual Paths Institute faculty embraced the InterSpiritual paradigm and developed an InterSpiritual purpose and curriculum. Soon, many courses and workshops were offered in Aspen and at several other locations in the US and Canada.

Once the Spiritual Paths Institute was well established, Ed wrote two books offering an abundance of InterSpiritual wisdom and practices: *InterSpiritual Meditation: A Seven-Step Process from the World's Spiritual Traditions* and *Mandala: Creating an Authentic Spiritual Path: An InterSpiritual Process.* It was during these formative years that the seven steps of InterSpiritual Meditation were created by Ed and his colleagues. They are based on his experiences with Thomas Keating and others at the Snowmass gatherings and on his collaboration with Spiritual Paths faculty and students. *InterSpiritual Meditation* is the text for the InterSpiritual Meditation e-course offered by Spiritual Paths. *Mandala* is the text for the Mandala e-course.

It was through two *Spirituality & Practice* e-courses that my contact with Ed and the Spiritual Paths community began. In 2010, I enrolled in the InterSpiritual Wisdom e-course with 42 reflections by members of the Spiritual Paths faculty: Dr. Ed Bastian, Swami Atmarupananda, Rabbi Rami Shapiro, Rev. Cynthia Bourgeault, Shaikha Camille Helminski, and Shaikh Kabir Helminski. There are Six themes offered for reflection, one for each of 6 weeks: Forgiveness; Self-knowledge; Self-emptying; Interdependence & Reciprocity; Courage; and Love & Compassion. Then in 2011, I enrolled in the InterSpiritual Meditation e-course which includes 42 lessons on the 7 steps of InterSpiritual Meditation. Ed is the sole teacher. They are excellent e-courses, and they are available for purchase at SpiritualityandPractice.com.

I was hooked. Never had I felt such a deep connection to so much of my journey. The Spiritual Paths e-courses based on Ed's two books mentioned above began in 2014, and I was there. I have participated in these two courses again and again since then.

Ed taught a weeklong seminar at the Omega Institute in 2013. It was a wonderful week. He told us about the InterSpiritual Mentor program which he was planning to begin that year. I signed up and was among a group of mentor students who met monthly for the next four years. In 2017, six of us became the first InterSpiritual mentors certified by the Spiritual Paths Institute. Now there are many more.

Many of you are familiar with the wonderful contribution to InterSpiritual Wisdom and Practices offered in the two forementioned books and in the 2 e-courses. The Spiritual Styles Profile Tool is a great way to get started. You can find it on the Spiritual Paths website as prompted there by the link "spiritual-styles-profile" and in the *Mandala* book. There are 60 questions. It takes 20 to 30 minutes. If you do it via the website, you get back a bar chart and a pie chart indicating which spiritual styles you naturally favor. I have done this several times over the years. It's interesting to see that some of my preferences stay the same and some move up or down.

[We look forward to sharing, in our Volume 3, the entirety of the Spiritual Practice prompts included in the extensive additional materials that accompany this Feature]

Putting Words to What Our Hearts Know
A Discussion with James Finley[1]
(transcribed by Karen J. Gordon)

As for me, I have but one desire, the desire for solitude to disappear into the secret of God's face. ~ Thomas Merton

As a young man, I was blessed to be mentored by mystic scholar and Trappist Monk Thomas Merton at the Abbey of Our Lady of Gethsemani in Kentucky. His teachings awakened in me the realization that our essence is a God-given godly nature, hidden with Christ and God before the origins of the universe.

At fourteen, in the midst of a traumatic home life in Akron, Ohio, I heard Merton's name mentioned by a high school teacher. Curious, I sought out Merton's *The Sign of Jonas* and was instantly captivated. On the first page of his beautiful journal, Merton says, "As for me, I have but one desire, the desire for solitude to disappear into the secret of God's face."

I didn't fully understand it — but something in me did. "Me too," I whispered.

I returned to that book daily, its pages sustaining me through adolescence as I prayed and longed for God. When I graduated from high school, I felt God calling me to live at the monastery. I dreamed I could go to Abbey of Our Lady of Gethsemani and sit at Merton's feet, believing with all my heart that he could help me find my way to "disappear into the secret of God's face."

Abbey of Our Lady of Gethsemani

I spent six years in the monastery, and that life of silence, discipline, and seeking left a lasting imprint on my soul. In this God-seeking life, Merton served as a living lineage holder of mystical tradition. He was my mentor and spiritual guide and introduced me to the core texts of both Christian and non-Christian mystics. His presence shaped the contemplative foundations of my life and work. His teachings placed him firmly in the Who's Who of awakened contemplative voices within Catholicism's timeless mystical heritage.

Born in France in 1915, Merton moved to the U.S. as an infant. He experienced great personal loss early — his mother died when he was six. His education at Cambridge and later Columbia led to mystical experiences and a deep engagement with metaphysical theology, particularly the works of Aquinas. Eventually, Merton was baptized into the Catholic Church and felt a calling of what direction to go with his life but didn't know to where. A professor directed him to the Abbey of Gethsemani, a Trappist monastery in Kentucky. Its spiritual lineage traces back through St. Bernard of Clairvaux and St. Benedict to the Desert Fathers. Merton once translated a story from that tradition:

> In a community of hermits in the desert, one of the monks came to the Abbot and said, "What can I do to save my soul?"
>
> And the Abbot said, "Keep the rule and love the brethren."
>
> The monk said, "I do that. What else do I do?"
>
> The Abbot stood up, stretching out all his fingers. They became like ten lamps of fire, and he said, "Why not become all fire?"

This image of divine transformation — becoming all fire — captures the heart of Merton's teachings on theosis.

The Contemplative Path Widens

Merton had entered the monastery at twenty-six, turning away from a promising literary career. His spiritual autobiography, *The Seven Storey Mountain*, became a bestseller, launching his public identity as a contemplative teacher. He taught that each moment holds the possibility of encountering God poured out and wholly given.

His later years reflected a widening of contemplative vision — first through interspiritual dialogue with figures like Abraham Heschel, Thích Nhất Hạnh, and D. T. Suzuki; then through a powerful moment of awakening in downtown Louisville where he realized a radical oneness with all people.

He wrote, "The only authentic withdrawal from the world is a withdrawal that radicalizes our oneness with the world."

Two Departures

Merton lived and breathed by this meeting place — a mystical awakening with a radicalized oneness with humanity. He saw this radicalization as Jesus: "God so loved the world, he sent His only begotten Son." Merton loved this world of infinite love, and he well understood that broken people are sustained by God in this way.

As the years went by, he became increasingly interested in social activism and wrote *Seeds of Destruction* (1964) and *Conjectures of a Guilty Bystander* (1966), works revealing his stance against the Vietnam War and atomic warfare. These books also portrayed him as being pro sentiments of Dr. Martin Luther King, and so on.

It was then that the hate mail began pouring in, mostly from Catholics, many threatening to come to the monastery to kill him. Simultaneously, he was thinking of leaving Our Lady of Gethsemani. He considered the bishop in Alaska's invitation to live there, but he also thought he might go East because of his interest in Buddhism.

And so, in this last stage of his life, he was given permission to attend an international conference on contemplative lineages and departed for Bangkok, Thailand. He planned to have person to person contact with the Buddhists in attendance, and he also ended up having several talks with His Holiness the Dalai Lama.

It was at that conference in Bangkok on the 10th of December, 1968, at the age of 58, that Thomas Merton departed this world from what was called "accidental" electrocution. But there were rumors founded upon his activist associations that he was actually killed by the CIA.

Reflections on "The General Dance"

For the world and time are the dance of the Lord in emptiness.

The silence of the spheres is the music of a wedding feast.

Behind these first two lines of "The General Dance,"[2] the last chapter from Merton's *New Seeds of Contemplation,* is a lineage of mystics of which Merton was a part. Speaking about creation, he said:

It's important to realize that when God, in the Torah, in the first words of Genesis, said, "Let there be light, let there be stones and trees and stars," it isn't that God just set all manifested reality into motion in that moment and then went off to let the Universe get by as best it could on its own.

"It's not like that," Merton said. "Creation is going on all the time. Creation is perpetual and absolute."

The infinite presence of God is pouring itself out and giving itself away whole and complete in and as the gift and miracle of the immediacy of our very presence, the presence of others, and the presence of all things in our communal nothingness without God.

So it's not that we *are* God. It's that we're absolutely nothing *without* God. But it's our nothing without God that makes our presence to *be* the presence of God.

Merton continues in "The General Dance":

What is serious to men is often very trivial in the sight of God.

What in God might appear to us as play is perhaps what God Himself takes most seriously.

At any rate, the Lord plays and diverts Himself in the mystery of His creation.

And if we could let go of our own obsession with what we think is the meaning of it all, we might be able to hear His call and follow Him in His mysterious cosmic dance.

We do not have to go very far to catch echoes of that game and of that dancing.

What if we could all close our eyes right now and be interiorly awakened out of this estrangement from the God-given godly nature of ourselves? What if we could see God in all we saw through our own awakened eyes, just as Jesus did?

There is your God-given godly nature of who you eternally are hidden with Christ and God before the origins of the universe. And then there is your God-given capacity to *see* it.

But it's fallen. You have eyes to see, but you don't see it. Jesus, in effect, says this is the source of all your sorrow and confusion. The prayer is, "O Lord, that I might see, that I might see through my own eyes the divinity of myself, others, and all things that you saw and everything."

It's through Merton's faith that we're able to realize that "the world and time are the dance of the Lord in emptiness" and that the silence of the spheres is the music of a wedding feast. This is what mystic teachers do. Merton is helping us put words to what our heart knows is true, and bears witness to it.

Depth Deprivation

When I was in the monastery, Merton said, "You know, the monastic life is very carefully crafted to nurture and protect this awakening and to live by it. But there are people in the world who are being led into this Oneness, and they have no one to help them understand what's happening to them. And they have no one to help them cooperate with."

When I left the monastery, I discovered that this is true, and it's what led me to write *Merton's Palace of Nowhere*. At the heart of Merton's teaching for all of us out in the world, is that in the complexities of trying to keep up with the day's demands, we get this feeling that we're skimming over the surface of the depths of our own life, that we're suffering from depth deprivation. And the mysterious thing is that God's unexplainable, sustaining Oneness with us is hidden in the very depths over which we're skimming.

"There is in faith, then," Merton says, "the healing of the depth deprivation of certain moments where we're momentarily healed."

Moments of Awakening

These moments of awakening — such as when we truly see children as children or when we know love in our own hearts — are subtle and utterly ordinary rather than moments of ecstasy.

Sometimes when quite young, we're granted an awakening that we spend the rest of our life learning to be faithful to. It isn't as if we're waiting for some big thing to happen. But we're trying to recalibrate our heart to an ever finer scale, so that in this way we can pick up on the incomprehensible stature of simple things. What Merton is referring to are realms of human existence.

The Realm of Nature

Say you're out walking alone in the midst of nature, and you turn to see a flock of birds descending. And as if out of the corner of your eye, you catch something in their descent that's primordial, vast, and true. To give faith language to it, we might say that God's the infinity of the bird's descent, and the bird's descent is the incarnate immediacy of God.

Extended out more inclusively to you, God's the infinity of your awareness of their descent, and your awareness of their descent is the incarnate mystery of God.

The Realm of Love

This is when we know love in our own hearts. There are moments between two people where they say to each other, "In love we are one." And in that Oneness, they get a sense of something primordial, vast, and true.

And we would say that the infinite love of God is the infinity of their love for each other. And holding each other in love is the incarnate presence of God. This is mystical marriage.

The Realm of Suffering and Death

A trauma psychotherapist said, "Sometimes in the very midst of drawn-out healing of the deep-seated trauma, there comes shining through the suffering intimations of the sustaining light that's guiding you and teaching you things you wouldn't know had you not gone through the trauma."

My wife died with in-house hospice right in the very living room where I'm writing this article. When you look into the face of a dying loved one, you sense you're looking into the gate of heaven. It's freedom from the tyranny of death in the midst of death, the eternality of ourselves, that which never passes away — this ribbon through all that's endlessly passing. And it shines bright.

Assuming the Stance

By knowing that we've already been granted the experience in nature, love, and birth and death, it's like we're tracing out a trail of these flashpoint moments of awakening.

Merton asks then, "How do we do this?" It is by assuming the stance.

Lovers cannot make their moments of oceanic oneness happen, but together they learn to assume the stance that offers the least resistance to being overtaken one more time by the oneness and love that gives meaning to everything they do.

Poets cannot make the poem happen. But they learn that inner stance and openness through which the poem flows out of them and through them out into the world.

This is the daily meditation. This is the rendezvous. We can't make any unique moment of awakening happen. But we can assume the stance that allows for it to happen.

Daily Rendezvous with the Divine

Reading Merton with a contemplative heart is a form of *lectio divina*. His words invite us to sit in quiet intimacy with mystery, to dwell in what we cannot comprehend, and to let that awaken us.

Merton distinguishes the ego from the false self: the ego is necessary; the false self is the illusion that the ego is all there is. Awakenings often happen in and through the ego — through love, art, or even suffering. And when they do, we are blindsided by the shining forth of that which transcends and is revealing itself to us.

Love is the key. Not love as escape, but love as radical presence to the world and to our brokenness. Merton taught me that even the part of ourselves that "doesn't get it" deserves our tenderness. That mercy is where healing begins.

He wrote: *Oh, how far I have to go to find you in whom I have already arrived!* That paradox of longing and arrival, of mystery and presence, defines his path — and mine.

Through Merton, I learned to be faithful to the daily rendezvous with the Divine, and to carry that thread of awareness into the ordinariness of life, even when it breaks. The oceanic mercy of God is great, and the brokenness vanishes away within God's mercy.

My Blessing

I'd like to share with you one last Merton quote that I particularly like:

> *Oh, how far I have to go to find you in whom I already arrived!*
>
> *I only wish it were over. I only wished it were begun.*

Merton has a poetic elegance of learning to be at home in this boundarylessness that we cannot comprehend, that's unexplainable and will be taking us to itself forever.

And having tasted it, to be evermore habitually abiding in it, being faithful to the rendezvous. And when we end our daily rendezvous with Merton or the mystic, whatever your practice is, ask God for the grace not to break the thread of that sensitivity as you go through your day.

You'll notice it breaks many times, but now you're aware that it breaks. Your faith is knowing that from God's end it never breaks as your faith deepens in this way. And so, I think this is the tonal quality for me of Merton, and how he helps us put words to this unexplainable immensity within ourselves, found in poverty and spirit of ordinariness.

He helps us live by and follow it. So I've been so blessed, really, so providential to me that I was in the monastery, and I sat with him. He changed my life.

Merton is one of these teachers whose deathless presence speaks to us this way, and I think that surely he belongs in the Who's Who of teachers.

Endnotes and References for James Finley Discussion Feature[xi]

In the Name of the Lord:
Towards an Interspiritual Theology
by Ben Bowler

What you seek is seeking you.
—Rumi

I. One Fine Morning

"Such a splendid morning," mused Jalāl al-Dīn as he strode into town. He was in particularly high spirits, having spent the past evening in spiritual fellowship with his beloved mentor — the one they called the Sun.

On his way to the bazaar to sip tea and break his fast, an ecstatic joy stirred within him. The laughter of children danced through the air as the morning sun warmed his face — reflecting the joy and divine love that had illuminated his soul throughout the night.

As he neared the heart of the marketplace, his attention was taken by the steady rhythm of the goldsmith's hammer. The vibrations struck him like a sacred drumbeat, and within his soul a chant began to rise, becoming a swelling chorus that whispered the names of God.

In that moment, his mind lifted, his spirit soared, and suspended in the levity of grace, he began to move. His right arm rose toward the heavens, his left dropped gently to his side. Turning left — into the heart — he began to whirl.

The world has never been quite the same since that fateful morning, nearly eight centuries ago in the heart of Anatolia, when Jalāl al-Dīn Rumi began to dance.

II. The Mystic Heart and the Question of the Divine

What compelled Rumi to whirl so freely in the marketplace? What is it that draws mystics across traditions to surrender their egos, dissolve the illusion of separateness, and drink so recklessly from the cup of divine love?

As we mark twenty-five years since the publication of Wayne Teasdale's *The Mystic Heart*, this anthology invites us to explore the depths of mystical experience across the world's traditions. What lies at the center of the mystic heart? What is that drumbeat that stirs awakening, that summons the soul to rise and whirl? But perhaps that is the wrong premise. The deeper question may not be *what* lies at the heart of the mystic journey — but *who*. For it is not the drumbeat we are ultimately seeking, but the Drummer.

These past twenty-five years — the Dawn of Interspirituality — have seen the emergence of a number of important evolutionary currents:

- The convergence of science and spirituality, as quantum physics, neuroscience, and cosmology echo the profound insights of ancient wisdom traditions.

- The reemergence of the Divine Feminine, restoring balance to spiritual discourse long dominated by patriarchal frameworks.

- The rise of eco-spirituality, a deepening reverence for Earth, water, land, and sacred sites as bearers of story and beings of spiritual presence.

- A maturing of the interfaith movement, evolving into a broader and more integrated interspiritual collective — one that is open toward indigenous traditions, established world religions, and emerging spiritual philosophies.

What remains underdeveloped, however, is a coherent interspiritual theology — a common language of divinity. This may be due to the movement's emphasis on shared experience over shared doctrine. Yet the time has come to articulate theological foundations capable of sustaining and deepening our unitive experience. If unity is our banner, upon what is it truly grounded? Are we united merely by our shared humanity and planetary home — or by something deeper, something transcendent? Is there, beneath all difference, a spiritual origin, a universal Source, that binds us in sacred kinship?

III. The Necessity of a Theological Center

For the interspiritual movement to flourish beyond the fringe, it must offer more than open-ended inclusivity. It must articulate the transcendent foundation that sustains our unity.

When Brother Wayne first coined the term *Interspirituality*, he was speaking from within the context of faith traditions and interfaith dialogue. At the time, he had not fully accounted for a global demographic shift toward non-affiliated forms of spirituality. And yet, even today, more than 80 percent of the world's population remains affiliated with a religion — and among them, over 80 percent profess belief in a Supreme Being.[1]

This alone is reason enough to engage the question of "God" with both courage and humility. Without acknowledging the spiritual language and symbols of the world's religions, the interspiritual movement risks being perceived as culturally detached or spiritually vague — confined to New Age enclaves rather than embraced by the broader human family.

And yet, merely adopting a universalist language is not enough. We need to discern what unites us — not just in metaphor, but in spiritual substance. What is the reality that holds us together in loving orbit?

IV. Ultimate Reality and the Personal God

Over recent decades, significant efforts have been made to craft inclusive spiritual narratives — emerging from the interfaith movement, early expressions of Interspirituality, and evolutionary cosmology. A recent example is *The Unitive Narrative*[2] — developed by thought leaders from the SDG Synergy Circle — which speaks of "*recognizing unity with the ultimate Great Mystery or Source of all being.*" Another notable effort is the Snowmass Interreligious Dialogues,[3] initiated under the leadership of Father Thomas Keating, which produced the Eight Points of Agreement — a foundational articulation of shared spiritual understanding.

In the Snowmass Dialogues, the term *Ultimate Reality* serves as an inclusive expression, embracing God, Source, the Absolute, and other transcendent conceptions found across traditions. Yet despite their depth and sincerity, both of these important initiatives do not address one essential question: **Is God personal**?

The question of divine personhood is not universally agreed upon, yet it remains foundational to how billions of people understand and relate to divinity. From Judaism, Christianity, and Islam to Hinduism and Sikhism — many faiths affirm a personal relationship with the Divine. Certain schools of Buddhism and many Indigenous traditions also speak of relational connection with divine Presence.

Challenges arise when the idea of a "personal God" is shaped by crude anthropomorphisms — often influenced by Western art and theology into the image of an old white man in the sky. Such projections have done immense damage.

Genesis declares that the Creator made human beings in the image of God — now through religion, we have returned the favor. Can we preserve the essential qualities of personhood without imposing the constructs of gender, race, age, and other deeply human lenses onto the Divine? Can we reclaim a vision of a personal God without falling back into simplistic anthropomorphic imagery? Can we envision a transpersonal Divine — one who is truly personal, yet not a projection; one who relates, but does not resemble?

Because here's the deeper truth: Love, trust, faith, and surrender are inherently relational. These sublime realities cannot truly exist between a person and an impersonal force. You cannot be loved by a law, confide in a force, or offer devotion to a field of energy. And if we ourselves are conscious, personal beings — made in the image of the Source of all being—how could that Source be anything less? Is it not an ontological absurdity to imagine that a creature could possess qualities the Creator does not?

In Bohmian terms, if conscious, relational being is so essential to the explicate world, how could it not also mirror a deeper reality within the implicate order?

The personal perspective opens the heart of theology — not as abstract speculation, but as a journey into divine relationship.

V. Love as the Supreme Secret

Two contemporary thinkers, Will Keepin and Ilia Delio, offer essential insights for the journey ahead — our unfolding path toward an interspiritual theology.

Will Keepin and his wife Cynthia Brix have conducted several signature events and published an important website under the name *Dawn of Interspirituality*.[4]

In his brilliant book *Belonging to God* (2016), Will Keepin — a mathematical physicist and interfaith mystic — draws profound parallels between the sacred texts of multiple traditions. At the heart of every mystical path, he finds the same radiant truth: devotion and divine love are the keys to spiritual realization — union with the Beloved.[5]

He highlights the resonances between Krishna's teachings in the *Bhagavad Gita*, Jesus' commandment to love God with heart, soul, and mind, and the Shema of Jewish faith:

"On Me fix thy mind, be thou My devotee... Thus

united to Me as thy Highest Goal, thou shalt be Mine
own."
— *Bhagavad Gita 9:34, repeated in Gita 18:65*

"You shall love the Lord your God with all your heart,
all your soul, and all your mind."
— *Matthew 22:37*

"Hear, O Israel... you shall love the Lord your God
with all your heart, with all your soul, and with all your
might."
— *Deuteronomy 6:4–5*

Across these traditions, the thread is unmistakable: love is the
path to union with the Divine. Keepin's central thesis is this: divine
truths are universal and are revealed not through analysis, but through
direct experience —through surrender to divine love. Devotion, he
suggests, is the sacred doorway — leading not to dogma, but to an
ever-deepening discovery of the Beloved.

Keepin goes on to point out that even in (non-theistic) Buddhism,
devotion remains a vital aspect. He quotes the Tibetan Dzogchen
master Tulku Urgyen Rinpoche: "realizing Buddha nature requires
devotion from the core of our hearts. ... It's extremely important."[6] A
modern revelation affirms Keepin's core idea:

> *"Human things must be known in order to be loved,*
> *but divine things must be loved in order to be known."*
> — *The Urantia Book* (102:1.1)

VI. God Ever Becoming

In her seminal 2024 work, *The Not Yet God*, Ilia Delio offers a
groundbreaking synthesis of spirituality, science, psychology, and

theology. Drawing on the insights of quantum physicist David Bohm, psychoanalyst Carl Jung, and philosopher–priest Teilhard de Chardin, Delio challenges static, classical notions of an unchanging deity.

Instead, she envisions a divinity that is dynamic, relational, and continually evolving. God, in this vision, is not a distant omnipotent ruler, but the "relational whole" — emerging through love, consciousness, and the unfolding cosmos. The phrase "not yet God" reflects a divinity in process, intimately woven into the evolutionary flow of the universe.

In Delio's framework, God is not fixed or finished, but actively participating in the becoming of the cosmos — ever luring creation toward a deeper completion, what Teilhard called "The Omega Point."[7]

This evolutionary perspective resonates deeply with the work of cosmologist Brian Swimme, whose Deeptime vision situates human consciousness within the vast unfolding of the universe. In works like *The Universe Story* and *Journey of the Universe*, Swimme invites us to recognize life, consciousness, and spirituality as integral expressions of the cosmos awakening to itself. This cosmic orientation shifts theology away from static absolutes toward a dynamic, participatory process — a universe in love with becoming. It echoes the process thought of John Cobb and the process theology of Alfred North Whitehead, envisioning God not as a distant, immutable object, but as an intimate, relational, co-creative Presence.

As Thomas Berry profoundly observed, *"The universe is a communion of subjects rather than a collection of objects."* While Berry was speaking to the foundations of an ecological civilization — the Ecozoic[8] — his insight equally illuminates the God-human relationship: not as an impersonal abstraction, but as a living communion between subjects within the sacred hoop of life.

In this view, we are not separate observers of a distant deity, but participants in a cosmic intimacy — co-creators within the unfolding story of divine love.

VII. The Lord Is One

It was another beautiful morning — this time spring in Rishikesh, India, in 2017. We were pioneering a spiritual immersion journey called *Mystic Express*, led by the legendary interfaith scholar Darrol M. Bryant. Our small group was full of anticipation as we crossed the Ganges on the iconic Lakshman Jhula footbridge, en route to meet the head Swami of the Divine Life Society.

Around the Ashram there were quotes from Swami Sivananda. One said, "*Detach the mind from the objects of the world, and attach it to the Lord.*" When the opportunity arose, I asked, "Who is the Lord referred to in your teachings?"

Swami Padmanabhananda's answer was immediate and emphatic: "*There is only one Lord. One Lord for all, actually.*"

He continued, *According to the Advaita concept, the Lord is within you. As it says in the Bible: "In the beginning was the Word, and the Word was with God, and the Word was God." God with us—that is Emmanuel. The Lord is an immanent reality, dwelling in each of us. The Lord is your inner core, your spiritual essence. This inner presence is not bound by space or time. God is omnipresent. The Lord is an all-pervading reality.*

That conversation left a lasting impression. Across every major spiritual tradition, the idea of the Lord appears again and again — Lord Jesus, Lord Buddha, Lord Krishna. In the Qur'an, *al-Rabb* ("the Lord") is one of the 99 names of God. In the Torah, Adonai — the

Lord — is invoked over 400 times. These are reverent expressions, drawn from different languages, cultures, and theologies.

And yet, what if — as the Swami suggested — beyond the diversity of names and forms, there is One Lord of All, transcending and including every human conceptualization?

VIII. The Feminine Divine

These reflections can equally be applied to the feminine dimensions of Divinity. Across cultures and traditions, we encounter sacred expressions of the Divine Feminine — Kuan Yin, Shakti, Pachamama, The Madonna, Shekinah, and many others. Whether revealed as nurturing mother, fierce protector, wise healer, destroyer of worlds or sacred lover, these archetypes reflect a universal presence — the Divine Mother Spirit — whose qualities of compassion, creative power, and intuitive knowing beautifully complement the masculine attributes traditionally associated with "the Lord."

As part of this renewed vision, it is essential to recognize the re-emergence of the Divine Feminine — not merely as a balance to the masculine, but as an essential, co-equal aspect of the Divine Whole. I recently interviewed spiritual teacher Andrew Harvey who spoke passionately of this sacred polarity:

> The tragedy of our time is the psychotic overvaluation of the masculine side of God, leading to the dismissal of nature, body, and sexuality. The antidote is the return of the Divine Feminine in her tender and ferocious aspects — reclaiming the sacred marriage within the One.

Harvey points to an ancient wisdom known to mystics across traditions: that Divinity is not a singular, static monolith, but a dynamic, living union of energies. He quoted a poem by the great Indian mystic Kabir:

> *My father is the absolute Godhead.*
> *My mother is the embodied Godhead.*
> *And I am their divine child, dancing for them both on*
> *their burning dance floor.*

In this luminous vision, God is not merely transcendent or immanent, not solely masculine or feminine, but the radiant union of both — birthing the universe anew through the sacred dance of love. In this sacred dance of Divine energies, we are invited to glimpse a deeper unity beyond all names, forms, and divisions.

It is toward this timeless mystery that the Swami's proclamation points: beyond all opposites, beyond all duality — **the Lord is One**. This realization naturally leads us inward as our journey toward interspiritual theology moves from the unity of the whole to the spark within the soul.

IX. God Within

At the heart of Jesus' teachings is this: *The Kingdom of God is within you.* The Swami echoed this same truth: *The Lord is within you.* This profound insight is also affirmed in the Fuji Declaration (2015): "We affirm the divine spark in the heart and mind of every human... The great spiritual traditions of the world have always told us that, at its root, human life is inextricably linked to its universal source."[9]

God's transcendence must always be remembered:

> *For my thoughts are not your thoughts, neither are*
> *your ways my ways,* declares the Lord. *As the heavens*
> *are higher than the earth, so are my ways higher than*

your ways and my thoughts than your thoughts. (Isaiah 55:8–9)

Yet God's immanence — the indwelling spark of Divinity — must equally become a foundational tenet of our emerging interspiritual theology. As God above inspires reverence, so too must God within inspire realization. The ancient maxim *As above, so below* may now be reimagined to frame our foundational theological position:

As Above, So Within.

If the Divine truly dwells within us, then every thought, every word, every act becomes a sacred opportunity to honor that Presence.

X. A Theology of Love and Unity

The task ahead is vast — but profoundly necessary. As we move deeper into the unfolding Interspiritual Age, the four key trends must continue to flourish: the re-emergence of the Mother Spirit, ongoing engagement with scientific discovery, the rise of ecological spirituality, and the growing movement toward greater spiritual unity across cultures, races, and nations.

These currents must be accompanied by philosophical and theological frameworks that honor the depth, diversity, and radiant wholeness of humanity's great wisdom traditions.

A generous interspiritual theology must be rooted in revelation, a plurality of sacred traditions, and the living flame of mystical experience. It must embrace both immanence and transcendence, the personal and the impersonal, the feminine and the masculine faces of the Divine. It must not erase the sacred names of different traditions, but honor them. It must not flatten difference, but hold space for mystery, paradox, and depth. It must be bold enough to speak of God — and humble enough to know that all our words fall short.

Humanity's spiritual inheritance is vast. To honor the sacred diversity of human spirituality is to recognize the unique jewel of each revelation: the chosenness of Abraham, the incarnation of Christ, the enlightenment of the Buddha, the prophethood of Muhammad, the deep ancestral wisdom of Indigenous traditions in sacred relationship with Mother Earth, and the eternal presence of the Divine Feminine — who has loved her children and taught them to dance through every age.

This is to embrace "collective revelation" — the expanded view that our manifold sacred histories are not in opposition, but are each a living facet of the Universal One, refracted through the prism of time, culture, and longing. This emerging planetary culture — expanded in vision and grounded in reverence for life — offers the foundation for realizing the deepest hopes of every generation: peace, justice, ecological renewal, and a luminous future in harmony with science, spirit, the Cosmos, and Earth herself.

In the end, we are not building a system — we are telling a love story. And at the center of that story is not a doctrine or an idea, but a Living Presence.

Call it God.

Call it the Beloved.

Call it Ultimate Reality.

But let us not be afraid to name the Divine, and to be known by that name in return. She is always calling us, ever inviting us all, to the joyful feast with the Lord of the Dance.

Endnotes and References in "Interspiritual Theology" Feature[xii]

Can Interspirituality Serve the Rebirth of Humanity?

by William Keepin

Humanity is struggling mightily to evolve to the next stage of our evolution. Today's horrific wars, political upheavals, social crises, and ecological disasters — taken together — are the birth pangs of a new humanity striving to be born.

What new forms of spiritual training, praxis, and community will truly serve humanity in this time of unprecedented polycrisis? As Archbishop Desmond Tutu has said, it is not enough to heal the past, we must also reinvent the future. Can the nascent field of "Interspirituality" rise to meet this twin challenge — not only to heal the wounds of our religious past, but also to reinvent spirituality itself, to serve the rebirth of humanity?

Controversial Priorities for Interspirituality

Interspiritual pioneers such as Fr. Thomas Keating, Wayne Teasdale, and numerous others have revealed remarkable common ground across the major religions, with corresponding elevated inspirations among their greatest mystics.[1] Many chapters in this anthology rightly highlight these major breakthroughs, and the crucial importance of contemplative practices, meditation and prayer, and inter-religious dialogue and collaboration.

Beyond these essential foundations, two additional priorities are also crucial for Interspirituality in the future, as outlined in this chapter. These are controversial, complex topics, and limited space allows for just a few key points to be summarized below.

Psychedelics and Interspirituality

Psychedelics and plant medicines have a long history within religion and spirituality, and likely played a far greater role in the origins and evolution of world religions than has generally been acknowledged. As Buddhist teacher Jack Kornfield observes:

> Sacred medicine is a part of spiritual paths on every continent. In spiritual communities, we need an honest exploration of this delicate and sometimes taboo topic. LSD, mushrooms, ecstasy [MDMA], or ayahuasca can bring healing and can grant us access to visionary and mystical realms of tremendous, transcendent understanding. They can bring a perception of unity, the reality of our connection with everything. Any methods that open the heart in this way and show us that we are not separate, that touch the realms of universal loving kindness, and compassion, can be valuable.[2]

The Eleusinian Mysteries

For two thousand years, the profound Eleusinian Mysteries were conducted annually outside Athens, from 1,600 BCE to 392 CE. The culmination of this secret initiation rite included drinking a potion called *kykeon*, "a mixture of water, barley, and mint — nothing more."[3] The *kykeon* was served up after a three-day fast in tiny chalices, only one inch high. This sounds perfectly benign except for one key fact: there exist powerful psychedelic strains of both mint (salvia divinorum) and barley (ergot, a precursor of LSD). If these strains were utilized, then no wonder those chalices were so tiny!

This would also explain the legendary power of the Eleusinian mysteries. Initiates frequently reported discovering their own immortality. Then, as now, the realization that death is an illusion is one of the major common breakthrough experiences in deep psychedelic journeys. As Professor Christopher Bache explains, "You lose all fear of death. You know in your bones from your own experience that death is not an end of anything. And there is absolutely nothing to fear. Death is homecoming."[4]

In an archaeological excavation of a Greek temple site at Mas Castellar des Pontos near Girona, Spain, dated to 300 BCE, traces of ergot were found in the small ceremonial chalices, and in the dental calculus and jawbone of a human skeleton found in the ceremonial space.[5] This provides the first direct evidence for a psychedelic *kykeon*. Similar results have emerged in other recent studies, such as an archaeo-chemistry study that found traces of three psychotropic plants in an Egyptian ritual Bes-vase from the 2nd century BCE, along with traces of human fluids, suggesting their direct involvement in rituals.[6] Although still highly controversial, even cautious scholars such as Harvard University's Charles Stang affirms that "the balance of evidence is tilting slightly in favor of the psychedelic hypothesis."[7]

A Psychedelic Eucharist?

For some 300 years after Jesus' resurrection, early Christians gathered in small 'house churches' in private homes. At that time, Christianity was a nascent illegal fringe religion, and worship ceremonies were conducted in secret. Officiants were usually women (as in Eleusis), and many had likely experienced Dionysian ceremonies, which entailed psychoactive wine. "Even by the most mainstream interpretations of the Dionysian Mysteries, the wine of Dionysius is a pharmakon that results in apotheosis."[8]

Pharmakon means "drug" or intoxicant, and apotheosis means to elevate or make into a god. "The wine is symbolic of something infinitely greater than itself," and is "rightly thought of as representing the blood of Dionysos himself. ... We partake of the essence of the God by drinking the wine."[9]

This is a remarkable precursor of the Christian Eucharist. Dennis McDonald and other scholars highlight several striking parallels between Jesus and Dionysius. Numerous passages in the *Gospel of John* are identical, word for word in Greek, to passages in the *Bachae* written by Euripides some 500 years earlier.[10] Thus, the "true drink" of John's Gospel has a strong precedent in Dionysian wine. Early Christians may have continued the use of psychoactive wine in their Eucharist, long before the Roman church emerged.

These complex questions are the focus of a controversial book by Brian Moraresku.[11] Scholarly reviews have been mixed. "It feels as if Muraresku is letting a narrative, rather than evidence, drive the inquiry," writes Charles Stang of Harvard University, "but to be fair to him, much of his book is also devoted to arguing — persuasively, I might add — that ancient beer and wine were much more powerfully psychoactive than their contemporary descendants."[12] Researchers Jerry and Judy Brown have documented extensive visual evidence of mushrooms and psychedelic images in Christian art throughout Europe and the Middle-East, suggesting that psychedelics may have played an important role in Christian history.[13]

Psychedelics in Contemporary Religion and Spirituality

Psychedelic sacraments are becoming increasingly common in

today's "psychedelic renaissance," with remarkable impacts in various religious communities.[14] Spring Washam, a Buddhist teacher authorized by Jack Kornfield, leads retreats in Costa Rica that combine Vipassana meditation and ayahuasca ceremonies. Washom opines that psychedelic plant medicines do not directly cause spiritual realization or enlightenment, but they can remove stubborn barriers that stand in the way. As Rabbi Shefa Gold explains, "Under the influence of psychedelics, I was given a profound glimpse of a larger Reality. Through psychedelics I learned to surrender my illusion of control and let my heart be ravished. In the ashes of my small self, a vision of my larger Self could emerge. And then the holy work (without drugs) could begin ... the work of becoming a clear channel for God's love to flow through in the forms of kindness and justice."[15]

Ligare is a Christian psychedelic society founded by Episcopal priest Hunt Priest, which aims "to empower and educate religious leaders and communities about the profound opportunities and significant challenges within the resurgence of psychedelics," and "aspires to create wisdom schools focused on the intersection of psychedelics and contemplative Christianity."[16] Organizations with similar missions in religion and spirituality include: *Shefa* (Judaism), *Psychedelic Sangha* (Buddhism), *Ruhani Spirit* (Islam), *GTUx* (Hinduism, yoga), *Sacred Plant Alliance* (interfaith churches), *Chacruna Institute* (indigenous), *Medicinal Mindfulness* (healing), *Beckley Retreats* (ceremonies and research), *Psychedelics and Spirituality* (Harvard Divinity School), and many others. An estimated 250 to 500 psychedelic churches are operating in the United States today.[17]

Santo Daime and UDV Churches

The Santo Daime and the União do Vegeta are syncretic Christian religions that have been integrating ayahuasca into Christian worship for 90 years and 63 years, respectively. Both traditions began in Brazil and spread to many countries. Professor William Barnard delved deeply into the Santo Daime tradition, concluding that "psychedelics can be used reverently, as genuine sacraments," and they reveal "how magical and mysterious the universe is."[18] Santo Daime provides "a powerfully transformative, and profoundly illuminative, spiritual path that centers on Christ, yet also affirms the Divine Mother so much so, that God's nature itself often appears to be understood as simultaneously masculine and feminine."[19] In their successful appeal to the U.S. Supreme Court, Santo Daime leaders argued that confiscating their (ayahuasca) tea amounted to treating Christ as contraband: "According to Church doctrine, the presence of Daime is the presence of Christ."[20] The Santo Daime and UDV churches are thriving legally in several countries.

Jack Kornfield collaborated with psychiatrist Stanislav Grof for decades, offering "Insight and Opening" retreats that combined holotropic breathwork with Vipassana meditation. My colleagues and I have implemented this same combination in our retreats for 35 years, and we consistently witness remarkable spiritual transformative breakthroughs with holotropic breathwork.[21] For individuals who are not inclined toward psychedelics, breathwork provides a remarkably effective drug-free alternative that delivers similar results.

A New Eleusis?

Humanity urgently needs effective ways to catalyze deep transformations of consciousness — on a massive scale, in a short amount of time. How might this happen?

A white supremacist leader was utterly transformed into a compassionate man via a single MDMA psychedelic session; afterwards he fully renounced his previous identity.[22] A long-awaited major clinical study from Johns Hopkins University was recently published, in which two sessions of psilocybin were administered under controlled conditions to religious leaders from multiple faith traditions.[23] The primary outcome assessment at 6 months showed that, compared with the control group, participants who had received psilocybin reported significantly greater positive changes in their religious practices, and effectiveness as religious leaders. In a second follow-up assessment 16 months later, 96 percent of these religious leaders rated the experience among the five most spiritually significant of their lives. Most also reported greater effectiveness in their jobs, lasting positive effects on their prayer or meditation (79%), and deeper appreciation of other religions (71%). This study challenges the notion that psychedelic experiences are not genuine spiritual encounters.

These and many similar examples raise a radical possibility: Could there be a contemporary "New Eleusis" in some form, suitably adapted to our time? Psychiatrist Stanislav Grof recently advocated for this possibility (originally suggested by Albert Hoffman). Grof proposes that skillful application of psychedelics could potentially help catalyze a global rebirth of human civilization.[24] Although psychedelics are not a panacea, they *can* facilitate life-changing transformations of consciousness, and dissolve major blocks to spiritual awakening — in short order.

A New Eleusis may seem implausibly extreme, but humanity is facing possible extinction, wrought by our own ignorance and escalating violence. The idea may not be so far-fetched. As the Roman statesman Cicero (106 – 43 BCE) observed:

*Among the many excellent and indeed divine institutions
which your Athens has brought forth and contributed
to human life, none, in my opinion, is better than those
[Eleusinian] mysteries. For by their means we have
been brought out of our barbarous and savage mode of
life and educated and refined to a state of civilization.
And as the rites are called 'initiations,' so in very truth
we have learned from them the beginnings of life, and
have gained the power not only to live happily, but also
to die with a better hope.*[25]

Sexuality and Interspirituality

Oppression and control of sexuality has a long, painful history in religion. Nevertheless, a few celebrated spiritual masters have praised and uplifted the sacred role and purpose of sexuality.

The Sufi master Ibn al Arabi (1165-1240) departs from many spiritual authorities — then *and* now — by declaring that sexual union based on a deep existential love can be "the greatest self-disclosure of God." In his words:

> [Each lover] dissolves in the other. ... Love has suffused
> all one's parts, so one's entire being is interconnected
> with the other. ... [T]hen your witnessing turns you
> back to God. ... Many of the sages are oblivious to this
> reality. Indeed, it is one of the secrets that none know,
> except a few of the people of divine favor (*'inaya*).[26]

After millennia of suppression, this secret needs to be revealed, with utmost integrity and impeccable ethics. As scholar Sa'diyya Shaikh summarizes Ibn Arabi's teaching: "The pleasure experienced during sex intimates the pleasure of union with God, who is the ultimate beloved. ... The potential for Divine participation in human sexuality a theophanic reality [that] allows for the experience of *conincidenta oppositorum'* [sacred union of 'opposites'], which ultimately is also the nature of the reality of God."[27]

Ibn Arabi is not alone. Tibetan doctor Nida Chenagtsang has published the first full exposition of "practical and safe styles of *karmamudra* [sexual practice] that do not require prior training in Tantric yoga," based on the revealed teachings of Yuthok Yönten Genpo (1126-1202).[28] Yuthok taught two forms of *karmamudra*: an advanced version that entails extensive training in subtle body 'channel winds' (*tsa loong*) and inner heat (*tummo*), and a basic 'entry-level' version for people without such training. Dr. Nida explains that this teaching was intended for non-celibate yogis and householders, and does not 'cut corners' for Westerners, but presents "Yuthok's own instructions."[29]

It is a supreme irony that most religions, both theistic and non-theistic, include an ancient esoteric tradition — usually hidden and suppressed — that specifically cultivates sexual alchemy for spiritual realization within a sacred context. These exalted sexual practices constitute a core element of the solution to the systemic crisis of sexuality in human societies, yet they have long been kept secret. Now, as the Dalai Lama has declared, "The time of secrecy is over. ... Unless these practices become better known they will be completely lost. That would be a great tragedy."[30]

> *Sexual pleasure is a "gift from God" that should be*
> *"disciplined with patience." —* Pope Francis

This recent papal declaration *alone* could help billions of Christians begin to release massive sexual guilt, shame, and associated intergenerational trauma.[31] Even more telling, the late Pope Francis further declared that the Church's "catechesis on sex is still in diapers."[32] It is a tremendous shame (in both senses of the word) that earlier Popes did not proclaim these self-evident truths long ago, so that the Church might have avoided promulgating its disastrous teachings and repression of sexuality — for two thousand years!

Christianity is not alone; most religions teach highly inadequate or destructive doctrines on sexuality, or else they avoid the topic altogether. Buddhist teacher Spring Washam (cited earlier) notes that in 20 years of diverse teachings and dharma talks at Spirit Rock Meditation Center, she heard sexuality addressed only once, for five minutes, and it was received with embarrassed snickers. Washam further concedes that many students privately confide with her that they grapple with intensive sexual energies, and that beyond the usual rote response (witness it until it passes), she does not know how to advise them.[33]

The human body is quite literally a sacred temple — a micro-cosmic *temenos* of the vast macrocosm, energized by sexual energy as the cosmic life force of creation itself. As the Bengali master Ajit Mukerjee puts it, "If you come to know the deep secrets of the body, you come to know the deep secrets of the entire cosmos." To realize this requires "completion stage" spiritual practices (borrowing the Vajrayana Buddhist term), which are *omitted* from most spiritual training — in *all* religions. As a result, "worldly sex and desire bind us to samsara," explains Dr. Nida, "but there is another way. If we know how, we can use sex differently … as an opportunity and method on the path to freedom."[34] Completion stage practices engage the entirety of the human body, including sexuality and dream states, as an integral part of meditative spiritual discipline.

For most people, sexual energy is quickly discharged soon after it arises, in a brief genital orgasm (or two). Most people never discover the vast depths of sexual energies, or experience sustained orgasms that expand throughout the entire body, nourishing every organ and muscle and cell. These orgasmic energies flow along the subtle energy channels of the body, concentrating in the chakras (or *Dan Tien* in Taoism), and they also expand beyond the physical body into the subtle energy bodies, becoming a transcendent radiant energy field that ultimately merges into blissful union with larger cosmic energies, culminating in union with the Divine.

This is the highest spiritual function and gift of sexuality, and it is the birthright of every human being. Yet tragically, most people never come anywhere near to this experience, nor do they know it is even possible. Sometimes people inadvertently encounter these sacred realms in ordinary love-making, but they generally have no context to understand or validate their experiences.[35]

Desire and Its Transmutation

Desire is often regarded as the cause of suffering (or dissatisfaction), and is therefore deemed to be the arch-enemy of spirituality, with sexual desire being the worst offender. But desire is not the cause of suffering; it is *attachment to the objects* of desire that causes suffering. Desire itself can be transmuted into the transcendent union of spiritual bliss and emptiness.[36]

Sexuality and Neurotheology

Although religions have often vehemently suppressed sexuality, the very origin of religion may *be* sexuality. Research in the emerging field of "neurotheology" has shown that prayer and spiritual practices change numerous structures and functions in the brain, which in turn increase feelings of security, compassion, and love while reducing stress and depression.[37] More recently, Andrew Newberg's pioneering brain-scan clinical studies of orgasmic meditation (OM) found that religious experiences and sexual practices activate the *same* brain regions. "The underlying biological mechanism of religious, spiritual, and sexual experiences are identical," suggesting a direct evolutionary link between sexuality and religion.[38]

As Above, So Below

If human beings are sacred, and sexuality is how we are created, then sexuality is also inherently sacred. The macrocosmic cycle of sacred energy flow from the divine plane to the human, and back again to the divine, is replicated on a microcosmic scale within every human body. Awakening to this ecstatic inner communion requires disciplined practice, and is the birthright of every human being. Because these practices work primarily with inner energies, they are equally applicable and effective for every human being including LGBTQ+ persons.

Interspiritual Training to Resacralize Sexuality

The time has come for authentic living masters of Taoist sexual alchemy, Hindu tantra, Buddhist tantra, and the Western esoteric traditions to join together and synthesize their wisdom into an unprecedented non-sectarian training curriculum that skillfully imparts the long-hidden secrets and practices of sexuality and spirituality. Trainings could be conducted in gender-balanced teams with full mutual accountability, sharing all power and decision-making, to implement this curriculum with maximum integrity, sensitivity, and safeguards. Some will dismiss this vision as utterly delusional, infeasible, or worse; but let those masters who know this is possible begin this collaborative mission now. It will take years to develop properly, but could become an unprecedented gift from Interspirituality to humanity — training earnest people everywhere to transmute sensual experience into spiritual communion, and pornographic distraction into passionate devotion.

Every human being is endowed with the requisite neuro-biological equipment, by Divine design, of the sexual organs and the cerebro-spinal axis from crown to perineum, plus the central nervous system and glands with their vast inner rivers of neuro-transmitters and hormones flowing through the intricate web of bio-spiritual pathways, concentrated in the chakras. Surely WHO-ever or WHAT-ever created these magnificent human bodies intended us to live in the fullness of our bio-chemical-hormonal-sexual-spiritual capacities — in dynamic flow and communion with their cosmic counterparts, for the highest human and divine purposes. As the celebrated Dzogchen master Tulku Urgyen Rinpoche has affirmed, *karmamudra* (sexual yoga) is an "incomparable path" for realizing the highest spiritual realization of Mahamudra or Dzogchen.[39]

Conclusion: What Way Forward for Interspirituality?

The goal of Interspirituality is not to replace the existing religions, but rather to:

1. identify universal spiritual truth(s) found across all major religions, and reveal the deeper common ground from which they all emerge;

2. uphold each religion as a unique, exquisite pathway to realization of ultimate spiritual reality (by whatever divine Name or concept is invoked);

3. overcome religious exclusivity, and cultivate mutual respect, love, and collaboration among the religions, so they unite rather than divide the human family;

4. reclaim the long-hidden esoteric spiritual traditions within most religions;

5. provide an alternative spiritual pathway for those seeking a multi-dimensional or inter-traditional spirituality;

6. correct the disastrous legacy of gender imbalance and male domination in virtually every religion;

7. establish feminine wisdom lineages and cultivate female spiritual mastery;

8. serve as refuge for healing and spiritual renewal for people who have been harmed by traditional religion(s);

9. cultivate new spiritual practices that restore and expand the scope of ecstatic religious ceremonies and praxis; and

10. serve as a transformative catalyst and shining example for existing religions to thoroughly renew themselves, reverse the damage they have caused, and ultimately fulfill their highest potential.

At a time when people are leaving traditional religion in droves, Interspirituality provides an unprecedented opportunity to uplift the best aspects of the religious traditions, and combine them with the best of esoteric spirituality and ancient wisdom — coupled with key insights from contemporary science and transpersonal psychology

— to create a truly comprehensive spirituality in new wineskins. Nothing less will suffice, if humanity is to be reborn anew in the third millennium.

Endnotes and References for "Can Interspirituality…" Feature[xiii]

The Interspiritual Milieu
by Netanel Miles-Yépez

"In the divine milieu all the elements of the universe touch each other by that which is most inward and ultimate in them." — Pierre Teilhard de Chardin, *The Divine Milieu*

In January of 1949, a French Benedictine monk, Henri Le Saux, traveled to southern India with a friend to visit the *ashram* of the great sage Sri Ramana Maharshi who lived at the foot of the holy mountain Arunachala. After a deeply moving encounter with the sage, Le Saux wrote in his diary that he felt he had been "initiated" there into the "Hindu monastic life."[1] Just two years later, he took the name Abhishiktananda (Sanskrit, "anointed with bliss") and founded Saccidananda Ashram on the banks of the Kaveri in Tamil Nadu, thus initiating the Christian *sannyāsa* movement for those who wished to live their Christianity in the manner of Hindu renunciates, as he would himself for the rest of his life.[2]

Not long after Abhishiktananda's death in the mid-1970s, a Hasidic *rebbe* and Holocaust survivor would meet with an unusual Indian-American Sufi *shaykh* in Northern California to do a thing rarely seen in the history of religions — to exchange initiations and lineages across traditions. The charismatic Hasidic rabbi, Rabbi Zalman Schachter-

Shalomi, dressed in the black silk caftan of his Polish Hasidic forbears, would be made a *shaykh* in the universalist Sufi lineage of Hazrat Inayat Khan; while the white-robed Sufi *shaykh,* Pir Vilayat Inayat Khan, would be initiated into the esoteric priesthood of Melchizedek and the study of *kabbalah.*[3]

In the Fall of 1976, Beverly Lanzetta, a young mother of three, recently separated, found temporary shelter in a friend's rustic cabin near the Pacific Ocean. One morning, while passing through the living room, she suddenly saw the wall to the kitchen dissolve, "revealing an endless expanse of palpable light." Falling to the floor, she lay immobile for the next several hours as waves of profound love and suffering poured through her entire body and being. It was an experience, she later described, of the "wounded heart" of the universe, of "a God without a name or a religion."[4] The experience would change the course of her life, leading her to study mystical theology, and later to found an ecumenically-oriented "new monastic" community.

Still later, in the 1980s, a Washington D.C.-born Christian pastor named Diane Wilson, fully in love with the Gospel, heard her Savior's voice calling from behind a door in a vision. Opening that door, she began an extraordinary journey through the "many rooms" of God's house, unexpectedly finding herself, after years of searching, at the feet of Buddhist masters in Nepal and China, and eventually being called the Venerable Pannavati, the first fully ordained African-American Theravadin Buddhist *bhikkhuni* in the West, embodying and teaching an unusually relational *dharma*, and ordaining a new generation of ecumenically-oriented *dharma* teachers.[5]

Interspirituality

Recognizing himself in such people, people who walk an unusual, though still committed path between religious traditions — sometimes *joining* and *unifying* them, sometimes *transcending* them — Brother Wayne Teasdale, an American monk of Abhishiktananda's Christian *sannyasa* movement, coined the word Interspiritual to describe their common experiences, as well as a range of ideas related to the internal and external dialogue between religious traditions.

For Teasdale, spiritual is not an oppositional word; it is not meant to emphasize contrasting perspectives, like religious or secular. It is used inclusively to unite them, to speak of the totality of human experience and possibility. "Being *spiritual,*" he writes, "is a personal commitment to a process of inner development that engages our totality."[6] The prefix *inter-*, then, "expresses the ontological roots that tie the various traditions together and that are responsible for religions influencing each other throughout history. It conveys a fundamental truth: the essential spiritual interdependence of the religions. Spiritual interdependence among the religions exists because an essential interconnectedness in being and reality exists."[7]

Basing himself on Buddhist philosophy, Teasdale is suggesting that the prefix *inter-* is merely an outward expression of a truth already resident in spirituality, and indeed, in all phenomena. Religions and spiritual traditions are not truly separate, having no independent existence from each other, because nothing does — everything is co-arising dependently. They share ultimate origins and common causation. Those ontological origins make them prone, as it were, to influence from one another. That is to say, it is in the DNA of religions to influence and absorb influence from one another, and to represent that possibility. Thus, all religions and spiritual traditions are interconnected because interconnectedness is the chief feature of reality.

And yet, Interspirituality is not defined solely by Brother Wayne Teasdale, who passed in 2004; nor is the word the only expression of the general notion he sought to encapsulate. Rather, it serves to connect a number of related ideas brought forth from the pioneers of interfaith dialogue, and the ideas of those who would continue the work of Interspirituality today.

Deep Ecumenism and Interspirituality

One of these related expressions is deep ecumenism, particularly as used by Father Matthew Fox and Rabbi Zalman Schachter-Shalomi. The word ecumenism—derived from the Greek *oikoumene*, "the whole world" — originally referred to cooperative dialogue and meaningful collaboration between different parts of the Christian *ecclesia,* the "congregation" of all Christians everywhere.[8] Eventually, however, its meaning among Christians expanded to include other religions, and to describe the dialogue between them. Adding the qualifier deep to ecumenism — inspired by Joanna Macy's "deep ecology"[9] — Father Matthew Fox, a former Dominican priest (officially silenced for his radical teachings and work with other religions), was also extending a metaphor of the Christian mystic Meister Eckhart: "Divinity is an Underground river that no one can stop and no one can dam up."[10] That river, Fox suggests, is the common and sacred source of all being, and thus all religion. "To go down a well," he says, "is to practice a tradition, but we would make a grave mistake (an idolatrous one) if we confused the well itself with the flowing waters of the underground river."[11] The depth of deep ecumenism refers to its emphasis on the sacred source giving birth to and connecting all of our sacred traditions.

But deep ecumenism is not merely a kind of perennial philosophy, focused on the common source of our traditions while neglecting their uniqueness and diversity; its depth is layered. We are indeed connected by a common source — some might say, unavoidably and unmistakably interconnected — but we are also connected structurally. Borrowing language from Noam Chomsky's transformational grammar, we might speak of "deep" and "surface structures" in religion. Deep structures are those themes and elements of teaching and practice that are common across traditions, like creation myths and prayer, even if expressed or emphasized differently. The unique expressions are surface structures, like the specific account of creation in the book of Genesis and the Gayatri *mantra* of the Hindu tradition. From deep structures, we learn to appreciate our common humanity; from surface structures, we learn to appreciate our creative diversity. Perhaps more importantly, in the witness of our juxtaposed diversity, our self-understanding as human beings is increased, and we may find options for getting unstuck when the path or practice of one tradition seems closed to us.

This latter perspective is closer to that of Rabbi Zalman Schachter-Shalomi, the founder of the Jewish Renewal movement, who spoke of deep ecumenism as a look beneath the surface to the inner workings of religion, to the scaffolding of the "generic religion" beneath our historical traditions.[12]

Hyphenated Spirituality and Multiple Religious Belonging

Another phenomenon of Interspirituality is something we might call "hyphenated spirituality." In a 1997 dialogue with Jewish-born Zen *roshi* Bernie Glassman, Schachter-Shalomi observed that there is hardly anyone today who does not "have some kind of a 'hyphen,' whether it be an African-American, a Hindu-Scientist, a Sufi-Jew, or a Jewish-Buddhist." The "hyphen," he suggests, is the expression of a planetary need for diversity, the ability to call on the "strength and resources" of more than one tradition, at all levels and in all aspects of society.[13] Thus, we find dedicated Christians who are also Jungian psychotherapists, resolved atheists with a deeply enriching Yoga practice, couples overcoming the demands of intermarriage for the sake of their love, and individuals integrating dual cultural identities.

So why should it be any different with religions? With all the jostling and bumping up against one another that happens in a globally connected world, new relationships are bound to form, just as atoms gain and lose electrons, or different chemical compounds are formed in seemingly random interactions. In the world of spirituality, increasingly frequent contacts and exposure have led to the development of hyphenated religious identities — Christian priests who have become recognized Zen roshis or rabbis who have become Sufi shaykhs, indigenous elders who have plumbed the theosophical depths.[14] In the struggle to define themselves — not by one identity or the other — some of them have chosen to call themselves interspiritual.

What we have called hyphenated here, others have called "Multiple Religious Belonging."[15] For some, the latter term has the advantage of sounding more formal and descriptive, but hyphenated may actually be the more significant and broadly applicable descriptor, in as much as it represents the individual as nexus, connecting two or more traditions. Moreover, those traditions are not necessarily religions. The hyphen may connect two normative religious traditions (like Christianity and Islam); it might also connect two supra-normative or esoteric traditions (such as Sufism and Hasidism), or a normative tradition and a supra-normative tradition (like Christianity and Zen). The hyphen is the "inter" in Interspirituality.

Interbeing and Nepantla

Perhaps the most accurate expression of Interspirituality's truth is the notion of interbeing, harkening back to Brother Wayne Teasdale's own definition. The Vietnamese Zen Buddhist monk Thích Nhất Hạnh says of a page in one of his own books: "If you are a poet, you will see clearly that there is a cloud floating in this sheet of paper. Without a cloud, there will be no rain; without rain, the trees cannot grow; and without trees, we cannot make paper. The cloud is essential for the paper to exist. If the cloud is not here, the sheet of paper cannot be here either. So we can say that the cloud and the paper *inter-are*."[16]

The notion of interbeing corrects a misapprehension of ourselves as independent and separate from anything else. For instance, Thích Nhất Hạnh might say, *a tree* is implicit in everything that we do and know, for there is no human life without an oxygen rich environment, no oxygen rich environment without trees and other flora. Thus, the phrase "I am," as it is usually applied, is inaccurate and incomplete without a tree. In truth, we *inter-are* or are *inter-being*. The same misapprehension holds true of our ordinary object relations. We tend to say, "I am sitting on a chair," believing that "I" am the subject sitting, and the chair is the object upon which I sit. But in reality, we are actually "inter-sitting." Subject and object are merely a matter of perspective; the reality is interactive.

The specific emphasis here is on the "between," and not what it connects. That is to say, interbeing and Interspirituality represent *liminality,* threshold spaces and identities defying conventional categorization, perhaps similar to Gloria Anzaldúa's notion of *nepantleras,* "threshold people, living within and among multiple worlds; through painful negotiations," developing what Anzaldúa calls "perspective[s] from the cracks."[17] Using the Nahuatl word *nepantla,* referring to "an in-between state," Anzaldúa describes "that uncertain terrain one crosses when moving from one place to another; when changing from one class, race, or sexual position to another; when changing from the present identity into a new identity."[18] In this sense, the Interspiritual may likewise understand themselves as "threshold people" who walk the liminal paths between complex religious and cultural identities, saying, "I am not *in* a tradition [or even *between* traditions]; I am simply *Interspiritual.*"

Interreligious and Interspiritual Dialogue

Although Interspirituality was, in a sense, born out of interfaith or interreligious dialogue, these terms no longer serve as adequate descriptors for the dialogue of Interspirituality. The dialogue between religions continues, of course, and must for obvious reasons. It is the work of Protestant ministers and Brahmin priests, Zen monks and Sunni imams, learning to share the planet and paving the way for their *ecclesia* to do the same; but the encounter of interspiritual dialogue does not take place between religions or representatives of religions. That is to say, religious ideas and information about one another's religion are not the focus of the dialogue; it is the individual in the act of dialogue, bearing all the complexities of their religio-spiritual identity.

As Rory McEntee and Adam Bucko write in their influential interspiritual manifesto, the word Interspirituality is "used to denote the phenomenon of the world's Wisdom Traditions moving beyond interfaith dialogue into a more intimate and symbiotic relationship."

For them, interfaith or interreligious dialogue is "a first step, allowing the traditions to learn about one another," thus engendering deep respect and trust.[19] Interspirituality, however, builds on that foundation and deepens the sharing to include what Rabbi Zalman Schachter-Shalomi has called "participatory epistemology," participation in the inner world and practices of another religious tradition.[20] The knowledge gained from such experiential learning, he suggests, can open one to an understanding of the "basic technology" beneath the religious exterior, allowing us to discern what is essential from what is accidental (in the philosophical sense) in our own religious traditions. In many ways, this is what the early Indologist Max Müller had in mind when he paraphrased Goethe, saying, "He who knows only one religion, knows none."[21]

Schachter-Shalomi called this the "dialogue of devoutness,"[22] meeting at the place of our devotion and longing for transformation. The "dialogue of theology," he says, begins where we should finish, and often inhibits actual dialogue because it begins with our conclusions rather than our questions.[23] Thus, we come to an ideal of individuals meeting in spiritual intimacy, with a mutual commitment to honest self-appraisal and genuine curiosity to learn through experimentation.

Of course, some might say that this was *always* the goal of interreligious dialogue, and such spiritual intimacy was the result of it. The latter is certainly true; but the former was a loftier goal, to which many were unable or unwilling to commit. A healthy pluralism was the proximate goal of interreligious dialogue, even with those who longed for more. Raimundo Panikkar, a forerunner of Interspirituality if ever there was one, and one of the leading thinkers in interreligious dialogue, wrote: "The aim of [interreligious] dialogue is understanding. It is not to win over the other or to come to a total agreement or a universal religion. The ideal is communication in order to bridge the gulfs of mutual ignorance and misunderstandings between the different cultures of the world, letting them speak and speak out their own insights in their own languages. Some may wish even to reach communion, but this does not imply at all that the aim is a uniform unity or a reduction of all the pluralistic variety [...]."[24]

Thus, interreligious dialogue has an external goal and orientation, which may be distinguished from its inner dimension and possible effect. One aspect of this inner dimension, Panikkar called the *intra-religious* dialogue, "an inner dialogue within myself, an encounter in the depth of my personal religiousness, having met another religious experience [in the form of another's testimony] on that very intimate level."[25] The intra-religious dialogue is seen as an opportunity to learn about *oneself* while in full engagement with another, creating an opening for growth and change.

Intra-religious dialogue, spiritual intimacy, and the dialogue of devoutness, are what might collectively be called the "inner dimension of interreligious dialogue." In *interspiritual* dialogue, these possible features or byproducts of interreligious dialogue become the goal. Thus, interspiritual dialogue might be seen as a kind of diagnostic to be run on one's spiritual life and tradition — to see how well each is functioning — and to be used as a tool for refining one's own understanding and experience.

And yet, as we have said, interspiritual dialogue is *not* between religions or representatives of religions. The identities and representation of the dialoguers is as complex and nuanced as our discussion of Interspirituality itself, ranging from multiple religious belonging (e.g., Christian-Muslim) to hyphenated identities connecting an exoteric tradition with an esoteric tradition historically bound to another exoteric tradition (e.g., Jewish-Sufi), to those "threshold people" who occupy and identify with the liminal.[26]

Is Interspirituality a New Religion?

In *The Mystic Heart,* Brother Wayne Teasdale writes: "The real religion of humankind can be said to be spirituality itself, because mystical spirituality is the origin of all the world religions. If this is so, and I believe it is, we might also say that *Interspirituality* — the sharing of ultimate experiences across traditions — is the religion of the third millennium."[27]

Witnessing the ever-increasing interactions between religions and spiritual traditions, the new configurations of spiritual identity announced in every social media post, it is hard to deny the apparent evolutionary trajectory of Interspirituality and the growth of a new "religion of spirituality."[28] As Beverly Lanzetta describes, "if it is a religion, it is unlike any we have known, for it is free of the universalist or exclusivist claim and without need of a determinate form or final name. Its underlying structure is dynamic and self-emptying, radically democratic and absent of one all-inspiring prophet."[29]

But I am not yet ready to declare, as some have done, that the dawn of this religion is upon us, or that such a prediction includes the necessary demise of our historical traditions. Teasdale speaks of a "religion of the third millennium" that honors the interconnectedness of religions, not of a religion that makes them irrelevant or spells their demise. We must assume that they will go on, continuing to evolve as we do, and to ends that will surprise us, because Interspirituality is not their replacement, it is the matrix of their evolution and interdependence.

Endnotes and References for "Interspiritual Milieu" Feature[xiv]

INTERVAL TO VOLUME 2

What a fitting way to conclude this first Volume — a capstone feature on "The Interspiritual Milieu" by the editor, Netanel Miles-Yépez, of the book *The Common Heart: An Experience of Interreligious Dialogue* [2006] that culminated the work of the Snowmass Interreligious Dialogues with the "Nine Points of Agreement" among the world's religions. It is especially apt as we move into Volume 2, *Interspirituality: The Future*.

In preparing these Volumes, we hoped that the "break" between Volume 1 and Volume 2 would include three elements: a natural break creating volumes of similar length; the emergence of a date that would represent a natural transition from the contents of the first volume to the second; and, the thematic transition from Interspirituality, solely in its religious and spiritual contexts, to the larger reality of our current world — the relationship of spirituality and science.

The emergent chronological partition between Volumes 1 and 2 and their contents, timelines, and benchmarks is @2015. That year is significant to both the growth of the global interspiritual experience *and* the relationship of spirituality and science. As recounted in the early pages of Volume 2, 2015 saw the first major international mergers of interspiritually-oriented organizations and networks on a global basis. And, as elaborated in detail as well in Volume 2, 2015 was the year that mainstream evolutionary science turned its understanding of "natural selection" ("survival of the fittest") — Darwin's driver of evolution itself — toward cooperation and partnership, not simply competition. It came to understand, as does the philosophy of science, that as a system complexifies, rules and norms can change, and in the case of our complex global culture of a somewhat intelligent species (*Homo sapiens*), "fitness" is potently connected to cooperation and partnership, not simply competition.

Moreover, given the strong relationship of the growing global interspiritual experience to international organizations and networks stressing international cooperation (*multi-lateralism*) like the United Nations — with its world-serving elements including UNESCO (the UN Economic and Social Council and its dynamic Culture of Peace Programme), UNEP (the UN Environmental Program), UNICEF (the UN Childrens Fund), the SDGs (the Sustainable Development Goals, themselves evolving toward not just the sustainable but the regenerative), and so many more — partnership is the name of the game. *And*, 2015 was also the year of the Papal Encyclical *Laudato Si'* ("On Care for Our Common Home"), a statement of solidarity with "all things interconnected."

In this context, we invite you to join us in Volume 2: *Interspirituality: The Future.*

ENDNOTES
Volume 1

i: Endnotes and References for Opening Message, Foreword, and Introduction

For the Opening Message: H. H. the 14th Dalai Lama authored the Foreword to Br. Teasdale's *The Mystic Heart* and for his Opening Message in the current Volumes we thank him, his staff, the creators of *The Wisdom of Happiness* film and Oneness of Humanity Awards for arranging this Opening Message.

For the Foreword: [1.] Matthew Fox, *Hildegard of Bingen, a Saint For Our Times,* (Vancouver: Namaste Publishing, 2012), p. 54. [2.] See Matthew Fox, *Meister Eckhart: A Mystic-Warrior for Our Times* (Novato, CA: New World Library, 2014) pp. 13, 223ff., 235f. [3.] Cited in Matthew Fox, *The Coming of the Cosmic Christ* (NY: HarperOne, 1988), p. 126.

For the Introduction: [1.] The "We" in these Volumes' commentaries — a journalistic "We" — refers both to the editorial staff of Light on Light listed on the Copyright Page and in the "Message from the Publisher" *and* the voices from the extensive material consulted in the preparation of these Volumes noted further below. Rather than listing specific editor or editors in title pages of these Volumes, the editorial staff is listed on the two pages noted above. We have wanted the Volumes themselves to "stand on their own" with the contributions of the Featured Authors. For the commentary sections of these Volumes we have taken a journalistic approach, the overall goal of which was to create a "conversational tone" giving the reader maximum accessibility to the breadth of materials in these books. We have not created commentaries "out of nowhere" but have drawn them by consulting extensive existing and extant materials, both published and unpublished, along with twenty-five years of correspondence among interspiritual leaders and the related unpublished attachments. Consequently, commentaries herein are drawn from multiple sources curated in a journalistic fashion to address the subject matter and thematics appropriate to this or that section of a Volume, the questions being asked, and the contexts being examined. Thus, as the Introduction notes, these Volumes are both a thematic and historical chronicle. As further noted there, we have employed commentary throughout the Volumes to enhance comprehensiveness of both history and thematics and to allow the books to be read with a sense of narrative, direction, and chronological and thematic coherence. The views of these commentaries may or may not agree with those of the Featured Authors, and the views of Featured Authors do not necessarily agree with, or represent, the views of the Publisher's editorial teams. But we have drawn from, and then striven to represent to the best of our abilities, the extensive materials consulted utilizing this kind of journalistic approach. [2.] H. H. the 14th Dalai Lama authored the Foreword to Br. Teasdale's *The Mystic Heart,* and for his Opening Message in the current Volumes we thank him, his staff, the creators of *The Wisdom of Happiness* film and Oneness of Humanity Awards for arranging this Introduction. [3.] Interspiritual Pioneers listing, illustrations, thecominginterspiritualage.com and isdna.org. [4.] Cover and Advanced Praise comments in Johnson, Kurt and David Robert Ord. 2013. *The Coming Interspiritual Age.* Vancouver, CN: Namaste Publishing. [5.] See lists of Riane Eisler's books on the domination to partnership cultural spectrum, like https://www.goodreads.com/author/list/2752081.Riane_Eisler.

ii: Endnotes and References for "History" Section

[1.] See Teasdale, Wayne. 2002. *A Monk in the World.* Novato, CA: New World Library. [2.] Interspiritual Pioneers listing, illustrations, thecominginterspiritualage.com and isdna.org; bulleted elements, see version from *Universal Principles and Action Steps* pp. 21-22 published in United Nations community, https://issuu.com/lightonlight. [3.] See Wilber, Ken. *Integral Spirituality: A Startling New Role for Religion in the Modern and Post-modern World.* Boston, MA: Shambhala, 2006. [4.] See citations and discussion in "Toward Unity Consciousness" in *The Coming Interspiritual Age,* pp. 225-238. [5.] See "Toward Unity Consciousness" in *The Coming Interspiritual Age,* pp. 225-238. [6.] Hawken, Paul. 2007. *Blessed Unrest, How the Largest Movement in the World Came into Being and Why No One Saw It Coming.* New York, NY: Penguin Books. [7.] See "Toward Unity Consciousness" and "The Great Coming Together" in *The Coming Interspiritual Age,* pp. 225-252. [8.] Küng, Hans. 1995. *Christianity: Essence, History, and Future.* New York, NY: Continuum International Publishing. ***Other Cited References:*** Br. Wayne Teasdale quotations: Teasdale, Wayne. 1999. *The Mystic Heart: Discovering a Universal Spirituality in the World's Religions*. Novato, CA: New World Library / Johnson, Kurt and David Robert Ord. 2013. *The Coming Interspiritual Age*. Vancouver, CN: Namaste Publishing / Ulfik, Rick, Kurt Johnson and Shannon Marie Winters (Ed.). 2021. *Universal Principles and Action Steps: A Historic Collection Gathered from Organizations, Networks, NGOs and Thought Leaders around the World*. Education Synergy Circle of the Evolutionary Leaders: https://issuu.com/lightonlight.

iii: Endnotes and References for "Interspirituality Itself" Section

[1.] Interspiritual Pioneers listing, illustrations, thecominginterspiritualage.com and isdna.org. [2.] See references and citations in "Scientific Consciousness Studies" pp. 157-161, "Toward Unity Consciousness" and "The Great Coming Together" pp. 225-252 and "Moving Toward the World Centric" pp. 297-309 in *The Coming Interspiritual Age*. [3.] See Wilber, Ken. *Integral Spirituality: A Startling New Role for Religion in the Modern and Post-modern World*. Boston, MA: Shambhala, 2006. [4.] See those named Sections in *Universal Principles and Action Steps*, https://issuu.com/lightonlight and re: Earth Charter Commission in *Sacred Sites and Spirituality in Nature*, https://issuu.com/lightonlight. [5.] See "Points of Agreement" Section in these Volumes and pp. 21-22 in *Universal Principles and Action Steps* published in United Nations community, https://issuu.com/lightonlight, re: original publications see Teasdale, Wayne. [6.] See data, citations and references in free publications at https://issuu.com/lightonlight and in Nautilus and "Best in Small Press" Nautilus Award winning books by Ervin Laszlo, and global thought leaders edited by Ervin Laszlo and David Lorimer (Chair, Galileo Commission) at lightonlight.us. *References*: Miles-Yépez, Netanel [Ed.]. 2006. *The Common Heart: An Experience of Interreligious Dialogue*. Brooklyn, NY: Lantern Books / Johnson, Kurt and David Robert Ord. 2013. *The Coming Interspiritual Age*. Vancouver, CN: Namaste Publishing / Laszlo, Ervin. 2024. *The Survival Imperative: Upshifting to Conscious Evolution*. New York, NY: Light on Light Press / Laszlo, Ervin and David Lorimer (Ed.). 2024. *The Great Upshift: Humanity's Coming Advance Toward Peace and Harmony on the Planet*. New York, NY: Light on Light Press / Laszlo, Ervin et al. 2024. *Humanity's Sacred Mission, Our Sacred Mission* e-publication anthologies at https://issuu.com/lightonlight / Teasdale, Wayne. 1999. *The Mystic Heart: Discovering a Universal Spirituality in the World's Religions*. Novato, CA: New World Library / Ulfik, Rick, Kurt Johnson and Shannon Marie Winters (Ed.). 2021. *Universal Principles and Action Steps: A Historic Collection Gathered from Organizations, Networks, NGOs and Thought Leaders around the World*. Education Synergy Circle of the Evolutionary Leaders: https://issuu.com/lightonlight; https://issuu.com/lightonlight/docs/universal_principles_and_action_steps.

iv: Endnotes and References for "Universal Principles" Section

[1.] Most relevant to this discussion, re: intersubjectivity [of which Interspirituality is a part]— in Physics, Roger Penrose, 2020 Nobel Prize (understanding dimensions of consciousness vis-a-vis quantum reality and wave functions); in 2022, Alain Aspect, John Clauser, and Anton Zeilinger Nobel Prize (re: quantum reality and human experience — quantum entanglement and non-locality); and in economics, Elinor Ostrom (re: human relations and the "tragedy of the commons," why humans trying to work together so often fail and how it can be remedied). **[2.]** See pp. 244-247 in "The Great Coming Together" in *The Coming Interspiritual Age*. ***References***: historically published versions of Points of Agreement have differed slightly. For this text's versions of Points of Agreement: Ulfik, Rick, Kurt Johnson and Shannon Marie Winters (Ed.). 2021. *Universal Principles and Action Steps: A Historic Collection Gathered from Organizations, Networks, NGOs and Thought Leaders around the World*. Education Synergy Circle of the Evolutionary Leaders: https://issuu.com/lightonlight; original versions Miles-Yépez, Netanel [Ed.]. 2006. *The Common Heart: An Experience of Interreligious Dialogue*. Brooklyn NY: Lantern Books / Teasdale, Wayne. 1999. *The Mystic Heart: Discovering a Universal Spirituality in the World's Religions*. Novato, CA: New World Library; other versions Johnson, Kurt and David Robert Ord. 2013. *The Coming Interspiritual Age*. Vancouver, CN: Namaste Publishing.

v: Endnotes and References for "Points of Agreement" Section

[1.] Historically published versions of Points of Agreement have differed slightly

— sometimes changed over time by subsequent convenings of authors. Many have been published widely in the interspiritual literature after their initial or early publications as noted below. All these Points of Agreement included herein were published together as "The Interspiritual Declaration" in Ulfik, Rick, Kurt Johnson and Shannon Marie Winters (Ed.). 2021. *Universal Principles and Action Steps: A Historic Collection Gathered from Organizations, Networks, NGOs and Thought Leaders around the World.* Education Synergy Circle of the Evolutionary Leaders: https://issuu.com/lightonlight assembled at the time of the 2018 Parliament of the World's Religions and published in 2021. [2.] For this text's version, *Universal Principles and Action Steps*, loc. cit.; original version Miles-Yépez , Netanel [Ed.]. 2006. *The Common Heart: An Experience of Interreligious Dialogue.* Brooklyn, NY: Lantern Books. [3.] For this text's version, *Universal Principles and Action Steps*, loc. cit.; original version: Teasdale, Wayne. 1999. *The Mystic Heart: Discovering a Universal Spirituality in the World's Religions.* Novato, CA: New World Library. The original Nine Elements were not listed by Teasdale in a list but used as subtitles (with additional comments) in *The Mystic Heart* (1999). [4.] These Points of Agreement had separate origins (see below) but were first published in these versions in Johnson, Kurt and David Robert Ord. 2013. *The Coming Interspiritual Age.* Vancouver, CN: Namaste Publishing and then in *Universal Principles and Action Steps*, loc. cit. (2021); The Seven Elements of Interspiritual Education were originally elucidated by One Spirit Interfaith Seminary (New York City) and The Community of the Mystic Heart (Br. Teasdale's association); The Eight Needed World Shifts in Consciousness and The Five Evolutionary Developmental Elements were derived from *The Mystic Heart* by Johnson and Ord and published in *The Coming Interspiritual Age.* Br. Teasdale did not use lists in *The Mystic Heart* but recognized sequential points in his texts.

vi: Endnotes and References for "Conferences..." Section

[1.] See "Towards Unity Consciousness (Origins of the Evolutionary Consciousness Movement)" pp. 226-240; data numbers from adherents.com, in *The Coming Interspiritual Age.* [2.] One Spirit Interfaith Seminary Curriculum on Interspirituality: Classroom handout on Distinguishing Religion and Spirituality. [3.] The Evolutionary

Leaders, a initiative of the Source of Synergy Foundation and their 31 Circles and Collaboratories for Social Engagement and Media Presence: evolutionaryleaders. net and evolutionaryleaders.net/synergy circles. **[4.]** More expansive list of elements of the global evolutionary and wholistic consciousness "movements": *Institutions and Organizations:* The founding of nearly a dozen interfaith seminaries, the California Institute of Integral Studies, Sofia University (formerly the Institute for Transpersonal Psychology), The Interspiritual Network, Satyana Institute, Spiritual Paths Institute, The Claritas Institute, Sophia Institute, Hoffman Institute, The Association for Global New Thought, World Wisdom Council, World Wisdom Alliance, World Commission on Global Consciousness, Alliance for a New Humanity, EnlightenNext, Conflict Transformation Collaborative, United Religions Initiative, The Foundation for Conscious Evolution, General Evolution Research Group, International Society for Systems Sciences, The Social Healing Project, The Oneness Project, the Institute of Noetic Sciences, the organizations built around *A Course in Miracles* and EST, the diverse network of the Evolutionary Leaders, an initiative of the Source of Synergy Foundation. *Centers and Associations:* Esalen and Tassajara Hot Springs in California, California Institute of Asian Studies, Naropa Institute in Colorado, the Snowmass Initiatives group, Omega Institute for Holistic Studies in New York, Blue Spirit Costa Rica, Edinburgh International Centre for Spirituality and Peace, Integral Institute and Integral Multiplex (virtual), Interspiritual Dialogue in Action, Interspiritual Multiplex (virtual), Spiritual Paths Institute, Evolutionary Leaders, Agape International Spiritual Center, the Contemplative Alliance, The Charter for Compassion, the Laszlo Institute, the Galileo Commission, the Occupy movement. *Publications and Media:* Shambala Publications, *Journal of Transpersonal Psychology, Journal of the Scientific Study of Religion, The Yoga Journal, What is Enlightenment?, Light on Light, Convergence,* and *Holomovement* magazines, New Dimension Radio, Namaste Radio, the journals *ReVision, Parabola, Somatics, Kosmos* and *Consciousness and Culture,* the State University of New York's book series on a holistic postmodernism; the Evolutionary Leaders Media Collaboratory including VoiceAmerica radio, Light on Light Publications and Media's commercial print books and free e-magazines and video series, *Humanity's Stream. Seminal World Conferences*: Revival of the Parliaments of the World's Religions, world religious summits of the Temple of Understanding, the Snowmass Dialogues, the Dawn of Interspirituality and other conferences of the Interspiritual Network and Evolutionary Leaders (noted farther below and in these Volumes); various issue-based global summits of the United Nations, first Conference on Voluntary Control of Internal States, first Association of Humanistic Psychology conference on the transpersonal, the international Transpersonal Conferences, the international conferences on A Unity of the Sciences, the Esalen conferences on Ecopsychology, the Kyoto World Conference on Religion and Peace, the Science and Nonduality Conference; diverse in-person and online conferences and media activity of members of The Evolutionary Leaders (ELs) global network, including the EL Synergy Circles and Collaboratories, Evolutionary Partners Network, The Holomovement, UNITY EARTH, Humanity's Team, One World, Connection Field, We.net, Founding Mothers Movement, UnGun Institute, One Planet Peace Forum and many more. Lists updated and adapted from "Selected Developments During the Emerging Holistic Epoch" in *The Coming Interspiritual Age*. **References**: Johnson, Kurt and David Robert Ord. 2013. *The Coming Interspiritual Age*. Vancouver CN: Namaste Publishing.

vii: Endnotes and References for "Timelines" and "Benchmarks" Sections

[1.] "Towards a Global Ethic: An Initial Declaration,"1993, from The Parliament of the World's Religions details ethical commitments shared by many of the world's religious, spiritual, and cultural traditions and is the Parliament's signature document: parliamentofreligions.org/globalethic. [2.] Fr. Thomas Keating O.C.S.O: "The Snowmass Agreements," *Contemplative Outreach News* Vol. 40. No. 2 June 2023; posted online July 23, 2023: https://www.contemplativeoutreach.org/ newsletter/2023-june-july-the-snowmass-agreements/; and Afterword in Miles-Yépez, Netanel [Ed.]. 2006. *The Common Heart: An Experience of Interreligious Dialogue*. Brooklyn NY: Lantern Books. [3.] *Namaste Insights*. October 4, 2015. "Namaste Insights, The Coming Interspiritual Age, Special Edition," Expanded ["Archive"] Edition. Originally posted at https://issuu.com/yorkmin/docs/the_ coming_interspiritual_age_archive_edition [original pagination p. 137 f.] [no longer online]. [4.] *Namaste Insights*. October 4, 2015. "Namaste Insights, The Coming Interspiritual Age, Special Edition," Expanded ["Archive"] Edition [no

longer online]. Originally posted [original pagination p. 214f.] at https://issuu.
com/yorkmin/docs/the_coming_interspiritual_age_archive_edition [5.] YouTube:
"Coming Together at the Crestone Convergence": https://www.youtube.com/
watch?v=xAVZtVD1sj0&t=30s; and re: Ken Wilber's video from the Self Care to
Earth Care Conference: https://www.youtube.com/watch?v=H4jcxxJ_0ok&t=137s.
Note also in *The Song of the Earth* (also previously cited) Harland and Keepin include
voices from this thematic. [6.] A fuller biography: Br. Wayne Teasdale (1945-2004).
After a decade of living the contemplative life at Hundred Acres Monastery in New
Hampshire, Br. Wayne Teasdale was invited in 1986 by Father Bede Griffiths, an
English Benedictine living in India and sharing the practice Advaita Vedanta in India,
to join him. From that time on, drawing on this and many other trans-traditional
relationships, particularly also with His Holiness the Dalai Lama, Br. Wayne shared,
and also published widely about, the common ground of contemplative experience.
He authored many books, among them *The Mystic Heart: Discovering a Universal
Spirituality in the World's Religions* and *A Monk in the World: Cultivating a
Spiritual Life*. His other books include: *Catholicism in Dialogue: Conversations
Across Traditions*; *Come and Sit: A Week Inside Meditation Centers*; *Hermitage of
the Heart: Contemplative Practices from Hundred Acres Monastery*; *Community of
Religions: Voices and Images of the Parliament of the World's Religions*; *Essays in
Mysticism; Yoga of Sound: Healing & Enlightenment Through the Sacred Practice
of Mantra* (with Russill Paul); *Bede Griffiths: An Introduction to His Interspiritual
Thought* (with Bede Griffiths); *Awakening the Spirit, Inspiring the Soul: 30 Stories
of Interspiritual Discovery in the Community of Faiths* (with Martha Howard, MD)
and *Mystic Hours: A Daybook Of Inspirational Wisdom And Devotion*. Taking a path
of service as well, Br. Wayne served on the Trustee board of the Parliament of the
World's Religions and the Bede Griffiths International Trust. He was also a leader
in the Interfaith Call for Freedom of Worship and Human Rights in Tibet and was
a member of the Monastic Interreligious Dialogue and helped draft their Universal
Declaration on Nonviolence. As a Christian sannyasa (renunciate), which vows
he took before Francis Cardinal George, the Archbishop of Chicago, in 2003, Br.
Wayne resided at the Catholic Theological Union in Chicago, where he taught as an
adjunct professor of Spirituality. He also taught at DePaul University and Columbia
College. Br. Wayne held an M.A. in philosophy from St. Joseph College and a Ph.D.

in theology from Fordham University. Members of the ISDnA network first met Br. Wayne in New York City in 2002. InterSpiritual Dialogue was founded under Br. Wayne's tutelage through members of the United Nations NGO community in 2003, and Br. Wayne was intended to host, with that group, a session on his interspiritual vision at the 2004 Parliament of the World's Religions in Barcelona, Spain. Too ill to attend, the session was hosted by members of the network, and Br. Wayne transitioned on October 20, 2004. In 2005, friends, persons, and groups inspired by Br. Wayne worldwide gathered at The Crossings retreat center in Austin, Texas, and as result of that meeting, the international network ISDnA was inaugurated. Source: About / Brother Wayne isdna.org. **[7.]** From "A Tribute to Fr. Thomas Keating: a legacy event July12-14, 2019." In *Change Makers: Leadership and Transformation. Light on Light Magazine* series, Fall 2019, Issue 5, pp. 52-54. https://issuu.com/lightonlight/docs/lightonlight_issue_5. **[8.]** *Universal Principles and Action Steps: A Historic Collection Gathered from Organizations, Networks, NGOs and Thought Leaders around the World.* Education Synergy Circle of the Evolutionary Leaders: https://issuu.com/lightonlight. **[9.]** Hellmich, Phillip and Kurt Johnson. 2016. "Sacred and Secular Activists are Now Joining their Strategies for Peacebuilding." pp. 27-41 in Cook, Bruce L. and Maria Cristina Azcona [Ed.]. *Strategies for Peace.* Elgin, IL: Cook Communication. **[10.]** The Awakening Trilogy by Lama Surya Das consists of three books: *Awakening the Buddha Within.* 1997. New York, NY: Broadway Books. *Awakening to the Sacred.* 1999. New York, NY: Broadway Books. *Awakening the Buddhist Heart.* 2000. New York, NY: Broadway Books. **[11.]** The Dawn of InterSpirituality [sic] Conference (aka Dawn of Interspirituality) September 29-October 4, 2013 at Cascadian Center, near Seattle, WA, sponsored by Satyana Institute and organized with a collective of international interfaith organizations was a foundational interspiritual event that brought together over 200 spiritual leaders from around the world. Extensive materials from the nearly 40 presentations at this conference: https://dawnofinterspirituality.org/2013-dawn-of-interspirituality/ **[12.]** Feature: "Dzieci Theatre: A Creative Experiment in Interspirituality" by Matt Mitler; excerpted in Volume 2, published in full in Volume 3 [subsequent e-publication]. **[13.]** *Universal Principles and Action Steps.* Ibid. loc. cit. **[14.]** *The Interfaith Observer* is an important resource for tracking the history and growth of Interspirituality. Accordingly, we share this extensive endnote that indexes all of the major articles published in TIO by these important interspiritual voices, all of whom are Featured Authors to these Volumes:

http://www.theinterfaithobserver.org/search?q=Kurt%20Johnson (for K. Johnson);

http://www.theinterfaithobserver.org/search?q=Diane%20Berke (for Diane Berke);

[Note: this includes "'Interfaith Seminaries' Chart New Territory" (Sept. 2012) by Diane Berke and Kurt Johnson (which includes a checklist, with links, to all international Interfaith Seminaries at the time of that publication) which was noted in particular in the text of these Volumes.]

http://www.theinterfaithobserver.org/search?q=Will%20Keepin (for Will Keepin);

http://www.theinterfaithobserver.org/search?q=Cynthia%20Brix (for Cynthia Brix);

http://www.theinterfaithobserver.org/search?q=Mirabai%20Starr   (for   Mirabai Starr); http://www.theinterfaithobserver.org/search?q=Adam%20Bucko (for Adam Bucko);   http://www.theinterfaithobserver.org/search?q=Rory%20McEntee   (for Rory McEntee); and http://www.theinterfaithobserver.org/search?q=Cynthia%20 Bourgeault (for Cynthia Bourgeault).

[15.] In our Volume 3, we will share in full the article "Interfaith and Interspiritual Clergy and Their Training" by Rev. Philip Waldrop. Here, to complete our contents on Interfaith Seminaries, we share these categories of important information from that piece: "The holistic clergy training paradigm has its roots in curriculum development at The New Seminary in the 1980s and 1990s, led by Rev. Dr. Diane Berke, Rev. Dr. Joyce Liechenstein, and Rev. Deborah Steen Ross. Of course, specific curriculum content evolves over time, but the holistic approach remains." **Groupings of Institutions: Gelberman Group**. The current four New York City-area interfaith / interspiritual seminaries have roots in the vision of Rabbi Joseph Gelberman: The New Seminary (1979), All Faiths Interfaith Seminary (1996), OneSpirit Interfaith Seminary (2001), and New Visions Interfaith Seminary (2011). Two others also have Gelberman roots: OneSpirit Interfaith Foundation in the UK (1996) and Tree of Life Interfaith Seminary (2006), Milford, NH. **Independently Developed Institutions.** Additional interfaith / interspiritual clergy training institutions include: The Chaplaincy Institute in Berkeley, CA (1999) founded by Rev. Gina Rose Halpern; the Chaplaincy Institute of Maine (2002), founded by Chaplaincy Institute grad, Rev. Jacob Watson; Rev. Dr. Katherine O'Connell's East-West Seminary (circa 2004); and the Seminary at HaShem's House (circa 2009) founded by Rev. Rabbi Dr. Raine Teller. Also, Rev. Dr. Barry King and Rev. Dr. Sandi King founded the iNtuitive Times Institute (2006) in Charlottetown, Prince Edward Island, to serve the interfaith movement in Canada they helped pioneer. Similarly, Doylestown, PA's interfaith Pebble Hill Church founded the School for Sacred Ministry (1999) for clergy development for itself, and similar other or new congregations. Two institutions follow mainly a distance-learning approach: American Institute of Holistic Theology (1992) founded by Michael Parker, which has offered ordination since 2011, and International Academy of Interfaith Studies (2011), founded by Rev. Dr. Thomas Lynch and Rev. Dr. Cynthia Lynch. **Profiles of Interfaith and Interspiritual Ministers.** Collectively, about 200 Interspiritual / Interfaith Ministers are ordained annually. Who are these people that pursue this? The details vary quite widely, but candidates often mention their heart and vision for spiritual service did not fit into a standard world religion. Also common is for candidates to have had a number of spiritual experiences / backgrounds, who then find that cross-traditional spiritual paths are not welcomed elsewhere. Sometimes gender or sexual orientation matters come into play. Typically, these are people in mid- or late-career who come to their ministry training with significant life and spiritual experience. Candidates often find this path via internet searches, or via an existing interfaith / interspiritual minister. **Types of Ministries.** Interfaith / interspiritual ministers pursue a wide range of activities. Forming / leading an interspiritual congregation, with regular worship services and community gatherings, is a minority choice among graduates. Other common ministry tracks include: ceremony-presiders (especially weddings); spiritual counselors (needs additional training); ministry with alternative healing arts modalities; hospital or military chaplaincy (again, requiring additional training); and social activist ministries, e.g. prison ministry, eco-ministry, women's shelters, homeless shelters. Typically, interfaith / interspiritual ministers are freelance, and conduct ministry part-time alongside other careers. **Organizations Serving Interspiritual Ministers and the Interspiritual Movement.** AWAIC: A World Alliance of Interspiritual Clergy (2004), the professional association and home for interfaith / interspiritual clergy. **[16.]** Booksellers' note, widely quoted, in some slightly different forms re: *The Monk Within: Embracing a Sacred Way of Life* by Beverly Lanzetta. 2018.Tucson, AZ: Blue Sapphire Books. Book notices, Amazon, Barnes and Noble, Indie Bound, beverlylanzetta.net. **[17.]** "Christian Spirituality Group." American Academy of Religion, October 2, 2008, Evan Howard, chairperson: "The New Monasticism." https://spiritualityshoppe.org/wp-content/pdfs/Introducing%20New%20 Monasticism.pdf. **[18.]** "The New Monastic Manifesto" was published prior to 2015 in serials, as in *Kosmos Journal* Spring/Summer issue, 2013 https://www. kosmosjournal.org/article/new-monasticism-an-interspiritual-manifesto-for-contemplative-life-in-the-21st-century/ and in PDF at https://www.kosmosjournal. org/wp-content/article-pdfsnew-monasticism-an-interspiritual   -manifesto-for-contemplative-life-in-the-21st-century.pdf and also published online by "Working With   Oneness"   https://www.scribd.com/doc/101981052/New-Monasticism-An-Interspiritual-Manifesto-for-Contemplative-Life-in-the-21st-Century. Original and current bookseller abstracts are well summarized in this version at https://orbisbooks. com/products/the-new-monasticism. **[19.]** As quoted in *A Matter of Spirit* (InterCommunity Peace and Justice Center), No. 117, Winter (Jan. 4. 2018) issue, "New Monasticism" https://issuu.com/ipjc/docs/amos_winter_2018-web. **[20.]** The Science and Nonduality Conference (SAND), scienceandnonduality.com is well known for its outstanding conferences on the relationship of science and spirit, held annually from 2009 until the Covid pandemic (and subsequently for online programming). During the in-person conference era attendees received a detailed printed program with outlines and abstracts of all programs, in this case, 2015. **[21.]** see Acknowledgments, pp. xv, 58-61 (Sannyasa, CMH) in Sw. Shraddhananda [Ed.]. *Mature Interspirituality.* 2017. Somerset, KY: Sacred Feet; and Sw. Prakashananda. *Sacred Feet Yoga Teachings with Meditations by Swami Prakashananda.* 2023. Somerset, KY: Sacred Feet. **[22.]** Br. Teasdale. As noted in TIMELINES, at a residential retreat of Community of the Mystic Heart in April 2016, Jeffrey Genung [later founder of contemplativelife.org] presented the Sannyas robes of Br. Teasdale to Sw. Shraddhananda and her Sacred Feet Slate Branch Ashram [now Sacred Feet Anugraha House] as part of a special ceremony that passed the Acclimation of the Universal Order of Sannyasa from its 2010 founding (see item 5 in 2007-2012 Timeline above), and thus Br. Teasdale's Universal Order of Sannyas lineage, to the care of Sw. Shraddhananda, Sacred Feet's full Sannyas program, and the Trustees of The Interspiritual Dialogue as founded by Br. Teasdale and his associates in 2002. **[22.]** Sw. Shraddhananda, her dharma heirs, and Jeffrey

Genung are all Featured Authors to the current Volumes. See Acknowledgments, pp. xv, 58-61 (Sannyasa, CMH) in Sw. Shraddhananda [Ed.]. *Mature Interspirituality*. 2017. Somerset, KY: Sacred Feet; and pp. i-iv in Sw. Prakashananda. *Sacred Feet Yoga Teachings with Meditations by Swami Prakashananda*. 2023. Somerset, KY: Sacred Feet. **[23.]** "Meditations by Swami Prakashananda" by Sw. Prakashananda of Sw. Shraddhananda's dharma heirs in *Sacred Feet Yoga Teachings with Meditations by Swami Prakashananda*. 2023. Somerset, KY: Sacred Feet. **[24.]** We want to acknowledge, and preview, in these Volumes 1 and 2 some key interspiritual innovators whose New Monastic modalities will be shared in more detail in Volume 3. These will include organizational documents from (1) Interspiritual Monastics in the World (Community of The Mystic Heart, from 2016) by James Hopkins, Timothy Olivieri and David Earnest Wachter (with a support group of Kurt Johnson, Yanni Maniates, Jeffrey Genung, T. S. Pennington, Dorothy Cunha [many original founders of CMH] along with Sw. Shraddhananda, Ma Shanti and others of the CMH Sannyas); (2) "The Sannyas Program of The Community of The Mystic Heart" by Sw. Shraddhananda; and (3) "The Charis Foundation for New Monasticism and Interspirituality" of Dr. Rory McEntee, Fr. Adam Bucko, Netanel Miles-Yépez, and Alejandra Warden. **[25.]** From original article in *Namaste Insights* "The Claritas Institute for Interspiritual Inquiry: Claritas Interspiritual Mentor Training Program" by Gordon Dveirin. and Joan Borysenko in *Namaste Insights*. October 4, 2015. "The Coming Interspiritual Age, Special Edition," Expanded ["Archive"] Edition [no longer online]. Originally posted at https://issuu.com/yorkmin/docs/the_coming_ interspiritual_age_archive_edition. **[26.]** Dr. Joni Dittrich (aka Rajashree Maa), psychologist and author of Light on Light Press's recent book on a new Divine Feminine Reiki Lineage: 2023. *May the Loveforce Be With You – Kali-Ki Reiki: Healing Through Divine Mother & Yogic Wisdom*. New York, NY: Light on Light Press. **[27.]** Scientific results from the Harvard DNA study were reported in the *Proceedings of the Royal Society (B: Biological Sciences)*, by Vila et al. (including Johnson as a co-author), 2011, issue 278 and reported in *The New York Times* and *New York Times Science Times*, (https://www.nytimes.com/2011/02/01/ science/01butterfly.html) among many other venues as "Nabokov Theory on Butterfly Evolution is Vindicated." **[28.]** Named *Namaste Insights* **References**: *Namaste Insights*. October 4, 2015. "Namaste Insights, The Coming Interspiritual

Age, Special Edition," Expanded ["Archive"] Edition [no longer online]. Originally posted at https://issuu.com/yorkmin/docs/the_coming_interspiritual_age_archive_ edition; *Namaste Insights*. December 6, 2014. "Namaste Insights, The Coming Interspiritual Age, a celebration of the 10th Anniversary of the transition of Bro. Wayne Teasdale" [no longer online, original posting url unknown].

viii: Endnotes and References for "Lost" and "Serial" Articles Section

[1.] A Wayne Teasdale article originally given to Kurt Johnson by Br. Teasdale. After Teasdale's transition, Johnson gave it to the online *Contemplative Journal* (CJ) where it was published online in 2015. CJ is no longer extant. A deletion notice at scribd.com notes the original version was at https://www.scribd.com/ document/314166285/Wayne-Teasdale-article-on-Swami-Abhishiktananda-pdf; A Hayashi and Johnson article originally published in online publication of Yasuhiko Genku Kimura, *Vision in Action*. Kimura, a well-known spiritual teacher noted in these Volumes re: the Parliaments of the World's Religions, is also founder and director of Vision-In-Action, LLC, committed to developing and implementing creative and transformative approaches to our world's problems and challenges. Early issues of the online publication are no longer online. The version here is from the original ms. Reference for this Feature: *The Mystic Heart: Discovering a Universal Spirituality in the World's Religions*. 1999. New World Library (Novato CA), xix + 293pp. (hereafter, "MH"). [2.] *Namaste Insights* **References**: *Namaste Insights*. October 4, 2015. "Namaste Insights, The Coming Interspiritual Age, Special Edition," Expanded ["Archive"] Edition [no longer online]. Originally posted at https://issuu.com/yorkmin/docs/the_coming_interspiritual_age_archive_ edition; *Namaste Insights*. December 6, 2014. "Namaste Insights, The Coming Interspiritual Age, a celebration of the 10th Anniversary of the transition of Bro. Wayne Teasdale" [no longer online, original posting url unknown]. [3.] In this special case the sequence of the "Author Name Cloud" is consistent with that of the original historical publications. Sources are as in Endnote 2 except for Johnson, Toth and Bucko which is from *The Interfaith Observer* at http://www.theinterfaithobserver. org/journal-articles/2013/9/15/pioneers-in-hindu-christian-interspirituality.html republished here, with permission, from the original ms. [4.] Endnotes for Mirabai

Starr: ¹*Rumi's Little Book of Life*, trans. Maryam Mafi & Azima Melita Kolin. ²*Song of Songs*, trans. Ariel Bloch and Chana Bloch. ³*The Shambhala Anthology of Women's Spiritual Poetry*, Ed. Alaki Barnstone. ⁴"Living Flame of Love," trans. Mirabai Starr, in *Be Love Now*, Ram Dass & Rameshwar Das. ⁵Mirabai, trans. Robert Bly and Jane Hirshfield. ⁶Johann Wolfgang von Goethe, trans. Robert Bly. Additional Resources: Mirabai Starr author page at Amazon.com: https://www.amazon.com/stores/author/B000APT4DY?. **[5.]** Ruth Broyde Sharone page at Amazon: https://www.amazon.com/stores/Ruth-Broyde-Sharone/author/ B0083J979U?; Broyde Sharone remembrance of Rabbi Zalman Schachter-Shalomi in *The Interfaith Observer*: http://theinterfaithobserver.org/journal-articles/2014/9/15/a-personal-reminiscence-of-rabbi-zalman-schachter-shalomi. html. **[6.]** Roger Housden's website: https://www.rogerhousden.com; Roger Housden page at Amazon: https://www.amazon.com/stores/Roger- Housden/ author/B001IGODW6?. **[7.]** Endnotes for Matthew Wright: ¹credit for the naming of this window of history as the "Axial Age" goes to Karl Jaspers in his seminal *The Origin and Goal of History* (Zurich: Artemis, 1949), 19-43. Additional Resources: Fr. Matthew Wright had an original column at *Contemplative Journal* which is no longer extant. Matthew Wright speaking at Dawn of Interspirituality Conference: http://www.youtube.com/watch?v=qKcWzIOpnJ8. **[8.]** Lama Surya Das websites: https://surya.org/; https://www.dzogchen.org/; Lama Surya Das's page at Amazon: https://www.amazon.com/stores/author/B002P4NOFW?. **[9.]** Ed Bastian websites —Spiritual Paths: http://www.spiritualpaths.net; Interspiritual Network: http://www.interspirituality.com. **[10.]** Endnotes for McEntee and Bucko: ¹Griffiths, Bede, *The New Creation in Christ*. Ed. by Robert Kiely and Laurence Freeman, OSB (Springfield: Templegate Publishers, 1994), 89. ²Griffiths, *The New Creation*, 91, 92, 94. ³Raimon Panikkar, *Blessed Simplicity: The Monk as Universal Archetype* (New York: Seabury, 1982). ⁴Cousins, Ewert, *Christ of the 21st Century* (New York: Continuum, 1998). Additional Resources: Pages for Fr. Adam Bucko and Dr. Rory McEntee at Amazon: Bucko, https://www.amazon.com/stores/author/ B00DDHID1K?; McEntee, https://www.amazon.com/stores/Rory-McEntee/author/ B00U854A76?; Websites: Fr. Adam Bucko, https://fatheradambucko.com/; Dr. Rory McEntee, https://charisinterspirituality.org/. **[11.]** Beverly J. Lanzetta author page at Amazon: https://www.amazon.com/stores/author/B001JS6E2A?. **[12.]** Websites for

Rabbi Roger Ross and Rev. Deborah Steen Ross: http://rabbirogerross.com/; https://www.facebook.com/InternationalSeminaryNYC/.

ix: Endnotes and References for "New Era" Section

[1.] Teasdale, Wayne. 1999. *The Mystic Heart: Discovering a Universal Spirituality in the World's Religions*. Novato, CA: New World Library. [2.] Bereshit 12:3. [3.] For us, Torah is a human document shaped over centuries by many writers and editors, and containing poems, parables, legends, laws, and philosophies. [4.] Bereshit 1:26. [5.] Bereshit 1:26. [6.] Bereshit 1:28. [7.] Bereshit 2: 5-7; 15. [8.] Talmud, *Shabbat* 31a. [9.] Isaiah 30:18. [10.] Talmud, *Sanhedrin* 97b. [11.] List of illustrations provided by Jeff Genung in his Feature which will be shared in our Volume 3 (from the Illustration Captions in the original ms.: (i) Photo of Br. Teasdale at a peace gathering of the Parliament (2 photos); (ii) Barbara Fields, The Dalai Lama, Br. Teasdale at the Synthesis Dialogues; (iii) Br. Teasdale at 1997 Parliament of the World's Religions; (iv) Br. Teasdale at 1997 Parliament of the World's Religions; (v) Br. Teasdale at 1997 Parliament of the World's Religions; (vi) Fr. Thomas Keating wearing Wayne's kavi at Synthesis Dialogues; (vii) Br. Teasdale, The Dalai Lama, Fr. Keating & other spiritual leaders; (viii) Profession of Vows, Benedictine Monastery, Chicago; (ix) Br. Teasdale taking sannyasa vows under Fr. Bede Griffiths in India with Russill Paul; (x) Profession of Vows under Cardinal George; (xi) Br. Teasdale & Cardinal George at a reception after Br. Teasdale's vows; (xii) *Global Ethic*, 1993 Parliament's signature document.

x: Endnotes and References for "Lineages" Feature

[1.] While being a challenge to comparativism in its emphasis on both rootedness and contextuality, poststructural and postmodern thought also brings to light the reality that knowledge and understanding are themselves the result of comparative processes located within cross cultural experiments. Hans Georg Gadamer's idea of the "fusion of horizons," which emphasizes the rootedness of all human discourse in tradition and culture and the interaction of such contextual views, is demonstrated well by the progression toward more sophisticated and complex models of religion and culture, especially when confronted by the ancient paradox of East meets West.

May it be so, then welcome the shamans, syncretists and animists back from the castaway island of misfits. [2.] Eliade, Mircea. *The Sacred and the Profane: The Nature of Religion*, trans. Willard R. Trask (New York: Harcourt Brace Jovanovich, 1959), 201–13. [3.] Habermas, Jürgen "Legitimation Problems in the Modern State," *Communication and the Evolution of Society* (Boston: Beacon Press, 1974). [4.] St. Paul who was gripped by his inner experience of evolving in Christ, exclaimed: "I live, not I, Christ lives in me" (Galatians 2:20). St. John proclaims in his gospel that Jesus himself promised us that he would be like "living streams welling up from the center of our being" (John 7:38). The post-Christendom Church needs to carve out oases of stillness, which could be spiritual recovery centers along the streets of a speedy and phrenetic postmodern life. "Contemplative prayer is the most urgent need of the Christian Church today." Abhishiktananda, *Hindu-Christian Meeting Point in the Cave of the Heart*. Delhi: ISPCK, 1975, p. 11. [5.] Griffiths, Bede "The Ashram as a Way of Transcendence," in Vandana (Ed.), Christian Ashrams, *A Movement with a Future?*. Delhi: ISPCK, 1993, p. 32. [6.] Abhishiktananda, Hindu- Christian Meeting Point in the Cave of the Heart. Delhi: ISPCK, 1975, p. 11. [7.] Griffiths, Bede "The Ashram as a Way of Transcendence," in Vandana (Ed.), *Christian Ashrams, A Movement with a Future?*. Delhi: ISPCK, 1993, p. 32. [8.] The sages of India speak of two inner faculties of perception: *manhi* (mind) and *buddhi* (intuitive intellect). *Manhi* objectifies everything and analyzes reality; *buddhi* enters into the reality by uniting it with the perceiving subject. *Manhi* looks at the structures and qualities of reality, while *buddhi* delves into the core of reality. *Manhi* pursues the logic of reality; *buddhi* seeks the mystique of reality. *Manhi* operates within the subject-object polarity and arrives at the knowledge of things (vijñāna); in *buddhi* this polarity is overcome: the subject and object merge into a unity of transpersonal consciousness in which wisdom (jhārna) emerges by welling up. *Manhi* speculates on the horizontal level; *buddhi* intuits vertically into the depth of reality. What the mind does is reflect over realities; what happens in the *buddhi* is meditation. The so called contradictions are such only at the mental level, but are in reality revelatory of a deeper complementarity of the superconsciousness (intuition) .... Truth is a hidden wholeness beyond words and concepts. Abhishiktananda, Journal, quoted by Emmanuel Vattakuzttv, *Indian Christian Sannyasa and Swami Abhishiktananda*. Bangalore: TPI, 1981, p. 187. [9.] Meditation is always on the verge of ekstasis presence within the heart of reality; the conscious movement to the sacred center of all beings; the disciplined immersion into the incomparable depth of consciousness; Return to the Center. Herewith, God is experienced not primarily as the divine Thou, object of veneration, but as the divine Self, the subject out of which one lives and moves and has ontology and teleology — final cause. All the interspiritual exercises, practices, and discipline of sadhana arising from interspiritual ashrams are meant for growing in this revelatory experience of universal consciousness. "The center of ashram life is not liturgy but contemplation." Three times a day (sandhyā kalas — sunrise, sunset, noonday) the ashramites come together to sit in meditative silence. All the works they do and their dealings with people, their prayers and studies evolve from this inner silence. Griffiths, Bede in Vandana [Ed.], *Christian Ashrams*, p. 31. **[10.]** Mysticism is the art of union with reality, transpiring from sacramentum to res and accidens to substens. The mystic is a person who has attained that union in greater or less degree; or who aims at and believes in such attainment. It is not expected that the inquirer will find great comfort in this sentence when first it meets his eye. The ultimate question, "What is Reality?" — a question, perhaps, which never occurred to him before — is already forming in his mind; and he knows that it will cause him infinite distress. Only a mystic can answer it: and he, in terms which other mystics alone will understand. Therefore, for the time being, the practical man may put it on one side. Additionally noted Reference: Griffiths, Bede. 1976 [1982]. *Return to the Center*. Springfield, IL: Template Publishers.

xi: Endnotes and References for James Finley Discussion Feature

1. See biographies of both Fr. James Finley and Karen J. Gordon. With regard to preparations for these Volumes, Fr. Finley joined Kurt Johnson and Jon Ramer (co-founder of The Compassion Games and Compassionate Cities) for an hour-long recorded discussion and retrospective on Thomas Merton and Interspirituality. Compassionate Cities is well established in Louisville, KY, and there is both a monument to Thomas Merton and a Thomas Merton Square in Louisville. It was agreed that this discussion with Fr. Finley could be transcribed for diverse educational purposes. The transcription above (part of a longer transcription) was prepared by Karen J. Gordon, a professional writer also editing for Light on Light and Inner

Traditions publishers. The transcription received Fr. Finley's approval, and more may likely be shared, with his permission, in Volume 3 of this series, whose format could also accommodate the many more lengthy, and inspiring, quotations from Fr. Merton and his work shared by Fr. Finley. [2.] Google AI summarizes Thomas Merton's "The General Dance" as a concept found in Thomas Merton's writings, particularly in *New Seeds of Contemplation*, which describes the interconnectedness of all things and the invitation to participate in a cosmic dance of love and creation. It is…a metaphor for the dynamic, ever-flowing, and interconnected nature of reality, where everything is participating in a divine activity.

xii: Endnotes and References in "Interspiritual Theology" Feature

[1.]https://www.ipsos.com/sites/default/files/ct/news/documents/2023-05/Ipsos%20Global%20Advisor%20-%20Religion%202023%20Report%20-%2026%20countries.pdf?utm_source=chatgpt.com. [2.] https://sdgthoughtleaderscircle.org/unitive-new-narrative/. [3.] *Snowmass Conferences,* convened by Father Thomas Keating, 1984–2004. [4.] https://dawnofinterspirituality.org/. [5.] *Will Keepin, Belonging to God: Spirituality, Science, and a Universal Path of Divine Love (2016).* [6.] Tulku Urgyen Rinpoche, Rainbow Painting (Hong Kong: Ranjung Yeshe Publications). [7.] *Ilia Delio, The Not Yet God (2024).* [8.] *Thomas Berry, The Dream of the Earth (1988).* [9.] *The Fuji Declaration* (2015), www.fujideclaration.org.

xiii: Endnotes and References for "Can Interspirituality....." Feature

[1]See, for example, Reza Shah-Kazemi, 2006. *Paths to Transcendence: According to Shankara, Ibn Arabi & Meister Eckhart,* World Wisdom. [2]Jack Kornfield, *Psychedelics and Spiritual Practice, https://www.dhammawheel.com/viewtopic.php?t=22652&start=40* [3]Simon Critchley, Athens in Pieces: What Really Happened in Eleusis? New York Times, March 13, 2019, nytimes.com/2019/03/13/opinion/ancient-greece-ritual-mystery-eleusis.htm. [4]Christopher Bache, 2019. *LSD and the Mind of the Universe: Diamonds from Heaven,* Park Street Press. Quotation from: accidentalgods.life/the-phoenix-always-rises-evolving-into-the-future-human-

with-prof-chris-bache-author-of-lsd-and-the-mind-of-the-universe/.[5]Giorgio Samorini, 2019. The oldest archeological data evidencing the relationship of *Homo sapiens* with psychoactive plants: A worldwide overview. *Journal of Psychedelic Studies* 3(2): 1-18. DOI:10.1556/2054.2019.008. Available online: akjournals.com/view/journals/2054/3/2/article-p63.xml (accessed on 27 August 2022). [6]D. Tanasi, B.F. van Oppen de Ruiter, F. Florian, et al., 2024. Multianalytical investigation reveals psychotropic substances in a ptolemaic Egyptian vase. Sci Rep 14, 27891 https://doi.org/10.1038/s41598-024-78721-8. [7]Charles Stang, 2024. "Psychedelic Futures and Altered States in the Religions of the Ancient Mediterranean," Harvard Theological Review, Cambridge University Press, published online. cambridge.org/core/journals/harvard-theological-review/article/psychedelic-futures-and-altered-states-in-the-religions-of-the-ancient-mediterranean/CFC771D700D6D7BEA8AD6D961BAC4F27. [8]Brian Moraresku, 2020. The Immortality Key, St. Martin's Press. hellenicgods.org/the-wine-of-bacchus-dionysus. [10]Dennis McDonald, 2017. The Dionysian Gospel: The Fourth Gospel and Euripides, Fortress Press. [11]Moraresku, op cit. [12]Charles Stang, Psychedelic Futures and Altered States in the Religions of the Ancient Mediterranean, Cambridge University Press, published online 31 December 2024. [13]Jerry Brown and Julie Brown, 2016. The Psychedelic Gospels: The Secret History of Hallucinogens in Christianity, Park Street Press. [14]See D. Osto, *Altered States: Buddhism and Psychedelic Spirituality in America,* Columbia University Press, 2019; and A. Badiner et al., *Zig Zag Zen: Buddhism and Psychedelics,* Synergetic Press, (2nd Edition), 2015. [15]https://www.rabbishefagold.com/invocation-jewish-psychedelic-summit/. [16]quoted from www.ligare.org/about. [17]Estimate of 250 churches: cswr.hds.harvard.edu/news/2025/03/charting-novel-psychedelic-spiritual-communities-0. Estimate of 500 churches: ecstaticintegration.org/p/a-new-wave-of-legal-psychedelic-churches. [18]G. William Barnard, 2022. Liquid Light: Ayahuasca Spirituality and the Santo Daime Tradition, Columbia University Press. [19]liquidlightbook.com/appendices/, "Santo Daime 101," accessed online Jan 16, 2025. [20]Ernesto Londoño, 2024. Trippy: The Peril and Promise of Medicinal Psychedelics, Celadon Books, Kindle edition, p. 179. [21]William Keepin, 2021. "Breathing New Life Into Social Transformation: Holotropic Breathwork for Social, Cultural, and Political Leaders," in Tarnas, R, and Kelly, S. (Eds), Psyche Unbound: Essays in Honor of Stanislav Grof, Synergia Press. [22]Rachel

Nuwer, 2023. "How a Dose of MDMA Transformed a White-Supremacist," BBC, bbc.com/future/article/20230614-how-a-dose-of-mdma-transformed-a-white-supremacist [23]Roland Griffiths, Robert Jesse, William Richards, Matthew Johnson, Nathan Sepeda, Anthony Bossis, and Stephen Ross, 2025. Effects of Psilocybin on Religious and Spiritual Attitudes and Behaviors in Clergy from Various Major World Religions, Psychedelic Medicine, published online: liebertpub.com/doi/10.1089/psymed.2023.0044 [24] Stanislav Grof, chapter in The Great Upshift, (Ervin Laszlo and David Lorimer, eds.), Light on Light Press, 2023. [25]Cicero, Laws II, xiv, 36; quoted in wikipedia.org/wiki/Eleusinian Mysteries. [26]Sa'diyya Shaikh, 2014. Sufi Narratives of Intimacy: Ibn 'Arabi, Gender, and Sexuality, University of North Carolina Press, pp. 186-88. Ibn Arabi's quotation has been edited for gender inclusivity. [27]Ibid., 189-90. [28]Nida Chenagtsang, 2018. Karamudra, The Yoga of Bliss: Sexuality in Tibetan Medicine and Buddhism, Sky Press. [29]Nida Chenagtsang, op cit. [30]H.H. Dalai Lama, personal communication to Dr. Ian Baker, quoted in: facebook.com/photo.php?fbid=576390281199331&set=a.281710518543502. [31]Laura Gozzi, 2024. "Pope Francis says sexual pleasure is 'a gift from God,'" BBC News, bbc.com/news/world-europe-68016311. [32]"Sex is 'divine': How Pope Francis is recasting Catholic Church's views on intimacy," Religion News Service, February 14, 2024, americamagazine.org/faith/2024/02/14/catholic-teaching-sex-sexuality-intimacy-247322. [33]Spring Washom and Rod Owens, "A liberated conversation about sexuality," Spirit Underground Podcast, Ep. 6, Sep 5, 2023, https://www.youtube.com/watch?v=TC_uxoEkn1E. [34]Nida Chenagtsang, op cit. [35]Jenny Wade, 2004. Transcendent Sex: When Lovemaking Opens the Veil, Gallery Books. [36]In Buddhism for example, an expanded version of the Four Noble Truths might be: 1. Suffering or dissatisfaction (dukkha) is inherent in life. 2. The cause (samudaya) of suffering is attachment to the objects of desire. 3. The cessation (nirodha) of this attachment leads to the end of suffering. 4. There are two pathways (marga) to accomplish this; either: (a) renunciation of desire, which is the traditional "Eight-fold path;" or (b) transmutation of desire into the union of bliss and emptiness (which is based on completion stage practices). [37]Andrew Newberg and Mark Waldman, 2009. How God Changes Your Brain, Ballentine Books. [38]Andrew Newberg, 2024. Sex, God, and the Brain: How Sexual Pleasure Gave Birth to Religion and a Whole

Lot More, Turner Publishing. [39]Personal communication from a close colleague, who was told this directly by Tulku Urgyen Rinpoche.

xiv: Endnotes and References for "Interspiritual Milieu" Feature

[1.] Diary entry, January 24th, 1949, in James Stuart, *Swami Abhishiktananda: His Life Told Through His Letters*, Delhi: ISPCK, 2000: 29. [2.] Letter to Joseph Lemarié, March 18th, 1952, in Stuart, *Swami Abhishiktananda: His Life Told Through His Letters*, 54. [3.] See Netanel Miles-Yépez, "The Merging of Two Oceans: The Making of a Sufi-Hasidic Lineage and a Universal Priesthood," the Foreword to Gregory Blann, *When Oceans Merge: The Contemporary Sufi and Hasidic Teachings of Pir Vilayat Inayat Khan and Rabbi Zalman Schachter-Shalomi*, Rhinebeck, NY: Adam Kadmon Books, 2019: xiii-xxxiv. [4.] Beverly Lanzetta. *Nine Jewels of Night: One Soul's Journey into God*. San Diego, CA: Blue Sapphire Books, 2014: 95-97. [5.] Personal conversation with the Venerable Pannavati Bhikkuni, Mepkin Abbey, Monck's Corner, South Carolina, October 2018. [6.] Wayne Teasdale. *The Mystic Heart: Discovering a Universal Spirituality in the World's Religions*. Novato, CA: New World Library, 2001: 17. [7.] Teasdale. *The Mystic Heart,* 27. [8.] In *The Intra-Religious Dialogue,* New York, NY: Paulist Press, 1978: 2-3, Raimundo Panikkar notes that in ancient Greece, *oikoumene* "referred to household management," and only grew into its later world-encompassing sense as the Greek notion of "we" grew over time. [9.] Personal correspondence with Matthew Fox, October 11th, 2021. [10.] Quoted in Matthew Fox, *One River, Many Wells: Wisdom Springing from Global Faiths*, New York, NY: Jeremy P. Tarcher/Putnam, 2000: 5. This is similar to the saying of Jerrahi Sufi master, Sheikh Muzaffer Ozak: "A river passes through many countries and each claims it for its own. But there is only one river." Muzaffer Ozak. *Love is the Wine: Talks of a Sufi Master in America*. Ed. Ragip Frager. Putney, VT: Threshold Books, 1987: 1. [11.] Fox, *One River, Many Wells,* 5. [12.] Zalman Schachter-Shalomi, with Shaya Isenberg. *Deep Ecumenism: An Elat Chayyim Week 1998*. Boulder, CO: Private Publication: Third Transcript, 7. Schachter-Shalomi was sometimes heard to call himself "a Jewish practitioner of generic religion." Zalman Schachter-Shalomi. *Paradigm Shift: From the Jewish Renewal Teachings of Reb Zalman Schachter-Shalomi*. Northvale, NJ: Jason Aronson Inc., 1993:

257. **[13.]** Zalman Schachter-Shalomi and Bernie Glassman. "Torah and Dharma: Torah Hyphen Dharma." *Spectrum: A Journal of Renewal Spirituality: Volume 2, Number 1:* Winter-Spring 2006. Boulder, CO: Albion-Andalus Books, 2019: 54. **[14.]** Thinking of Robert Kennedy (Jesuit priest and Zen roshi), Zalman Schachter-Shalomi (Hasidic rabbi and Sufi *shaykh),* and Maestro Manuel Rufino (Taino elder and teacher of the Universal Initiatic Academy). **[15.]** A term possibly coined by professor of comparative theology, Catherine Cornille. **[16.]** Thích Nhất Hạnh. *Peace is Every Step: The Path of Mindfulness in Everyday Life.* New York: Bantam Books, 1991: 95. **[17.]** Gloria E. Anzaldúa. *Light in the Dark / Luz en lo Oscuro: Rewriting Identity, Spirituality, Reality.* Ed. Analouise Keating. Durham, NC: Duke University Press, 2015: 245. **[18.]** Anzaldúa, *Light in the Dark / Luz en lo Oscuro,* 56. **[19.]** Rory McEntee and Adam Bucko. *The New Monasticism: An Interspiritual Manifesto for Contemplative Living.* Maryknoll, NY: Orbis Books, 2015: 25. **[20.]** Heard directly from Rabbi Zalman Schachter-Shalomi. **[21.]** Well-known quote by Max Müller. **[22.]** Zalman Schachter-Shalomi, with Shaya Isenberg. *Deep Ecumenism: An Elat Chayyim Week 1998.* Boulder, CO: Private Publication: First Transcript, 9. **[23.]** Schachter-Shalomi, *Deep Ecumenism,* First Transcript, 9, and also heard directly from Rabbi Zalman Schachter-Shalomi. **[24.]** Panikkar, *The Intra-Religious Dialogue,* xxvii. **[25.]** Panikkar, 40. **[26.]** It was for this reason that the Snowmass Interreligious Conference, one of the oldest continuous interreligious dialogues, begun in 1984 by Fr. Thomas Keating, transitioned (with the latter's blessing) in 2016, to become the Charis Snowmass Dialogues, maintaining much of the form and traditions of the original Snowmass Dialogues, but with a new emphasis on the interior experience and complex interspiritual identities of the dialoguers, as well as the "deep structures" shared by different spiritual traditions, spiritual experience, and the techniques used to achieve it. **[27.]** Teasdale, *The Mystic Heart,* 26. **[28.]** See Netanel Miles-Yépez, *The End of Religion and Other Writings.* Des Moines, NM: Charis Mandala Publishing, 2023: 17-23. **[29.]** Beverly Lanzetta. *Emerging Heart: Global Spirituality and the Sacred.* Minneapolis, MN: Fortress Press.

FEATURED AUTHORS

Robert Atkinson. Robert Atkinson, PhD, is an award-winning author, educator, and developmental psychologist. He is a 2020 Gold Nautilus Book Award winner for *Our Moment of Choice* (co-editor), a 2023 Silver winner for *A New Story of Wholeness*, and a 2017 Silver winner for *The Story of Our Time*. Author or co-editor of nine other books, his works include *Year of Living Deeply*, *Mystic Journey*, and *The Gift of Stories*. Atkinson is professor emeritus at the University of Southern Maine, director of StoryCommons, founder of the One Planet Peace Forum, and a member of the Evolutionary Leaders Circle. See *robertatkinson.net*; *lightonlight.us*.

DeShannon Barnes-Bowens. Iya Rev. DeShannon Barnes-Bowens is a psychotherapist, professional development trainer, and spiritual counselor. She is founder of ILERA Counseling & Education Services, and her work focuses on spiritual development, healing from sexual abuse, vicarious trauma, and sustainable self-care. An initiated priestess of Ifá-Òrìṣà spirituality, she was ordained in 2010 as an Interfaith Minister and later served as co-director of One Spirit Interfaith Seminary. Barnes-Bowens is author of *Hush Hush: An African American Family Breaks their Silence on Sexuality and Sexual Abuse* and was the first recipient of the Bill T. Jones Award from AASECT. She coordinated CONNECT Faith's Ending Child Sexual Abuse Collaborative and has taught at national and international events, including the Parliament of the World's Religions and the American Academy of Religion. See *ilera.com*.

JoAnn Barrett. Rev. JoAnn Barrett, ordained in 1995 from what is now One Spirit Interfaith Seminary, is the founder and spiritual director of Gathering of Light Interspiritual Fellowship. With degrees in human services, social policy, and substance abuse counseling, she has served on numerous interfaith and state faith-based task forces, including the Interfaith Institute of Long Island and Faith Leaders Task Force for NY State. A long-time student and teacher of *A Course in Miracles*, she founded programs like Voices of Faith for Peace, STARTER Packs for the homeless, and Bedding for Babes. Barrett is also the founder and spiritual director of Lightpaths Wisdom Studies Interspiritual Seminary. She served in pastoral care and clinical roles and contributed to *Mature Interspirituality* and *Guideposts*. See *gatheringoflight.org*.

Edward Bastian. Edward Bastian, PhD, is founder and president of Spiritual Paths Foundation. With a PhD in Buddhist Studies, he has spent over forty years studying and teaching in dialogue with teachers from many faith traditions. He developed InterSpiritual Meditation and Mandala processes, and the well-known books associated with them, and has led retreats and educational programs since 2002. A former co-director of the Forum on Biodiversity for the Smithsonian and the National Academy of Sciences, he has also produced religion-focused documentaries for the BBC and PBS. His most recently premiered film is *The Dalai Lama's Gift*. Bastian is author of *InterSpiritual Meditation* and *Mandala: Creating an Authentic Spiritual Path: An InterSpiritual Process*, and co-author of *Living Fully, Dying Well*. Bastian was also instrumental in forming the Interspiritual Network and its current web resource *interspiritiuality.com*. See *spiritualpaths.net*; *interspirituality.com*.

Diane Berke. Rev. Diane Berke is the founder and spiritual director of One Spirit Learning Alliance and One Spirit Interfaith Seminary who have played a pivotal role in the development of Interspirituality and interspiritual education. Ordained in 1988, she has trained and ordained nearly 1,500 interfaith / interspiritual ministers. She holds advanced degrees in sociology, psychology, and therapeutic counseling, and is a licensed mental health counselor in New York State. A certified facilitator of Circles of Trust® through the Center for Courage and Renewal, Berke also maintains a private spiritual counseling practice. She is the author of *Love Always Answers*, *The Gentle Smile*, and *Developing and Deepening Your Spiritual Practice*. She is a founding member of the Contemplative Alliance of the Global Peace Initiative of women, and a core team member of Transformation365 and ProSocial Spirituality. Rev. Berke was also part of the group who created the Interspiritual Network, and its current web resource interspirituality.com. See *1spirit.org*; *interspirituality.com*; *prosocial.world/prosocial-initiatives/prosocial-spirituality*.

Joan Borysenko. Joan Borysenko, PhD, is president and founding partner of MindBody Health Sciences, LLC. A Harvard-trained cell biologist and licensed psychologist, she taught at Harvard Medical School until 1988. She is the author or co-author of seventeen books on integrative medicine, psychology, spirituality, and women's studies. Her work bridges science and mysticism, and she is widely regarded as a pioneer in mind-body medicine. Borysenko lives in New Mexico with her husband Gordon Dveirin. Close friends of Br. Wayne Teasdale, Borysenko and Dveirin co-founded the Claritas Institute for Interspiritual Inquiry and she co-authored with Dveirin *Saying Yes to Change* and *Your Soul's Compass: What is Spiritual Guidance?* See *joanborysenko.com*; *claritasinstitute.com*.

Cynthia Bourgeault. Cynthia Bourgeault is an Episcopal priest, author, and modern-day mystic known for reviving the Christian contemplative and Wisdom traditions. She is founding director of an international network of wisdom schools that blend Christian mystical and monastic teachings with practices of mindfulness and embodied presence. A globally respected retreat leader, Bourgeault divides her time between her seaside hermitage in Maine and an international teaching schedule. She is a faculty member emeritus of the Center for Action and Contemplation and was named one of the 100 most spiritually influential living people in 2021. See *cynthiabourgeault.org*.

Ben Bowler. Ben Bowler is a unity-activist, spiritual entrepreneur, and founder of spiritual programs that foster interfaith immersion. In 2008, he and his wife founded Blood Foundation to support communities along the Thai-Burma border. He later launched Monk for a Month and Muslim for a Month, immersive spiritual programs in Thailand and Turkey. Bowler founded World Weavers and the U DAY Festival, bringing together spiritual leaders and musicians in global celebration. He co-founded 1GOD.com and *The Convergence* radio series, and helped launch Sacred Australia. A "Social Entrepreneur in Residence" at INSEAD Business School and blogger for *HuffPost*, he is active in building interspiritual unity. See *UNITY.earth*; *1 GOD.com*; *interspirituality.com*.

Cynthia Brix. Rev. Cynthia Brix, PhD (hon.), is co-founder and co-director of Gender Equity and Reconciliation International (GERI), which has offered more than 280 intensive trainings in 12 countries. She is an ordained interfaith minister and co-director of Satyana Institute. A long-time student of Eknath Easwaran's Passage Meditation, she also leads retreats on interfaith spirituality. Brix co-organized 5 international conferences on interspirituality and produced *Cultivating Women's Spiritual Mastery*. She holds a Master of Divinity from Iliff School of Theology, a double M.A. in wellness management and gerontology, and an honorary doctorate from CIIS. See *Satyana.org*, *GRworld.org*, *DawnofInterSpirituality.org*; *interspirituality.com*.

Adam Bucko. Rev. Adam Bucko is an Episcopal priest, contemplative activist, spiritual director, and author or co-author of *Let Your Heartbreak Be Your Guide*, *The New Monasticism*, and *Occupy Spirituality: A Radical Vision for a New Generation* (with Matthew Fox). In 2004, he co-founded The Reciprocity Foundation, an award-winning nonprofit for homeless youth in New York City. He also founded HAB, an interspiritual fellowship for young people focused on radical spirituality and sacred activism. Bucko has been featured in ABC News, CBS, *Shambhala Sun*, *Yoga International*, and *Sojourners*. He collaborates with spiritual leaders across traditions, helping youth discover their spiritual paths and live in service to compassion and justice. See *fatheradambucko.com*; *spiritualimagination.org*; *interspirituality.com*.

Paul Chaffee. Rev. Paul Chaffee, ordained in the United Church of Christ, began his interfaith ministry in 1975 at the Church for the Fellowship of All People. Over nearly five decades, he has served as co-founder and executive director of the Interfaith Center at the Presidio, ambassador for the Parliament of the World's Religions, and founding editor of *The Interfaith Observer*. He also co-founded United Religions Initiative and served on the board of the North American Interfaith Network. His *Interfaith Observer* team has published multiple articles on the interspiritual experience. His books include *Accountable Leadership* and *Remembered Light*. See *theinterfaithobserver.org*.

Richard Clugston. Rick Clugston, PhD, is co-director of the Association of University Leaders for a Sustainable Future and a member of the Earth Charter International Council. A founding member of the SDG Thought Leaders Circle, he has led sustainability initiatives globally for decades. He directed the Sustainability and Global Concerns program at the Center for Earth Ethics and served twenty years as executive director of the Center for Respect of Life and Environment where he assisted religious and academic institutions in transforming their teaching and practices to support strong sustainability. Clugston holds a doctorate in higher education policy and planning from the University of Minnesota. See *ulsf.org.*

Matthew M. Cobb. Rev. Matthew M. Cobb is an Episcopal priest and director of the Bede Griffiths Trust, which promotes the contemplative, interspiritual vision of Benedictine monk and mystic Fr. Bede Griffiths. Through Cobb's leadership, the Trust supports dialogue and understanding across spiritual traditions by preserving and sharing Griffiths's teachings. Cobb curates digital archives, organizes educational offerings, and fosters connection among a global community of seekers. His ministry draws on the Christian contemplative tradition while engaging in broader interreligious conversation. Deeply committed to the transformative potential of Interspirituality, he works to create spaces where people of all faiths — and none — can explore the sacred together. See *bedegriffiths.org.*

H. H. the 14th Dalai Lama. His Holiness the 14th Dalai Lama, born Lhamo Thondup and later named Tenzin Gyatso, is the spiritual leader of Tibetan Buddhism. Recognized as the reincarnation of Avalokiteshvara, he was enthroned in 1940 and later fled to India in 1959 following the continued oppression of Tibet, and Tibetan culture, by the Chinese communist regime. He continues to lead the Tibetan government-in-exile and advocates tirelessly for peace, non-violence, and interfaith dialogue. In 1989, he was awarded the Nobel Peace Prize for his dedication to nonviolent resistance against Chinese occupation and for his broader message of compassion, tolerance, and universal responsibility. His Holiness has had close long-term relationships with many key pioneers of Interspirituality, including Fr. Thomas Keating, Br. Wayne Teasdale and others, and has been a major part of seminal interreligious and interspiritual dialogues and initiatives around the world. See *dalailama.com.*

Gordon Dveirin. Gordon Dveirin, EdD, is an educator, organizational consultant, and spiritual mentor whose work spans systems change and transpersonal development. Educated in literature and the history of ideas at the University of Toronto, and in organizational development at the University of Northern Colorado, he has consulted in both private and public sectors for forty years. Dveirin co-founded the Claritas Institute for Interspiritual Inquiry with his wife, Dr. Joan Borysenko, and co-authored with Borysenko *Saying Yes to Change* and *Your Soul's Compass: What is Spiritual Guidance?* He is a founding member of the Evolutionary Leaders Circle. See *claritasinstitute.com.*

James Finley. James Finley is a clinical psychologist, former Trappist monk, and student of Thomas Merton. He teaches contemplative spirituality through the Center for Action and Contemplation, where he hosts the *Turning to the Mystics* podcast. Finley is the author of *Merton's Palace of Nowhere* and *The Contemplative Heart*, and leads retreats and online courses that help people connect with their divine indwelling. See *cac.org.*

Matthew Fox. Matthew Fox, PhD, is a spiritual theologian, Episcopal priest, and activist for gender and ecological justice. He has authored thirty-seven books, including *Original Blessing, The Coming of the Cosmic Christ*, and *The Hidden Spirituality of Men.* A pioneer of Creation Spirituality, he founded the Institute in Culture and Creation Spirituality and later the University of Creation Spirituality. He is co-founder of the Order of the Sacred Earth and creator of The Cosmic Mass, a reinvention of Western ritual. Fox has taught at major universities and inspired the rediscovery of mystics like Hildegard of Bingen and Meister Eckhart. His honors include the Abbey Courage of Conscience Award and the Gandhi King Ikeda Award. He is consistently listed among Watkins' Top 100 Most Spiritually Influential People. See *matthewfox.org.*

Ashok Gangadean. Ashok Gangadean, PhD, is professor and chair of Philosophy at Haverford College, where he has taught for over forty years. His work explores common ground across worldviews and expands philosophy into global consciousness. He is founder-director of the Global Dialogue Institute and co-convener of the World Commission on Global Consciousness and Spirituality. He is also co-chair of the World Wisdom Council. Gangadean's current work includes deep dialogue initiatives and hosting the television series *Global Lens*. His most recent book is *The Awakening of the Global Mind*. See *awakeningmind.org*; *global-dialogue.com*; *globalspirit.org*.

Jeffrey Genung. Jeffrey Genung is managing director and chief architect of Prosocial World, a nonprofit advancing global cooperation and well-being. He is co-founder of Contemplative Life, a hub connecting people with transformative practices, and of Transformation365.org, an experiential practice network. His newest initiative, Prosocial Spirituality, integrates evolutionary science with evolutionary spirituality through training and research. A longtime entrepreneur and technology executive, Jeff has developed partnerships with major global companies. He now focuses on the intersection of science, spirituality, art, and technology to help create a more caring and balanced world. Long associated with the Wayne Teasdale legacy, he has now also joined with The Interspiritual Network and Light on Light. See *prosocial. world*; *contemplativelife.org*; *interspirituality.com*, *lightonlight.us*.

Charles P. Gibbs. The Rev. Canon Dr. Charles P. Gibbs is an Episcopal priest, Sufi by adoption, poet, visionary, and peacebuilder devoted to serving the sacred in the world, particularly through interreligious and intercultural engagement for peace, healing and justice. He is senior partner and poet-in-residence at Catalyst for Peace and founding executive director emeritus of United Religions Initiative. An internationally respected spiritual leader, speaker, and writer, he has dedicated his life to serving the sacred in all beings. His most recent poetry collection is *Light Reading – Poems from a Pilgrim Journey*, with a forthcoming volume titled *Living Water – Poems to Help Grow a Transformed Tomorrow*. See *uri.org*; *catalystforpeace.org*.

Philip Goldberg. Philip Goldberg has explored the world's spiritual traditions for over fifty years as a practitioner, teacher, and author. As an interfaith minister, spiritual counselor, and public speaker, he has presented at major venues and been widely published. He has written or co-written over twenty-five books, including *American Veda: The Life of Yogananda, Roadsigns on the Spiritual Path*, and *Spiritual Practice for Crazy Times*. He teaches on various online platforms, co-hosts the *Spirit Matters* podcast, and serves on the board of the Association for Spiritual Integrity. His work bridges Eastern and Western wisdom for contemporary seekers. See *philipgoldberg.com*.

Karen Gordon. Karen Gordon is a writer, copy editor, and proofreader with extensive experience in spirituality, metaphysics, and conscious living. She provides editorial services for Inner Traditions / Bear & Company, Light on Light Press, and individual authors, and is a member of the Editorial Freelancers Association. Karen also serves as administrative manager for Seven Sisters Mystery School. With a deep passion for transforming creative vision into polished prose, she supports writers in bringing their work into the world with clarity and heart. She is a contributing author to the *Interspirituality Volumes* project.

Andrew Harvey. Andrew Harvey is a renowned religious scholar, spiritual teacher, and author of over forty books, including the critically acclaimed *The Hope, Son of Man*, and *Savage Grace* with Carolyn Baker. Born in South India, he has studied and practiced deeply within the world's mystical traditions, including Hinduism, Buddhism, and Sufism. He is the founder of the Institute of Sacred Activism, an international organization dedicated to uniting spiritual insight with action for justice, sustainability, and planetary healing. Through Sacred Activism, he encourages individuals to become compassionate agents of transformation by fusing inner wisdom with courageous service. His work calls for a collective response to global crises rooted in love and awakened consciousness. See *andrewharvey.net*.

Gorakh Hayashi. Gorakh Hayashi is an interspiritual educator, artist, writer, and meditation teacher, whose visionary work bridges spiritual practice and cultural transformation. A close colleague of Wayne Teasdale, he co-authored *The Heart of*

Brother Wayne Teasdale's Vision of the Interspiritual Age alongside Kurt Johnson, contributing foundational insights to the InterSpiritual Dialogue in Action (ISDnA) movement. Hayashi's approach to Interspirituality is deeply experiential, integrating elements from Eastern and Indigenous traditions. He collaborates across platforms that foster inner awakening and collective transformation. Hayashi has helped create educational programs rooted in Teasdale's interspiritual philosophy, including the InterSpiritual Multiplex and the Community of the Mystic Heart order. He also leads guided meditation sessions in Chicago, carrying forward the contemplative legacy of Teasdale for contemporary seekers. See *gorakhuniverse.com*.

Philip M. Hellmich. The late Philip M. Hellmich was a global peacebuilder and thought leader known for bridging inner transformation with international peace. As director of peace at The Shift Network, he helped create global programs such as the Summer of Peace, Yoga Day Summit, and World Peace Library. A former Peace Corps volunteer in Sierra Leone, he also worked with Search for Common Ground for fourteen years. He authored *God and Conflict: A Search for Peace in a Time of Crisis*, and advised The Global Peace Initiative of Women. Hellmich's legacy lives on through his teachings on the Peace Continuum — from inner peace to international harmony. Hellmich transitioned in 2022. See *theshiftnetwork.com*.

Camille Hamilton Adams Helminski. Camille Hamilton Adams Helminski is co-founder of the Threshold Society and a respected translator, poet, and spiritual teacher in the Sufi tradition. She is the author of *Women of Sufism*, *The Way of Mary*, and several volumes of poetry, including *Ninety-Nine Names of the Beloved*. She co-translated *Rumi's Sun: The Teachings of Shams of Tabriz* and holds the distinction of being the first woman to translate a substantial portion of the Qur'an into English, published as *The Light of Dawn*. Helminski continues work on a full Qur'an translation and teaches widely on Sufism in interspiritual contexts alongside her husband and collaborator, Kabir Helminski. See *sufism.org*.

Kabir Helminski. Kabir Helminski is a Mevlevi Shaikh in the Sufi tradition of Rumi, a translator of classical Sufi texts, and author of widely respected books on spirituality. His titles include *Living Presence, The Knowing Heart, The Mysterion:*

Rumi and the Secret of Becoming Fully Human, and *Holistic Islam*. His work focuses on spiritual psychology and sacred presence, integrating Sufi wisdom with contemporary spiritual life. Kabir has co-translated volumes of Rumi's work with Camille Helminski, and together they founded the Threshold Society. In 2009, he was named one of "The 500 Most Influential Muslims in the World." See *sufism.org*.

Roger Housden. Roger Housden is a spiritual writer and traveler from England known for his *Ten Poems* series. He has traveled widely, studying with spiritual masters of both East and West — from Indian nondual teachers to Mevlevi Sufis and Orthodox Christian monks. He is the author of over twenty books, including *Chasing Love and Revelation* and the widely acclaimed *Ten Poems* series (*Ten Poems to Change Your Life* through *Ten Poems to Say Goodbye*). His work explores the intersection of poetry, spirituality, and personal transformation, and has been featured in *The Oprah Magazine*, *The New York Times*, and *The Los Angeles Times*. See *rogerhousden.com*.

Kurt Johnson. Rev. Kurt Johnson, PhD, has worked in professional science and comparative religion for more than fifty years. Author, and co-founder of the award-winning Light on Light Press, he is a prominent figure on international committees, particularly at the United Nations. He has published over 200 scientific articles and seven books including co-authoring or co-editing award winners *The Coming Interspiritual Age, Our Moment of Choice, Nabokov's Blues* and *Fine Lines*. Johnson served on the faculty of New York's Interfaith Seminary for fifteen years and was on the staff of the American Museum of Natural History in New York City for twenty-five years. As part of UNITY EARTH and the Interspiritual Dialogue Network, he co-edits two magazines, *The Convergence* and *Light on Light,* and cohosts the Convergence series on VoiceAmerica. He serves on core teams of the Evolutionary Leaders, The Holomovement and Prosocial World. See *EvolutionaryLeaders. net/leaders/KJohnson*; *lightonlight.us*; *issuu.com/LightonLight*; *isdna.org*; *thecominginterspiritualage.com*; *sdgthoughtleaderscircle.org*; *interspirituality.com*.

Thomas Keating. Fr. Thomas Keating (1923–2018) was a Trappist monk and one of the most influential figures in modern Christian contemplative practice. Born in

New York, he studied at Yale and Fordham before joining the Cistercian Orders in 1944. From 1961 to 1981, he served as Abbot of St. Joseph's Abbey in Spencer, Massachusetts, later residing at St. Benedict's Monastery in Snowmass, Colorado. A founding member of Contemplative Outreach, he played a central role in developing and teaching Centering Prayer, a method of silent meditation rooted in ancient Christian traditions. Fr. Keating was also a pioneer of interreligious dialogue, collaborating with spiritual leaders from diverse traditions through forums such as the Snowmass InterSpiritual Dialogue. He was closely associated with both H. H. The Dalai Lama and Br. Wayne Teasdale (who considered Fr. Keating a "spiritual father," along with Fr. Bede Griffiths). He, and other contributors to these Volumes, were pivotal in planning the 2013 Dawn of Interspirituality Conference. Fr. Keating authored important books, including *Open Mind, Open Heart* and *Invitation to Love*, and remained a dedicated monastic at St. Benedict's Monastery in Snowmass, Colorado, until his passing. See *contemplativeoutreach.org*; *interspirituality.com*.

William Keepin. Dr. William Keepin is an interspiritual author, physicist, environmental scientist, and co-founder of Gender Equity and Reconciliation International (GERI), endorsed by Archbishop Desmond Tutu. Formerly a researcher in sustainable energy and whistleblower on nuclear power bias, he has testified before the U.S. Congress and helped found the Energy Foundation. Keepin holds a PhD and honorary doctorate and co-founded (with Cynthia Brix) the Gender Equity & Reconciliation International (GERI) project. A practitioner of interspiritual mysticism, he co-founded the Dawn of Interspirituality project and has facilitated holotropic breathwork for over thirty years. He has practiced Eastern and Western contemplative spiritual disciplines for decades, and his "Principles of Spiritual Activism" have been widely circulated. He is author of several books, including *Belonging to God* and *Divine Duality*. See *satyana.org*; *grworld.org*; *dawnofinterspirituality.org*; *interspirituality.com*.

Ken Kitatani. Ken Kitatani is Chief of Executive Board and Committee of i-ceed. org (International Council on Environmental Economics and Development) and Founder, Executive director of the Forum 21, both affiliated with the United Nations. Deeply engaged in spiritual advocacy at the United Nations, he serves on the executive boards of the Committee for Spirituality, Values and Global Concerns and the Committee of Religious NGOs. He also co-chairs the Advisory Board of the Center for Earth Ethics at Union Theological Seminary. A Columbia University graduate in East Asian Studies, Kitatani supports global dialogue on ethics, sustainability, and spiritual values through diplomacy, education, and partnership. He is also co-founder of the Bio-Cultural Sacred Sites circle of the Evolutionary Leaders, proactive internationally with First Peoples and foundational cultures. See *i-ceed.org*; *forum21.co*.

Beverly Lanzetta. Beverly Lanzetta is a theologian, contemplative scholar, spiritual teacher, and author of seven influential books on global spirituality and new monasticism. She is the founder of Schola Divina and the Community of a New Monastic Way, and has dedicated nearly four decades to guiding seekers in universal contemplative practice. A vowed "monk of peace living in the world" and interfaith chaplain, Lanzetta has served on faculty at Villanova, Prescott College, and Grinnell College. Her teaching and writing emphasize theological openness and spiritual nonviolence and have earned acclaim for their mystical insight and inclusive approach. She has been guiding others in the universal call to contemplation for almost forty years. See *beverlylanzetta.net*.

Frank Levy. Frank Levy is co-founder and co-director of the One River Foundation, an organization dedicated to interspiritual wisdom and spiritual growth, founded alongside Rabbi Rami Shapiro. He also serves as vice chair of the Human Relations Commission in Huntsville, Alabama, where he supports efforts toward equity and inclusion. Through One River Foundation, Levy helps lead workshops and retreats that explore universal spiritual principles and contemplative practices drawn from many traditions. His work fosters interspiritual dialogue, ethical reflection, and personal transformation through a non-dogmatic, heart-centered approach. He is particularly interested in building inclusive spiritual communities that transcend religious boundaries while honoring diverse paths to the sacred. Levy has also contributed to collaborative efforts supporting spiritual resilience, justice, and compassionate living in local and global contexts. See *new.oneriverfoundation.org/*.

Kay Lindahl. Kay Lindahl is founder director of The Listening Center (now the Global Listening Centre), an ordained interfaith minister, and spiritual leader based in Long Beach, California. She pioneered the "Sacred Art of Listening," teaching Centering Prayer, reflective listening, and the practice of listening presence through workshops, retreat facilitation, and training at global interfaith gatherings, including the Parliament of the World's Religions. She co-founded the Alliance for Spiritual Community, later helping to launch SARAH (Spiritual and Religious Alliance for Hope). Lindahl served as a trustee of URI's Global Council and chair of the North American Interfaith Network, and is a board member of Women of Spirit and Faith and the Rumi Educational Center. She is author of *The Sacred Art of Listening* and *Practicing the Sacred Art of Listening.* See *sacredlistening.com.*

Yanni Maniates. Yanni Maniates is chair of the UNITY EARTH USA board and a long-time spiritual teacher, author, and publisher. He directed New ERA and the International Religious Foundation from 1979–1985, then served as director of Paragon House Publishers in New York. Earlier in his career, he helped build a 100,000-volume theological seminary library and worked as a rare book librarian at Yale. For over 35 years, he has taught meditation, intuitive development, and Hermetic and Perennial Wisdom teachings. Manniates is the author of six books, numerous articles and courses, and meditation CDs. His work centers on guiding people into "The Embrace" — a direct experience of the Divine. He and his wife recently opened a spiritual and healing center in Williamstown, NJ. See *insideoutjourneys.com*; *unity.earth.*

Rory McEntee. Dr. Rory McEntee is an author, educator, new monastic, and contemplative activist working at the intersection of spirituality, education, and culture. A close friend and mentee of Br. Wayne Teasdale, he helped seed the Interspiritual Movement and currently serves as administrator for the Snowmass InterSpiritual Dialogue, founded in 1984 by Father Thomas Keating. He is also executive director of the Foundation for New Monasticism. McEntee collaborates with spiritual leaders across the religious spectrum, helping to form young people in contemplative and prophetic depth. He has worked as a teacher and vice principal in secondary education, blogs for *Huffington Post,* and co-authored *The New*

Monasticism: An Interspiritual Manifesto for Contemplative Living with Adam Bucko. He holds a PhD in Theological and Philosophical Studies in Religion from Drew University and PhD (ABD) in Applied Mathematics from the University of Southern CA. See *charisinterspirituality.org*; *interspirituality.com*.

Dena Merriam. Dena Merriam is the founder of the Global Peace Initiative of Women (GPIW), a spiritual and interfaith organization working for peace and ecological sustainability. In 2002, she convened a meeting of women religious and spiritual leaders at the Palais des Nations in Geneva from which emerged the GPIW. A veteran of the interfaith movement, she served as vice chair of the Millennium World Peace Summit of Religious and Spiritual Leaders at the United Nations. Merriam holds a master's degree in sacred literature from Columbia University and has organized forums alongside global climate and development gatherings, including the UN Climate Change Conferences and G20 meetings. Her work emphasizes spiritual leadership, the sacred feminine, and the evolution of consciousness. She is the author of *My Journey Through Time: A Spiritual Memoir of Life, Death and Rebirth*. See *gpiw.org*.

Netanel Miles-Yépez. Netanel Miles-Yépez is an artist, philosopher, religion scholar, and spiritual teacher. He heads the Inayati-Maimuni lineage of Sufism, studied under spiritual luminaries such as Rabbi Zalman Schachter-Shalomi and Fr. Thomas Keating, and is a prominent voice in the Interspiritual and New Monasticism movements. Miles-Yépez holds academic degrees in History of Religions and Contemplative Traditions. He is the author of *The End of Religion and Other Writings* (2023), which explores the evolving future of spirituality and sacred practice. He is chair of Wisdom Traditions and director of the Keating-Schachter Center for Interspirituality at Naropa University, a project of the Charis Foundation. See *charisinterspirituality.org*.

Matt Mitler. Matt Mitler is an actor, director, therapist, and founder of Dzieci Theatre, an experimental ensemble dedicated to the work of sacred theater and service. Integrating performance with spiritual practice and care for the dying, Dzieci combines ritual, improvisation, and physical theater rooted in Grotowskiinspired methodologies. Mitler has led workshops throughout the U.S. and Europe, guiding individuals in creative and spiritual self-discovery. His work bridges artistic expression and contemplative practice, often offering theater as both transformative journey and healing balm. See *dziecitheatre.org*.

Leslie Reambeault. Leslie Reambeault, LCSW, is a licensed clinical social worker and ordained Interspiritual Minister practicing near Santa Fe, New Mexico (also licensed in Illinois). She founded *InsideOut Healing Happens*, offering psychotherapy, energy work, eco-spiritual mentoring, and Light Body practices. Reambeault has advanced training in Internal Family Systems (IFS), Somatic Experiencing, and Integral Somatic Practice, and works with first responders and survivors of abuse. She served as dean and co-director at One Spirit Interfaith Seminary, ordained in 2012, and supports ceremonies and life-event rituals across traditions. Reambeault lives in La Cieneguilla with her partner and their poodle, Lahli. See *lesliereambeault.com*.

Roger Ross. Rabbi Roger Ross is chair of the board & CFO at the New Vision Interspiritual Seminary and serves as a United Nations representative for the United Religions Initiative (URI). He holds a BA in psychology and philosophy from New York University and a Certificate in Spiritual Counseling from The New Seminary. Ordained by Rabbinical Seminary International, he offers spiritual counseling, officiates interfaith life-cycle ceremonies, and has conducted weddings and baby namings for over three decades through Loving Hearts Ceremonies. He also sits on the UN Committee on Spirituality, Values & Global Concerns and co-chairs URI's UN interfaith delegation. His leadership fosters interfaith harmony through education, ritual, and global diplomacy. See *rogerross.online*; *1spirit.org*.

Deborah Steen Ross. Deborah Steen Ross is director and founder of ISIS Interfaith Seminary (International Seminary for Interfaith Studies) and an ordained interfaith minister based in Elmsford, New York. She is co-owner, alongside Rabbi Roger Ross, of Loving Hearts Ceremonies, offering personalized interfaith weddings, civil unions, and life-event services. A trained energy healer and educator, Ross has led spiritual healing workshops at the Center of the Shining Light since 1991, and has been guiding interfaith formation at ISIS since its founding. Her work integrates contemplative interspiritual practices, reflective listening, and sacred ceremony to support couples and seekers across traditions. See *insideout-healinghappens.com*.

Sacred Feet Dharma Heirs. The Sacred Feet Dharma Heirs are the ordained spiritual successors of Swami Shraddhananda (Rev. Dr. Sonya L. Jones), who founded the interspiritual lineage known as Sacred Feet Yoga. These heirs — Chamatkara (Sandra Simon) (also Dharma Books Editor at Light on Light Press), Amrita (Jenny Williams), and Swami Prakashananda (The Right Rev. Bishop Christine Deefholts) — continue her legacy through teaching, writing, publishing, and spiritual leadership. They carry forward Shraddhananda's vision — guiding practitioners in the Sacred Feet Yoga Teachings and supporting practices that focus on kindling and facilitating the universal sacred energy within (Maha Kundalini Shakti, Tara, Windhorse, the Holy Spirit, Ruah, Ruh, etc.) which, by the grace of the divine, plumbs the depths of the soul, releases emotional or behavioral patterns which no longer serve, and helps us to "hold our seat" along bumps in the road until we are free and able to live every moment from our natural, innate state of divinity. See *jefifoundation.org/sacred-feet-yoga/; lightonlight.us*.

Rami Shapiro. Rabbi Rami Shapiro is an award-winning author, poet, and teacher of Perennial Wisdom — the core truths found across the world's spiritual traditions. Ordained as a rabbi in the Reform Jewish tradition, he served as a congregational rabbi for twenty years before co-founding the One River Foundation and Wisdom School. Holding a PhD in religious studies from Union Graduate School, Rabbi Shapiro has lectured at Harvard, the US Air Force, and the United Nations, and received the 2020 Huston Smith Award for Excellence in Interfaith Education. His books include *Perennial Wisdom for the Spiritually Independent*, *The Divine Feminine in Biblical Wisdom Literature*, and *Holy Rascals*. Rabbi Shapiro bridges tradition with spiritual freedom and currently writes a regular column for *Spirituality & Health* magazine and hosts the *Essential Conversations* podcast. See *rabbirami.com*.

Ruth Broyde Sharone. Ruth Broyde Sharone, long associated with the Parliament of the World's Religions and their "Partner Cities" program, is an interfaith leader, documentary filmmaker, journalist, and author, honored internationally for her contributions to cultural education, peace and justice. Her memoir, *Minefields and Miracles: Why God and Allah Need to Talk*, is a chronicle of the history and personalities of the interfaith movement. Sharone's well-known documentary film work has taken her around the globe and has been featured on CNN and other major international media outlets. A passionate speaker and advocate, she continues to inspire unity through storytelling, film, and global engagement. See *minefieldsandmiracles.com*.

Swami Shraddhananda. Sw. Shraddhananda, also known as Rev. Dr. Sonya L. Jones, founder of Sacred Feet Yoga, entered mahasamadhi on February 16, 2021. She established Sacred Feet Yoga in 2010 as an interspiritual system. A major leader in the interspiritual experience, she was a co-founder and director of Sannyas for the Community of the Mystic Heart, host of its retreats, and editor of its book, *Mature Interspirituality: Wayne Teasdale's Nine Elements and Beyond*. She also served as Book Review Editor for *Light on Light* magazine. A dedicated teacher, writer, and spiritual guide, she inspired students worldwide through her compassionate service, deep interspiritual wisdom, and steadfast commitment to spiritual practice. She is survived by three ordained Dharma Heirs: Jenny Williams (Amrita), Sandra Simon (Chamatkara) (now Dharma Books Editor for Light on Light), and Sw. Prakashananda (Rt. Rev. Christine Deefholts), who continue her work through Sacred Feet Yoga and The Sacred Feet Publishing Imprint under the umbrella of The Jones Educational Foundation. Hundreds of former students and colleagues remember her with affection and gratitude for her joyful presence and enduring legacy. See *jefifoundation.org/sacred-feet-yoga/*; *lightonlight.us*.

Mirabai Starr. Mirabai Starr is the author of critically acclaimed translations of the mystics and pioneering books on the interspiritual paradigm. She is well known for the breadth of her involvement in all aspects of the sixties counterculture phenomenon, from traveling internationally during the seminal period of East/West spiritual convergence, involvement in the protests of the Vietnam War and Civil Rights eras, residence at the historic Lama Foundation, and her close life-long friendship with counterculture icon Ram Das. She taught Philosophy and World Religions at the University of New Mexico, Taos, and now speaks and teaches nationally and internationally on the teachings of the mystics and contemplative practice. She is also a certified bereavement guide and conducts contemplative retreats and spiritual events throughout the world. See *mirabaistarr.com*; *interspirituality.com*.

Melissa Stewart. Melissa Stewart is an educator, minister, and spiritual leader associated with One Spirit Interfaith Seminary. With extensive experience in interfaith education, she offers formation programs for spiritual directors and ministers across traditions. As a faculty member, Stewart integrates contemplative practice, pastoral care, and spiritual accompaniment into her teaching. She supports emerging ministers in developing skills for guiding others in sacred presence, compassionate listening, and community building. Her work emphasizes deep spiritual formation and empowering interspiritual leadership from a foundation of awareness and service. See *melissastewart.com*.

Lama Surya Das. Lama Surya Das is one of the foremost Western Buddhist meditation teachers and scholars and a pioneer in bringing Tibetan Buddhism to the West. Dubbed "the American Lama" by the Dalai Lama, he has spent over forty-five years studying Zen, Vipassana, Yoga, and Tibetan Buddhism with many of Asia's great masters. An authorized lama and founder of the Dzogchen Center, he is also a poet, translator, chant master, and spiritual activist. Lama Surya Das is the author of the international bestselling *Awakening* trilogy and several other books, including *Buddha Standard Time*. He co-founded the Western Buddhist Teachers Network with the Dalai Lama in 1993, and leads retreats and workshops worldwide. He is also a regular contributor at *Huffington Post*. See *dzogchen.org*; *surya.org*; *askthelama.com*.

Wayne Teasdale. Br. Wayne Teasdale (1945–2004) was a Catholic monk, mystic, and leading voice in the interspiritual movement. These Volumes are published on the 25th anniversary of his naming the "Interspirituality" paradigm. After ten years as a lay monk associated with St. Joseph's Abbey under Abbot Thomas Keating, he studied at Bede Griffiths's ashram in India. Teasdale coined the term Interspirituality to describe a mystical path embracing wisdom from multiple religious traditions, rather than merging doctrines. His books *The Mystic Heart* and *A Monk in the World* are considered foundational to contemporary interspiritual dialogue and practice. In 2002, he co-founded The Interspiritual Dialogue network with international colleagues (which is now also the parent of the Light on Light Press). A close associate of H. H. the Dalai Lama, Br. Teasdale was also a social justice activist and educator, promoting compassion-in-action rooted in contemplative awareness. He served on the Parliament of the World's Religions Board, was part of the Monastic Interreligious Dialogue, co-authored the Universal Declaration on Nonviolence, and taught at DePaul University and Catholic Theological Union. See *isdna.org*; *interspirituality.com*.

Robert Toth. Robert Toth is a contemplative writer, educator, and interfaith explorer. He served as executive director of the Merton Institute for Contemplative Living and later as director of Special Initiatives, guiding its expansion. He co-edited *Bridges to Contemplative Living*, a popular series for group spiritual practice, and has contributed to *The Interfaith Observer*, writing on Hindu–Christian interspiritual pioneers with Kurt Johnson and Adam Bucko. Toth holds degrees in classics and education from John Carroll University and has served in high schools, healthcare administration, and contemplative centers for over four decades. Toth supports a vision of unity and reverence that honors the sacred in all forms.

"We". We refers to the editorial team of the Light on Light Press listed on the copyright page and in the "Message from the Publisher" at the end of each Volume. For History, Commentary and Interval sections, this team employed a "journalistic approach," studying available printed and online resources along with twenty-five years of saved correspondence and attachments. The goal was a "We" voice that would communicate these sections to readers in a conversational tone.

Claudia Welss. Claudia Welss is Executive Chair and former Interim CEO of the Institute of Noetic Sciences (IONS), founded by Apollo 14 astronaut Edgar Mitchell to advance the scientific study of consciousness. She is the lead citizen scientist for the Global Consciousness Project 2.0, and serves as Vice Chair of

Space for Humanity. A co-founder of HeartMath's Global Coherence Initiative, she also initiated the Invest in Yourself working group at NEXUS Global to bring consciousness research into philanthropic and systems-change contexts. Her work explores the intersection of collective intelligence, social transformation, and planetary-scale coherence. Previously, she pioneered the collaboratory model by founding NextNow.org — described by MIT's Center for Collective Intelligence as "a new kind of collective intelligence" — as well as corporate social responsibility and sustainability curriculum as Director of Executive Education Center at UC Berkeley's Haas School of Business. She is a Featured Author to *Our Moment of Choice* (Simon & Schuster, 2020). See *noetic.org*.

Ken Wilber. Ken Wilber, a visionary thinker of inspired genius, is the developer of an integral "theory of everything" that embraces the truths of all the world's great spiritual, scientific, and philosophical traditions. Often called the "Einstein of consciousness studies," Wilber is the most widely translated academic writer in the U.S., with twenty- five books published in over thirty languages. He is the founder of the Integral Institute, a multidisciplinary think tank addressing global issues through the Integral Approach, and co-founder of Integral Life, a platform for advancing integral awareness and practice. A preeminent scholar of the Integral stage of human development, Wilber has been a close friend of the interspiritual movement for many years, participating in programs and publications with Br. Wayne Teasdale, Kurt Johnson & Light on Light, and many others. Based in Denver, he remains an active author, teacher, and leading voice in the evolution of human consciousness. See *kenwilber.com*; *integrallife.com*.

John A. Wilde. Rev. Dr. John A. Wilde is an InterSpirituality Mentor with the Spiritual Paths Institute and a retired Presbyterian pastor whose work centers on spiritual practice and environmental reverence. With a long-standing commitment to the interspiritual movement, he documents sacred sites, rituals, and teachings across the world's wisdom traditions. Founder of AbundanceTrek.com, Wilde blends traditional Christianity with a broader spiritual vision through retreats, blog writing, and teaching conferences at organizations such as the Center for Action and Contemplation and St. Margaret's House. He is based in Seattle, and his work fosters interfaith understanding and contemplative spirituality within faith communities — undefining religious labels while honoring spiritual roots. See *abundancetrek.com*; *spiritualpaths.net/mentor-bios/*.

Matthew Wright. Rev. Matthew Wright is a dynamic voice in the interfaith and interspiritual community. An Episcopal priest and interspiritual teacher, he is committed to renewing the Christian Wisdom tradition within a broader interspiritual context. His divinity thesis on "Multiple Belonging" informs his inclusive spiritual approach, drawing deeply from Sufism and Vedanta alongside Christian practice. Wright serves as priest-in-charge at St. Gregory's Episcopal Church in Woodstock, NY, and lives in community with his wife, Yanick, alongside the brothers of Holy Cross Monastery. A frequent retreat leader and public speaker, he has spoken and written internationally on themes of Christian mysticism and interspirituality. See *awakingheart.com/about*.

MESSAGE FROM THE PUBLISHER

Light on Light Press produces enhanced content books spotlighting the sacred ground upon which all religious and wisdom traditions intersect. Its foundational aim has been to stimulate and perpetuate engaged interspiritual and perennial wisdom dialogue for the purpose of assisting the dawning of a unitive consciousness that will inspire compassionate action toward a just and peaceful world.

In this express context, we are delighted to publish *Interspirituality: The Heritage* and *Interspirituality: The Future* on the 25th anniversary of Br. Wayne Teasdale's now classic book, *The Mystic Heart: Discovering a Universal Spirituality in the World's Religions*, in which he named "Interspirituality." It also commemorates the 10th anniversary of *The Coming Interspiritual Age* whose generative organization, The Interspiritual Dialogue, was founded with Br. Wayne Teasdale in 2002 by members of this editorial group, and became the charity that is now the parent of The Light on Light Press.

We deeply thank the more than 120 Featured Authors gathered in these Volumes. Their articles, excerpts, abridgements, and twenty-five years of correspondence and attachments have made the books possible. Honoring them, we expressly have not distinguished particular editors from our own Light on Light team other than our list below. It worked as a team, with a journalistic approach, aiming to curate these wonderful materials and, as the "We" voice in these Volumes, "report *on,*" and share, this last quarter century of interfaith and interspiritual expansion and impact.

In the spirit of Br. Wayne Teasdale's identification of Interspirituality as "The common heritage of humankind's spiritual wisdom; the sharing of mystical resources across traditions" and The Interspiritual Age as "the age we are now entering, where people are no longer isolated within their home tradition but are exploring other traditions, finding what is useful to their own growth," we feel privileged to present the content herein. It bears on the critical topics of our global landscape today: partnership consciousness, peace, justice, governance, economic equality, environmental health, science and the wisdom traditions, and a sustainable and regenerative future – in a phrase, "a world that works for all." May it be so.

The Editors
Rev. Shannon Marie Winters MS
Rev. Kurt Johnson PhD
Robert Atkinson PhD
Nomi Naeem MA
Chamatkara (aka Sandra Simon)
Karuna (aka Rev. Caroline Ashley)
Karen J. Gordon
Roger P. Briggs